How to access your on-line resources

Kaplan Financial students will have a MyKaplan account and these extra resources will be available to you online. You do not need to register again, as this process was completed when you enrolled. If you are having problems accessing online materials, please ask your course administrator.

If you are not studying with Kaplan and did not purchase your book via a Kaplan website, to unlock your extra online resources please go to www.en-gage.co.uk (even if you have set up an account and registered books previously). You will then need to enter the ISBN number (on the title page and back cover) and the unique pass key number contained in the scratch panel below to gain access.

You will also be required to enter additional information during this process to set up or confirm your account details.

If you purchased via the Kaplan Publishing website you will automatically receive an e-mail invitation to register your details and gain access to your content. If you do not receive the e-mail or book content, please contact Kaplan Publishing.

Your code and information

This code can only be used once for the registration of one book online. This registration and your online content will expire when the final sittings for the examinations covered by this book have taken place. Please allow one hour from the time you submit your book details for us to process your request.

Please scratch the film to access your unique code.

Please be aware that this code is case-sensitive and you will need to include the dashes within the passcode, but not when entering the ISBN.

CIMA

Subject F3

Financial Strategy

Study Text

Published by: Kaplan Publishing UK

Unit 2 The Business Centre, Molly Millars Lane, Wokingham, Berkshire RG41 2QZ

Acknowledgements

This Product includes propriety content of the International Accounting Standards Board which is overseen by the IFRS Foundation, and is used with the express permission of the IFRS Foundation under licence. All rights reserved. No part of this publication may be reproduced, stored in a retrieval system, or transmitted in any form or by any means, electronic, mechanical, photocopying, recording, or otherwise, without prior written permission of Kaplan Publishing and the IFRS Foundation.

Trade Marks

The IFRS Foundation logo, the IASB logo, the IFRS for SMEs logo, the "Hexagon Device", "IFRS Foundation", "eIFRS", "IAS", "IASB", "IFRS for SMEs", "NIIF" IASs" "IFRS", "IFRSs", "International Accounting Standards", "International Financial Reporting Standards", "IFRIC", "SIC" and "IFRS Taxonomy".

Further details of the Trade Marks including details of countries where the Trade Marks are registered or applied for are available from the Foundation on request.

British Library Cataloguing in Publication Data

A catalogue record for this book is available from the British Library.

ISBN: 978-1-78740-355-0

Printed and bound in Great Britain.

Contents

Introduction

How to use the Materials

These official CIMA learning materials have been carefully designed to make your learning experience as easy as possible and to give you the best chances of success in your objective tests.

The product range contains a number of features to help you in the study process. They include:

- a detailed explanation of all syllabus areas

- extensive 'practical' materials

- generous question practice, together with full solutions.

This Study Text has been designed with the needs of home study and distance learning candidates in mind. Such students require very full coverage of the syllabus topics, and also the facility to undertake extensive question practice. However, the Study Text is also ideal for fully taught courses.

The main body of the text is divided into a number of chapters, each of which is organised on the following pattern:

- **Detailed learning outcomes.** These describe the knowledge expected after your studies of the chapter are complete. You should assimilate these before beginning detailed work on the chapter, so that you can appreciate where your studies are leading.

- **Step-by-step topic coverage.** This is the heart of each chapter, containing detailed explanatory text supported where appropriate by worked examples and exercises. You should work carefully through this section, ensuring that you understand the material being explained and can tackle the examples and exercises successfully. Remember that in many cases knowledge is cumulative: if you fail to digest earlier material thoroughly, you may struggle to understand later chapters.

- **Activities.** Some chapters are illustrated by more practical elements, such as comments and questions designed to stimulate discussion.

- **Question practice.** The text contains three styles of question:

  - Exam-style objective test questions (OTQs).

  - 'Integration' questions – these test your ability to understand topics within a wider context. This is particularly important with calculations where OTQs may focus on just one element but an integration question tackles the full calculation, just as you would be expected to do in the workplace.

- 'Case' style questions – these test your ability to analyse and discuss issues in greater depth, particularly focusing on scenarios that are less clear cut than in the objective tests, and thus provide excellent practice for developing the skills needed for success in the Management Level Case Study Examination.

- **Solutions.** Avoid the temptation merely to 'audit' the solutions provided. It is an illusion to think that this provides the same benefits as you would gain from a serious attempt of your own. However, if you are struggling to get started on a question you should read the introductory guidance provided at the beginning of the solution, where provided, and then make your own attempt before referring back to the full solution.

If you work conscientiously through this Official CIMA Study Text according to the guidelines above you will be giving yourself an excellent chance of success in your objective tests. Good luck with your studies!

Quality and accuracy are of the utmost importance to us so if you spot an error in any of our products, please send an email to mykaplanreporting@kaplan.com with full details, or follow the link to the feedback form in MyKaplan.

Our Quality Co-ordinator will work with our technical team to verify the error and take action to ensure it is corrected in future editions.

Icon explanations

Definition – These sections explain important areas of knowledge which must be understood and reproduced in an assessment environment.

Key point – Identifies topics which are key to success and are often examined.

Supplementary reading – These sections will help to provide a deeper understanding of core areas. The supplementary reading is **NOT** optional reading. It is vital to provide you with the breadth of knowledge you will need to address the wide range of topics within your syllabus that could feature in an assessment question. **Reference to this text is vital when self-studying.**

Test your understanding – Following key points and definitions are exercises which give the opportunity to assess the understanding of these core areas.

Illustration – To help develop an understanding of particular topics. The illustrative examples are useful in preparing for the Test your understanding exercises.

Exclamation mark – This symbol signifies a topic which can be more difficult to understand. When reviewing these areas, care should be taken.

 New – Identifies topics that are brand new in subjects that build on, and therefore also contain, learning covered in earlier subjects.

 Tutorial note – Included to explain some of the technical points in more detail.

Study technique

Passing exams is partly a matter of intellectual ability, but however accomplished you are in that respect you can improve your chances significantly by the use of appropriate study and revision techniques. In this section we briefly outline some tips for effective study during the earlier stages of your approach to the objective tests. We also mention some techniques that you will find useful at the revision stage.

Planning

To begin with, formal planning is essential to get the best return from the time you spend studying. Estimate how much time in total you are going to need for each subject you are studying. Remember that you need to allow time for revision as well as for initial study of the material.

With your study material before you, decide which chapters you are going to study in each week, and which weeks you will devote to revision and final question practice.

Prepare a written schedule summarising the above and stick to it!

It is essential to know your syllabus. As your studies progress you will become more familiar with how long it takes to cover topics in sufficient depth. Your timetable may need to be adapted to allocate enough time for the whole syllabus.

Students are advised to refer to the examination blueprints (see page P.13 for further information) and the CIMA website, www.cimaglobal.com, to ensure they are up-to-date.

The amount of space allocated to a topic in the Study Text is not a very good guide as to how long it will take you. The syllabus weighting is the better guide as to how long you should spend on a syllabus topic.

Tips for effective studying

(1) Aim to find a quiet and undisturbed location for your study, and plan as far as possible to use the same period of time each day. Getting into a routine helps to avoid wasting time. Make sure that you have all the materials you need before you begin so as to minimise interruptions.

(2) Store all your materials in one place, so that you do not waste time searching for items every time you want to begin studying. If you have to pack everything away after each study period, keep your study materials in a box, or even a suitcase, which will not be disturbed until the next time.

(3) Limit distractions. To make the most effective use of your study periods you should be able to apply total concentration, so turn off all entertainment equipment, set your phones to message mode, and put up your 'do not disturb' sign.

(4) Your timetable will tell you which topic to study. However, before diving in and becoming engrossed in the finer points, make sure you have an overall picture of all the areas that need to be covered by the end of that session. After an hour, allow yourself a short break and move away from your Study Text. With experience, you will learn to assess the pace you need to work at. Each study session should focus on component learning outcomes – the basis for all questions.

(5) Work carefully through a chapter, making notes as you go. When you have covered a suitable amount of material, vary the pattern by attempting a practice question. When you have finished your attempt, make notes of any mistakes you made, or any areas that you failed to cover or covered more briefly. Be aware that all component learning outcomes will be tested in each examination.

(6) Make notes as you study, and discover the techniques that work best for you. Your notes may be in the form of lists, bullet points, diagrams, summaries, 'mind maps', or the written word, but remember that you will need to refer back to them at a later date, so they must be intelligible. If you are on a taught course, make sure you highlight any issues you would like to follow up with your lecturer.

(7) Organise your notes. Make sure that all your notes, calculations etc. can be effectively filed and easily retrieved later.

Progression

There are two elements of progression that we can measure: how quickly students move through individual topics within a subject; and how quickly they move from one course to the next. We know that there is an optimum for both, but it can vary from subject to subject and from student to student. However, using data and our experience of student performance over many years, we can make some generalisations.

A fixed period of study set out at the start of a course with key milestones is important. This can be within a subject, for example 'I will finish this topic by 30 June', or for overall achievement, such as 'I want to be qualified by the end of next year'.

Your qualification is cumulative, as earlier papers provide a foundation for your subsequent studies, so do not allow there to be too big a gap between one subject and another. For example, F3 *Financial strategy* builds on your knowledge of long-term sources of finance from F2 *Advanced financial reporting* as well as risks and control and capital investment decision making from P2 *Advanced management accounting.*

We know that exams encourage techniques that lead to some degree of short term retention, the result being that you will simply forget much of what you have already learned unless it is refreshed (look up Ebbinghaus Forgetting Curve for more details on this). This makes it more difficult as you move from one subject to another: not only will you have to learn the new subject, you will also have to relearn all the underpinning knowledge as well. This is very inefficient and slows down your overall progression which makes it more likely you may not succeed at all.

In addition, delaying your studies slows your path to qualification which can have negative impacts on your career, postponing the opportunity to apply for higher level positions and therefore higher pay.

You can use the following diagram showing the whole structure of your qualification to help you keep track of your progress. Make sure you carefully review the 2019 CIMA syllabus transition rules and seek appropriate advice if you are unsure about your progression through the qualification.

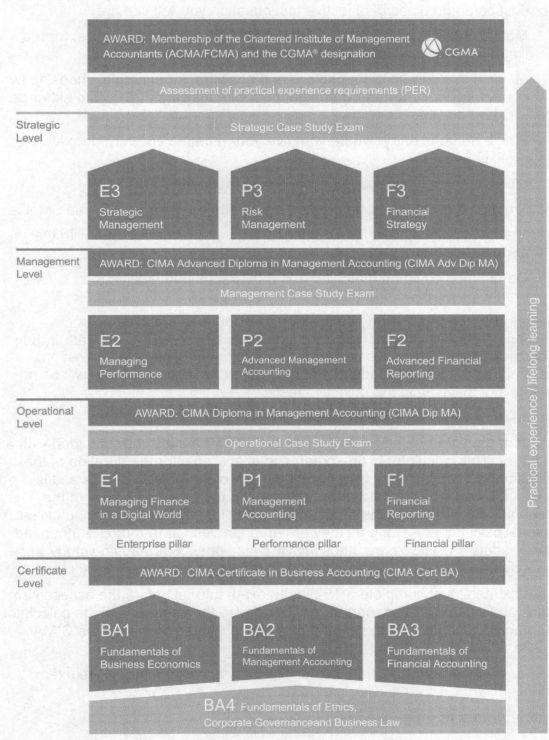

Reproduced with permission from CIMA

Objective test

Objective test questions require you to choose or provide a response to a question whose correct answer is predetermined.

The most common types of objective test question you will see are:

- Multiple choice, where you have to choose the correct answer(s) from a list of possible answers. This could either be numbers or text.

- Multiple choice with more choices and answers, for example, choosing two correct answers from a list of eight possible answers. This could either be numbers or text.

- Single numeric entry, where you give your numeric answer, for example, profit is $10,000.

- Multiple entry, where you give several numeric answers.

- True/false questions, where you state whether a statement is true or false.

- Matching pairs of text, for example, matching a technical term with the correct definition.

- Other types could be matching text with graphs and labelling graphs/diagrams.

In every chapter of this Study Text we have introduced these types of questions, but obviously we have had to label answers A, B, C etc. rather than using click boxes. For convenience, we have retained quite a few questions where an initial scenario leads to a number of sub-questions. There will be no questions of this type in the objective tests.

Guidance re CIMA on-screen calculator

As part of the CIMA objective test software, candidates are now provided with a calculator. This calculator is on-screen and is available for the duration of the assessment. The calculator is available in each of the objective tests and is accessed by clicking the calculator button in the top left hand corner of the screen at any time during the assessment. Candidates are permitted to utilise personal calculators as long as they are an approved CIMA model. Authorised CIMA models are listed here: https://www.cimaglobal.com/Studying/study-and-resources/.

All candidates must complete a 15-minute exam tutorial before the assessment begins and will have the opportunity to familiarise themselves with the calculator and practise using it. The exam tutorial is also available online via the CIMA website.

Candidates may practise using the calculator by accessing the online exam tutorial.

Fundamentals of objective tests

The objective tests are 90-minute assessments comprising 60 compulsory questions, with one or more parts. There will be no choice and all questions should be attempted. All elements of a question must be answered correctly for the question to be marked correctly. All questions are equally weighted.

CIMA syllabus 2019 – Structure of subjects and learning outcomes

Details regarding the content of the new CIMA syllabus can be located within the CIMA 2019 professional syllabus document.

Each subject within the syllabus is divided into a number of broad syllabus topics. The topics contain one or more lead learning outcomes, related component learning outcomes and indicative knowledge content.

A learning outcome has two main purposes:

(a) To define the skill or ability that a well prepared candidate should be able to exhibit in the examination.

(b) To demonstrate the approach likely to be taken in examination questions.

The learning outcomes are part of a hierarchy of learning objectives. The verbs used at the beginning of each learning outcome relate to a specific learning objective, e.g.

Calculate the break-even point, profit target, margin of safety and profit/volume ratio for a single product or service.

The verb '**calculate**' indicates a level three learning objective. The following tables list the verbs that appear in the syllabus learning outcomes and examination questions.

The examination blueprints and representative task statements

CIMA have also published examination blueprints giving learners clear expectations regarding what is expected of them.

The blueprint is structured as follows:

- Exam content sections (reflecting the syllabus document)

- Lead and component outcomes (reflecting the syllabus document)

- Representative task statements.

A representative task statement is a plain English description of what a CIMA finance professional should know and be able to do.

The content and skill level determine the language and verbs used in the representative task.

CIMA will test up to the level of the task statement in the objective tests (an objective test question on a particular topic could be set at a lower level than the task statement in the blueprint).

The format of the objective test blueprints follows that of the published syllabus for the 2019 CIMA Professional Qualification.

Weightings for content sections are also included in the individual subject blueprints.

CIMA VERB HIERARCHY

CIMA place great importance on the definition of verbs in structuring objective tests. It is therefore crucial that you understand the verbs in order to appreciate the depth and breadth of a topic and the level of skill required. The objective tests will focus on levels one, two and three of the CIMA hierarchy of verbs. However, they will also test levels four and five, especially at the management and strategic levels.

Skill level	Verbs used	Definition
Level 5 Evaluation How you are expected to use your learning to evaluate, make decisions or recommendations	Advise	Counsel, inform or notify
	Assess	Evaluate or estimate the nature, ability or quality of
	Evaluate	Appraise or assess the value of
	Recommend	Propose a course of action
	Review	Assess and evaluate in order, to change if necessary
Level 4 Analysis How you are expected to analyse the detail of what you have learned	Align	Arrange in an orderly way
	Analyse	Examine in detail the structure of
	Communicate	Share or exchange information
	Compare and contrast	Show the similarities and/or differences between
	Develop	Grow and expand a concept
	Discuss	Examine in detail by argument
	Examine	Inspect thoroughly
	Interpret	Translate into intelligible or familiar terms
	Monitor	Observe and check the progress of
	Prioritise	Place in order of priority or sequence for action
	Produce	Create or bring into existence
Level 3 Application How you are expected to apply your knowledge	Apply	Put to practical use
	Calculate	Ascertain or reckon mathematically
	Conduct	Organise and carry out
	Demonstrate	Prove with certainty or exhibit by practical means
	Prepare	Make or get ready for use
	Reconcile	Make or prove consistent/compatible

Skill level	Verbs used	Definition
Level 2 **Comprehension** What you are expected to understand	Describe	Communicate the key features of
	Distinguish	Highlight the differences between
	Explain	Make clear or intelligible/state the meaning or purpose of
	Identify	Recognise, establish or select after consideration
	Illustrate	Use an example to describe or explain something
Level 1 **Knowledge** What you are expected to know	List	Make a list of
	State	Express, fully or clearly, the details/facts of
	Define	Give the exact meaning of
	Outline	Give a summary of

Information concerning formulae and tables will be provided via the CIMA website, www.cimaglobal.com.

SYLLABUS GRIDS

F3: Financial Strategy

Create financial strategy, evaluate and manage financial risk and assess organisational value

Content weighting

Content area		Weighting
A	Financial policy decisions	15%
B	Sources of long-term funds	25%
C	Financial risks	20%
D	Business valuation	40%
		100%

F3A: Financial policy decisions

The overall strategy of the organisation must be supported by how its finances are organised. This requires an understanding of the different strategic financial objectives and policy options that are open to organisations. The choice of these objectives and policy options will be heavily influenced by the financial market requirements and the regulatory environment in which the organisation operates. This section examines these issues.

Lead outcome	Component outcome	Topics to be covered	Explanatory notes
1. Advise on strategic financial objectives.	a. Analyse different types of organisations and their objectives. b. Advise on financial objectives. c. Advise on non-financial objectives.	• Profit and not-for-profit organisations • Quoted and unquoted companies • Private and public sector organisations • Value for money, maximising shareholder wealth • Earnings growth, dividend growth • Impact of underlying economic conditions and business variables on financial objectives • Enhancing the value of other non-financial capitals (human capital, intellectual capital and social and relationship capital) • United Nations Sustainability Development Goals	This section is about aligning financial objectives and policies to the strategies of the organisation. The key aim is to make sure that the organisation has a proper basis to determine what types of funds to access and how to use those funds. To do this effectively finance professionals must be able to evaluate the opportunities and constraints placed on them in the operating environment – particularly financial market requirements, the impact of taxation and the requirements of industry and financial market regulators.
2. Analyse strategic financial policy decisions.	Analyse the following policy decision areas: a. Investment b. Financing c. Dividends d. Interrelationships between policy decision areas	• Use of policy decisions to meet cash needs of entity • Sensitivity of forecast financial statements and future cash position to these policy decisions • Consideration of the interests of stakeholders	
3. Discuss the external influences on financial strategic decisions.	Discuss the influence of the following on financial strategic decisions a. Market requirements b. Taxation c. Regulatory requirements	• Lenders' assessment of creditworthiness • Consideration of domestic and international tax regulations • Consideration of industry regulations such as price and service controls	

F3B: Sources of long-term funds

What types of funds are available to organisations to finance the implementation of their strategies? How much of each type should they go for? And what is the impact on the organisation? Where and how do they get these funds? And how do they provide incentives to providers of such funds so that the funds are available at the right time, in the right quantities and at the right cost? These are some of the questions covered by this section.

Lead outcome	Component outcome	Topics to be covered	Explanatory notes
1. Evaluate the capital structure of a firm.	Evaluate: a. Choice of capital structure b. Changes in capital structure	• Capital structure theories (traditional theory and Miller and Modigliani (MM) theories) • Calculation of cost of equity and weighted cost of capital to reflect changes in capital structure • Impact of choice of capital structure on financial statements • Structuring debt/equity profiles of companies in a group	How should important elements of the financial statement be treated in the books? What principles should underpin these? How do financial reporting standards help to ensure this? Using financial reporting standards terminology this part will be looking at issues of recognition and measurement. The most important issues will be considered here.
2. Analyse long-term debt finance.	Analyse: a. Selecting debt instruments b. Target debt profile c. Issuing debt securities d. Debt covenants e. Tax considerations	• Types of debt instruments and criteria for selecting them • Managing interest, currency and refinancing risks with target debt profile • Private placements and capital market issuance of debt • Features of debt covenants	
3. Evaluate equity finance.	a. Evaluate methods of flotation b. Discuss rights issues	• Methods of flotation and implications for management and shareholders • Rights issues, choice of discount rates and impact on shareholders • Calculation of theoretical ex-rights price (TERP) and yield adjusted TERP	
4. Evaluate dividend policy.	Evaluate policy in the following areas: a. Cash dividends b. Scrip dividends c. Share repurchase programmes	• Features and criteria • Impact on shareholder value and entity value, financial statements and performance	

F3C: Financial risks

There is always a risk that the organisation will not be able to attract enough funds to finance its operations and in extreme conditions will fail to survive as a result. This section covers the sources of such risks and how to evaluate and manage such financial risks appropriately.

Lead outcome	Component outcome	Topics to be covered	Explanatory notes
1. Discuss the sources and types of financial risks.	Discuss: a. Sources of financial risk b. Types of financial risk	• Economic risk • Political risk • Currency risk • Interest rate risk	Managing risks related to finances is similar to managing other types of risks in general approach and methodology. However, there are specific differences such as the sources and types of financial risks, how they can be quantified and ways in which they are managed. This section looks at the very specific issues related to managing financial risks within a general risk management framework
2. Evaluate financial risks.	a. Evaluate how financial risks are quantified	• Theory and forecasting of exchange rates (e.g. interest rate parity, purchasing power parity and the Fisher Effect) • Value at risk	
3. Recommend ways of managing financial risks.	a. Recommend ways to manage economic and political risks b. Discuss currency risk instruments c. Discuss interest rate risk instruments	• Responses to economic transaction and translation risks • Operations and features of swaps, forward contracts, money market hedges, futures and options • Techniques for combining options in order to achieve specific risk profile such as caps, collars and floors • Internal hedging techniques	

F3D: Business valuation

The primary objective of all strategic activity is to create and preserve value for organisations. How does the organisation know whether it has succeeded in this objective? Sometimes, in order to implement strategies, organisations have to acquire other organisations. How does the acquirer determine the value of its acquisition? This section covers how to use techniques in business valuation to answer such questions.

Lead outcome	Component outcome	Topics to be covered	Explanatory notes
1. Discuss the context of valuation.	Discuss: a. Listing of firms b. Mergers and acquisitions (M&A) c. Demergers and divestments	• Reasons for M&A and divestments • Taxation implications • Process and implications of management buy-outs • Acquisition by private equity and venture capitalist	This section looks at the conditions under which organisations need to calculate their own value or the value of other organisations or sub-units thereof. It introduces candidates to valuation techniques. Of particular importance in the digital world is the valuation of intangibles. This links also to how to report intangible value and their drivers in integrated reporting. In addition, how should digital assets be valued? One of the reasons for valuation is when merging or acquiring firms. How should such deals be structured, implemented and closed? For example what should the forms of the consideration be? What are the terms of the acquisition? How does one enable benefit realisation, particularly for synergies once the acquired organisation has been integrated into the acquiring organisation?
2. Evaluate the various valuation methods.	a. Evaluate different valuation methods b. Discuss the strengths and weaknesses of each valuation method	• Asset valuation • Valuation of intangibles • Different methods of equity valuation (share prices, earnings valuation, dividend valuation, discounted cash flow valuation) • Capital Asset Pricing Model (CAPM) • Efficient market hypothesis	
3. Analyse pricing and bid issues.	Analyse: a. Pricing issues b. Bid issues	• Forms of consideration • Terms of acquisition • Target entity debt • Methods of financing cash offer and refinancing target entity debt • Bid negotiation	
4. Discuss post-transaction issues.	Discuss: a. Post-transaction value b. Benefit realisation	• Post-transaction value incorporating effect of intended synergies • M&A integration and synergy benefit realisation • Exit strategies	

Strategic financial objectives

Chapter learning objectives

Lead outcome	Component outcome
A1: Advise on strategic financial objectives	(a) Analyse different types of organisations and their objectives
	(b) Advise on financial objectives
	(c) Advise on non-financial objectives

Topics to be covered

- Profit and not for profit (NFP) organisations
- Quoted and unquoted companies
- Private and public sector organisations
- Value for money, maximising shareholder wealth
- Earnings growth and dividend growth
- Impact of underlying economic conditions and business variables on financial objectives

1   Overview of chapter

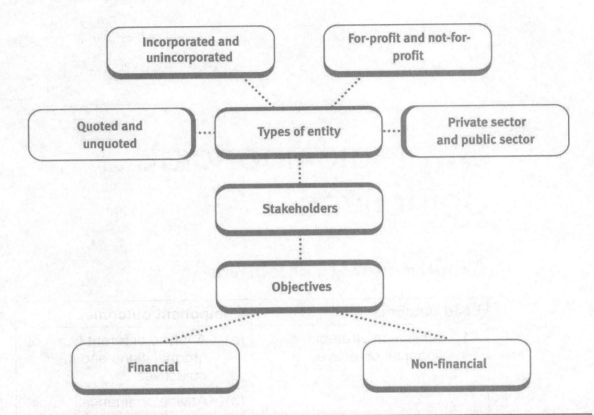

 Definitions of key terms

Mission: Fundamental objective(s) of an entity, expressed in general terms. (CIMA Official Terminology, 2005)

Mission statement: Published statement, apparently of the entity's fundamental objective(s). This may or may not summarise the true mission of the entity. (CIMA Official Terminology, 2005)

Objectives, hierarchy of: Arrangement of the objectives of an entity into a number of different levels, with the higher levels being more general and the lower levels more specific. These levels may be mission, goals, targets or, alternatively: strategic objectives, tactical objectives or operational objectives.

 ## 2   The mission and objectives of an entity

The mission and objectives of an entity will differ depending on:

- the type of entity (for example for-profit or not-for-profit)

- the needs of the entity's different stakeholders.

This chapter defines the different types of entity and considers who the entity's key stakeholders are. It then looks at different objectives, both financial objectives and non-financial.

Definitions of different types of entity

For-profit and not-for-profit entities

Most companies operate on a for-profit, or profit seeking basis. This means that their primary objective is to make a profit and therefore to satisfy their shareholders.

Most public sector entities operate on a not-for-profit basis, in that they usually have other primary objectives, often non-financial in nature.

Unincorporated and incorporated entities

An incorporated entity (sometimes called a company or corporation) is legally a separate entity from its owner(s).

Conversely, an owner and an unincorporated entity are legally the same, so the owner personally bears all the risks of the business.

Unincorporated entities are usually sole traders or partnerships.

Quoted and unquoted entities

Once an entity has been incorporated, it can apply to a stock exchange to have its shares quoted (or listed) on the exchange. It can be expensive to secure a stock exchange listing, so only large companies tend to become quoted.

A listing on an exchange makes it much easier for shareholders to buy and sell the entity's shares.

Private sector and public sector entities

A private sector entity is owned by private investors, whereas a public sector entity is owned by the government of a country.

Other types of entity

A **charitable entity (charity)** is a type of not-for-profit entity. It differs from other types of not-for-profit entities in that it centres on not-for-profit and philanthropic goals as well as social well-being (e.g. activities serving the public interest or common good).

An **association** or **union** is a group of individuals who enter into an agreement to form an entity to accomplish a purpose. Common examples include trade associations, trade unions and professional associations (like CIMA).

3 Objectives of different types of entity

It is generally accepted that the primary strategic objective of a for-profit entity (i.e. a commercial company) is the long-term goal of the **maximisation of the wealth of the shareholders.**

Entities such as public sector bodies (e.g. schools, hospitals), charities, trade unions and associations (such as accountancy bodies) are not run to make profits but to benefit prescribed groups of people. For example, the primary objective of a charity is to pursue whatever charitable objectives it was set up for.

Since the services provided are limited primarily by the funds available, secondary objectives are to raise the maximum possible funds each year (net of fund-raising expenses), and to use the funds efficiently to maximise the benefit generated.

Objectives of specific types of entity

There are some interesting extra points to note regarding objectives when we consider the issues facing the following specific types of entity:

Incorporated v unincorporated

An incorporated entity is likely to have several owners, and therefore there is the potential for greater conflict of stakeholder objectives than with an unincorporated entity.

Quoted v unquoted

A quoted company faces far more scrutiny from its many investors and from the financial market in general.

Also, because of this increased scrutiny, it is arguably more important that a quoted company sets appropriate non-financial objectives relating to its relationship with the environment and its staff.

Charities

Charites are usually established to raise money for a specific cause, and to spend the money raised in the most effective way.

However, increasingly charities are setting up retail outlets and trying to generate profits through trading. In some cases, the charities are making investments and therefore taking risks in order to try to increase returns. This sort of strategy used to be associated only with profit seeking organisations and would have once seemed inappropriate behaviour for charities. However, it has become the norm for most charities now.

4 Objectives and stakeholders

Definition of stakeholders

Stakeholders: Those persons and entities that have an interest in the strategy of an entity. Stakeholders normally include shareholders, customers, staff and the local community. (CIMA Official Terminology, 2005)

The decisions made by an entity's managers depend on the ultimate objectives of the entity.

Academic studies have shown that entities often have many, **sometimes conflicting**, objectives.

This is a consequence of having many stakeholders with both long- and short-term goals, such as:

- Equity investors (ordinary shareholders)
- The community at large
- Company employees
- Company managers/directors
- Customers
- Suppliers
- Finance providers
- The government

Stakeholder conflicts

Faced with a broad range of stakeholders, managers are likely to find they cannot simultaneously meet all the stakeholders' objectives.

For example the managers of a for-profit entity will find it difficult to maximise the wealth of their shareholders and keep all the other stakeholders content.

In this case, the main strategic objective may be interpreted as achieving the maximum profit possible, consistent with balancing the needs of the various stakeholders in the entity.

Such a policy may imply achieving a satisfactory return for shareholders, whilst (for example) establishing competitive terms and conditions of service for the employees, and avoiding polluting the environment.

> ### Example of conflicts of objectives – agency theory
>
> **Agency theory:** Hypothesis that attempts to explain elements of organisational behaviour through an understanding of the relationships between principals (such as shareholders) and agents (such as company managers and accountants). A conflict may exist between the actions undertaken by agents in furtherance of their own self-interest, and those required to promote the interests of the principals. (CIMA Official Terminology, 2005)
>
> ### Agency theory
>
> A possible conflict can arise when ownership is separated from the day-to-day management of an entity. In larger entities, the ordinary shares are likely to be diversely held, and so the actions of shareholders are likely to be restricted in practical terms. The responsibility of running the entity will be with the board of directors, who may only own a small percentage of the shares in issue.
>
> The managers of an entity are essentially agents for the shareholders, being tasked with running the entity in the shareholders' best interests. The shareholders, however, have little opportunity to assess whether the managers are acting in the shareholders' best interests.

5 For-profit entities

Introduction to objectives of for-profit entities

As stated above, the primary objective of a for-profit entity is the maximisation of shareholder wealth.

However, this objective always has to be balanced with other objectives, driven by the needs of the other key stakeholder groups.

For-profit entities will therefore have a mix of financial and non-financial objectives.

Financial objectives of for-profit entities

The financial objectives of a for-profit entity will be created after considering the following factors:

Equity investors (ordinary shareholders)

Within any economic system, the equity investors provide the risk finance. There is a very strong argument for maximising the wealth of equity investors. In order to attract funds, the company has to compete with other risk-free investment opportunities, e.g. government securities. The shareholders require returns from the company in terms of dividends and increases in share prices.

Finance providers

Providers of loan finance (banks, loan creditors) will primarily be interested in the ability of the firm to repay the finance including interest. As a result it will be the firm's ability to generate cash both long and short term that will be the basis of the goals of these providers.

Risk exposure

Risk can be measured according to finance theory.

Some risks – for example exchange-rate risk and interest-rate risk – can be managed by the use of hedging mechanisms. Shareholders and entities can therefore choose how much risk they wish to be exposed to for a given level of return. However, risk can take many forms, and the theory does not deal with risk exposure to matters such as recruitment of senior personnel or competitor activity.

Directors should set risk policies according to an agreed risk appetite which reflects the risk appetite of the shareholders.

Examples of specific financial objectives of for-profit entities

In order to achieve the overall objective of maximising shareholder wealth, but also to address the other issues identified above, entities should set specific financial targets in order to both communicate direction and measure performance.

For example:

Profitability

e.g. annual 10% improvement in earnings, or earnings per share.

Dividends

e.g. annual 5% increase in dividends.

Cash generation

e.g. annual 10% improvement in operating cash flow.

Gearing

e.g. a maximum [debt to (debt + equity)] ratio of 40%.

In order to assess whether the entity has achieved its financial objectives, ratio analysis can be used (covered in more detail towards the end of this chapter).

More on financial objectives of for-profit entities

Financial performance indicators

Return to investors

The return from ownership of shares in a profit-making entity can be measured by the formula:

$$\text{Annual return to investors} = \frac{P_1 - P_0 + \text{Dividend}}{P_0}$$

This is the capital appreciation on the shares (the difference between P_1 and P_0 – the share price at the end and the start of the year respectively), plus dividends received during the year. The measure reflects the fact that both share price growth and dividends are important to investors. In fact, investors can still make gains (through the capital appreciation of their shares) even if the entity never pays out a dividend.

Cash generation

Poor liquidity is a greater threat to the survival of an entity than is poor profitability. Unless the entity is prepared to fund growth with high levels of borrowings, cash generation is vital to ensure investment in future profitable ventures. In the private sector the alternative to cash via retained earnings is borrowing.

Value added

This is primarily a measure of performance. It is usually defined as revenues less the cost of purchased materials and services. It represents the value added to an entity's products by its own efforts. A problem here is comparability with other industries – or even with other entities in the same industry.

Profitability

Profitability may be defined as the rate at which profits are generated. It is often expressed as profit per unit of input (e.g. investment). However, profitability limits an entity's focus to one output measure – profit. It overlooks quality, and this limitation must be kept in mind when using profitability as a measure of success. Profitability as a measure of decision-making has been criticised because:

- it fails to provide a systematic explanation as to why one business sector has more favourable prospects than another;

- it does not provide enough insight into the dynamics and balance of an entity's individual business units, and the balance between them;

- it is remote from the actions that create value, and cannot therefore be managed directly in any but the smallest entities;

- the input to the measure may vary substantially between entities.

Nevertheless, it is a well-known and accepted measure which, once the input has been defined, is readily understood. Provided the input is consistent across entities and time periods, it also provides a useful comparative measure.

Return on assets (RoA)

This is an accounting measure, calculated by dividing annual profits by the average net book value of assets. It is therefore subject to the distortions inevitable when profit, rather than cash flows, is used to determine performance. Distorting factors for interpretation and comparison purposes include depreciation policy, inventory revaluations, write-off of intangibles such as goodwill, etc. A further defect is that RoA ignores the time value of money, although this may be of minor concern when inflation is very low.

RoA may not adequately reflect how efficiently assets were utilised: in a commercial context, taking account of profits but not the assets used in their making, for whatever reason, would overstate an entity's performance.

Market share

Market share is often seen as an objective for an entity in its own right. However, it must be judged in the context of other measures such as profitability and shareholder value. Market share, unlike many other measures, can take quality into account – it must be assumed that if customers do not get the quality they want or expect, then the entity will lose market share.

Gaining market share must be seen as a long-term goal of entities to ensure outlets for their products and services, and to minimise competition. However, market share can be acquired only within limits if a monopoly situation is to be avoided.

Competitive position

The performance of an entity must be compared with that of its competitors to establish a strategic perspective. A number of models and frameworks have been suggested by organisational theorists as to how competitive position may be determined and improved. A manager needing to make decisions must know by whom, by how much, and why he is gaining ground or being beaten by competitors.

Conventional measures, such as accounting data, are useful but no one measure is sufficient. Instead, an array of measures is needed to establish competitive position. The most difficult problem to overcome in using competitive position as a success factor is in collecting and acquiring data from competitors.

Non-financial objectives of for-profit entities

The non-financial objectives of a for-profit entity will be created after considering the following stakeholder issues:

Company employees

Returns = wages or salaries. However, maximising the returns to employees does assume that finance can be raised purely on the basis of satisficing the returns to finance providers. The employees' other interests also include job security and good conditions of employment.

Company managers/directors

Such senior employees are in an ideal position to follow their own aims at the expense of other stakeholders. Their goals will be both long-term (defending against takeovers, sales maximisation) and short-term (profit margins leading to increased bonuses).

Suppliers

Suppliers to the organisation will have short-term goals such as prompt payment terms alongside long-term requirements including contracts and regular business. The importance of the needs of suppliers will depend upon both their relative size and the number of suppliers.

The government

The government will have political and financial interests in the firm. Politically it will wish to increase exports and decrease imports whilst monitoring companies via the competition authorities. Financially it requires long-term profits to maximise taxation income.

The community at large

The goals of the community will be broad but will include such aspects as legal and social responsibilities, pollution control and employee welfare.

Environmental concerns

In pursuit of shareholder wealth maximisation, historically decisions have often been made that led to pollution or other environmental problems. Increasingly, entities are becoming aware of their environmental responsibilities. Many entities now produce environmental reports alongside their financial statements to emphasise their commitment to environmental issues. This is covered in more detail in Chapter 2: 'Integrated Reporting'.

Customer pressure

Entities are increasingly coming under pressure from knowledgeable customers. Customers are more and more keen to ensure that entities they trade with behave ethically and responsibly. Therefore, decision makers have to take account of customers' wishes, even if there appears to be a short-term conflict with the shareholder wealth maximisation objective.

Customer satisfaction

If customers are not satisfied they will take their business elsewhere and the entity will lose market share and go into liquidation. Measuring customer satisfaction is difficult to do formally, as the inputs and outputs are not readily defined or measurable. Surveys and questionnaires may be used but these methods have known flaws, mainly as a result of respondent bias.

Examples of specific non-financial objectives of for-profit entities

Non-financial objectives can be used to direct managers' attention towards key stakeholder requirements, to ensure that the entity balances the needs of its different stakeholders and minimises the conflict between the different stakeholder groups.

Also, achievement of non-financial objectives can improve the image of the entity from the perspective of its stakeholders. This can have a knock-on effect on sales and profitability and hence can help to create additional wealth for shareholders in the longer term.

Non-financial objectives can be categorised under the following headings:

Human

This considers the relationship of the entity with its staff, so objectives could cover increasing the amount of training provided, or reducing the level of staff turnover

Intellectual

This considers the intangible assets of the entity, such as its brand and reputation. Objectives could focus on improving the brand recognition.

Natural

This considers the entity's responsibility towards the environment, so objectives might include reducing the level of pollution and increasing the amount of recycling.

Social

This considers the entity's responsibility towards its local community. A social objective could be to make sure at least 50% of the employees live within a 5 mile radius of the entity's premises.

Relationship

This considers the entity's responsibility towards key stakeholders such as suppliers and customers. A relationship objective could be to pledge to offer all suppliers longer term contracts and to pay them on time, in order to improve the relationships.

6   Not-for-profit entities

Objectives of not-for-profit entities

Not-for-profit entities such as public sector bodies (e.g. schools, hospitals), charities, trade unions and associations (such as accountancy bodies) are not run to make profits but to benefit prescribed groups of people. For example, the primary objective of a charity is to pursue whatever charitable objectives it was set up for.

Since the services provided are limited primarily by the funds available, secondary objectives are to raise the maximum possible funds each year (net of fund-raising expenses), and to use the funds efficiently to maximise the benefit generated.

This can be measured as the 'value for money' (VFM) generated.

Satisfying many different stakeholders

Before we look at VFM in detail, it is worth noting that not-for-profit entities will still have a mix of financial and non-financial objectives (just like for-profit entities discussed above) and will still have to try to satisfy many different stakeholder groups.

There will often be different views of what the objectives of a not-for-profit entity should be, and therefore, whether appropriate objectives have been achieved. What value does one put on curing an illness, or saving a life? Should the success of a hospital be measured by shorter waiting lists? These are societal matters, the discomfort being one of the reasons they are placed firmly in the public sector, rather than being left to the 'survival of the fittest' philosophy associated with the competitive markets.

A public sector college will set objectives relating to the number of students, the number of courses, the ratio of lecturers to students, and so on. It will also seek its customers' assessments of the standard of, for example it's lecturing and catering, and compare them with preset targets. In the language of strategic financial management, these are answers to the question 'How well did we do what we chose to do?' that is, 'how **effective** were we in meeting the objectives?'

Public sector entities

Public sector entities are bodies such as nationalised industries and local government organisations. They represent a significant part of many countries' economies and sound financial management is essential if their affairs are to be conducted efficiently. The major problem here lies in obtaining a measurable objective.

Financial objectives in the public sector

For a stock market listed company we can take the maximisation of shareholder wealth as a working objective and know that the achievement of this objective can be monitored with reference to share price and dividend payments. For a public sector entity the situation is more complex.

The entity's mission statement will lay out its key objectives. However, generally such entities are run in the interests of society as a whole and therefore we should seek to attain the position where the gap between the benefits they provide to society and the costs of their operation is the widest (in positive terms).

The cost is relatively easily measured in accounting terms. However, many of the benefits are intangible. For example, the benefits of such bodies as the National Health Service or Local Education Authorities are almost impossible to quantify.

Such government organisations tend to use a low discount rate in investment appraisals (to take account of 'time preference') and have complex methods of quantifying non-financial benefits in a standard NPV analysis.

Economists have tried to evaluate many public sector investments through the use of cost benefit analysis, with varying degrees of success. Problems are usually encountered in evaluating all the benefits.

Regulation

It is worth remembering that organisations that have had a public sector history or are themselves natural monopolies are often regulated in order to ensure the public are not the victims of the monopoly power these companies enjoy. This regulation can take many forms but can include the capping of the selling prices, the taxing of super profits or simply a limit on the profits these entities are allowed to make.

Specific objectives of public sector entities

Traditionally, managers have focused on financial measures of performance and progress, but increasingly, entities in both the private and public sectors are using non-financial indicators to assess success across a range of criteria, which need to be chosen to help an entity meet its objectives.

A number of common objectives are discussed below, in the context of public sector entities.

Cash generation

Poor liquidity is a greater threat to the survival of an entity than is poor profitability. Unless the entity is prepared to fund growth with high levels of borrowings, cash generation is vital to ensure investment in future profitable ventures. In the private sector the alternative to cash via retained earnings is borrowing.

In the public sector this choice has not been available in the past, and all growth has been funded by government. However, in the face of government-imposed cash limits, local authorities and other public-sector entities are beginning to raise debt on the capital markets, and are therefore beginning to be faced with the same choices as profit-making entities.

Value added

Value added represents the value added to an entity's products by its own efforts.

A problem here is comparability with other industries – or even with other entities in the same industry.

Many public sector entities – for example those in the health service – are now publishing information on their own value added.

Profitability

Although the concept of profit in its true sense is absent from most of the public sector, profitability may be used to relate inputs to outputs if a different measure of output is used – for example: surplus after all costs, to capital investment.

Return on assets (RoA)

In the public sector, the concept of profit is absent, but it is still not unrealistic to expect entities to use donated assets with maximum efficiency. If depreciation on such assets were to be charged against income, this would depress the amount of surplus income over expenditure. Other points which may affect interpretation of RoA in the public sector are:

- difficulty in determining value;

- there may be no resale value;

- are for use by community at large;

- charge for depreciation may have the effect of 'double taxation' on the taxpayer.

Market share

Market share is a measure that is becoming increasingly relevant to the public sector – for example universities and health provision. Health providers must now 'sell' their services to trusts established to 'buy' from them. Those providers which are seen to fail their customers will lose market share as the trusts will buy from elsewhere (within certain limits).

Competitive position

The public sector is increasingly in competition with other providers of a similar service both in the private and public sectors.

For example hospitals now have to compete for the funds of health trusts. Their advantage is that it is easier to gain access to data from such competitors than it is in the private sector.

Risk exposure

Public sector entities tend to be risk averse because of the political repercussions of failure and the fact that taxpayers, unlike shareholders, do not have the option to invest their money in less (or more) risky ventures.

Assessing value for money in not-for-profit entities

Not-for-profit entities are often appraised according to the 'value for money' (VFM) that they generate.

Value for money may be defined as "performance of an activity in such a way as to simultaneously achieve economy, efficiency and effectiveness." (CIMA Official Terminology, 2005)

This means making the optimum use of available resources to achieve the intended outcome.

VFM has three constituent elements:

Economy: minimising the cost of resources used or required (inputs) – spending less

Efficiency: the relationship between the output from goods or services and the resources to produce them – spending well

Effectiveness: the relationship between the intended and actual results of public spending (outcomes) – spending wisely.

These elements can be referred to by the umbrella term **'cost effectiveness'**.

Besides these three 'Es, a fourth 'E' is applied in some places:

Equity: the extent to which services are available to and reach all people that they are intended to – spending fairly. Some people may receive differing levels of service for reasons other than differences in their levels of need.

Overview of VFM

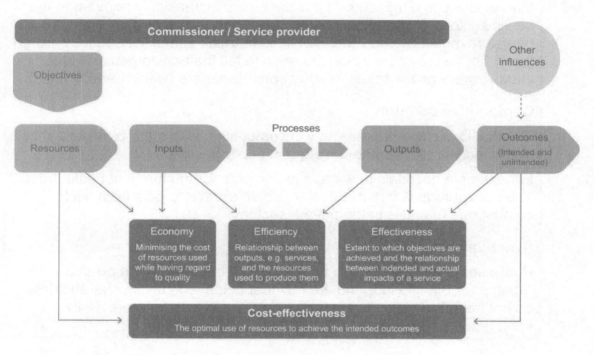

Source: UK National Audit Office website

More detail on VFM

Measurement of VFM

In practice, value for money is difficult to measure, and it is a relative rather than an absolute measure.

Value for money audit or study

A value for money audit is defined as an "investigation into whether proper arrangements have been made for securing economy, efficiency and effectiveness in the use of resources." (CIMA Official Terminology, 2005)

A value for money study focuses on a specific area of expenditure, and seeks to reach a judgement on whether value for money has been achieved. Good value for money can be defined as the optimal use of resources to achieve the intended outcomes.

The purpose of a VFM study is not to question policy objectives, but to provide independent and rigorous analysis on the way in which money has been spent to achieve those policy objectives.

As well as reaching an overall conclusion on value for money, a VFM study will make recommendations on how to achieve better value for money and to improve the services under examination. In some circumstances, a follow-up study is conducted to measure progress against the recommendations made.

Typically, a study will use a mix of quantitative and qualitative methods. The methods commonly used include:

- Financial analysis
- Analysis of management information
- Interviews or focus groups with departmental and other staff
- General research
- Surveys of practitioners or service users
- Benchmarking with other organisations or other countries.

Real world difficulties

In reality, a VFM audit will usually focus on either effectiveness or on economy and efficiency. This is because the two sides of VFM are often in partial conflict; you can have a better service (but spend more) or a cheaper service (often of lower quality). Therefore the different elements are typically looked at within separate VFM audits.

Illustration 1 – A practical example of VFM

Practical example: Value for money (taken from the website of the UK National Audit Office)

A local authority sets up a new programme to reduce litter dropping. One of its early steps is to agree with stakeholders a set of outcomes for the programme. The effectiveness of the programme is to be judged on the extent to which it reaches its outcomes in a year.

In this case, the programme achieves 97% of its outcomes and councillors declare they have 'come within a whisker of winning the battle against litter'. The programme was effective.

However, the programme cost more than expected and overspent its budget by 25 per cent. This was because the programme managers allowed costs to over-run in their drive to meet the outcome. The programme was not economical.

The cost over-run prompts a review of the service. This concludes that, outcome for outcome, it was more expensive than similar programmes in neighbouring areas. The programme was not efficient.

If programme objectives had been exceeded sufficiently, the programme may have been cost-effective despite the overspend. However, programme managers could still be criticised for exceeding the budget.

The most disadvantaged parts of the area were also those with the biggest litter problems and these neighbourhoods improved more, from a lower base, than wealthier places. The programme was equitable.

Note how effectiveness (achieving the outcomes) partly conflicted with the economy and efficiency (high overspends and cheaper projects in other regions).

7 International operations

Increasingly in the modern business environment, entities are expanding across national boundaries into many different countries.

Although there are risks associated with such strategies, the strategic and financial benefits to an entity can be enormous.

In many ways, the objectives of an entity trading internationally will be the same as those of an entity based in just one country. However, there are some additional considerations.

Strategic implications of international expansion

The main strategic implications of international expansion are:

Competition

Foreign markets may have weaker competition. A firm facing a competitive domestic market will benefit from finding a foreign market where it has a monopoly.

Country factors

Some countries have cheap sources of natural raw materials and cheap labour costs. Locating production facilities in these countries will bring significant cost savings. Also, some countries' governments offer grants and cheap loans to foreign investors to attract inward investment.

Benefits to the customer

Locating in a different country could move an entity closer to existing customers, so reducing delivery times and improving relationships. Also, it is likely to bring an entity closer to a pool of potential new customers.

Economies of scale

As the entity gets bigger, international expansion might be the best way of continuing to generate economies of scale.

Risk management

International expansion will leave an entity less exposed to a single economy. Factors such as interest rates, inflation, government policy and exchange rates from more than one economy will impact a business with international operations. This will reduce the economic and political risk to the entity.

Financial implications of international expansion

The primary corporate objective – to maximise shareholder wealth – has been referred to earlier in this chapter.

The main financial benefit of an international investment is the positive NPV and consequent gain to shareholders of undertaking an attractive project.

However, also consider the following other financial implications of international investment:

Impact on the financial statements

If the foreign project assets are denominated in foreign currency, they will have to be converted into the domestic currency for the purposes of consolidation. If exchange rates fluctuate from one year to the next, the value of these assets will also fluctuate, giving (unrealised) exchange gains or losses in the entity's accounts. This is known as translation risk, however it does not impact the actual cash flows of the business and is often left unmitigated.

Impact on the cost of capital

International investments will often be more risky to an entity than its normal domestic investments. Therefore, it is likely that the entity's cost of capital will change to reflect this increased risk.

8 Financial performance evaluation

Introduction

Investors (both shareholders and lenders) will often appraise the financial performance of an organisation, to assess whether the organisation represents a good investment. If it is shown that the organisation's financial performance is declining, the shareholders may decide to sell their shares, and the lenders might change their assessment of the organisation's creditworthiness.

In an exam question, you might also be asked to use ratio analysis to assess whether an entity has met its financial objectives.

 To appraise financial performance, it is necessary to first calculate ratios under the following headings:

- profitability ratios,
- lender ratios,
- investor ratios.

The calculation of these ratios is covered in the rest of this chapter.

However, as well as performing the calculations, it will also be important to be able to interpret the figures, so you will find detailed explanations of how to interpret the ratios throughout.

9 Profitability ratios

Several profit figures (gross profit, operating profit, net profit) can be identified in a typical statement of profit or loss.

Profitability is a key performance indicator for an entity. In order to assess performance accurately, it is important to compare figures consistently from one year to the next.

 Definitions of different profit figures

Profit figures in the statement of profit or loss

Gross profit = Sales − Cost of Sales

$$\text{Gross profit margin} = \frac{\text{Gross profit}}{\text{Revenue}} \times 100$$

Generally, a high profit margin is perceived to be indicative of good performance.

Operating profit = profit from the trading activities of an entity i.e. sales – operating costs, but before finance costs (interest) and tax.

Net profit = Profit after deduction of the finance costs (interest) and tax

EBITDA

EBITDA is an acronym for earnings before interest, tax, depreciation and amortization. In recent years many large entities have adopted EBITDA as a key measure of financial performance. Sceptics suggest that they do this in order to publicise a higher measure of earnings than profit from operations (this type of measurement is sometimes cynically referred to as EBB – earnings before the bad bits).

However, it does make some sense to measure EBITDA, provided that the user fully understands what is included and what is left out. Depreciation and amortization are accounting adjustments, not representing cash flows that are determined by management. It can therefore be argued that excluding these items in assessing earnings eliminates a major area where management bias can operate. Unfortunately, EBITDA is consequently often misunderstood as being a measurement of cash flow, which of course it is not. Even though two categories of non-cash adjustment are eliminated, financial statements are prepared on an accruals basis. EBITDA makes no adjustments in respect of accruals or working capital movements, and so is emphatically not a cash flow measurement.

 There are two measures critical to any analysis of profitability:

1   **Return on Capital Employed (ROCE)**

2   **Return on Equity (ROE)**

Return on capital employed (ROCE)

Return on capital employed (ROCE) is a measurement that is frequently used in the analysis of financial statements.

It shows the overall performance of the entity, expressed as a percentage return on the total investment. It measures management's efficiency in generating profits from the resources available.

ROCE is expressed as a percentage, and is calculated as follows:

$$\text{ROCE} = \frac{\text{Operating profit}}{\text{Capital employed}} \times 100$$

where Capital employed = The total funds invested in the business, i.e. shareholders' funds + long term debt, or total assets less current liabilities.

Return on equity (ROE)

ROE gives an indication as to how well the company has performed in relation to its shareholders, the most important stakeholder.

ROE is expressed as a percentage, and is calculated as follows:

$$ROE = \frac{Net\ profit}{Equity} \times 100$$

where Equity = The book value of shareholders' funds

It is useful to compare the ROE to the ROCE to measure the amount of the return underlying the business that pertains to the shareholder. Note, however, that they are not directly comparable, ROE being based on net profit and ROCE based on operating profit.

Asset turnover

$$Asset\ turnover = \frac{Revenue}{Capital\ employed}$$

This calculation is usually expressed as a simple ratio, rather than as a percentage. It shows how much revenue is produced per $ of investment in capital employed.

Return on capital employed – Further analysis

When trying to analyse ROCE, it can be useful to break it down as follows into two component ratios:

ROCE = Operating profit margin × Asset turnover

The relationship becomes clear when we put the ratio calculations into the formula:

$$\frac{Operating\ profit}{Capital\ employed} \times 100 = \frac{Operating\ profit}{Revenue} \times 100 \times \frac{Revenue}{Capital\ employed}$$

Analysing the component ratios may throw some light on the cause of a change in ROCE.

For example, a fall in ROCE could be caused by:

- generating lower sales from the company's capital (lower asset turnover), and/or

- generating a lower profit margin on the sales which have been achieved (lower operating profit margin).

Test your understanding 1 (Integration question)

A company is considering two funding options for a new project. The new project may be funded by GBP10m of equity or debt. Below are the forecast financial statements reflecting both methods of funding.

Statement of financial position extract

	Equity GBPm	Debt GBPm
Long term liabilities (10% bonds)	0.0	10.0
Capital		
Share capital (50 pence)	11.0	3.5
Share premium	4.0	1.5
Reserves	5.0	5.0
	20.0	10.0

Statement of profit or loss extract

	GBPm
Revenue	100.0
Gross profit	20.0
Less expenses (excluding finance charges)	(15.0)
Operating profit	5.0

Corporation tax is charged at 30%.

Required:

(a) Calculate the operating profit margin and the asset turnover.

(b) Calculate Return on Capital Employed and Return on Equity, and compare the financial performance of the company under the two funding methods.

(c) What is the impact on the company's performance of financing by debt rather than equity?

Interpretation of profitability ratios

In general terms, high levels of profitability are desirable.

An entity with high profit margins and a high ROCE is usually perceived to be performing well. Similarly, if the ratios grow over time, this is usually perceived to be positive.

The ideal value for the profitability ratios will vary from industry to industry, so be sure to compare the figures to previous years and to other similar businesses if possible.

10 Lender ratios

Definition of gearing
CIMA's Official Terminology provides the following definition of gearing: "... the relationship between an entity's borrowings, which includes both prior charge capital and long-term debt, and its shareholders' funds."

 Gearing is the mix of debt to equity within a firm's permanent capital. There are two particularly useful measures:

1   Capital gearing – a statement of financial position (balance sheet) measure.

2   Interest cover – a statement of profit or loss measure.

Capital gearing – a measure of capital structure

There are two key measures of capital gearing:

$$\text{Capital gearing} = \frac{\text{Debt}}{\text{Equity}} \times 100$$

$$\frac{\text{Debt}}{\text{Debt + Equity}} \times 100$$

The calculation of capital gearing can be done in a number of different ways. In the exam, you'll be told which formula to use.

The most commonly used formula in practice and in the exam is debt/(debt + equity) i.e. the second formula here.

Constituent elements of debt and equity

Debt includes redeemable preference shares, bank borrowings and bonds (overdrafts may be included if they are long-term finance sources).

Equity includes ordinary and irredeemable preference shares (plus reserves if the valuation is at book value).

Market values and book values

Wherever possible, market values should be used in preference to book values for the capital gearing ratio.

When using market values, care must be taken when calculating the market value of equity:

When equity is valued using book values it must include any reserves and retained profits that are attributable to the ordinary shareholders that is:

Book value of equity = ordinary share capital + reserves

When market values are used, reserves must be excluded since they are considered to be already incorporated into the market price of the shares, that is:

Market value of equity = Number of shares × Share price

 ## Interest cover

The interest cover ratio indicates the number of times profits will cover the interest charge; the higher the ratio, the better.

$$\text{Interest cover} = \frac{\text{Profit before interest and tax}}{\text{Interest payable}}$$

The interest cover ratio is used by lenders to determine the vulnerability of interest payments to a drop in profit.

As an alternative to the formula shown here, investors often use EBITDA rather than profit before interest and tax in the formula, because EBITDA is a better approximation to the cash generated by the business (and available to pay interest with).

 ### The debt ratio

Another useful ratio is the ratio of long-term debt to total assets, which is calculated as follows:

$$\text{Debt ratio} = \frac{\text{Total long term debt}}{\text{Total assets}}$$

This can provide very useful information for creditors as it measures the availability of assets in the business in relation to the total debt.

Test your understanding 2 (Integration question)

Statement of financial position for X Co

	USDm
Non-current assets (total)	23.0
Current assets (total)	15.0
TOTAL ASSETS	**38.0**
Equity and Liabilities	
Ordinary share capital	10.0
Ordinary share premium	4.0
Preference share capital (irredeemable)	1.5
Reserves	1.5
Non-current liabilities	
10% bonds	8.0
Current liabilities	
Trade creditors	8.0
Bank overdraft	5.0
TOTAL EQUITY & LIABILITIES	**38.0**

X Co statement of profit or loss extract

	USDm
Operating profit (PBIT)	4.0
Finance Charges	(1.0)
Profit before tax (PBT)	3.0
Tax @ 30%	(0.9)
Net profit	2.1

Required:

(a) Calculate the interest cover for X Co, and the capital gearing ratio (on the assumption that the overdraft is to be used in the long term so should be included within debt).

(b) Comment on the results of your calculations in part (a).

11 Investor ratios

Investors will wish to assess the performance of the shares they have invested in (against competing entities in the same sector, against the market as a whole, and over time).

There are a number of ratios which will be of specific interest to investors (both debt investors and equity investors).

Market price per share

The market price per share used throughout the following ratio formulae is the ex-dividend market price.

Ex-dividend means that in buying a share today, the investor will not participate in the forthcoming dividend payment.

Sometimes in an examination, the market price may be quoted cum-dividend which means with dividend rights attached. Here the investor will participate in the forthcoming dividend if purchasing the share today. Arguably the investor will be willing to pay a higher price for the share, knowing that a dividend payment is forthcoming in the near future.

The relationship between the cum-dividend price and the ex-dividend price is then:

Ex-dividend market price = Cum-dividend market price – Forthcoming dividend per share.

Earnings per share (EPS)

Before we can calculate any ratios we need to calculate a key measure of return, the Earnings per share (EPS).

$$EPS = \frac{Earnings}{Number\ of\ ordinary\ shares\ in\ issue}$$

where Earnings = Profit distributable to ordinary shareholders, i.e. after interest, tax and any preference dividend.

More details on EPS

An important point to remember is that EPS is a historical figure and can be manipulated by changes in accounting policies, mergers or acquisitions, etc.

Market analysts and company executives occasionally appear obsessed about EPS as a performance measure, an obsession which many think is quite disproportionate to its true value.

It is future earnings which should concern investors, a figure far more difficult to estimate.

P/E ratio

The P/E ratio is a measure of growth; it compares the market value (a measure of future earnings) to the current earnings.

$$P/E\ ratio = \frac{Current\ share\ price}{EPS}$$

or, alternatively, Total market capitalisation/Total earnings.

The higher the P/E ratio, the greater the market expectation of future earnings growth. This may also be described as market potential.

Earnings yield

The P/E ratio is the reciprocal (in maths, a number or quantity divided into 1) of the earnings yield.

$$\text{Earnings yield} = \frac{\text{EPS}}{\text{Current share price}}$$

or, alternatively, Total earnings/Total market capitalisation.

The market price will incorporate expectations of all buyers and sellers of the entity's shares, and so this is an indication of the future earning power of the entity.

Dividend-payout rate

The cash effect of payment of dividends is measured by the dividend-payout rate.

$$\text{Payout rate} = \frac{\text{Dividend per share}}{\text{EPS}}$$

or, alternatively, Total dividend/Total earnings.

The relationship between the above investors' ratios is usually that an entity with a high P/E ratio has a low dividend payout ratio as the high growth entity needs to retain more resources in the entity. A more stable entity would have a relatively low P/E ratio and higher dividend-payout ratio.

When analysing financial statements from an investor's point of view it is important to identify the objectives of the investor. Does the investor require high capital growth and high risk, or a lower risk, fixed dividend payment and low capital growth?

Dividend yield

This is the relationship of the dividend paid to the current market value of a share.

$$\text{Dividend yield} = \frac{\text{Dividend per share}}{\text{Current share price}}$$

or, alternatively, Total dividend/Total market capitalisation.

However, the dividend represents only part of the overall return from a share.

The other part of the return is the capital gain from an increase in the value of the share. The capital gain from a share may well be far more significant than the dividend.

Dividend cover

Dividend cover measures the ability of the entity to maintain the existing level of dividend and is used in conjunction with the dividend yield.

$$\text{Dividend cover} = \frac{\text{Earnings per share}}{\text{Dividend per share}}$$

or, alternatively, Total earnings/Total dividend.

The higher the dividend cover the more likely it is that the dividend yield can be maintained.

Dividend cover also gives an indication of the level of profits being retained by the entity for reinvestment by considering how many times this year's dividend is covered by this year's earnings.

 Test your understanding 3 (Integration question)

Lilydale Co has 5m ordinary shares in issue. Its results for the year are:

	USD000
Profit before tax	750
Tax	(150)
Profit after tax (PAT)	600
Ordinary dividend – proposed	(150)
Retained profit	450

The market price per share is currently 83 cents cum-dividend.

Required:

Calculate the following ratios:

(a) Price/earnings ratio

(b) Dividend payout rate

(c) Dividend yield, and

(d) Dividend cover.

Earnings growth and dividend growth

An analysis of growth rates of earnings and dividends can enable investors to make an assessment of the performance of an entity.

High growth rates in earnings and dividends are usually viewed positively.

Calculations

The growth rate for a single year is:

[(current figure/last year's figure) − 1] × 100%

Over a number of years (n), the implied compound annual growth rate is:

$[\sqrt[n]{(\text{current figure/earliest year's figure})} - 1] \times 100\%$

So for example, if earnings per share have grown from $0.28 to $0.33 over a 4 year period, the implied compound annual growth rate is:

$[\sqrt[4]{(0.33/0.28)} - 1] \times 100\% = 4.19\%$ per year

Test your understanding 4 (Objective test question)

ALB Co has the following financial objectives:

- to achieve an average earnings growth of at least 6% per annum

- to keep its gearing, measured as [debt/(debt + equity)] by market value, below 35%

In the last three years, ALB Co's operating profit has grown from $4.0 million to $4.6 million, and its profit after tax has grown from $2.3 million to $2.9 million.

ALB Co has 1 million $1 shares in issue, trading at $1.88, and $1,000,000 of bonds, trading at $106 per cent.

Which of the objectives has ALB Co achieved?

A   Both objectives

B   Just the gearing objective

C   Just the earnings growth objective

D   Neither objective

---

12 Sensitivity of the attainment of financial objectives to changes in economic and business variables

Changes to economic and business variables

When economic variables (such as inflation rates and interest rates) and / or business variables (such as margins and volumes) change, it is important to be able to assess the likely impact on the entity and its chances of achieving its financial objectives.

For example a change in interest rates in the economy might cause an entity's financing costs to rise, and therefore might make it more difficult for the entity to achieve a profitability target.

More detail on interest rates and inflation

The effects of interest rate changes

Changes in interest rates affect the economy in many ways. The following consequences are the main effects of an increase in interest rates:

Spending falls – expenditure by consumers, both individual and business, will be reduced. This occurs because the higher interest rates raise the cost of credit and deter spending. If we take incomes as fairly stable in the short term, higher interest payments on credit cards/mortgages, etc., leave less income for spending on consumer goods and services. This fall in spending means less aggregate demand in the economy and thus unemployment results.

Asset values fall – the market value of financial assets will drop, because of the inverse relationship (between bonds and the rate of interest) explained earlier. This, in turn, will reduce many people's wealth. It is likely that they will react to maintain the value of their total wealth and so may save, thereby further reducing expenditure in the economy. This phenomenon seems to fit the UK recession of the early 1990s when the house-price slump deepened the economic gloom. For many consumers today a house, rather than bonds, is their main asset.

Foreign funds are attracted into the country – a rise in interest rates will encourage overseas financial speculators to deposit money in the country's banking institutions because the rate of return has increased relative to that in other countries. Such funds could be made available as loans to firms in that country by the banking sector.

The exchange rate rises – the inflow of foreign funds raises demand for the domestic currency and so pushes up the exchange rate. This has the benefit of lowering import prices and thereby bearing down on domestic inflation. However, it makes exports more expensive and possibly harder to sell. The longer-term effect on the balance of payments could be beneficial or harmful depending on the elasticity of demand and supply for traded goods.

Inflation falls – higher interest rates affect the rate of inflation in three ways. First, less demand in the economy may encourage producers to lower prices in order to sell. This could be achieved by squeezing profit margins and/or wage levels. Second, new borrowing is deferred by the high interest rates and so demand will fall. Third, the higher exchange rate will raise export prices and thereby threaten sales which in turn pressurises producers to cut costs, particularly wages. If workers are laid off then again total demand is reduced and inflation is likely to fall.

The effects of inflation

Inflation is defined simply as 'rising prices' and shows the cost of living in general terms.

If the rate of inflation is low, then the effects may be beneficial to an economy. Business people are encouraged by fairly stable prices and the prospect of higher profits. However, there is some argument about whether getting inflation below 3% to, say, zero, is worth the economic pain (of, say, higher unemployment). There is agreement, though, that inflation above 5% is harmful – worse still if it is accelerating. The main arguments are that such inflation:

Distorts consumer behaviour – people may bring forward purchases because they fear higher prices later. This can cause hoarding and so destabilise markets, creating unnecessary shortages.

Redistributes income – people on fixed incomes or those lacking bargaining power will become relatively worse off, as their purchasing power falls. This is unfair.

Affects wage bargainers – trades unionists on behalf of labour may submit higher claims at times of high inflation, particularly if previously they had underestimated the future rise in prices. If employers accept such claims this may precipitate a wage–price spiral which exacerbates the inflation problem.

Undermines business confidence – wide fluctuations in the inflation rate make it difficult for entrepreneurs to predict the economic future and accurately calculate prices and investment returns. This uncertainty handicaps planning and production.

Weakens the country's competitive position – if inflation in a country exceeds that in a competitor country, then it makes exports less attractive (assuming unchanged exchange rates) and imports more competitive. This could mean fewer sales of that country's goods at home and abroad and thus a bigger trade deficit. For example the decline of Britain's manufacturing industry can be partly attributed to the growth of cheap imports when they were experiencing high inflation in the period 1978–1983.

Redistributes wealth – if the rate of interest is below the rate of inflation, then borrowers are gaining at the expense of lenders. The real value of savings is being eroded. This wealth is being redistributed from savers to borrowers and from payables to receivables. As the government is the largest borrower, via the national debt, it gains most during inflationary times.

Interest rate parity theory

In economic theory, the impact of interest rates on the expected exchange rate is given by the interest rate parity theory.

Interest rate parity formula

$$F_0 = S_0 \times \frac{(1 + r_{var})}{(1 + r_{base})}$$

where

S_0 = spot rate of exchange

F_0 = forward rate of exchange

r_{var} and r_{base} are the interest rates associated with the variable and base currencies respectively. For example, if an exchange rate is quoted as GBP/USD 1.65 (i.e. GBP 1 = USD 1.65) then the GBP is the base currency and the USD is the variable one.

The interest rate parity theory shows that the forward rate of exchange can be found by adjusting the spot rate of exchange to reflect the differential in interest rates between the two countries.

Test your understanding 5 (Objective test question)

BBL Co is based in country G, where the functional currency is the G$.

Some of BBL Co's suppliers are based in the UK, and they invoice BBL Co in British pounds (GBP). Therefore, the directors of BBL Co keep a close eye on the exchange rate between the G$ and the GBP, and they use the interest rate parity theory to estimate the likely future exchange rates.

The current spot rate is G$/GBP 1.88 (that is G$ 1 = GBP 1.88), and the expected interest rates in the UK and country G respectively are 5% and 8% over the next year.

What is the forecast spot rate in one year's time using the interest rate parity theory and assuming that the current forward rate is the best forecast of the future spot rate?

A G$/GBP 1.18

B G$/GBP 1.83

C G$/GBP 1.93

D G$/GBP 3.01

Test your understanding 6 (Objective test question)

The financial director of JW Co is attempting to estimate the likely exchange rate in 1 years' time, so that he can assess the likely value of the entity's foreign currency income.

JW Co is based in country C (functional currency C$) and it makes some sales in the USA, denominated in US dollars (USD). Sales in 1 year's time are expected to be USD 400,000.

The spot rate of exchange is C$/USD 23.35 (that is C$ 1 = USD 23.35). Interest rates in the USA and country C are expected to be 2% and 6% respectively over the next year.

What is the expected exchange rate in 1 years' time, using the interest rate parity theory, and what is the expected value of the USD sales when translated into C$?

A   Exchange rate: C$/USD 24.27, value of sales: C$ 9.708 million

B   Exchange rate: C$/USD 24.27, value of sales: C$ 16,481

C   Exchange rate: C$/USD 22.47, value of sales: C$ 8.988 million

D   Exchange rate: C$/USD 22.47, value of sales: C$ 17,802

Interest rate parity and other similar theories are covered in more detail in Chapter 9: 'Currency risk management'.

The impact on financial ratios of changes in interest rates, exchange rates and inflation

A change in economic variables such as interest rates, exchange rates and inflation can have an impact on an entity's ability to meet its objectives.

For example, a change in exchange rates could impact selling prices and hence profitability ratios, and could prevent an entity from achieving an earnings objective.

If you are asked in the exam to assess the likelihood of an entity achieving a given objective, you should revise the financial statements to reflect the expected change and then recalculate the necessary ratios.

Test your understanding 7 (Objective test question)

Tillman Co is an unquoted manufacturing company based in country T, whose functional currency is the T$.

Extracts from its most recent financial statements are shown below:

Statement of profit or loss extract

	T$ m
Revenue	100.0
Gross profit	20.0
Less expenses (excluding finance charges)	(15.0)
Operating profit	5.0

Corporation tax is charged at 30%.

Tillman has T$ 8 million of long term borrowings, on which it paid interest of 10% last year, and it has 20 million T$ 1 shares in issue.

Tillman Co expects its interest rate to rise by two percentage points next year (to 12%). Also, a strengthening of the currency in Tillman Co's main export market will cause the T$ value of Tillman Co's gross profit to rise to T$ 25 million next year.

What is the likely impact on Tillman Co's earnings per share (EPS), assuming that all other factors remain the same next year?

A   Increase by 20%

B   Increase by 25%

C   Increase by 115%

D   Increase by 215%

The impact on financial ratios of changes in margins and volumes

A change in business variables such as margins and volumes of activity can also have an impact on an entity's ability to meet its objectives.

For example, a fall in sales volume can impact profitability ratios and could prevent an entity from achieving an earnings growth objective.

If you are asked in the exam to assess the likelihood of an entity achieving a given objective, you should revise the financial statements to reflect the expected change and then recalculate the necessary ratios.

Test your understanding 8 (Objective test question)

MATT Co is a manufacturing company based in country M, whose functional currency is the M$.

Extracts from its most recent financial statements are shown below:

Statement of financial position extract

	M$ m
Long term liabilities (10% bonds)	8.0
Capital	
Share capital (M$ 0.50 par)	10.0
Share premium	1.0
Reserves	3.0
	14.0

Statement of profit or loss extract

	M$ m
Revenue	100.0
Gross profit	20.0
Less expenses (excluding finance charges)	(15.0)
Operating profit	5.0

Corporation tax is charged at 30%.

MATT Co expects its volume of sales to increase by 5% next year, and its gross profit margin to reduce by 4 percentage points (so for example if the margin were currently 40%, it would reduce to 36% next year).

What is the likely impact on MATT Co's earnings per share (EPS), assuming that its capital structure, tax rate and other expenses stay constant?

A   Increase by 5%

B   Increase by 1%

C   Decrease by 20%

D   Decrease by 76%

13 The use of published accounts for ratio analysis

When external stakeholders, such as potential investors and lenders, try to assess the performance of an entity, the most readily available source of information is the published accounts of the entity.

In trying to interpret the ratios calculated from the published accounts figures, it is important to understand the limitations of the published figures.

Limitations of published accounts figures for ratio analysis

- Published accounts are historic records, not forward looking. However, in many countries there are additional local regulations which require or encourage companies to present additional information as part of their published accounts. This may include the directors' view of the company's prospects, environmental data, market information, gender pay gaps and much more. This fits with the global drive towards integrated reporting, which is discussed more in Chapter 2.

- The statement of profit or loss is prepared using the accruals concept, so it is difficult to relate the figures to the entity's cash position. However the inclusion of the cash flow statement in the published accounts helps to give an impression of the cash position.

- The published accounts have historically contained only financial information. In recent years entities have been encouraged to report on wider issues (such as environmental and social issues), so users of the accounts are able to see a fuller view of the entity's performance.

These points are covered more fully in the next chapter.

14 End of chapter objective test questions

> **Test your understanding 9 (Objective test question)**
>
> The share price of Woundale Co rose from $2.00 to $2.30 last year. During the year, the company paid out a dividend of $0.12 per share.
>
> **What was the annual return to investors last year?**
>
> A   15%
>
> B   21%
>
> C   30%
>
> D   42%

Test your understanding 10 (Objective test question)

Q Co is an entity that was set up by the government of Country Q to produce electricity for the country's citizens.

Five years ago it was privatised as the government of Country Q opened up the energy market to competition. The shares of Q co are now owned by both private investors and institutions, and are traded on Country Q's stock market.

What kind of entity is Q Co?

A   Public sector, for-profit entity

B   Public sector, not-for-profit entity

C   Private sector, for-profit entity

D   Private sector, not-for-profit entity

Test your understanding 11 (Objective test question)

Value for money is an important objective for not-for-profit organisations.

Which action is LEAST consistent with increasing value for money?

A   Using a cheaper source of goods without decreasing the quality of not-for-profit organisation services

B   Searching for ways to diversify the finances of the not-for-profit organisation

C   Decreasing waste in the provision of a service by the not-for-profit organisation

D   Focusing on meeting the objectives of the not-for-profit organisation

Test your understanding 12 (Objective test question)

Blunderbuss Co is a listed company with 1 million $1 shares in issue and long term bank borrowings of $5 million. The bank interest rate in the most recent year was 8%, but this is expected to change to 10% for the whole of next year.

The company made an operating profit of $1.84 million last year.

What will be the change in the interest cover of Blunderbuss Co next year, on the assumption that operating profits will stay constant?

A   25% increase

B   20% decrease

C   25% decrease

D   20% increase

Test your understanding 13 (Objective test question)

Angela Co is a listed company.

It has 1 million $0.25 par value ordinary shares in issue, and $100,000 worth of $100 par value bonds.

The shares were originally issued at a premium of $0.05 per share, and the bonds were issued at a 10% discount to par value. The shares and the bonds are trading at $1.22 and $102 respectively.

What is the gearing ratio of Angela Co, calculated as [debt / (debt + equity)] and using market values?

A   7.7%

B   8.4%

C   23.1%

D   28.6%

Test your understanding 14 (Objective test question)

Your manager has asked you to compute the Return on Capital Employed for your company.

Which of the following profit figures would you use in the calculation?

A   Gross profit

B   Net profit

C   Operating profit

D   EBITDA

Test your understanding 15 (Objective test question)

Shepley High School had a problem with high levels of pupil absenteeism in the last academic year, so the senior management team decided to implement a new rewards programme in an attempt to reduce the number of pupils missing classes.

The plan was to reward all pupils with a sticker on a chart for every day that they attended all their classes. Then, at the end of each week, all pupils with five stickers on the chart (i.e. those with a perfect attendance record) were entered into a prize draw with a tablet computer as the prize for the winner.

The end of the academic year is now approaching, and the value for money (VFM) of the programme is being assessed.

Key observations:

- The cost of the programme has been lower than budgeted, because the school managed to get an unexpected bulk discount on purchases of the prize tablet computers.

- The level of absenteeism has remained almost constant compared with the previous year.

- A local newspaper has run a negative campaign about the programme, accusing the school of wasting money and 'bribing' pupils to attend classes. The head teacher has defended the programme, but has admitted that other schools in the area manage to achieve lower levels of absenteeism despite not running such expensive rewards programmes.

Which of the following is the best summary of the results of this Value for Money review?

A   Economy, effectiveness and efficiency have all been achieved

B   Economy and efficiency have been achieved, but not effectiveness

C   Economy and effectiveness have been achieved, but not efficiency

D   Only economy has been achieved

Test your understanding 16 (Objective test question)

The most recent statement of financial position of Johnson Co is as follows:

Assets	$000
Non-current assets	23,600
Current assets	8,400
	32,000

Equity and liabilities	
Capital and reserves	
$1 Ordinary shares	8,000
Retained earnings	11,200
	19,200
Non-current liabilities	
6% Unsecured bond	8,000
Current liabilities	4,800
	32,000

Johnson Co made an operating profit of $3.0 million and a net profit of $2.5 million in the year.

What is the return on equity of Johnson Co?

A   13.0%

B   15.6%

C   31.3%

D   37.5%

Test your understanding 17 (Objective test question)

The P/E ratios of AA Co and BB Co are 7.8 and 9.8 respectively.

Which TWO of the following statements are definitely correct based on this information?

A   AA Co's share price is lower than BB Co's

B   The market perception of BB Co is better than that of AA Co

C   AA Co is an unquoted company and BB Co is a quoted company

D   The risk associated with BB Co must be higher than the risk associated with AA Co

E   BB Co's earnings yield is lower than AA Co's

Test your understanding 18 (Objective test question)

Josh Co is an all equity financed company. It made sales in the most recent accounting period of $10.5 million, and achieved an operating profit margin of 12%.

The directors expect sales to increase by 10% next year, and the operating profit margin to fall to 10% in difficult trading conditions.

What is the likely change in operating profit, assuming all else remains the same?

A   No change

B $0.105 million decrease

C $0.100 million increase

D $1.050 million increase

Test your understanding 19 (Objective test question)

Ghoo Co is a company that has 50,000 shares in issue (nominal value $0.50 per share). The value of its capital employed in the most recent statement of financial position was $0.35 million.

Statement of profit or loss for the most recent accounting period

	$000
Revenue	285.1
Cost of sales	(120.9)
Gross profit	164.2
Operating expenses	(66.9)
Operating profit	97.3
Finance costs	(10.0)
Profit before tax	87.3
Taxation	(21.6)
Profit after tax	65.7

A trainee accountant has computed the return on capital employed (ROCE) and the earnings per share (EPS) of Ghoo Co.

Select the TWO numbers that are incorrect in the workings.

$$\text{ROCE} = \frac{\$87,300}{\$350,000} \times 100$$

$$\text{EPS} = \frac{\$65,700}{\$25,000}$$

Test your understanding 20 (Objective test question)

An investor in Hook Co has calculated that the company's dividend payout ratio is 25% and that the current dividend yield is 4%.

What is the P/E ratio of Hook Co?

A   100

B   16

C   6.25

D   29

Test your understanding 21 (Objective test question)

Cherry Co has the following accounting ratios, based on its most recent financial statements:

Gross profit margin = 18.6%

Operating profit margin = 10.4%

Asset turnover = 1.5

Interest cover = 4.3

What is the return on capital employed of Cherry Co?

A   It is impossible to tell from such limited information

B   15.6%

C   21.8%

D   27.9%

15   End of chapter case style questions

Test your understanding 22 (Case style question)

(a)   You are a newly appointed Finance Manager of an Educational Institution that is mainly government-funded, having moved from a similar post in a service entity in the private sector. The objective, or mission statement, of this Institution is shown in its publicity material as:

'To achieve recognized standards of excellence in the provision of teaching and research.'

The only financial performance measure evaluated by the government is that the Institution has to remain within cash limits. The cash allocation each year is determined by a range of non-financial measures such as the number of research publications the Institution's staff have achieved and official ratings for teaching quality.

However, almost 20% of total cash generated by the Institution is now from the provision of courses and seminars to private sector entities, using either its own or its customers' facilities. These customers are largely unconcerned about research ratings and teaching quality as they relate more to academic awards such as degrees.

The Head of the Institution aims to increase the percentage of income coming from the private sector to 50% over the next 5 years. She has asked you to advise on how the management team can evaluate progress towards achieving this aim as well as meeting the objective set by the government for the activities it funds.

Required:

Discuss the main issues that an institution such as this has to consider when setting objectives. Advise on whether a financial objective, or objectives, could or should be determined; and whether such objective(s) should be made public.

(30 minutes)

(b)   The following is a list of financial and non-financial performance measures that were in use in your previous profit-making entity:

Financial	**Non-financial**
Value added	Customer satisfaction
Profitability	Competitive position
Return on investment	Market share

Required:

Choose two of each type of measure, explain their purpose and advise on how they could be used by the Educational Institution over the next 5 years to assess how it is meeting the Head of the Institution's aims.

(30 minutes)

Note: A report format is not required in answering this question.

Test your understanding 23 (Case style question)

The directors of ABC, a conglomerate listed on a stock exchange, are appraising one of their wholly-owned subsidiaries, XYZ, with a view to disinvestment. The subsidiary is primarily involved in the manufacture and distribution of car care products.

Financial data for XYZ are shown in the table below.

Required:

(a)   Calculate three ratios for each of the two years 20X1 and 20X2 which you consider to be appropriate for the evaluation of the subsidiary's gearing and profitability over the two-year period. Your selection of ratios should ensure measurement of the company's performance in both areas.

(30 minutes)

(b) Prepare a report for the management of ABC. This report should discuss the following:

(i) the performance of the subsidiary during the past two years, using the ratios calculated in part (a) to guide your comments;

(ii) the limitations of the type of historical analysis you have just provided;

(iii) suggestions for the parent company's future course of action in respect of the subsidiary, including comment on an appropriate procedure for valuing the company;

(iv) other, non-financial information which would be useful to the directors of ABC before they make any decision.

(30 minutes)

Summary accounts for XYZ

Statements of financial position at 31 December

	20X2	20X1
	£000	£000
Non-current assets (plant & equip)	2,650	2,255
Other long-term assets **(Note 1)**	750	675
Cash and marketable securities	195	162
Receivables	765	476
Inventory and work-in-progress	1,250	893
Other current assets	150	91
Total assets	5,760	4,552
Shareholders' funds	2,520	1,726
Long-term debt	2,250	1,976
Other long-term liabilities **(Note 2)**	275	206
Current liabilities	715	644
Total equity & liabilities	5,760	4,552

Extracts from the statement of profit or loss for the years ended 31 December

	20X2	20X1
	$000	$000
Turnover	6,575	5,918
Cost of goods sold	5,918	5,444
Other expenses	658	592
Other income	23	20
Earnings before finance charges and tax	22	(98)
Finance Charges	395	339
Tax on ordinary activities **(Note 3)**	(120)	(149)
Net loss	(253)	(288)

Notes:

1   Other long-term assets are motor vehicles and office equipment.

2   Other long-term liabilities are finance leases.

3   The tax shown in the 20X1 profit and loss extract will be recovered in 20X2.

Other financial information

	$000
Depreciation 20X2	175
Net realisable value of inventory	1,091
Net realisable value of plant and equipment	3,907
Inventory and work-in-progress at 1 January 20X1	850
Receivables at 1 January 20X1	435

Test your understanding answers

Test your understanding 1 (Integration question)

(a) Asset turnover   = 100m/20m   = 5.0 times

      Operating profit margin   = 5m/100m × 100   = 5%

		Equity finance	**Debt finance**
(b)	Return on capital employed	= 5m/20m × 100	= 5m/20m × 100
		= 25%	= 25%

Working:

	GBPm	GBPm
Operating profit	5.0	5.0
Interest	0.0	(1.0)
	5.0	4.0
Tax (@30%)	(1.5)	(1.2)
Net profit	3.5	2.8

Return on equity   = 3.5m/20m × 100   = 2.8m/10m × 100

                    = 17.5%   = 28%

The financial performance of the two funding options is exactly the same for ROCE. This should not be a surprise given that ROCE is an indication of performance before financing, or underlying performance.

(c) When considering the ROE we see that the geared option achieves a higher return than the equity option. This is because the debt (10%) is costing less than the return on capital (25%). The excess return on that part funded by debt passes to the shareholder enhancing their return.

The only differences between ROCE and ROE will be due to taxation and gearing.

Test your understanding 2 (Integration question)

(a) **Capital gearing ratio**

Debt	=	5m + 8m	= USD13m
Equity	=	10m + 4m + 1.5m + 1.5m	= USD17m
Either	=	13m/17m × 100	= 76.5%
Or	=	13m/(13m + 17m) × 100	= 43.3%

Interest cover = 4m/1m = 4 times

(b) The capital gearing figure looks to be a high percentage, but without further analysis of trends and industry average figures, it is difficult to conclude whether the gearing is too high or whether it is at an acceptable level based on this value alone.

The interest cover measure attempts to equate the earning of profits with ability to pay interest as it falls due. There will be some correlation between the two; however, it is very risky to equate profits earned to cash flow.

However, a value of 4 indicates that the entity was easily able to meet its interest obligations in the most recent accounting period, and that the interest payments are not particularly vulnerable to a drop in profits.

Test your understanding 3 (Integration question)

$$EPS = \frac{\text{Profit distributable to ordinary shareholders}}{\text{Number of ordinary shares in issue}}$$

= 600,000/5m = USD 0.12

$$DPS \text{ (dividend per share)} = \frac{\text{Ordinary dividend}}{\text{Number of shares}}$$

= 150,000/5m = USD 0.03

Share price (ex-dividend) = 0.83 – 0.03 = USD 0.80

(a) Price/earnings ratio = 0.80/0.12 = 6.7

(b) Dividend payout rate = 0.03/0.12 = 25%

(c) Dividend yield = 0.03/0.80 = 3.75%

(d) Dividend cover = 0.12/0.03 = 4

Test your understanding 4 (Objective test question)

The answer is (C).

Earnings growth:

Focus on earnings, so profit after tax. From $2.3 million to $2.9 million amounts to approximately 26% growth in total (= [2.9/2.3] − 1).

Over three years, the annual growth is found by taking [3√ 1.26] − 1 = 8%, so above the target of 6% − objective achieved.

Gearing:

Debt value is $1 million × (106/100) = $1.06 million

Equity value is 1 million × $1.88 = $1.88 million

So [debt/(debt + equity)] = [1.06/(1.06 + 1.88)] = 36%, so above the target of 35% − objective not achieved.

Test your understanding 5 (Objective test question)

The answer is (B).

The G$ is the base currency and the GBP is the variable, so the forward rate is 1.88 × (1.05/1.08) = 1.83

Test your understanding 6 (Objective test question)

The answer is (D).

$$23.35 \times \frac{1.02}{1.06} = 22.47$$

so 400,000 USD equates to (400,000/22.47 =) C$17,802

Test your understanding 7 (Objective test question)

The answer is (C).

Earnings per share is (profit after tax (PAT)/no. of shares)

Current situation

Current profit before tax = T$ 5.0 m (operating profit) − T$ 0.8 m (interest) = T$ 4.2 m

Therefore PAT = 70% × T$ 4.2 m = T$ 2.94 m.

There are 20 million shares in issue, hence EPS = (T$ 2.94 m/20 m) = T$ 0.147.

Next year's forecast

Gross profit will be T$ 25m and interest will be (12% × T$ 8 m)
= T$ 0.96 m.

Profit before tax = T$ 25 m – T$ 15 m – T$ 0.96 m (interest) = T$ 9.04 m

Therefore PAT = 70% × T$ 9.04 m = T$ 6.33 m. Hence EPS
= (T$ 6.33 m/20 m) = T$ 0.3165

This EPS of T$ 0.3165 is 215% of the previous year's T$ 0.147, so this is
an increase of 115%.

Test your understanding 8 (Objective test question)

The answer is (D).

Earnings per share is (profit after tax (PAT)/no. of shares)

Current situation

Current profit before tax = M$ 5.0 m (operating profit) – M$ 0.8 m
(interest) = M$ 4.2 m

Therefore PAT = 70% × M$ 4.2 m = M$ 2.94 m.

There are 20 million shares in issue, hence EPS = (M$ 2.94 m/20 m)
= M$ 0.147.

Next year's forecast

Revenue will be M$ 100 m × 1.05 = M$ 105 million.

Current gross profit margin is 20% (20/100) so next year's margin will be
16%.

Profit before tax = (16% × M$ 105 m) – M$ 15 m – M$ 0.8 m (interest)
= M$ 1.0 m

Therefore PAT = 70% × M$ 1.0 m = M$ 0.70 m. Hence EPS
= (M$ 0.70 m/20 m) = M$ 0.035

The EPS of M$ 0.035 is only 24% of the previous year's M$ 0.147, so this
is a decrease of 76%.

Test your understanding 9 (Objective test question)

The answer is (B).

The annual return to investors is:

$$\text{Annual return to investors} = \frac{(P_1 - P_0) + \text{Dividend}}{P_0}$$

where P_0 is $2.00, P_1 is $2.30 and Dividend is $0.12.

Test your understanding 10 (Objective test question)

The answer is (C).

When the entity was privatised, it changed from being a public sector to a private sector entity. The fact that its shares are traded on the stock market and that it operates in a competitive market place suggests that it is a for-profit entity.

Test your understanding 11 (Objective test question)

The answer is (B).

VFM is about achieving economy, effectiveness and efficiency.

(A) achieves economy, (C) achieves efficiency and (D) achieves effectiveness.

Test your understanding 12 (Objective test question)

The answer is (B).

Interest cover is (operating profit/interest payable)

Last year = $1.84m/($5m × 8%) = 4.60

Next year = $1.84m/($5m × 10%) = 3.68

i.e. a decrease of 20%

Test your understanding 13 (Objective test question)

The answer is (A).

Market value of debt is $100,000 × (102/100) = $102,000

Market value of equity = 1 million × $1.22 = $1,220,000

Therefore, gearing is [102/(102 + 1,220)] = 7.7%

Test your understanding 14 (Objective test question)

The answer is (C).

Test your understanding 15 (Objective test question)

The answer is (D).

Economy – achieved since the cost of the programme was below budget.

Effectiveness – not achieved since there has been no improvement in the level of absenteeism.

Efficiency – not achieved. Other schools manage to get better results at a lower cost, so this programme has not been an efficient use of resources.

Test your understanding 16 (Objective test question)

The answer is (A).

Return on equity uses the net profit figure. ($2.5 million) and the equity value is equal to the value of the ordinary share capital plus reserves ($19.2 million).

Test your understanding 17 (Objective test question)

The answer is (B) and (E).

A high P/E ratio shows that investors have confidence in the company.

Earnings yield is the reciprocal of P/E ratio, so a high P/E will correspond to a low earnings yield.

Test your understanding 18 (Objective test question)

The answer is (B).

Last year's operating profit was $10.5 million × 12% = $1.260 million

Next year's is expected to be ($10.5 million × 1.10) × 10% = $1.155 million

i.e. a decrease of $0.105 million

Test your understanding 19 (Objective test question)

The workings have been corrected below. The bold figures are the ones that were incorrect.

$$ROCE = \frac{\$97,300}{\$350,000} \times 100$$

$$EPS = \frac{\$65,700}{\$50,000}$$

Explanation:

ROCE uses operating profit, not profit after interest. EPS uses the number of shares, not the value of them.

Test your understanding 20 (Objective test question)

The answer is (C).

Dividend pay-out ratio is (dividend per share/earnings per share), dividend yield is (dividend per share/share price) and P/E ratio is (share price/earnings per share).

Therefore, P/E ratio = (dividend pay-out ratio/dividend yield).

Alternatively, make up some numbers to help you manipulate the formulae.

For example, if dividend pay-out ratio is 25%, assume that dividend per share is $0.25 and EPS is $1. Then, if dividend yield is 4%, the share price must be $6.25 since we have already assumed that dividend per share is $0.25.

Hence P/E ratio = Share price/EPS = $6.25/$1 = 6.25

Test your understanding 21 (Objective test question)

The answer is (B).

ROCE can be found by multiplying asset turnover and operating profit margin.

Test your understanding 22 (Case style question)

(a) The main issues to consider are:

- Who are the main stakeholders?

- Where is the financing coming from, and in what proportions?

- Are there other, higher level objectives that will supersede those set by the Institution, for example political aims/goals by the government?

- Does the objective need to be measurable?

- How can one objective meet all the competing aims of the stakeholders?

- Will information on the Educational Institution's performance be publicly available?

Setting a financial objective has the main advantage of being measurable. If it is made public, it can also be compared with other, similar, institutions if they also set and make public their objective and their subsequent performance. One objective will probably be insufficient, especially as the Institution has two main markets with very different requirements, costs and revenue structures.

The disadvantages of setting and making public an organisation's objectives are:

- The Educational Institution may not be allowed freedom to choose its own policies, for example on charging fees or selection of state-funded students.

- Political decisions may not affect all publicly funded institutions in the same way or to the same extent.

- Cost allocation between state-funded business and private-sector business may be difficult and politically sensitive.

(b) **Examiner's Note**

The question asks for comments on two performance indicators from each list, four criteria in all. In this answer comments are provided for all six criteria. Candidates may only receive marks for a maximum of two indicators from each list (i.e. no compensation between the lists.)

Introduction

Traditionally, financial measures have been the focus of management attention. Increasingly companies are using non-financial indicators to assess success across a range of criteria, which need to be chosen to help a company meet its objectives. However, an indicator, which is appropriate for one group of stakeholders in an organisation, may not be suitable for another group.

Also, indicators that are suitable for short-term performance assessment may be unsuitable, or not optimum, for the long term.

The objective, or mission statement, of this institution is entirely qualitative (and subjective) and makes no concession to financial considerations or constraints.

Financial performance measures

Value added

This is primarily a measure of performance. It is usually defined as sales value less the cost of purchased materials and services. It represents the value added to a company's products by its own efforts. A problem here is comparability with other industries or even other companies in the same industry.

It is less common in the public sector, although the situation is changing and many public sector organisations are now publishing information on their own value added, for example, in the health service.

In respect of teaching, value added could be measured by the percentage of students who leave with a qualification. In post-graduate or executive education, it could be the increase in salary or improved jobs/job prospects obtained by graduates on obtaining their qualification. This may not precisely measure the qualitative aspects of the Institution's objectives, but could provide a close approximation.

In respect of research, the measure is much easier to apply and interpret. Research output can be measured by the number of staff publications in various categories of journal.

Profitability

Profitability may be defined as the rate at which profits are generated. It is often expressed as profit per unit of input (e.g. investment). However, profitability limits an organisation's focus to one output measure – profit. It overlooks quality and this limitation needs to be kept in mind when using it as a measure of success. Profitability as a measure of decision-making has been criticised because

– it fails to provide a systematic explanation as to why one business sector has more favourable prospects than another;

– it does not provide enough insight into the dynamics and balance of an enterprise's individual business units and the balance between them;

– it is remote from the actions that actually create value and cannot therefore be managed directly in all but the smallest of organisations;

– the input to the measure may vary substantially between organisations.

However, it is a well-known and accepted measure that, once the input has been defined, is readily understood. Provided the input is consistent across organisations and time periods it also provides a useful comparative measure. Although the concept of profit in its true sense is absent from most of the public sector, profitability may be used to relate inputs to outputs if a different measure of output is used, for example surplus after all costs to capital investment.

In the case of the educational institution, a problem may be determining the value of the initial investment, which may have been purchased by the government many years ago and appear to have cost nothing. A notional value could be attached to these assets for the purpose. Profits would be fees and other income less costs of salaries and other expenses. Notional rents or depreciation would also have to be estimated.

This measure would have little relevance to the Institution's only stated objective and its calculation is fraught with uncertainties and unknowns. This would be a measure that the organisation might wish to introduce some time in the future, but first it needs to estimate the value of its assets and the true nature of its costs.

Return on investment (ROI)

This is an accounting measure, which is calculated by dividing annual profits by the average net book value of assets. It is, therefore, subject to the distortions inevitable when profit rather than cash flows are used to determine performance. Distorting factors for interpretation and comparison purposes include depreciation policy, stock revaluations, write off of intangibles such as goodwill. A further defect is that ROI ignores the time value of money, although this may be of less concern when inflation rates, and therefore money discount rates, are very low.

Return on assets may not adequately reflect how efficiently assets were utilised; in a commercial context taking account of profits, but not the assets used in their making, for whatever reason, would overstate a company's performance. In the public sector, the concept of profit is absent, but it is still not unrealistic to expect organisations to use donated assets with maximum efficiency. If depreciation on such assets were to be charged against income, this would depress the amount of surplus income over expenditure. Other points which may affect interpretation of ROI in any public sector organisation, including educational institutions are: difficulty in determining value; assets may have no re-sale value; they are, or were originally intended, for use by the community at large and any charge for depreciation may have the effect of 'double taxation' on the taxpayer.

As with profitability, the relevance of this measure at the present time and to the stated objective is limited. First of all, it needs to estimate the value of its assets and the true nature of its costs.

Non-financial performance measures

Customer satisfaction

This measure can be linked to market share. If customers are not satisfied, they will take their business elsewhere and the company will lose market share or go into liquidation. Measuring customer satisfaction is difficult to do formally, as the inputs and outputs are not readily defined or measurable. Surveys and questionnaires may be used, but these methods have known flaws, mainly as a result of respondent bias. It can, of course, be measured indirectly by the level of sales and increase in market share.

In the United Kingdom, the Citizens' Charter was designed to help 'customers' of public services gain satisfaction and redress if they do not, for example refunds on late trains. There are many criteria for determining customer satisfaction in an educational institution, if we assume the 'customer' is the student. For example:

- Evaluations by students at the end of modules or entire programmes. There are problems of bias with this type of measure, but this is true of all surveys.

- Quality audits by government agencies and other regulatory bodies.

- Internal peer reviews.

However, the customer could also be the employer or sponsor of the graduating student. Surveys of satisfaction from this type of customer are less likely to be biased.

This type of measure will already be in place and possibly to a greater extent than in many private-sector institutions. If the Institution wishes to increase its proportion of private funding, then it needs to focus on developing its surveys of employers and likely providers of research funding.

Competitive position

The performance of a business needs to be compared with that of its competitors to establish a strategic perspective. A number of models and frameworks have been suggested by organisational theorists as to how a competitive position may be determined and improved. A manager needing to make decisions must know by whom, by how much and why he is gaining ground or being beaten by competitors.

Conventional measures such as accounting data are useful, but no one measure is sufficient. Instead, an array of measures is needed to establish competitive position. The most difficult problem to overcome in using competitive position as a success factor is in collecting and acquiring data from competitors.

The public sector is increasingly in competition with other providers of a similar service, both in the private and public sector. For example, universities must now compete for government funding on the basis of research output as well as meeting a range of targets for student recruitment. Their advantage is that it is easier to gain access to data from such competitors than is possible in the private sector, as all this information is ultimately in the public domain. Less publicly available is data on the amount of privately-funded teaching obtained by public-sector educational institutions.

This measure will also be already extensively used by the Institution, certainly in respect of its competitive position for students worldwide. Where it might need to develop its measures and improve its measurement data is in respect of privately-funded or sponsored students or courses.

Market share

Market share, a performance indicator that could conceivably be included under the financial heading as well as non-financial, is often seen as an objective for a company in its own right. However, it must be judged in the context of other measures such as profitability and shareholder value. Market share, unlike many other measures, can take quality into account as, it must be assumed, if customers do not get the quality they want or expect the company will lose market share.

Gaining market share must be seen as a long-term goal of companies to ensure outlets for their products and services and to minimise competition. However, market share can only be acquired within limits if a monopoly situation is to be avoided.

It is a measure that is becoming increasingly relevant to the public sector, for example universities and the health service. In educational institutions, the market share within the home country can be measured quite easily by reference to student numbers, in total and by programme/course. It is more difficult to compare market share worldwide. However, this measure of market share is on volume not value. Some institutions have high value programmes, such as MBAs, that distort this simple volume measure.

This institution needs to determine its mix of programmes and courses and set targets aimed at specific markets, for example to achieve x per cent of the market share of home-based MBA students by 2xxx. Such a target by itself will not be a guide to the quality of teaching and would need to be combined with other measures, such as customer satisfaction.

Test your understanding 23 (Case style question)

Key answer tips

Part (a): There are many other alternative ratios which could have been calculated (other than those below), as long as between them the five ratios cover the efficiency, profitability and liquidity of the company. It would also be possible to calculate different figures for each ratio, depending on whether the 'other financial information' was used, whether year-end or average statement of financial position figures were used, etc. What is important is that you show clearly how you have derived each of your chosen ratios, and that you do not overrun the time allowed for this part of the question.

(a)　The following ratios can be calculated from the figures in the summary accounts:

Profitability ratios

		20X2	20X1
Return on Capital Employed =	Opening profit	22	(98)
	Capital employed	2,520 + 2,250	1,726 + 1,976
		= 0.0046	= (0.0265)
Operating profit margin	Operating profit	22	(98)
	Sales	6,575	5,918
		= 0.33%	= (1.66%)

Gearing ratios

At 31 Dec 20X2, gearing = $\dfrac{2,250}{2,250 + 2,520}$ = 47%

At 31 Dec 20X1, gearing = $\dfrac{1,976}{1,726 + 1,976}$ = 53%

(b)

Report

To:　　The Management of ABC

From:　The Management Accountant

Date:　X-X-20XX

Subject: Proposed disinvestment of XYZ

Introduction

This report has been prepared to appraise the financial performance of our wholly-owned subsidiary XYZ, with a view to recommending whether the company should be divested. The analysis has used XYZ's summary accounts for 20X1 and 20X2.

Analysis of recent performance

Gearing has fallen over the period as a result of the new equity injection exceeding the increase in net borrowings.

At 31 Dec 20X2, gearing $= \dfrac{2{,}250}{2{,}250 + 2{,}520} = 47\%$

At 31 Dec 20X1, gearing $= \dfrac{1{,}976}{1{,}726 + 1{,}976} = 53\%$

The company was struggling to pay its finance charge in 20X1 out of available profits; although the profitability situation has improved slightly in 20X2, finance charges payable still exceeds available profits so that a net loss is reported.

Limitations of historical analysis

The analysis above has been carried out on the summary accounts of XYZ for 20X1 and 20X2 which were presumably drawn up under the historical cost convention. In a period of changing prices such accounts can become misleading, for instance with the depreciation charge being calculated on the out-of-date historical cost of the fixed assets. Capital gearing ratios such as calculated above do not give the true picture; it would be more helpful if the summary accounts could be restated under a current cost basis.

There is the further conflict that a decision is to be made about the future based on an analysis of the past. The summary accounts give a historical record of what has happened over the last two years, but give no evidence of the company's likely future prospects. The decision as to whether XYZ should be divested should be taken on the basis of future opportunities and threats to which the company will be exposed.

A final weakness of analysis from accounts is that conventional accounting statements do not recognise a number of important assets that a company might have – a trained workforce, a new product about to be launched on to the market which has been fully researched, other sorts of inherent goodwill. It is impossible to look at the full picture of a company's situation while these assets have been ignored.

Future course of action

Given that ABC has subscribed an extra $1m of share capital of XYZ within the past 12 months, it seems premature to be considering divesting the company. It is perhaps more reasonable to allow the newly invested funds to settle down and reap the benefits for which, presumably, the investment was made. However, if ABC insists on divestment, there is a choice between closing the business (and selling the assets piecemeal) or selling the business as a going concern. If the assets are to be sold piecemeal, their relevant values are their net realisable values, e.g. inventory $1.091m and plant and equipment $3.907m. An aggregate total of the net assets valued at net realisable value would be the minimum acceptable offer.

In the more likely situation of selling the business as a going concern, the value of the business forgone if sold would be the aggregate of the forecast cash flows arising to ABC from XYZ, discounted at ABC's cost of capital. Such a computation requires many estimates to be made, including future growth of XYZ's business and of the car care products business sector as a whole. It may only be possible to identify a range of possible values, but even if it contains a degree of estimation the exercise will still be valuable.

Other valuable non-financial information

Several valuable items of non-financial information have already been identified above which would be useful to the directors of ABC before they make any decision:

(i)   the financial results of XYZ on a current cost basis, i.e. after the effects of price changes have been eliminated;

(ii)   whether the company has significant intangible assets not currently recognised in the accounts;

(iii)   the future prospects for the company and its place in its business sector if it is retained within the ABC group;

(iv)   whether a prospective purchaser of the company has already been identified;

(v)   the effect on the morale of the remaining workforce if the company is closed or sold.

Please let me know if I can be of any further assistance.

Signed: The management accountant

Non-financial objectives

Chapter learning objectives

Lead outcome	Component outcome
A1: Advise on strategic financial objectives	(c) Advise on non-financial objectives

Topics to be covered

- Enhancing the value of other non-financial capitals (human capital, intellectual capital and social and relational capital)

- United Nations Sustainability Development Goals

1   Overview of chapter

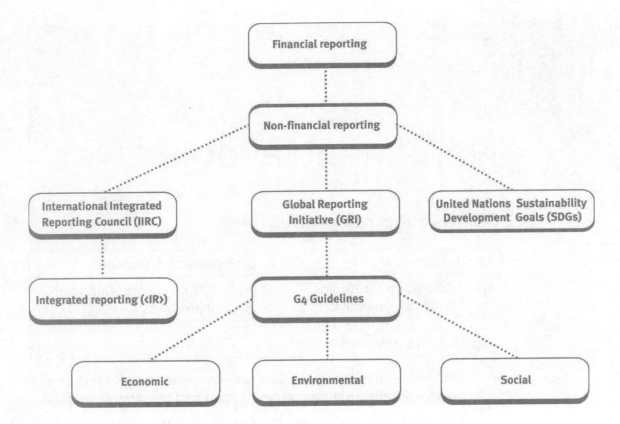

2   Financial and non-financial reporting

Financial reporting

According to the International Accounting Standards Board's (IASB's) conceptual framework, the objective of financial reporting is to 'provide information about the reporting entity that is useful to existing and potential investors, lenders and other creditors in making decisions about providing resources to the entity'.

Financial statements provide historic financial information, but they do not provide a full picture of how the entity is performing.

To help users make decisions, it may be helpful to provide information relating to other aspects of an entity's performance, such as:

- how the business is managed;
- its future prospects;
- the entity's policy on the environment;
- its attitude towards social responsibility etc.

There has been increasing pressure for entities to provide more information in their annual reports beyond just the financial statements since non- financial information can also be important to users' decisions.

Non-financial reporting

The important additional non-financial information can be reported in a number of ways.

For example, the Global Reporting Initiative (GRI) has produced guidelines that propose additional disclosures in addition to the standard disclosures required in the financial statements. In particular, the GRI guidelines suggest that entities should disclose economic, environmental and social performance indicators.

Alternatively, the International Integrated Reporting Council (IIRC) has produced a revolutionary framework known as the Integrated Reporting framework (<IR> framework). The <IR> approach proposes a fundamental change to the way that entities are managed and report to stakeholders.

This chapter first looks at the limitations of financial statements as a basis for performance appraisal. It then explains the GRI guidelines and the concept of Integrated Reporting (<IR>).

3 Limitations of financial statements in reflecting the value and stewardship of the non-financial capital base

Introduction

Capitalism relies on the efficient allocation of capital to deliver returns to investors over the short, medium and long term. It is the job of companies to manage the financial capital that investors provide and also to create and preserve the value generated from other forms of non-financial capital such as people, trademarks/copyrights and natural resources.

The western model of capitalism has been questioned following the onset of the banking crisis in 2007 because of its apparent dependence on short term financial factors over other forms of capital and longer time scales.

Financial statements have traditionally only reported the financial capital of companies in detail, and have not presented detailed information on the non-financial capital base.

Unfortunately, this type of corporate reporting no longer reflects the needs of users of accounting information in the 21st century.

Link to Integrated Reporting (<IR>)

Resilient capitalism needs financial stability and sustainability in order to succeed – and Integrated Reporting is intended to underpin both of these problems through communicating to providers of financial capital the information that they need.

At the heart of <IR> is the growing realisation that a wide range of factors determine the value of an organisation – some of these are financial or tangible in nature and are easy to account for in financial statements (e.g. property, cash), while many such as intellectual capital, competition and energy security are not.

<IR> reflects the broad and longer-term consequences of the decisions organisations make, based on a wide range of factors, in order to create and sustain value. <IR> enables an organisation to communicate in a clear, articulate way how it is drawing on all the resources and relationships it utilises to create and preserve value in the short, medium and long term, helping investors to manage risks and allocate resources most efficiently.

Link to the GRI guidelines

The GRI guidelines encourage organisations to disclose extra information when communicating with key stakeholders. Economic, environmental and social factors disclosed alongside the standard financial statements enable investors and other stakeholders to make a much better assessment of an organisation's overall performance.

The extra disclosures can be made in a separate environmental / sustainability or corporate social responsibility document, or as part of the management commentary presented with the financial statements. The disclosures are usually made by reference to the GRI guidelines, but this is not mandatory in all jurisdictions.

4   The Global Reporting Initiative (GRI)

Overall aim of the GRI

The GRI suggests that entities report performance indicators so that users can monitor their performance from economic, environmental and social perspectives.

GRI guidelines

- The most accepted framework for reporting sustainability is the Global Reporting Initiative's (GRI's) Sustainability Reporting Guidelines. 'G4' – the fourth version of the guidelines – was issued in May 2013.

- The G4 Guidelines provide universal guidance for reporting on sustainability performance. They are applicable to all entities including SMEs and not-for-profit entities worldwide.

- The G4 Guidelines consist of principles and disclosure items. The principles help to define report content, quality of the report, and give guidance on how to set the report boundary. The disclosure items include disclosures on management of issues, as well as performance indicators themselves.

- Applying these guidelines is mandatory in some jurisdictions but voluntary in others.

Further information

The Global Reporting Initiative website is www.globalreporting.org.

The financial statements of companies that have applied the GRI guidelines are listed (in the 'Disclosure Database') with a link to their reports.

Background to and objectives of the G4 guidelines

Preface to the G4 guidelines

The following quote from the preface to the G4 guidelines explains the background to the G4 update of the GRI guidelines:

"The GRI Sustainability Reporting Guidelines are periodically reviewed to provide the best and most up-to-date guidance for effective sustainability reporting. The aim of G4, the fourth such update, is simple:

> to help reporters prepare sustainability reports that matter, contain valuable information about the organization's most critical sustainability-related issues, and make such sustainability reporting standard practice.

It is crucial for society and markets that sustainability reporting evolves in terms of content, and from an exceptional activity undertaken by a minority of leading companies to a standard practice.

Together with being more user-friendly than previous versions of the Guidelines, G4 has an increased emphasis on the need for organizations to focus the reporting process and final report on those topics that are material to their business and their key stakeholders. This 'materiality' focus will make reports more relevant, more credible and more user-friendly. This will, in turn, enable organizations to better inform markets and society on sustainability matters."

Materiality considerations

Materiality is placed at the centre of the new sustainability reporting guidelines issued by the Global Reporting Initiative (the so-called 'G4' guidelines).

G4 aims to improve the common language of corporate reporting, focusing heavily on the issues that are material to the organisation and important for stakeholders.

CEOs worldwide have identified the need to build public trust as a crucial part of improving operational effectiveness and engaging with customers following the financial crisis. Sustainability reporting, says the GRI, plays a key role in this, with non-financial reporting being singled out as a particularly effective means of communicating long-term commitment to sustainability.

G4 does not reward reporting of large quantities of indicators but requires companies to indicate and explain omissions of standard or material disclosures.

Overview of the GRI's G4 Guidelines document

The GRI's G4 Guidelines were published in May 2013, in a 94 page document in 7 sections. A brief, section-by-section overview of the contents of the G4 document is given immediately below, followed by a more detailed overview of the key elements.

Overview of the GRI's G4 Guidelines

Sections 1 and 2: The purpose of the Guidelines and how to use the Guidelines

These sections explain that there are two elements to the Guidelines, namely:

- Reporting Principles and Standard Disclosures (covered in Section 4 and the first part of Section 5), and

- Implementation Manual (covered in detail in Section 5).

They then give a step-by-step guide to using the Guidelines and preparing a sustainability report.

Section 3: Criteria to be applied by an organization to prepare Its sustainability report 'in accordance' with the Guidelines

This section explains that an entity can either prepare its sustainability report using Core disclosures or Comprehensive disclosures.

Both options can be applied by all entities, regardless of their size, sector or location.

The Core option provides the background against which an entity communicates the impacts of its economic, environmental and social and governance performance. The Comprehensive option builds on the Core option by requiring more extensive reporting of the entity's strategy and analysis, governance, and ethics and integrity.

A table in this section shows which of the detailed disclosures from the later Section 5 are needed for each of the Core and Comprehensive options.

Section 4: Reporting principles

In this section, the key reporting principles are outlined. These are essentially the required characteristics of the Report Content and the Report Quality.

The Principles for Defining Report Content are given as:

- Stakeholder Inclusiveness

- Sustainability Context

- Materiality

- Completeness

The Principles for Defining Report Quality are given as:

- Balance
- Comparability
- Accuracy
- Timeliness
- Clarity
- Reliability

Section 5: Standard Disclosures

This is the largest section of the G4 Guidelines document, covering 65 pages.

It covers in specific detail the Standard Disclosures required, after first explaining that there are two different types of Standard Disclosures (General Standard Disclosures and Specific Standard Disclosures), and outlining the subheadings that should be used within each type.

General Standard Disclosures

- Strategy and Analysis
- Organizational Profile
- Identified Material Aspects and Boundaries
- Stakeholder Engagement
- Report Profile
- Governance
- Ethics and Integrity

Specific Standard Disclosures

- Disclosures on Management Approach
- Indicators

Then, the Guidelines explain how to separate the Indicators into three Categories – Economic, Environmental and Social. The Social Category is further divided into four sub-Categories, which are Labor Practices and Decent Work, Human Rights, Society and Product Responsibility.

Sections 6 and 7: Quick links and definitions of key terms used

These final sections show how the G4 Guidelines link to other important sustainability reporting guidelines, such as the OECD Guidelines for Multinational Enterprises, and the UN's Guiding Principles on Business and Human Rights.

Then, the document finishes with a glossary of key terms.

Disclosures required by the GRI guidelines

The **Specific Standard Disclosures** are divided into two parts (Disclosures on Management Approach and Indicators). These disclosures cover the specific performance of the entity.

Disclosures on Management Approach (DMA)

The DMA is intended to give the entity an opportunity to explain how the economic, environmental and social impacts related to material Aspects are managed. The DMA also provides context for the performance reported by Indicators (see below).

Indicators

Indicators give information on the economic, environmental and social performance of an entity related to its material Aspects. Disclosures have to be made in each of these three categories (economic, environmental and social performance).

- **Economic**

  The **economic** dimension of sustainability concerns the entity's impacts on the economic conditions of its stakeholders, and on economic systems at local, national, and global levels.

  The **Economic Category** illustrates the flow of capital among different stakeholders, and the main economic impacts of the entity throughout society.

- **Environmental**

  The **environmental** dimension of sustainability concerns the entity's impact on living and non-living natural systems, including land, air, water and ecosystems.

  The **Environmental Category** covers impacts related to inputs (such as energy and water) and outputs (such as emissions, effluents and waste). In addition, it covers biodiversity, transport, and product and service-related impacts, as well as environmental compliance and expenditures.

- **Social**

  The **social** dimension of sustainability concerns the impacts the entity has on the social systems within which it operates.

  The **Social Category** includes the sub-Categories:

  1   Labor Practices and Decent Work

  2   Human Rights

  3   Society

  4   Product Responsibility

  Most of the content in the sub-Categories is based on internationally recognised universal standards or other relevant international references.

Examples of disclosures

The G4 guidelines encourage disclosure of various 'aspects' in the three key categories: Economic, Environmental and Social.

Based on the above guidance, the sort of disclosures entities might make to comply with the G4 guidelines are:

Economic

Aspect	Example of disclosures
Economic performance	Revenues/costs, levels of pension contributions, taxes paid and subsidies received
Market presence (i.e. the economic impact on the local area)	Comparison of wage rates to other firms locally, proportion of senior managers hired from the local community
Indirect economic impacts	Extent of investment in infrastructure projects
Procurement practices	Proportion of spending with local suppliers

Environmental

Key aspect	Example of disclosures
Materials	Materials used by weight or volume, and the proportion of materials used in production that are recycled
Energy	Total fuel consumption, reductions in the energy requirements of sold products and services
Biodiversity	The nature of significant impacts on biodiversity e.g. species affected and duration of impact
Emissions	Total emissions of greenhouse gases and ozone depleting substances, emissions reductions achieved as a direct result of initiatives to reduce emissions
Products and services (environmental aspects)	How the environmental impact of products services is mitigated, and what proportion of products and packaging materials is reclaimed
Supplier Environmental Assessment	The percentage of new suppliers that were screened using environmental criteria

Social – Labor practices and decent work

Key aspect	Example of disclosures
Employment (i.e. an overview of the entity's staff and policies)	Rate of staff turnover, number of new staff appointed, benefits provided to staff (e.g. life insurance, parental leave)
Training and education	Average hours of training provided per employee
Diversity and equal opportunity	Analysis of employees (and members of the entity's governance bodies) by age, gender, ethnic background, disability etc.

Social – Human rights

Key aspect	Example of disclosures
Investment	The number/percentage of the entity's investments and contracts that underwent human rights screening
Freedom of association and collective bargaining	Measures taken to support rights to exercise freedom of association (e.g. joining a trade union) and collective bargaining
Assessment (of the entity's operations)	The number/percentage of the entity's operations that have been subject to human rights reviews (e.g. by groups such as Amnesty International)

Social – Society

Key aspect	Example of disclosures
Local communities	Operations with local community engagement and those with significant actual/potential negative impacts on local communities
Public policy	Financial donations to political parties analysed by country and by recipient
Anti-competitive behaviour	Number of legal actions faced by the entity relating to anti-competitive behaviour and violations of monopoly legislation

Social – Product responsibility

Key aspect	Example of disclosures
Customer health and safety	A summary of breaches of health and safety legislation reported by customers, and a summary of the results of any investigations
Marketing communications	A list of products sold by the entity that are banned or restricted in some markets, a summary of any investigations by the authorities into non-compliance with regulations on advertising/promotions
Customer privacy	The number of complaints received regarding customer privacy issues (for example leaks, thefts or losses of customer data)

Detailed list of aspects and categories of disclosures

Categories and aspects in the G4 guidelines

The examples in the tables above show some of the key disclosures under the G4 guidelines. For completeness, the lists below show all the aspects listed in the guidelines. For more examples, see the GRI's website (www.globalreporting.org).

Economic

- Economic Performance
- Market Presence
- Indirect Economic Impacts
- Procurement Practices

Environmental

- Materials
- Energy
- Water
- Biodiversity
- Emissions
- Effluents and Waste
- Products and Services
- Compliance
- Transport
- Overall
- Supplier Environmental Assessment
- Environmental Grievance Mechanisms

Social – the Social category is split into four sub-categories, each with several aspects associated with it as follows:

Labor Practices and Decent Work

- Employment
- Labor/Management Relations
- Occupational Health and Safety
- Training and Education
- Diversity and Equal Opportunity
- Equal Remuneration for Women and Men
- Supplier Assessment for Labor Practices
- Labor Practices Grievance Mechanisms

Human Rights

- Investment
- Non-discrimination
- Freedom of Association and Collective Bargaining
- Child Labor
- Forced or Compulsory Labor
- Security Practices
- Indigenous Rights
- Assessment
- Supplier Human Rights Assessment
- Human Rights Grievance Mechanisms

Society

- Local Communities
- Anti-corruption
- Public Policy
- Anti-competitive Behaviour
- Compliance
- Supplier Assessment for Impacts on Society
- Grievance Mechanisms for Impacts on Society

Product Responsibility

- Customer Health and Safety
- Product and Service Labelling
- Marketing Communications
- Customer Privacy
- Compliance

General Standard Disclosures

As well as the Specific Standard Disclosures identified above, the GRI guidance proposes seven **General Standard Disclosures**. These disclosures cover general issues related to the entity, rather than information specific to its performance.

General Standard Disclosures

Strategy and Analysis

These disclosures provide a general strategic view of the entity's sustainability, in order to provide context for subsequent, more detailed reporting.

Organisational Profile

These disclosures provide an overview of organisational characteristics, in order to provide context for subsequent more detailed reporting.

Identified Material Aspects and Boundaries

These disclosures provide an overview of the process that the entity has followed to define the Report Content, the identified material Aspects and their Boundaries. (Note that the word Aspect is used throughout the Guidelines to refer to the list of subjects covered by the Guidelines.)

Stakeholder Engagement

These disclosures provide an overview of the entity's stakeholder engagement during the reporting period.

Engaging with stakeholders is the basis for good corporate governance but this is often something that entities either ignore or underestimate.

There are many ways to engage with stakeholders, especially as social media channels become more sophisticated. A direct dialogue with stakeholders is important for two reasons:

- as a PR and marketing exercise
- to take a direct pulse of the entity's performance and to assess how well its products are received.

Report Profile

These disclosures provide an overview of the basic information about the report, such as the reporting period, date of previous report and whether Core or Comprehensive disclosure has been used.

Governance

These disclosures provide an overview of the highest governance body of the entity (for example, the Board of Directors).

> ### Ethics and Integrity
>
> These disclosures provide an overview of the entity's values, principles, standards and norms, along with its internal and external mechanisms for seeking advice or reporting concerns on ethics and matters of integrity.

Principles for defining content of the GRI disclosures

Section 4 of the G4 Guidelines provides the following principles for defining report content:

Stakeholder inclusiveness

The reporting entity should identify its stakeholders and explain in the report how it has responded to their expectations and interests.

Sustainability context

The report should present the entity's performance in the wider context of sustainability.

Materiality

Organisations are faced with a wide range of topics on which they could report. Relevant topics are those that may reasonably be considered important for reflecting the organisation's economic, environmental and social impacts, or influencing the decisions of stakeholders, and, therefore, potentially merit inclusion in the report. Materiality is the threshold at which Aspects become sufficiently important that they should be reported.

Completeness

Coverage of all the material topics and indicators should be enough to reflect significant impacts and allow stakeholders to assess the reporting entity's performance.

Non-disclosure

In exceptional cases, if it is not possible to disclose certain required information, the report should clearly:

- Identify the information that has been omitted.

- Explain the reasons why the information has been omitted.

In addition, the applicable explanation of omission from the list below should be provided:

- A Standard Disclosure, part of a Standard Disclosure, or an Indicator is not applicable; the reason why it is considered to be not applicable should be disclosed

- The information is subject to specific confidentiality constraints; those constraints are to be disclosed by the organisation

- The existence of specific legal prohibitions; a reference to the specific legal prohibitions should be made

- The information is currently unavailable. In the case of the unavailability of data, the organization should disclose the steps being taken to obtain the data and the expected timeframe for doing so

The organisation should recognise, however, that a large number of omitted Standard Disclosures may invalidate its ability to claim that its sustainability report has been prepared 'in accordance' with the Guidelines.

Principles for defining report quality

As well as the principles for defining report content identified above, Section 4 of the G4 Guidelines provides the following principles for defining report quality:

Balance

The report should reflect both positive and negative aspects of an entity's performance to enable a reasoned overall assessment.

Comparability

Issues and information should be reported consistently. Reported information should be presented in a way which allows stakeholders to assess trends over time and compare the entity to other organisations.

Accuracy

The reported information should be sufficiently accurate and detailed for stakeholders to assess the entity's performance.

Timeliness

Reporting should occur regularly and in time for stakeholders to make informed decisions.

Clarity

Information should be understandable and accessible.

Reliability

The entity should gather, record, compile, analyse and disclose information and processes used in the preparation of a report in a way that they can be subject to examination and that establishes the quality and materiality of the information.

The process of putting together a report in accordance with the GRI guidelines

The GRI's 'G4' Guidelines document sets out the following four step approach to putting together a report.

Step 1: Identification

- Consider the GRI Aspects list and other topics of interest
- Apply the Principles of Sustainability Context and Stakeholder Inclusiveness: Identify the Aspects – and other relevant topics – based on the relevant economic, environmental and social impacts related to all of the organisation's activities, products, services, and relationships, or on the influence they have on the assessments and decisions of stakeholders
- Identify where the impacts occur: within or outside of the organisation
- List the Aspects and other topics considered relevant, and their Boundaries

Step 2: Prioritisation

- Each Aspect and other topic considered relevant for:
  - the significance of the organisation's economic, environmental and social impacts
  - the influence on stakeholder assessments and decisions
- Identify the material Aspects by combining the assessments
- Define and document thresholds (criteria) that render an Aspect material
- For each material Aspect identified, decide the level of coverage, the amount of data and narrative explanation to be disclosed
- List the material Aspects to be included in the report, along with their Boundaries and the level of coverage

Step 3: Validation

- Apply the Principles of Completeness and Stakeholder Inclusiveness: Assess the list of material Aspects against Scope, Aspect Boundaries and Time to ensure that the report provides a reasonable and balanced representation of the organisation's significant economic, environmental and social impacts, and enables stakeholders to assess the organisation's performance
- Approve the list of identified material Aspects with the relevant internal senior decision-maker
- Prepare systems and processes to gather the information needed to be disclosed
- Translate the identified material Aspects into Standard Disclosures – DMA and Indicators – to report against.
- Determine which information is available and explain those for which it still needs to establish management approaches and measurements systems

Step 4: Review

- Apply the Principles of Sustainability Context and Stakeholder Inclusiveness: Review the Aspects that were material in the previous reporting period

- Use the result of the review to inform Step 1 Identification for the next reporting cycle

5 Integrated Reporting (<IR>)

Background

The objective of integrated reporting is to try to create a more holistic and balanced view of the company being reported upon, bringing together material aspects such as strategy, governance, performance and prospects in a way that reflects the commercial, social and environmental context within which it operates.

The basics of integrated reporting were covered earlier in the CIMA syllabus.

Link between sustainability and <IR>

Sustainability reporting (in accordance with the GRI guidelines explained above) is an intrinsic element of integrated reporting.

Sustainability reporting is fundamental to an organisation's integrated thinking and reporting process, in providing input into the organisation's identification of its material issues, its strategic objectives, and the assessment of its ability to achieve those objectives and create value over time.

 More on the link between sustainability and <IR>

From the **GRI 'G4' Guidelines**

"Sustainability reporting is a process that assists organizations in setting goals, measuring performance and managing change towards a sustainable global economy – one that combines long term profitability with social responsibility and environmental care. Sustainability reporting – mainly through but not limited to a sustainability report – is the key platform for communicating the organization's economic, environmental, social and governance performance, reflecting positive and negative impacts.

The Aspects that the organization deems to be material, in response to its stakeholders' expectations and interests, drive sustainability reporting. Stakeholders can include those who are invested in in the organization as well as those who have other relationships with the organization.

Integrated reporting is an emerging and evolving trend in corporate reporting, which in general aims primarily to offer an organization's providers of financial capital with an integrated representation of the key factors that are material to its present and future value creation.

Integrated reporters build on sustainability reporting foundations and disclosures in preparing their integrated report. Through the integrated report, an organization provides a concise communication about how its strategy, governance, performance and prospects lead to the creation of value over time. Therefore, the integrated report is not intended to be an extract of the traditional annual report nor a combination of the annual financial statements and the sustainability report. However, the integrated report interacts with other reports and communications by making reference to additional detailed information that is provided separately.

Three fundamental concepts

There are three fundamental concepts underpinning integrated reporting:

Value creation for the organisation and for others

An organisation's activities, its interactions and relationships, its outputs and the outcomes for the various capitals it uses and affects influence its ability to continue to draw on these capitals in a continuous cycle.

The capitals

The capitals are the resources and the relationships used and affected by the organisation, which are identified in the <IR> Framework as financial, manufactured, intellectual, human, social and relationship, and natural capital. However, these categories of capital are not required to be adopted in preparing an entity's integrated report, and an integrated report may not cover all capitals – the focus is on capitals that are relevant to the entity.

The value creation process

At the core of the value creation process is an entity's business model, which draws on various capitals and inputs, and by using the entity's business activities, creates outputs (products, services, by-products, waste) and outcomes (internal and external consequences for the capitals).

 More on the capitals

The stock and flow of capitals

All organisations depend on various forms of capital for their success. In the <IR> Framework, the capitals comprise financial, manufactured, intellectual, human, social and relationship, and natural, although as explained below, organisations preparing an integrated report are not required to adopt this categorisation.

The capitals are stocks of value that are increased, decreased or transformed through the activities and outputs of the organisation. For example, an organisation's financial capital is increased when it makes a profit, and the quality of its human capital is improved when employees become better trained.

The overall stock of capitals is not fixed over time. There is a constant flow between and within the capitals as they are increased, decreased or transformed. For example, when an organisation improves its human capital through employee training, the related training costs reduce its financial capital. The effect is that financial capital has been transformed into human capital. Although this example is simple and presented only from the organisation's perspective, it demonstrates the continuous interaction and transformation between the capitals, albeit with varying rates and outcomes.

Many activities cause increases, decreases or transformations that are far more complex than the above example and involve a broader mix of capitals or of components within a capital (e.g. the use of water to grow crops that are fed to farm animals, all of which are components of natural capital).

Categories and descriptions of the capitals

For the purpose of the <IR> Framework, the capitals are categorised and described as follows:

- **Financial capital** – The pool of funds that is:
    - available to an organization for use in the production of goods or the provision of services
    - obtained through financing, such as debt, equity or grants, or generated through operations or investments

- **Manufactured capital** – Manufactured physical objects (as distinct from natural physical objects) that are available to an organisation for use in the production of goods or the provision of services, including:
    - buildings
    - equipment
    - infrastructure (such as roads, ports, bridges, and waste and water treatment plants)

- Manufactured capital is often created by other organisations, but includes assets manufactured by the reporting organisation for sale or when they are retained for its own use.

- **Intellectual capital** – Organisational, knowledge-based intangibles, including:
    - intellectual property, such as patents, copyrights, software, rights and licences
    - 'organizational capital' such as tacit knowledge, systems, procedures and protocols

- **Human capital** – People's competencies, capabilities and experience, and their motivations to innovate, including their:
    - alignment with and support for an organization's governance framework, risk management approach, and ethical values

- – ability to understand, develop and implement an organization's strategy

- – loyalties and motivations for improving processes, goods and services, including their ability to lead, manage and collaborate

- **Social and relationship capital** – The institutions and the relationships within and between communities, groups of stakeholders and other networks, and the ability to share information to enhance individual and collective well-being. Social and relationship capital includes:

  - – shared norms, and common values and behaviours

  - – key stakeholder relationships, and the trust and willingness to engage that an organisation has developed and strives to build and protect with external stakeholders

  - – intangibles associated with the brand and reputation that an organisation has developed

  - – an organisation's social licence to operate

- **Natural capital** – All renewable and non-renewable environmental resources and processes that provide goods or services that support the past, current or future prosperity of an organisation. It includes:

  - – air, water, land, minerals and forests

  - – biodiversity and eco-system health.

Not all capitals are equally relevant or applicable to all organisations. While most organisations interact with all capitals to some extent, these interactions might be relatively minor or so indirect that they are not sufficiently important to include in the integrated report.

Role of the capitals in the <IR> Framework

The Framework does not require an integrated report to adopt the categories identified above or to be structured along the lines of the capitals. Rather, the primary reasons for including the capitals in the Framework are to serve:

- As part of the theoretical underpinning for the concept of value creation

- As a guideline for ensuring organisations consider all the forms of capital they use or affect.

Organisations may categorise the capitals differently. For example, relationships with external stakeholders and the intangibles associated with brand and reputation (both identified as part of social and relationship capital here), might be considered by some organisations to be separate capitals, part of other capitals or cutting across a number of individual capitals.

> Similarly, some organisations define intellectual capital as comprising what they identify as human, 'structural' and 'relational' capitals.
>
> Regardless of how an organisation categorises the capitals for its own purposes, the categories identified above are to be used as a guideline to ensure the organisation does not overlook a capital that it uses or affects.

6   How should the extra information be presented?

Introduction

This chapter has so far explained the benefits of using either the GRI guidelines and/or the <IR> framework to enhance the quality of information presented to stakeholders. However, a question remains regarding what form the extra information should take, and whether it should be presented as a separate document or as part of the entity's published financial statements.

Within the introduction to the <IR> framework document, it says:

> "An integrated report should be a designated, identifiable communication, and should be more than just a summary of information in other communications. Critically, it must make explicit the connectivity of information to communicate how value is created over time.
>
> An integrated report may be either a standalone report or be included as a distinguishable, prominent and accessible part of another report or communication. For example, it may be included at the front of a report that also includes the entity's financial statements."

Therefore, the information is often presented as part of an entity's management commentary (MC) and included as part of the report containing the entity's financial statements.

Purpose of the Management Commentary (MC)

The International Financial Reporting Standards (IFRS) Practice Statement on Management Commentary provides a broad, non-binding framework for the presentation of management commentary that accompanies financial statements that have been prepared in accordance with International Financial Reporting Standards.

It sets out the principles, qualitative characteristics and elements that are necessary to provide users of financial statements with useful information. As the guidance is in the form of a practice statement (rather than an IFRS) compliance with it is voluntary, however where an entity chooses to apply the practice statement it should explain the extent to which it has been applied.

Management commentary is a narrative report that provides a context within which to interpret the financial position, financial performance and cash flows of an entity. Management are able to explain their objectives and strategies for achieving those objectives. Users routinely use the type of information provided in management commentary to help them evaluate an entity's prospects and its general risks, as well as the success of management's strategies for achieving the entity's stated objectives. For many entities, management commentary is already an important element of their communication with the capital markets, supplementing as well as complementing the financial statements.

The practice statement helps management to produce the management commentary that will be reported alongside the financial statements prepared in accordance with IFRS. The users are identified as existing and potential shareholders, together with lenders and creditors.

Framework for presentation of the MC

The following principles should be applied when considering the content of the management commentary:

(a) it should provide management's perspective of the entity's performance, position and progress;

(b) it should supplement and complement information presented in the financial statements;

(c) it should have an orientation to the future;

(d) it should possess the qualitative characteristics of relevance and faithful representation as described in the IASB's Conceptual Framework for Financial Reporting.

The management commentary should provide information to help users of the financial reports to assess the performance of the entity and the actions of its management relative to stated strategies and plans for progress. That type of commentary will help users of the financial reports to understand risk exposures and strategies of the entity, relevant non-financial factors and other issues not otherwise included within the financial statements.

Management commentary should provide management's perspective of the entity's performance, position and progress and therefore should derive from the information that is important to management in managing the business.

Error
Error

Test your understanding 1 (Integration question)

Many entities produce a 'Management Commentary' (known in the UK as the Operating and Financial Review).

Required:

(a) Explain why entities produce such a commentary together with a brief description of the typical information that it might contain.

(b) From the perspective of a user of financial statements, explain the advantages and disadvantages of such a report.

7 Future developments

Problems with the current approach to non-financial reporting

The sections above have highlighted the developments in non-financial reporting.

Due to the voluntary nature of these disclosures their impact and effectiveness will depend on various factors:

- **Relevance:** how much weight do/will investors, employees and consumers give to these factors, compared with that given to financial factors (so return on investment, employee benefits and price, respectively)?

- **Reliability:** how much can the performance measured in these areas be relied on? How sure can users of this information be that it is a faithful representation of what has occurred, as opposed to a selective view focusing on the successes? Are there external assurance processes that can validate the information, perhaps using the GRI guidelines?

- **Comparability:** is the information produced by different entities pulled together on a comparable basis, using similar measurement policies, so that the users can make informed choices between entities? If not, all that can be measured is an entity's performance compared with its own performance in previous periods.

The fact that there are two complementary sets of guidelines (GRI and <IR>) is certainly a problem, as is the fact that compliance with the guidelines is voluntary in many jurisdictions.

Future developments

The International Accounting Standards Board (IASB) and International Integrated Reporting Council (IIRC) have recently announced an agreement that will see the two organisations deepen their cooperation on the IIRC's work to develop an integrated corporate reporting framework. The agreement formalises the strong relationship that already exists at multiple levels between the two organisations.

As part of the agreement, the two bodies will work together to communicate about work on their respective frameworks and to aim for complementarity and compatibility in the ongoing development of the two standards.

They have also agreed to work together to identify ways in which <IR> and financial reporting standards can be aligned to strengthen corporate reporting, and have committed to having regular, frequent and meaningful information exchanges on what they are each doing.

This will ensure that, where there are overlapping interests, they express a common opinion where possible.

It is likely that at some point in the future, regulation will be introduced to formalise this link between the two organisations.

Test your understanding 2 (Case style question)

Company B owns a chemical plant, producing paint.

The plant uses a great deal of energy and releases emissions into the environment. Its by-product is harmful and is treated before being safely disposed of. The company has been fined for damaging the environment following a spillage of the toxic waste product. Due to stricter monitoring routines set up by the company, the fines have reduced and in the current year they have not been in breach of any local environment laws.

The company is aware that emissions are high and has been steadily reducing them. They purchase electricity from renewable sources and in the current year have employed a temporary consultant to calculate their carbon footprint so they can take steps to reduce it.

Required:

(a) Explain why companies may wish to make social and environmental disclosures in their annual report. Discuss how this content should be determined.

(b) Discuss the information that could be included in Company B's environmental report.

(30 minutes)

8   United Nations Sustainability Development Goals

Introduction

In September 2015 the 193 member states of the United Nations adopted a new global 15 year plan to help "end extreme poverty, fight inequality and injustice, and to protect our planet". At the heart of this plan were 17 Sustainability Development Goals (SDG):

The UN recognises that to achieve these goals it will require strong links between governments, companies and the general public. These SDGs are now frequently being reported on within an integrated reporting framework (as of Feb 2018, 40% largest 250 global companies discussed SDGs in their corporate reports). Companies who adopt and support these goals can see many long term benefits such as:

- Improved reputation with customers for being socially responsible

- A healthier and more skilled workforce

- Greater growth opportunities in developing countries as their economy strengthens, giving the population more disposable income

- Continued supply of raw materials from a sustainable source, helping to secure the long term future of the business

- Reduced risks of regulatory breaches and bad publicity

Linking the SDGs with integrated reporting

Integrated reporting provides a framework to help senior management focus on SDGs and build them into the organisation's long term strategy.

Integrated reporting encourages management to look at external factors that may impact the organisation's ability to create value for its stakeholders.

Both the <IR> Framework and GRI G4 Guidelines requires organisations to consider how the external environment (and explicitly social and environmental issues) impact value creation. Many of these factors, such as population, human rights, poverty, education and climate change all relate directly to a number of the SDGs.

Once these external factors are examined, management should identify and evaluate which SDGs will help the organisation to create the most value to its capitals, then develop medium and long term strategies to achieve this.

This is likely to create more integrated thinking and build relationships both between internal departments within the organisation, and also between the organisation and external stakeholders.

These targets, strategies and value creation can and should be reported within the integrated report, along with both the positive and negative ways in which the organisation impact the SDGs

Two real life examples (prepared by Vodafone and Samsung) are shown below.

Case Study – Vodafone's Sustainable Business Report

Vodafone's "Sustainable Business Report" (which can be found on the company's website) starts by setting out the report's aims:

"In our Sustainable Business Report, we give an overview of our ambition of what we are trying to achieve through our sustainable business strategy, together with our progress to date.

The Report also provides an overview of the full range of background information and material non-financial disclosures, including insights into the ethical challenges that inform our business principles and that influence the controls we have put in place to ensure our operating practices meet our (and our stakeholders') expectations."

UN SDGs

The Vodafone report acknowledges the importance of the UN SDGs and has a section explaining how the company addresses five of these goals in particular. The detail from this section of the report is shown below:

"We focus on five of the UN SDGs

We believe our business can have the greatest impact on five of the UN SDGs through our networks, products and services and through the work of the Vodafone Foundation.

SDG 4: Quality education

Ensure inclusive and equitable quality education and promote lifelong learning opportunities for all.

Vodafone and the Vodafone Foundation use mobile technology to enable young people to have access to develop their digital skills and to provide learning opportunities for students. The provision of free or subsidised education resources and technology – particularly to marginalised groups, including refugees – offers enhanced opportunities to achieve academic success and therefore improved life opportunities.

Examples of our contribution:

Over 419,000 people have enrolled in the Vodafone Egypt Foundation's *Knowledge is Power* adult literacy programme.

Over 500,000 refugee students have accessed free, quality education content with no data charges as part of the Vodafone Foundation's *Instant Schools for Africa* programme.

SDG 5: Gender equality

Achieve gender equality and empower all women and girls.

Vodafone provides women with access to life-enhancing services unlocking socio-economic opportunities and helping to address inequality. We also champion the inclusion of women in the workplace, highlighting their vital role in our success and adopting a progressive stance to encourage others.

Examples of our contribution:

We have connected an additional 13.3 million female customers to mobile in our emerging markets since 2016.

29% of our management and leadership roles are held by women.

SDG 8: Decent work and economic growth

Promote sustained, inclusive and sustainable economic growth, full and productive employment and decent work for all.

Youth unemployment is a significant global social and economic challenge in many of our markets. At the same time, the nature of work is changing as advances in technology are leading to the automation of many job categories and digital skills become ever more important in the workplace today. Those skills are in short supply and as a result, many digital jobs remain unfilled. Urgent action is needed to support young people to understand how they can contribute to the digital economy.

Examples of our contribution:

Over 111,000 unique users completed of our *Future Jobs Finder* platform in the first ten days since launch.

We estimate over 14,000 young people were provided with a digital workplace experience during the year.

SDG 9: Industry, innovation and infrastructure

Build resilient infrastructure, promote sustainable industrialisation and foster innovation.

Extending Vodafone's networks to connect the unconnected and improve broadband access enhances global infrastructure and the opportunities that flow from that. Many of our products and services promote sustainable industrial development and foster innovation.

Examples of our contribution:

Our network infrastructure comprises 310,000 base station sites, 65,000 computer servers, 4,200 buildings (including 500 technology centres).

We invested EUR 7.3 billion during the year to maintain and upgrade our digital infrastructure to deliver improved coverage and access to high-speed networks.

SDG 13: Climate action

Take urgent action to combat climate change and its impacts.

We aim to reduce the energy required to run our networks while meeting increasing customer demand for data and are seeking to increase the proportion of our electricity that comes from renewable sources, through the launch of two new energy goals. In parallel, our Internet of Things (IoT) services play a significant role in helping our customers to operate more efficiently and reduce their greenhouse gas (GHG) emissions.

Examples of our contribution:

During the year, we reduced the amount of GHG emissions per petabyte of data carried on our network by 40%.

We have helped our customers to save an estimated 2.1 tonnes of CO_2e for every tonne we generated through our own activities.

Case Study – Samsung's Sustainability Report

The "Sustainability" section on Samsung's website explains the company's approach to sustainability by using a formula:

Value of Samsung sustainability = Economic Value + Social Value

Where

- Economic Value is "Maximise profits and shareholder values (products and services innovation)"

and

- Social Value is "Contribute to a sustainable society (Attainment of the UN SDGs)"

The company goes on to explain how both Economic Value and Social Value are created, as follows:

"Economic Value Creation

Our endeavours to bring innovative technology and products pave the way to generate profits and secure new growth drivers. We strive to embed innovation into the fabric of our corporate culture while creating synergies through the use of external resources to pursue open innovation. In so doing, we take a step closer to building an ecosystem to develop innovative products that cater to the needs of today's rapidly-shifting market.

Social Value Creation

As a global corporate citizen, we at Samsung create social values in a way that is aligned with the UN Sustainable Development Goals (SDGs): Especially, we pinpointed goals that are highly relevant to our business conduct and are analysing our negative/positive impact in attaining these goals. Furthermore, we will discover and fully explore business opportunities that contribute to reaching the UN SDGs."

Focus on UN SDGs

As mentioned in this Social Value Creation introduction, in Samsung's detailed "Sustainability Report" (which can be accessed from a link on the company's website) each of the UN SDGs is highlighted and assessed in terms of how relevant it is to Samsung. Once the relevance has been graded (on a three point scale – low, medium or high) the report then looks at the potential impact (either positive or negative) and explains Samsung's status and future plan. An extract from the report is shown below.

Extract from Samsung's "Sustainability Report" showing UN SDGs

Goal	Relevance	Potential impact	Our status	Future plan
SDG 1: No poverty	Medium	(+) Improve access through technology, information and communication services. (-) Exert a direct or indirect impact on environmental destruction that may affect local residents' livelihood.	Operate citizenship programs that guarantee access to information to all regardless of abilities or economic status. Operate the Tech Institute digital skills program to offer employment training to underprivileged / marginalized populations so that they become economically independent.	Pursue technological innovation that meets social needs. Improve the quality of employment training programs and expand employment support.
SDG 4: Quality education	High	(+) Increase access to education by using ICT.	Provide quality education / training in the EU. Provide career development programs aligned with the life cycle needs of employees.	Expand and improve education and digital skills program. Support individuals with strengthening their job expertise.
SDG 5: Gender equality	High	(+) Strengthen female leadership in the workplace and support female-led businesses.	Operate education programs for females - Designer School in Nepal, programs for women domestic violence in Italy. Operate work programs that ensure maternity protection (Mommy Room in Vietnam).	Expand support for digital education for women. Strengthen gender equality as part of our corporate culture.
SDG 6: Clean water and sanitation	Medium	(+) Ensure the sustainable use and management of water resources. (-) Exert an indirect impact on the shortage of water resources in local communities.	Manage water resource risks in the workplace and monitor the quality of effluent.	Reach 50 tons/KRW 100 million in intensity based use of water resources by 2020.

Summary

This enables the reader of the "Sustainability Report" to see at a glance which of the UN SDGs are most important from Samsung's point of view and should help to reassure the reader that the company takes its sustainability responsibilities very seriously.

9 End of chapter objective test questions

Test your understanding 3 (Objective test question)

HRJ Co is about to prepare a sustainability report for the first time, following the Global Reporting Initiative Guidelines.

The directors are currently preparing the section covering General Standard Disclosures.

Which TWO of the following headings should NOT appear in this section?

A   Society

B   Strategy and Analysis

C   Human Rights

D   Stakeholder Engagement

E   Governance

Test your understanding 4 (Objective test question)

Which THREE of the following are Content Elements as defined by the International Integrated Reporting Council's <IR> Framework?

A   Strategic focus and future orientation

B   Performance

C   Business model

D   Governance

E   Stakeholder relationships

Test your understanding 5 (Objective test question)

Eunice Co has followed the Global Reporting Initiative (GRI) G4 guidelines and is preparing to issue a sustainability report in accordance with the guidelines.

Which of the following statements relating to incomplete disclosure is correct?

A   Information may only be omitted if it is subject to either legal prohibitions or confidentiality constraints

B   Where legal restrictions prohibit disclosure, no further disclosure is required

C   Where information is omitted due to confidentiality constraints, these should be explained

D   Where information is unavailable, it is sufficient to state that this is the case

Test your understanding 6 (Objective test question)

Which THREE of the following are defined by the Global Reporting Initiative as being Principles for Defining Report Quality:

A   Timeliness

B   Materiality

C   Clarity

D   Reliability

E   Completeness

Test your understanding 7 (Objective test question)

Which THREE of the following are objectives of Integrated Reporting, as identified by the International Integrated Reporting Council (IIRC)?

A   To support integrated thinking and decision making

B   To communicate the impacts of economic, environmental and social and governance performance

C   To improve the quality of information available to providers of financial capital

D   To increase the quantity of information available to providers of financial capital

E   To provide a more cohesive and efficient approach to corporate reporting

Test your understanding 8 (Objective test question)

Which THREE of the following are Guiding Principles as defined by the International Integrated Reporting Council's <IR> Framework?

A   Conciseness

B   Materiality

C   Connectivity of information

D   Outlook

E   Basis of preparation and presentation

Test your understanding 9 (Objective test question)

Vinus Co is a UK based company. It is preparing a sustainability report in accordance with the Global Reporting Initiative's G4 guidelines.

The company recently made a political donation to the opposition party during the UK general election campaign.

Under which category would this information be disclosed in Vinus Co's sustainability report?

A   Economic

B   Social – Society

C   Social – Human rights

D   There is no requirement in the G4 guidelines to disclose political donations

Test your understanding 10 (Objective test question)

QQ Co has prepared a draft Integrated Report following the International Integrated Reporting Council's <IR> Framework.

Which THREE of the headings below have been placed in the wrong section of the report?

Guiding principles

A   Strategic focus and future orientation

B   Stakeholder relationships

C   Governance

D   Disclosures on Management Approach (DMA)

Content elements

E   Organisational overview and external environment

F   Strategy and resource allocation

G   Outlook

H   Consistency and comparability

Test your understanding 11 (Objective test question)

Which THREE of the following are defined by the Global Reporting Initiative as being Principles for Defining Report Content:

A   Sustainability context

B   Materiality

C   Stakeholder inclusiveness

D   Reliability

E   Balance

Test your understanding 12 (Objective test question)

Yootha Co is preparing an Integrated Report for the first time.

The directors feel that the eight 'Content Elements' headings listed in the <IR> Framework won't enable them to present the information about their company in the most user-friendly way. Hence, they are planning to use a different set of headings to structure their Integrated Report.

What does the <IR> Framework say about using different report headings?

A   Companies are not allowed to use different headings. The eight 'Content Elements' headings must be used to enable users to compare different companies' Integrated Reports easily.

B   Companies can use different report headings for the 'Content Elements'. The given headings are only provided as suggestions.

C   The eight 'Content Elements' headings must be used if a company is presenting Core Disclosures, but different headings can be used for Comprehensive Disclosures.

D   Different headings can be used in a company's first Integrated Reports, but by the time a company produces its third annual Integrated Report, the eight 'Content Elements' headings listed in the <IR> Framework have to be used.

Test your understanding 13 (Objective test question)

Which TWO of the following headings are not one of the 17 United Nations Sustainable Development Goals (SDGs)?

A   Zero hunger

B   Quality education

C   Internet for all

D   Climate action

E   Recycling more

F   Gender equality

10   End of chapter case style questions

Test your understanding 14 (Case style question)

It is becoming increasingly common for listed entities to provide non-financial disclosures intended to inform stakeholders about the business's environmental policies, impacts and practices. Supporters of such voluntary disclosures argue that stakeholders have a right to be informed about environmental issues in this way. However, there are also arguments against this type of disclosure.

Required:

Identify and explain the principal arguments against voluntary disclosures by businesses of their environmental policies, impacts and practices.

(15 minutes)

Test your understanding 15 (Case style question)

The directors of World Energy, a public limited company, feel that their financial statements do not address a broad enough range of users' needs. The company's main business is the generation and supply of electricity and gas.

They have reviewed the published financial statements and have realised that there is very little information about their corporate environmental governance.

The company discloses the following social and environmental information in the financial statements:

Corporate Environmental Governance

- the highest radiation dosage to a member of the public

- total acid gas emissions and global warming potential

- contribution to clean air through emission savings

The company wishes to enhance its disclosures but is unsure as to what the benefits would be for the company and what constitutes current practice. The problem that the directors envisage is how to measure and report the company's performance.

Required:

Explain the factors that provide encouragement to companies to disclose social and environmental information in their financial statements, briefly discussing whether the content of such disclosure should be at the company's discretion.   **(30 minutes)**

Describe how the current disclosure by World Energy of its 'Corporate Environmental Governance' could be extended and improved.

(30 minutes)

Test your understanding 16 (Case style question)

The directors of Glowball, a public limited company, have discussed a study by the Institute of Environmental Management which indicated that over 35% of the world's 250 largest corporations are voluntarily releasing green reports to the public to promote corporate environmental performance and to attract customers and investors. They have heard that their main competitors are applying the 'Global Reporting Initiative'(GRI) in an effort to develop a worldwide format for corporate environmental reporting.

However, the directors are unsure as to what this initiative actually means. Additionally they require advice as to the nature of any legislation or standards relating to environmental reporting as they are worried that any environmental report produced by the company may not be of sufficient quality and may detract and not enhance their image if the report does not comply with recognised standards.

Glowball has a reputation for ensuring the preservation of the environment in its business activities.

Required:

Prepare a report suitable for presentation to the directors of Glowball in which you discuss the current reporting requirements and guidelines relating to environmental reporting. **(30 minutes)**

Test your understanding answers

Test your understanding 1 (Integration question)

(a) **The need for management commentary**

Financial statements, although useful, have limitations in that they are highly summarised and provide historic information. Management commentary (MC) aims to overcome these limitations by having a forward looking focus and enabling management to expand on the information presented in the financial statements.

The management commentary provides a narrative to the financial statements. It can therefore be used to explain the financial results within the context of the environment in which the entity operates. For example, whilst the financial results may not on their own be viewed as positive, the management commentary provides directors with the opportunity to explain that, within the context of the economic climate, the results should be considered positive.

The typical information contained within management commentary would be:

– description of the nature of the entity's activities

– the entity's objectives and strategies to achieve those objectives

– description of the entity's resources and the risks facing the business

– narrative review of the current year's results

– key performance indicators

– non-financial information such as employment and environmental policies

– outline plan for the future development of the business

(b) **Advantages and disadvantages to users**

Advantages

The MC will provide information regarding the future prospects of an entity. This should enhance the users' ability to make more appropriate investment decisions.

The narrative information should give users a better understanding of the performance and position of the entity.

Producing an MC voluntarily shows the entity as being transparent and willing to communicate. Users may wish to consider such factors, as well as financial information, when making investment decisions.

Users can gain information on non-financial factors addressed by the entity such as how the skills of the workforce contribute to the performance of the entity and whether the entity have a responsible attitude to the environment.

Disadvantages

Since the MC is voluntarily produced, it is unlikely to be prepared in a consistent manner between entities. Therefore users may not be able to perform any meaningful comparison between different entities.

Disclosing information regarding future prospects of an entity may raise the expectations of users. Users may be disadvantaged in the future if the performance does not meet these expectations.

The content of an MC is at the discretion of the directors. They may therefore choose to only disclose positive information. This reduces the reliability of the document for the users.

The content of the MC is not audited. Again, this reduces the level of reliance that users may be willing to place on the information.

Test your understanding 2 (Case style question)

(a) The way in which companies manage their social and environmental responsibilities is a high level strategic issue for management. Companies that actively manage these responsibilities can help create long-term sustainable performance in an increasingly competitive business environment.

Reports that disclose transparent information will benefit organisations and their stakeholders. These stakeholders will have an interest in knowing that the company is attempting to adopt best practice in the area. Institutional investors will see value in the 'responsible ownership' principle adopted by the company.

Although there is no universal 'best practice', there seems to be growing consensus that high performance is linked with high quality practice in such areas as recruitment, organisational culture, training and reduction of environmental risks and impact. Companies that actively reduce environmental risks and promote social disclosures could be considered to be potentially more sustainable, profitable, valuable and competitive. Many companies build their reputation on the basis of social and environmental responsibility and go to substantial lengths to prove that their activities do not exploit their workforce or any other section of society.

Governments are encouraging disclosure by passing legislation, for example in the area of anti-discrimination and by their own example in terms of the depth and breadth of reporting (also by requiring companies who provide services to the government to disclose such information). External awards and endorsements, such as environmental league tables and employer awards, encourage companies to adopt a more strategic approach to these issues. Finally, local cultural and social pressures are causing greater demands for transparency of reporting.

There is no IFRS that determines the content of an environmental and social report. While companies are allowed to include the information they wish to disclose, there is a lack of comparability and the potential that only the positive actions will be shown.

A common framework that provides guidelines on sustainability reporting would be useful for both companies and stakeholders.

The Global Reporting Initiative (GRI) provides guidelines on the content of a sustainability report, but these are not mandatory. However, a number of companies prepare their reports in accordance with the guidelines and the GRI is becoming the unofficial best practice guide in this area.

(b) Company B's environmental report should include the following information.

(i) A statement of the environmental policy covering all aspects of business activity. This can include their aim of using renewable electricity and reducing their carbon footprint – the amount of carbon dioxide released into the environment as a result of their activities.

(ii) The management systems that reduce and minimise environmental risks.

(iii) Details of environmental training and expertise.

(iv) A report on their environmental performance including verified emissions to air/land and water, and how they are seeking to reduce these and other environmental impacts. Company B's activities have a significant impact so it is important to show how this is dealt with. The emissions data could be graphed to show it is reducing. If they have the data, they could compare their carbon dioxide emissions or their electricity usage over previous periods. Presenting this information graphically helps stakeholders see how the business is performing in the areas it is targeting.

(v)   Details of any environmental offence that resulted in enforcement action, fine, etc. and any serious pollution incident. They can disclose how fines have been reducing and state that there have not been any pollution incidents in the current period.

(vi) A report on historical trends for key indicators and a comparison with the corporate targets.

Test your understanding 3 (Objective test question)

The answer is (A) and (C).

These two sections should appear in the social category of the specific standard disclosures, not the general standard disclosures.

Test your understanding 4 (Objective test question)

The answer is (B), (C) and (D).

The other two headings are Guiding Principles, not Content Elements, as defined by the <IR> Framework.

Test your understanding 5 (Objective test question)

The answer is (C).

Where information is omitted due to confidentiality constraints, these should be explained.

Test your understanding 6 (Objective test question)

The answer is (A), (C) and (D).

The other two are Principles for Defining Report Content according to the GRI.

Test your understanding 7 (Objective test question)

The answer is (A), (C) and (E).

(B) is an objective of sustainability reporting.

(D) is irrelevant – investors are more interested in the quality, not the quantity, of information available.

Test your understanding 8 (Objective test question)

The answer is (A), (B) and (C).

The other two headings are Content Elements, not Guiding Principles, as defined by the <IR> Framework.

Test your understanding 9 (Objective test question)

The answer is (B).

Political donations have to be disclosed as part of the Public Policy aspect of the Social (Society) category.

Test your understanding 10 (Objective test question)

The answer is (C), (D) and (H).

(C) and (H) are simply the wrong way round i.e. Governance is really a content element and Consistency and comparability is a guiding principle.

(D) should not appear in an Integrated Report. However it would appear as a specific standard disclosure in a sustainability report prepared using the GRI Guidelines.

Test your understanding 11 (Objective test question)

The answer is (A), (B) and (C).

The other two are Principles for Defining Report Quality according to the GRI.

Test your understanding 12 (Objective test question)

The answer is (B).

Note that the Core and Comprehensive Disclosures mentioned in (C) relate to the GRI G4 guidelines, not the <IR> Framework.

Test your understanding 13 (Objective test question)

The answers are (C) and (E).

Internet for all is not one of the specific goals, however improving access to technology would form part of the 'Industry, Innovation and Infrastructure' goal.

Similarly recycling is not a specific goal, however it could come under the goals for ' Responsible consumption and production', ' Life on land' and 'Life below water'

Test your understanding 14 (Case style question)

Many of the arguments against disclosure stem from the fact that disclosure is still voluntary. Even in countries such as the UK, where many companies are now legally required to disclose relevant information, there may be few actual requirements as to what exactly should be disclosed.

Several problems result:

- The information disclosed may not be complete or reliable. Environmental disclosures normally appear in the Chairman's Statement, in the Operating and Financial Review or in a 'stand alone' environmental report. Therefore they do not normally have to be audited and can be framed in very general terms. Entities can present information selectively so as to present their activities in a positive light.

- A wide variety of information is disclosed and this may be both narrative and numerical (in the form of key performance indicators). This means that is difficult to compare the performance of different entities. Non-financial performance indicators may not be well understood by users and the basis of their calculation may not be adequately explained.

- The information may not be disclosed consistently from year to year. This means that users cannot assess any progress that is being made.

- Not all businesses disclose information. Those that do are often under particular pressure to prove their 'green' credentials (for example, large public utility companies whose operations directly affect the environment) or because they have deliberately built their reputation on environmental friendliness or social responsibility. This means that (understandably) the public may view environmental reporting as little more than a cynical public relations exercise and not pay much attention to any information presented.

Some believe that there are fundamental problems to do with disclosure itself, rather than with the relevance or reliability of the information:

- Separate environmental reports and/or disclosure in the Operating and Financial Review are no substitute for clear disclosure of environmental costs in the financial statements themselves. This would provide a far greater incentive for entities to act responsibly.

- Equally, disclosure does not solve the environmental problems that are disclosed. There is a school of thought that believes that encouraging and praising voluntary disclosure could create the impression that disclosure, in itself, is enough.

Management may also have arguments against disclosure:

- Producing environmental disclosures is time consuming and costly, particularly where these are intended to be genuinely useful. It may also harm a company's reputation, rather than enhancing it. A useful report must be even handed, and must publish bad news as well as good. Even if the company acts in good faith, there is a danger that disclosure will be seen as merely a public relations exercise.

- A company that presents itself as environmentally responsible in a 'standalone' report may find that this has an impact on the financial statements. Undertaking publicly to carry out particular courses of action (for example, to clean up environmental damage) will create a constructive obligation to do so, even where there is no legal obligation.

Test your understanding 15 (Case style question)

Answer to the first task

The way in which companies manage their social and environmental responsibilities is a high level strategic issue for management. Companies that actively manage these responsibilities can help create long term sustainable performance in an increasingly competitive business environment.

Greater transparency in this area will benefit organisations and their stakeholders. These stakeholders will have an interest in knowing that the company is attempting to adopt best practice in the area. Institutional investors will see value in the 'responsible ownership' principle adopted by the company. Although there is no universal 'best practice' there seems to be growing consensus that high performance is linked with high quality practice in such areas as recruitment, organisational culture, training and reduction of environmental risks and impact. Companies that actively reduce environmental risks and promote social disclosures could be considered to be potentially more sustainable, profitable, valuable and competitive.

Many companies build their reputation on the basis of social and environmental responsibility and go to substantial lengths to prove that their activities do not exploit their workforce or any other section of society. Governments are encouraging disclosure by passing legislation, for example in the area of anti-discrimination and by their own example in terms of the depth and breadth of reporting (also by requiring companies who provide services to the government to disclose such information).

External awards and endorsements, such as environmental league tables and employer awards, encourage companies to adopt a more strategic approach to these issues. Finally, local cultural and social pressures are causing greater demands for transparency of reporting.

There are arguments for giving organisations the freedom to determine the contents of such reports and for encouraging common practices and measures. Standardised reports may fail to capture important information in individual organisations and may lead to 'compliance' rather than 'relevance'. At the same time, best practice would encourage consistency, comparability and reliability, providing a common framework which companies and stakeholders might find useful.

Answer to the second task – Corporate environmental governance

The reporting of corporate environmental governance by World Energy could be improved by including the following information in the financial statements:

- a statement of the environmental policy covering all aspects of business activity

- the management systems which reduce and minimise environmental risks (reference should be made to internationally recognised environmental management systems)

- details of environmental training and expertise

- a report on their environmental performance including disclosing verified emissions to air/land and water, and how they are seeking to reduce these and other environmental impacts. Operating site reports could be prepared for local communities for businesses with high environmental impacts

- details of any environmental offence that resulted in enforcement action, fine, etc., and any serious pollution incident

- a report on historical trends for key indicators and a comparison with the corporate targets

- a simple environmental statement of comprehensive income and statement of financial position including income and value derived from the environment, expenditure on natural resources, licences etc., investment in anti-pollution equipment.

The environmental performance statements and report should be audited and verified to recognise environmental and auditing standards, and companies should perhaps have a health, safety and environment committee.'

Test your understanding 16 (Case style question)

Report to the Directors of Glowball – Environmental Reporting

Introduction

The following report details the current reporting requirements and guidelines relating to Environmental Reporting.

Current reporting requirements and guidelines

The initial goal of environmental reporting was simply to demonstrate a company's commitment to the environment. However, the debate has moved on and the central objective of any environmental report is now to communicate environmental performance.

Wider ranging objectives may also be attributed to the report, such as acknowledging shared responsibility for the environment, differentiating the company from its competitors, obtaining social approval for operating practices and demonstrating regulatory compliance.

Reports in practice vary from a simple public relations statement to a detailed examination of the company's environmental performance. Environmental accounting disclosure is an assortment of mandatory and voluntary requirements.

Not all companies report on environmental performance and those that do report often focus on only selected aspects of performance. It is typically only the leaders in environmental reporting that report in a comprehensive manner.

In the UK, environmental reporting is voluntary although disclosure of environmental matters such as the business's impact on the environment is encouraged in a company's 'Operating and Financial Review' by the ASB's Reporting Statement on best practice on the operating and financial review. Accounting standards on non-current assets, provisions, and research and development costs mention the need to disclose environmental effects.

This voluntary position contrasts with the situation in Denmark and the Netherlands, which have passed legislation making environmental disclosure mandatory for the larger companies. In the USA, the SEC/FASB environmental accounting standards are obligatory, although the standards may not be policed as closely as other accounting standards. The International Accounting Standards Board has not as yet issued a standard in this area. However, IAS 37 Provisions, Contingent Liabilities and Contingent Assets requires disclosure of potential environmental liabilities in certain circumstances.

There is a range of codes of practice and environmental reporting guidelines that have been published. The Global Reporting Initiative's Sustainability Reporting Guidelines, published by the Coalition of Environmentally Responsible Economies (CERES), has become the de facto standard worldwide. The GRI provides a set of principles to enable investors and others to assess environmental performance.

There is a whole range of governmental, academic, professional body and international agencies that have published reports and guidelines that can be accessed and downloaded from the Web. Under the Eco Management and Audit Scheme (EMAS), companies can sign up to agree to a specific code of practice, but the report must be validated by an accredited environmental verifier.

The Companies Act 2006 now requires the directors of UK quoted companies to report on environmental matters, the company's employees and social/community issues.

Conclusion

In summary, environmental reports can enhance a company's reputation and standing, and the use of environmental reporting will expand. Currently, except in a few specific countries, this form of activity reporting is voluntary and, therefore, the extent of disclosure varies significantly.

However, until regulation and standards are developed, the completeness and consistency of environmental reports will not be achieved. Similarly best practice in the attestation of the reports also needs establishing.

Environmental reporting is important to large companies as it is no passing phase. The main question is as to the form and content of the environmental report.

3

Development of financial strategy

Chapter learning objectives

Lead outcome	Component outcome
A2: Analyse strategic financial policy decisions	Analyse the following policy decision areas: (a) Investment (b) Financing (c) Dividends (d) Interrelationships between them
A3: Discuss the external influences on financial strategic decisions	Discuss the influence of the following on financial strategic decisions (a) Market requirements (b) Taxation (c) Regulatory requirements

Topics to be covered

- Use of policy decisions to meet cash needs of entity
- Sensitivity of forecast financial statements and future cash position to these policy decisions
- Considerations of the interests of stakeholders
- Lenders' assessment of creditworthiness
- Consideration of domestic and international taxation regulations
- Consideration of industry regulations such as price and service controls

1 Overview of chapter

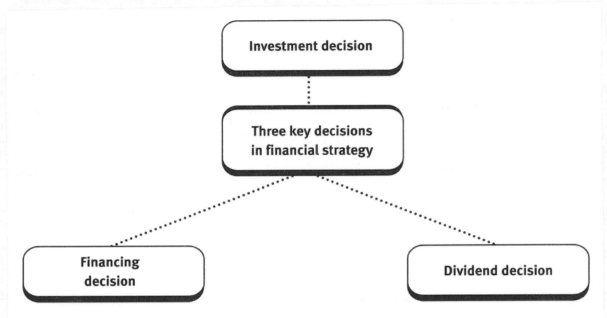

Definitions of key terms

Strategy: A course of action, including the specification of resources required, to achieve a specific objective. (CIMA Official Terminology, 2005)

Financial strategy is the aspect of strategy which falls within the scope of financial management, which will include decisions on investment, financing and dividends.

Strategic financial management: The identification of the possible strategies capable of maximising an entity's net present value, the allocation of scarce capital resources among the competing opportunities and the implementation and monitoring of the chosen strategy so as to achieve stated objectives. (CIMA Official Terminology, 2005)

The importance of financial strategy to an entity

An entity's financial managers must plan their courses of action to achieve the entity's financial objectives.

The key consideration is how should the entity generate cash, and what is the best use of this key finite resource?

For example, should new investments be undertaken, and how large a dividend should be paid?

This chapter identifies the three key decisions in financial strategy and looks at the links between them.

2 The key decisions of financial strategy

We saw in the earlier Chapter 1: 'Objectives', that entities usually have financial objectives that encourage investment and growth.

However, before any investment decisions can be made, the entity's managers will have to assess whether they have enough cash to make the new investments, or whether additional finance will have to be raised.

Therefore, the three key decisions in financial strategy are:

- Investment – what projects should be undertaken by the organisation?

- Financing – how should the necessary funds be raised?

- Dividends – how much cash should be allocated each year to be paid as a return to shareholders, and how much should be retained to meet the cash needs of the business?

These three areas are very closely interlinked.

Investment decision

Financial managers have responsibility for the allocation of financial resources to achieve the organisation's objectives. An important part of their job is to understand the short, medium and long-term capital requirements for investment in fixed assets and working capital that fits with the overall strategy.

Whilst financial managers are unlikely to be solely responsible for the final choice of capital investment projects to be undertaken, they will be actively involved in the evaluation of possible investment opportunities.

 More detail on the investment decision

When considering whether a project is worthwhile, a company must consider its implications. Any potential investment is likely to affect:

- **The liquidity of the company** – All projects involve cash flows in and out. The size and timing of such flows should be considered when appraising projects. If an aim of investment appraisal is to satisfy shareholders then it is important to remember that, if a company has no cash, it cannot pay a dividend.

- **The reported profit and earnings** – All projects will change the revenues, expenses and asset values shown in the financial accounts. If shareholders are concerned about such statistics as earnings per share, then the effect of investments on reported figures must be part of the investment appraisal.

> - **The variability of cash flows and earnings** – Investors are concerned about the variability of returns from their investments. The greater the variability, the greater the risk, and therefore the greater the return they will require. Thus, when appraising potential projects, managers should consider not only the likely size and direction of cash flows and profits but also whether they are likely to add to or reduce the variability of such flows.

Financing decision

For both non-current asset and working capital investment, the financial manager must decide on the most appropriate type and source of funding.

This will include such considerations as:

- the extent to which requirements can be funded internally, from the organisation's operations. This will involve considerations of dividend policy and tax implications;

- if new, externally provided, finance is required, whether it should be in the form of equity or debt finance. This may affect the level of gearing (the ratio of debt to equity finance) which can have implications for returns required by the providers of capital;

- the extent to which working capital should be financed by long-term finance or short-term credit.

More detail on the financing decision

Financing decisions relate to acquiring the optimum finance to meet financial objectives and seeing that non-current assets and working capital are effectively managed.

Optimum level of cash to hold

The first decision that the financial manager will have to make is how much cash should be held by the business as a buffer against unexpected costs.

Key considerations are:

- **Trade off (too much cash v too little cash)**

  Holding too little cash will potentially leave the entity subject to liquidity problems and possible liquidation. However, holding too much cash has an opportunity cost (lost interest on deposits, or returns on attractive investments) and leaves an entity vulnerable to a takeover bid. The financial manager has to balance the trade-off between these issues and identify the optimum level of cash to hold.

- **Flexibility**

  Holding cash means that the entity can adjust its business plan (for example pursue a takeover opportunity or invest in a new project) rapidly without needing to raise finance first.

- **Expectations of shareholders**

  An entity needs to consider whether its shareholders could make better use of the cash themselves. The shareholders invest money in the expectation that the entity will invest it to create wealth. Theoretically, the entity should only hold cash if the managers expect to be able to use it to increase the wealth of the shareholders.

Sources of finance

The financial manager must possess a good knowledge of the sources of available funds and their respective costs, and should ensure that the entity has a sound capital structure, that is, a proper balance between equity capital and borrowings. Such managers also need to have a very clear understanding of the difference between profit and cash flow, bearing in mind that profit is of little avail unless the entity is adequately supported by cash to pay for assets and sustain the working capital cycle.

Financing decisions also call for a good knowledge of evaluation of risk: excessive borrowing carries high risk for an entity's equity because of the priority rights of the lenders.

A major area for risk-related decisions is in establishing foreign subsidiaries, where an entity is vulnerable to currency fluctuations. Foreign debt is often appropriate to create a hedge of the change in value of the net investment in the subsidiary as a result of currency movements.

Benefits of matching characteristics of investment and financing

The matching approach to financing is where the profile of the of the entity's financing matches the profile of the assets being funded.

This principle can be applied to the matching of maturities.

For example, using long-term finance to fund both non-current assets and permanent current assets, and financing fluctuating current assets by short-term borrowings.

It makes sense to fund long term assets with long term finance since it gives security that the finance will be in place for the life of the asset, and also so that the economic benefits from the assets can help repay the finance.

The finance will mature (and hopefully be repaid where applicable) at a similar time to the asset being disposed of. New finance can then be obtained to fund the replacement asset.

> Nearly all companies will have a certain level of current assets and working capital permanently tied up in the business (e.g. a minimum level of receivables and inventory). Since this is always required, it is often called 'permanent current assets' and is often funded with long term finance.

Dividend decision

Dividends provide important returns to shareholders and can be seen as an indicator of success of the business. Shareholder returns comprise both increase in share price and cash in the form of dividends.

When deciding on the type of investment and level of finance needed, the financial manager must have regard for the potential effects on the risk and level of dividends payable to shareholders. If the shareholders are not happy with their return, they will be reluctant to invest further, which in turn will affect the funding available for future investment. However, the cash needs of the business must also be considered.

The business may wish to retain cash resources to finance investments rather than increase gearing by raising new funding. Cash resources may also be retained in order to provide rapid access to funds to respond to investment opportunities that might arise in the future or to provide flexibility in the face of poor trading conditions.

The dividend decision thus has two elements:

- the amount to be paid out, and
- the amount to be retained to support the growth of the entity (note that this is also a financing decision).

The level and regular growth of dividends represent a significant factor in determining a profit-making entity's market value, that is, the value placed on its shares by the stock market.

 ## Links between the three key decisions

It is clear from the discussions above that the three areas are closely interrelated.

Investment decisions cannot be taken without consideration of where and how the funds are to be raised to finance them. The type of finance available will, in turn, depend to some extent on the nature of the project – its size, duration, risk, capital asset backing, etc.

Dividends represent the payment of returns on the investment back to the shareholders, the level and risk of which will depend upon the project itself, and how it was financed.

Debt finance, for example, can be cheap (particularly where interest is tax deductible) but requires an interest payment to be made out of project earnings, which can increase the risk of the shareholders' dividends.

3 The impact of investment, financing and dividend decisions on financial ratios

It is important to consider the inter-relationship between investment, financing and dividend decisions when assessing the impact of the decisions on the entity's ratios.

Examples of inter-relationships

1   An investment decision to undertake a profitable project, financed by raising new debt or equity finance, may impact several important investor and lender ratios such as earnings per share, earnings yield and interest cover.

Test your understanding 1 (Integration question)

Seed Co is considering an investment of $20m which is expected have an NPV of $8m, and is expected to increase profit before interest and tax by $4m per annum.

Extracts from the most recent financial statements of Seed Co:

Statement of financial position extracts	$m
Share capital ($1 shares)	16
Reserves	48
Long term borrowings	56
Statement of profit or loss extracts	**$m**
Profit before interest and tax	15.0
Interest	(4.0)
Profit before tax	11.0
Tax at 30%	(3.3)
Profit after tax (earnings)	7.7

The current share price of Seed Co is $2.70 per share.

The directors of Seed Co are considering two alternative ways of financing the new investment.

*   borrow the $20m at an interest rate of 6% per annum,

*   raise the funds using a 1 for 2 rights issue at $2.50 per share. Assume that this would cause the share price after the issue (BEFORE taking account of the project NPV) to fall to $2.63.

> **Required:**
>
> (a) Prepare profit forecasts for Seed Co for next year under both financing options, assuming that the new project goes ahead. Use the forecasts to calculate the impact of the project and each financing option on Seed Co's interest cover, earnings per share and earnings yield ratios.
>
> (b) Based on the results of your calculations, discuss the likely reaction of the shareholders and the lenders to each of the possible financing options.

2   Financing requirements and cash available for payment of dividends are determined based on the overall consideration of the forecast future cash flows arising from investment decisions, business strategy and forecast business and economic variables.

Test your understanding 2 (Objective test question)

The Finance Director of CP has calculated that the company needs to raise some additional long term funds to provide finance for the following three proposals.

- CP's trade payables are currently $3.15 million. Suppliers have expressed dissatisfaction that the company currently takes 45 days to pay. They would like to be paid 10 days quicker.

- The bank overdraft has been close to its limit for the last 6 months, and the bank is putting pressure on CP to reduce the overdraft from its current level of $2.2 million to $2 million.

- Over the past three years the annual revenue of CP has stagnated, so the directors are considering expanding operations. Capital expenditure of $1 million would be required to expand the existing distribution facilities.

How much finance needs to be raised in total to fund these three proposals?

A $1.90 million

B $3.65 million

C $4.35 million

D $6.35 million

3   A change in dividend policy can have an immediate impact on some investor ratios such as dividend cover and dividend yield. However, there may also be other, less obvious, impacts. For example, reducing the level of dividend paid out one year could increase the amount of funds available for re-investment, so there might well be an increased level of growth in profit which could impact ratios such as earnings per share.

Illustration 1 (Integration question)

Elbow Co is an all equity financed company with a functional currency of British pounds (GBP). It has 10 million GBP 1 shares in issue. The directors of Elbow Co are considering a change in dividend policy at the end of this year.

Historically the company has paid out 30% of its profits as a dividend. However, the directors have identified a new project that they want to invest in. The necessary funds for investment could be found by cutting the dividend payout ratio to 10% of profits for this year only.

Forecast profits for the current year are GBP 10 million. Next year's profits will be 15% higher if the dividend is cut and the new project undertaken. Otherwise, profits will stay constant.

Required:

Calculate the dividend per share and the earnings per share for this year and next year, on the assumption that:

(a)   the dividend is cut and the project is invested in.

(b)   the dividend pay-out is left unchanged and the project is not undertaken.

Solution:

Current year:

The current year's profit is forecast to be GBP 10 million, so whether the dividend is cut and the project is undertaken or not, the earnings per share (EPS) will be

GBP 10m/10m = GBP 1.

If the dividend is cut, to 10% of profits, the dividend per share (DPS) will therefore be 10% of this, i.e. GBP 0.10.

If the dividend is not cut, so remains at 30% of profits, the dividend per share (DPS) will be 30% of this, i.e. GBP 0.30.

Next year:

No project:

Next year's profit is forecast to stay at GBP 10 million if the project is not undertaken, so EPS will be

GBP 10m/10m = GBP 1.

DPS is expected to stay at 30% of this, so will be GBP 0.30.

With project:

Next year's profit is forecast to grow by 15% (to GBP 11.5 million) if the project is undertaken, so EPS will be

GBP 11.5m/10m = GBP 1.15

We are told that the dividend cut is expected to be for only one year, so DPS next year will revert to 30% of EPS, i.e. 30% × GBP 1.15 = GBP 0.345

4 Objectives and economic forces

When setting the company's financial strategy the financial manager is often influenced by external economic forces.

For example, significant expansion and an increase in dividends may become uneconomic if interest rates are set to rise (thus increasing the amount payable to banks and other debt finance providers).

External influences on financial strategy

Major influences include:

- The need to maintain good investor relations and provide a satisfactory return on investment

- Limited access to sources of finance, either due to weak creditworthiness or lack of liquidity in the banking sector and capital markets

- Gearing level. The main argument in favour of gearing is that introducing borrowings into the capital structure attracts tax relief on interest payments. The argument against borrowing is that it introduces financial risk into the entity. Financial managers have to formulate a policy that balances the effects of these opposing features.

- Debt covenants. These are clauses written into debt agreements which protect the lender's interests by requiring the borrower to satisfy certain criteria (e.g. a minimum level of interest cover)

- Government influence (see below)

- Regulatory bodies (see below)

- Major economic influences, such as interest rates, growth in GDP, inflation rates and exchange rates. The effects of interest rate and inflation changes on the economy are covered below.

- Accounting concepts.

Government influence

Governments often play a large part in influencing business activity. Some examples of the way in which governments can have an influence are as follows:

- Employment policy. Governments play a major role in attempting to stimulate employment. They can do this by funding vocational training programmes and funding employment programmes.

- Regional policy. Governments may make funds available to support regions of high unemployment and social deprivation.

- Taxation policy. The government raises taxes on the profits generated by profit-making entities and on shareholders' dividends.

- Legislation. Laws set out how people can and should behave towards one another, and particularly, how business should be conducted.

Regulatory requirements

Developing financial strategy in the context of regulatory requirements

The financial manager must have a proper understanding of those aspects of legislation which impact upon entities. Such legislation will include the Companies Acts, health and safety regulations, laws relating to consumer protection and consumer rights, laws relating to contract and agency, employment law and laws relating to protection of the environment and promoting competition.

Listed companies also have to comply with Stock Exchange regulations, and entities which operate in some high profile industries will also find regulatory bodies monitoring their performance. For example, in the UK, Oftel (telecommunications), Ofcom (media) and Ofwat (water) have been set up by the government to monitor and regulate their respective industries.

Regulatory bodies

A clear set of objectives is required for each regulatory body. In general terms, a regulatory body will have the power to impose price controls or service controls (i.e. to dictate prices or the quality of service delivered).

The objectives may be classified under three headings:

1   The promotion of competition.

2   The protection of customers from monopoly power.

3   The promotion of social and macroeconomic objectives.

1   **Competition**

Where a market is not competitive, or is in the early stages of becoming so, there is a need for regulators whose role is to try to balance the interests of the various stakeholders.

Important issues for regulation are the prevention of 'cross-subsidy', that is the transferring or offloading of portions of overhead costs from lower- to higher-margin products, the limitation of non-price barriers affecting the entry of new competitors, and assuring reasonable quality of product in relation to price. Non-price barriers could include trade restrictions, or restricted access to supplies or distribution channels.

2   **Monopoly power**

Where market participants are judged to possess significant market power, and where there is no other protection for customers, controls on prices and on quality of service may be considered.

3   **Social objectives**

Government objectives may include the availability and affordability of services in particular areas and to particular groups such as customers in remote rural areas. Regulators often use a 'public interest test' to assess whether an entity's strategy is acceptable – for example strategies compromising national security could be blocked.

5   The impact of taxation on financial strategy

The financial manager will have to consider the taxation implications of all his decisions when setting the entity's financial strategy. For companies with operations in several countries, there will be both domestic and international tax implications.

Specific tax rules differ from country to country, but some general points are explained below.

Domestic tax implications

Any profits generated by a new investment project will be taxable. However, tax allowable depreciation will normally be available on assets purchased, to reduce the overall tax liability.

Debt interest is tax deductible. Therefore if the entity decides to finance new investments through debt finance, there will be tax savings when the interest is paid. This is not the case with dividends to shareholders (if equity finance is used).

Dividends to shareholders will be taxed under income tax rules. However, if the entity chooses not to pay out a dividend, any increases in share price will be taxed under capital gains tax rules when the shares are sold. Therefore, most investors have a preference as to whether they'd like the entity to pay out a dividend or not.

Where the entity meets certain conditions its shares may be issued under special schemes that allow the investor tax relief on the investment, and/or when the shares are sold. An example is the Enterprise Investment Scheme in the UK, which is intended to encourage investors to subscribe for new shares in unquoted trading companies.

International tax implications

The main additional tax consideration for an entity with international operations is how to minimise the overall tax liability of the international entity.

For example, a decision will need to be made as to where the head office of the entity should be located. Multinational companies are often attracted to set up their operations in a low tax economy.

Also, the group's transfer pricing policy will be an important consideration. Tax authorities only allow transfer prices that are set at a fair, 'arm's length' level, so there is no opportunity to manipulate the entity's tax liability. The authorities will disallow any transfer prices that are considered to be set purely for the purposes of moving as much profit as possible into the lowest tax country.

The tax authorities also monitor royalties and management charges alongside transfer prices. Any royalties or management charges paid from one group company to another will not be allowed if the authorities feel that they are being used to increase profits in one group company (based in a low tax country) at the expense of another (based in a higher tax country).

6 The lender's assessment of creditworthiness

When an entity (a borrower) is seeking to raise debt finance, the lender (for example the bank) will carry out an assessment of the borrower to decide whether to lend.

Information presented by the borrower to the lender

In order to apply for the debt finance from a bank or other lender, an entity will have to put together a business plan. This will contain important information regarding the borrower's plans, such as:

- the purpose, amount and duration of the borrowing

- detailed cash flow forecasts, showing the likely cash flows of the borrower and aiming to show the lender that the prospects for the borrower are good

- an explanation of how the borrower is proposing to repay the borrowing.

Assessment of creditworthiness by the lender

The lender will carry out an assessment of the potential borrower by considering the following information:

- **Analysis of business plan**

  The lender will perform a detailed analysis of the business plan presented by the potential borrower. This will include detailed ratio analysis of the potential borrower's recent accounts and forecasts (see detail on ratio analysis below).

- **Business prospects of the potential borrower**

  An analysis of the business plan will give the lender an initial insight into the business prospects of the borrower. However, it will be important for the lender to carry out further analysis in an attempt to build up an independent assessment of the prospects of the borrower. For example, the lender will assess

  - the quality and track record of the borrower's management

  - the risk profile of the company

  - the prospects for the industry sector – e.g. competitor growth, market share trends etc.

- **Security available**

  The lender will look at the statement of financial position of the potential borrower to assess whether there are assets that could be used to provide security for the borrowings. Lending the money secured on assets of the borrower would significantly reduce the risk to the lender.

- **Credit rating**

  The credit rating of the borrower is also an important factor. An entity with a poor credit rating will find it more difficult to borrow money. If the lender does decide to lend, a higher interest rate would be charged to compensate for the risk taken on by the lender.

- **Other borrowings and covenants**

  The risk to the lender will be higher if the potential borrower is already highly geared and has debt covenants attached to its existing borrowings.

  If the potential borrower has other borrowings and hence interest commitments, this could increase the risk to the new lender by reducing the amount of cash available to pay the interest on the new borrowing and possibly reducing the availability of assets to be used as security.

  The existence of covenants on existing borrowings could also cause problems for a new lender, especially if the covenants give priority to existing lenders over any new lenders.

Use of ratio analysis

The analysis undertaken by the lender will use many of the ratios that were covered in Chapter 1: 'Objectives'.

The key objective of the lender will be to assess the liquidity of the potential borrower i.e. whether the borrower's cash flows will be sufficient to pay the interest and repay the capital according to the proposed repayment schedule.

For example, the interest cover ratio will be particularly important, since it gives an idea of how likely it is that the firm will continue to be able to meet its interest payments even if profits fall.

Lenders might be even more interested in calculating interest cover with regard to EBITDA or cash (rather than profits) to give a more practical measure of cover.

Other ratios such as the stock market ratios (P/E ratio in particular) will also give the lender a feel for how the rest of the market views the firm. If the firm has a high P/E ratio, its growth prospects are good, so lending to such a firm would be perceived as low risk.

Rationale for analysing gearing

Analysis of capital structure

The gearing ratio is an important measure of risk. It is important to analyse, particularly for users such as shareholders and creditors, the ability to satisfy debts falling due after one year. There are two elements to consider: repayment of capital and payment of interest.

The assessment of an entity's gearing risk can be identified from two areas. The statement of financial position shows the current liquidity and capital structure of the entity, that is the short-term liquidity and the level of fixed prior charge capital. The statement of profit or loss shows the profitability of the entity generally, indicating its ability to generate cash, some of which may be available to repay debt.

The capital structure of the entity provides information about the relative risk that is accepted by shareholders and creditors. As long-term debt increases relative to share-holders' funds then more risk is assumed by long-term creditors and so they would require higher rewards, thereby decreasing resources available for the shareholders. As risk increases, creditors require higher interest in order to compensate for the higher risk.

However, the use of debt by management in their capital structure can assist in increasing profits available to shareholders. Cash received into the business from lenders will be used to generate revenue and profits. As interest costs are fixed, any profits generated in excess of the interest costs will accrue to the shareholders. There is, however, a negative side to the use of debt in the business. If the cash from the debt does not raise sufficient profits then the fixed interest cost must be paid first and so profits available to shareholders are decreased, and may be extinguished completely.

Interpretation of gearing ratios

Statement of financial position

A high proportion of debt finance in the entity's capital structure is seen as being risky by the entity's shareholders (which causes them to demand higher returns on their equity – see the later chapter: 'Financing – Capital structure' for more details).

However, it is difficult to give any practical guidance as to what a 'safe' level of gearing might be. Compare the gearing ratio to prior years and budgets, and to the gearing ratio of similar entities, to assess whether it looks too high. Also, consider in particular the level of non-current assets on the statement of financial position which could be used for security. A high level of non-current assets (much higher than the current value of debt finance) indicates that potentially the entity should be able to raise more debt finance quite easily.

Statement of profit or loss

An interest cover ratio less than 1 indicates that the entity is having trouble servicing its debt finance. The higher the ratio is above 1, the easier it should be for the entity to continue paying its interest, so the less risky the entity appears to be.

However, note that a lack of cash, rather than a lack of profit, is usually the reason why a company fails to meet its interest obligations. This is why analysts often substitute EBITDA (or even cash flow) into the formula instead of profit, to give a more useful measure of cover.

Independent credit rating agencies

In order to help with the assessment of creditworthiness, credit ratings issued by an independent credit rating agency will often be considered.

Moody's and Standard and Poor's (S&P) are the two biggest credit rating agencies. Each of these agencies aims to provide a rating system to help investors determine the risk associated with investing in a specific company, investing instrument or market.

So for example, for a public issue of bonds, the company will obtain a specific rating for that issue from a rating agency before the issue takes place.

Setting credit ratings

These large credit rating agencies monitor the performance of all major businesses and rate them according to how likely it is that they will be able to afford to repay any debts.

The rating agency will focus on:

- Plans and forecasts of the company

- The strength and trends in the industry in which the company operates and the company's competitive position within that industry.

- Country risks – the political and regulatory risks

- The quality of the management team, including experience and track record

- Corporate attitude to risk taking

- Financial position – including capital structure and current debt profile

- Financial ratios

- Any parental support such as guarantees.

Updating of credit ratings

The ratings agencies are constantly assessing the performance of entities, and will update their ratings regularly.

For example, if an entity releases some worse-than-expected financial results, or if market analysts predict that an entity is likely to perform worse than previously thought, the ratings agencies may react by downgrading the entity's credit rating, or warning of a possibly future downgrade by issuing a Negative Outlook statement.

This could have a significant impact on the entity's plans to raise new finance e.g. the entity might have to delay a planned debt issue until such time that the rating rises again, or an issue currently in progress might not be fully subscribed.

The meaning of credit ratings

The different credit rating agencies use different terms to describe high risk and low risk companies or issues, as shown by the following table:

Moody's	S & P	Grade	Risk
Aaa	AAA	Investment	Lowest risk
Aa	AA	Investment	Low risk
A	A	Investment	Low risk
Baa	BBB	Investment	Medium risk
Ba, B	BB,B	Junk	High risk
Caa, Ca, C	CCC,CC,C	Junk	Highest risk
C	D	Junk	In default

A rating can refer to an entity's specific financial obligation or to its general creditworthiness.

Thus, for S&P, an 'AAA' rating signifies the highest investment grade and means that there is very low credit risk. 'AA' represents very high credit quality; 'A' means high credit quality, and 'BBB' is good credit quality. These ratings are considered to be investment grade, which means that the security or entity being rated carries a quality level that many institutions require when considering investments.

Ratings that fall under 'BBB' (for S&P) are considered to be speculative or junk grade. This is indicative of high risk.

The link between credit ratings and interest rates

An entity rated 'AAA' (the best rating) by Standard and Poor's is a very low risk investment.

Consequently, a lender would generally set a relatively low interest rate on a loan to an 'AAA' entity. By contrast, a lower rated entity would generally have to pay higher rates of interest (or might struggle to raise debt finance at all if its rating were especially low).

This is because risk and return are always linked: if an investor is likely to face high risks, he demands a high return to compensate him for this risk.

7 End of chapter objective test questions

Test your understanding 3 (Objective test question)

Which of the following financial ratios is likely to be of LEAST interest to a lender when assessing the creditworthiness of a borrower?

A   Interest cover

B   Gearing

C   Operating profit margin

D   EBITDA to finance charges ratio

Test your understanding 4 (Objective test question)

White Co has 1 million shares in issue. The shares have a nominal value of $1 and are currently trading at $2.00. White Co's P/E ratio is 7.05.

The directors are considering raising $400,000 in order to undertake a new project. It is expected that the new project will cause earnings to rise by $30,000 each year.

If White Co uses a 1 for 4 rights issue to raise the finance, what is the expected earnings per share (EPS) of White Co after the finance has been raised and the project undertaken?

A $1.60

B $1.41

C $0.28

D $0.25

Test your understanding 5 (Objective test question)

A company has 20 million $0.50 ordinary shares in issue and the current share price is $1.33.

A proposed new project is expected to have an IRR of 15% and an NPV of $8 million and requires an initial investment of $10 million.

If the market is efficient and the share price moves to reflect this information on the day that the project is announced, what is the theoretical movement in the share price on that day?

A   No change

B $0.40 increase

C $0.90 increase

D $0.20 increase

Test your understanding 6 (Objective test question)

Lazaretto Co is a listed company. It has 1 million $1 shares in issue, trading at $3.01, and 10,000, 5% coupon bonds with par value $100 and market value $95.

The company made an operating profit of $1.33 million last year.

The directors are considering issuing 5,000 new secured bonds at their par value of $100. The coupon rate will be 4%.

What will be the interest cover of Lazaretto Co in the year after the bonds are issued, on the assumption that operating profits will stay constant?

A   19.0

B   26.6

C   28.0

D   66.5

Test your understanding 7 (Objective test question)

Company X's bonds have a BBB credit rating according to Standard and Poor's credit rating agency, while Company Y's bonds have an A rating.

Which THREE of the following statements are true?

A   Both companies' bonds are investment grade

B   Both companies' bonds carry a low level of risk

C   The investors in Company X's bonds will require a higher rate of return than those in Company Y's bonds

D   The coupon rate on Company X's bonds will be higher than the coupon rate on Company Y's bonds

E   A movement to a BB rating would represent a downgrade for both companies

Test your understanding 8 (Objective test question)

The directors of McCombs Co, an unlisted company, have identified an attractive (positive NPV) project which is expected to generate positive cash flows for the company over a five year period. Finance is needed to fund the purchase of a new machine to use in the project.

Which of the following financing decisions would be most appropriate in these circumstances?

A   Extend the overdraft to fund the investment

B   Issue new shares to existing shareholders

C   Issue some new bonds on the market

D   Arrange a term loan with the bank

Test your understanding 9 (Objective test question)

Which TWO of the following actions are MOST likely to increase shareholder wealth?

A   The average cost of capital is decreased by a recent financing decision

B   The financial rewards of directors are linked to increasing earnings per share

C   The board of directors decides to invest in a project with a positive net present value

D   The annual report declares full compliance with the corporate governance code

Test your understanding 10 (Objective test question)

BB Co hopes to pay out an increased dividend to satisfy its shareholders, despite the fact that earnings have fallen by 3% this year.

Which of the following is NOT a likely consequence of this action?

A   The company will have less cash available for new investment projects

B   The shareholders' wealth will increase

C   The company is more likely to have to raise finance from new sources if it wants to make new investments

D   The gearing of the company will increase

Test your understanding 11 (Objective test question)

MFW is considering a $1 million expansion of its business.

The directors are considering either debt finance in the form of a 7% bond, or issuing 400,000 ordinary shares at a price of $2.50 to raise the necessary funds.

The expansion will generate $500,000 of extra operating profit each year. MFW pays tax at 25%. Key investor ratios for MFW are currently as follows:

Gearing = (debt/equity) = $2.5m/$7.2m = 34.7%

Interest cover = (Earnings before interest and tax/Interest payable) = $2,522,000/$223,000 = 11.3 times

Earnings per share (EPS) = (Profit after tax/No. of shares) = $1,724,000/3,000,000 = $0.575

Which of the following statements is correct?

A   Interest cover is reduced using either source of finance

B   EPS increases more by using debt

C   Equity reduces gearing and gives the best EPS

D   EPS and interest cover both worsen using debt

8   End of chapter case style question

Test your understanding 12 (Case style question)

CCC is a local government entity.

It is financed almost equally by a combination of central government funding and local taxation. The funding from central government is determined largely on a per capita (per head of population) basis, adjusted to reflect the scale of deprivation (or special needs) deemed to exist in CCC's region. A small percentage of its finance comes from the private sector, for example from renting out City Hall for private functions.

CCC's main objectives are:

- to make the region economically prosperous and an attractive place in which to live and work

- to provide service excellence in health and education for the local community.

DDD is a large listed entity with widespread commercial and geographical interests. For historic reasons, its headquarters are in CCC's region. This is something of an anomaly as most entities of DDD's size would have their HQ in a capital city, or at least a city much larger than where it is.

DDD has one financial objective: To increase shareholder wealth by an average 10% per annum. It also has a series of non-financial objectives that deal with how the entity treats other stakeholders, including the local communities where it operates.

DDD has total net assets of $1.5 billion and a gearing ratio of 45% (debt to debt plus equity), which is typical for its industry. It is currently considering raising a substantial amount of capital to finance an acquisition.

Required:

Discuss the criteria that the two very different entities described above have to consider when setting objectives, recognising the needs of each of their main stakeholder groups.

Make some reference in your answer to the consequences of each of them failing to meet its declared objectives.

(30 minutes)

MS is a private entity in a computer-related industry. It has been trading for six years and is managed by its main shareholders, the original founders of the entity.

Most of the employees are also shareholders, having been given shares as bonuses. None of the shareholders has attempted to sell shares in the entity so the problem of placing a value on them has not arisen. Dividends have been paid every year at the rate of 60 cents per share, irrespective of profits. So far, profits have always been sufficient to cover the dividend at least once but never more than twice.

MS is all-equity financed at present although $15 million new finance is likely to be required in the near future to finance expansion. Total net assets as at the last balance sheet date were $45 million.

Required:

Discuss and compare the relationship between dividend policy, investment policy and financing policy in the context of the small entity described above, MS, and DDD, the large listed entity described in the first part of this question.

(30 minutes)

Test your understanding answers

Test your understanding 1 (Integration question)

(a) **Pre-project ratios:**

Interest cover = $15m/$4m = 3.75 times

Earnings per share (EPS) = $7.7m/16m = 48.1 cents per share

Earnings yield = EPS/Share price = $0.481/$2.70 = 0.178, or 17.8%

Statement of profit / loss forecasts	$m – debt used	$m – rights issue
Profit before interest and tax ($15m + $4m)	19.0	19.0
Interest **(W1)**	(5.2)	(4.0)
	___	___
Profit before tax	13.8	15.0
Tax at 30%	(4.1)	(4.5)
	___	___
Profit after tax (earnings)	9.7	10.5
	___	___

(W1) Interest on the new debt is 6% of $20m i.e. $1.2m. Assume that interest on the existing borrowings stays constant.

Share price workings: Rights issue

If the rights issue goes ahead, the value of the shares after the rights issue will be the theoretical ex-rights price (TERP) of $2.63 (given). **NB:** The calculation of this TERP will be covered in detail in the later chapter: 'Financing – Equity finance'.

> **Workings** (for illustration only at the moment):
>
> TERP = [(N × cum rights price) + issue price]/(N+1)
>
> = [(2 × 2.70) + 2.50]/3 = $2.63

However, since the rights issue will be used to fund the new project with an NPV of $8m, the value of the project will also be reflected in the new share price, increasing the share price to

$2.63 + [$8m/(16m shares + 8m new shares)] = $2.96

Debt finance

If debt finance is used to fund the new project, the share price should rise after the project has been taken on, to reflect the NPV of the new project.

Expected share price = $2.70 + ($8m/16m shares) = $3.20

Post project ratios – using debt finance:

Interest cover = $19m/$5.2m = 3.65 times

Earnings per share (EPS) = $9.7m/16m = 60.6 cents per share

Earnings yield = $0.606/$3.20 = 0.189, or 18.9%

Post project ratios – using equity finance:

Interest cover = $19m/$4m = 4.75 times

Earnings per share (EPS) = $10.5m/(16m + 8m) = 43.8 cents per share

Earnings yield = $0.438/$2.96 = 0.148, or 14.8%

(b) **Debt financing option**

If debt is used to fund the new project, the shareholders are likely to see the change in EPS and earnings yield as positive.

The EPS increases from 48.1 cents per share to 60.6 cents per share, and the earnings yield increases from 17.8% to 18.9%. This indicates that Seed Co will potentially be able to pay out a higher dividend to the shareholders in future.

On the other hand, the reduction in interest cover indicates that Seed Co will face a higher level of risk if the debt financing option is used i.e. the chance of Seed Co being unable to meet its interest obligations is higher. The higher risk to shareholders could lead to a fall in the share price if considered to be significant.

However, in practice it is unlikely that this issue will worry either the shareholders or the lenders greatly, given that the movement in interest cover is extremely small (3.75 to 3.65 times).

Overall, it is likely that both shareholders and lenders will be quite happy with the EPS, earnings yield and interest cover ratios if the debt finance option is used (assuming that the expected $4m increase in profit and $8m NPV are achieved).

Equity finance option

The lenders will be happy if the rights issue goes ahead, because there will be no additional interest payable and yet profits will increase, so the interest cover ratio will rise significantly. This means that the chances of Seed Co defaulting on its interest payments will be less if this option goes ahead.

At first glance, it appears that the shareholders will not be happy with this option, given that EPS reduces from 48.1 cents per share to 43.8 cents per share, and also given that earnings yield falls from 17.8% to 14.8%.

However, in this situation, where a 1 for 2 rights issue has been used, a shareholder who owned 2 shares before the rights issue will now own 3 shares (assuming he took up his rights). The rights issue itself makes no difference to the shareholder's return or wealth. However, the positive NPV of the project undertaken causes the shareholder return and wealth to increase.

The increase in earnings attributable to each shareholder's shareholding will be viewed positively by shareholders, who might expect to see increased overall dividends in the future.

Once again, overall it is likely that both shareholders and lenders will be quite happy with the EPS, earnings yield and interest cover ratios if this financing option is used (assuming that the expected $4m increase in profit and $8m NPV are achieved).

Test your understanding 2 (Objective test question)

The answer is (A).

Financing requirement is:

Reduction in payables = ($3,150,000 × 10/45) = $700,000

Reduction in overdraft = (2,200,000 – 2,000,000) = $200,000

New capital expenditure = $1,000,000

Therefore, total = $1,900,000

Test your understanding 3 (Objective test question)

The answer is (C).

Lenders are particularly interested in the level of gearing (B) and the ability of the borrower to meet its interest commitments ((A) and (D)).

Test your understanding 4 (Objective test question)

The answer is (D).

Currently P/E is 7.05 and share price is $2.00. Therefore, EPS = (2.00/7.05 =) $0.284

With 1 million shares in issue, this amounts to total earnings of approximately $284,000

After the issue, the project will add $30,000 earnings to this, so earnings will become $314,000.

Total shares will be 1 million existing shares + 250,000 new ones (1 for 4 rights). Therefore 1,250,000 in total.

Hence EPS will be 314,000/1,250,000 = $0.25

Test your understanding 5 (Objective test question)

The answer is (B).

The NPV of the project is equal to the increase in wealth of the shareholders (i.e. the increase in share price).

Therefore, an NPV of $8 million, split between 20 million shares means an increase of 8/20 = $0.40 per share.

Test your understanding 6 (Objective test question)

The answer is (A).

Interest cover is (operating profit/interest payable)

= $1.33m/[(10,000 × $100 × 5%) + (5,000 × $100 × 4%)] = 19.0

Test your understanding 7 (Objective test question)

The answer is (A), (C) and (E).

Both companies' bonds are indeed investment grade bonds (A) – all ratings of BBB and above are investment grade. However, BBB is considered to be a medium level of risk, so both companies' bonds do not carry a low level of risk (B).

The investors in Company X's bonds will indeed require a higher rate of return (C) because of this higher level of risk, but that does not necessarily mean that the coupon rate on Company X's bonds will be higher than the coupon rate on Company Y's bonds (D) (for example the extra return could be paid in the form of a premium on redemption, rather than necessarily as an increased coupon rate).

BB is a lower grading than both A and BBB so a movement to a BB rating would represent a downgrade for both companies (E).

Test your understanding 8 (Objective test question)

The answer is (D).

An unlisted company cannot issue bonds (C). An overdraft (A) is too short term and equity (B) is too long term for the funding of a five year project.

Test your understanding 9 (Objective test question)

The answer is (A) and (C).

Test your understanding 10 (Objective test question)

The answer is (B).

Shareholder wealth is not affected by a dividend payment. Gearing will increase though, as there is less equity within the company. Also, the financing and investment policies will have to change since less cash is available within the company.

Test your understanding 11 (Objective test question)

The answer is (B).

Debt

Interest = $70,000 and value of debt increases by $1m, so the ratios become:

Gearing = (debt/equity) = $3.5m/$7.2m = 48.6%

Interest cover = (Earnings before interest and tax/Interest payable) = $3,022,000/$293,000 = 10.3 times

Earnings per share (EPS) = (Profit after tax/No. of shares) = $2,047,000/3,000,000 = $0.682

Note that profit after tax = (EBIT – Interest) × (1 – 0.25)

Equity

400,000 extra shares and value of equity increases by $1m, so the ratios become:

Gearing = (debt/equity) = $2.5m/$8.2m = 30.5%

Interest cover = (Earnings before interest and tax/Interest payable) = $3,022,000/$223,000 = 13.6 times

Earnings per share (EPS) = (Profit after tax/No. of shares) = $2,099,000/3,400,000 = $0.617

Test your understanding 12 (Case style question)

Answer to the first task:

The key criteria that need to be considered when objective setting are as follows:

Stakeholder expectations

All organisations need to identify key stakeholders, examine their expectations and try to set objectives to meet them. For CCC stakeholders include:

- Local residents want to see the provision of quality health

- Local businesses who will be interested in local infrastructure when deciding whether to invest in the area. In particular, CCC may be keen to ensure that DDD does not close its local offices, with resulting job losses, and move to the capital city.

- Central Government committees who make funding decisions based on local population and deprivation.

For DDD stakeholders include:

- Shareholders want to see their wealth increased through a mixture of growing dividends and an increasing share price. DDD has reflected this in the objective to increase shareholder wealth by 10% per annum.

- Customers will expect a certain level of quality and value for money, depending on the nature of products sold.

- The local communities affected by DDD will expect them to be good citizens and operate at high levels of corporate social responsibility.

Stakeholder power

All organisations will find conflicts between stakeholders, so they need to consider how to prioritise them. For a company like DDD the expectations of shareholders come first for the following reasons:

- This is usually reflected in companies' legislation where directors have a duty in law to put shareholder interests first. Many governance recommendations focus on protecting shareholder interests.

- Failure to deliver shareholder expectations will result in a falling share price and difficulties raising finance. Ultimately, shareholders have the power to remove directors should they feel dissatisfied.

However, this does not mean that other stakeholders' needs are ignored. Clearly, if customers are unhappy, then sales will be lost with a resulting fall in profitability and shareholder wealth.

For CCC the problem is more complex:

- It is much more difficult to prioritise stakeholder expectations. For example, given limited funds, should community health care needs come before educational ones?

- Even individual stakeholder groups have multiple conflicting objectives. For example, residents want to pay less tax and have better provision of services. Thus, even if some groups are satisfied, others may still vote for changes in CCC.

- With companies, customers pay directly for the products they receive, ensuring that customer needs are addressed. With CCC the bulk of its funding comes from central government, not the local community that benefits from CCC's actions. Thus the needs of the funding body may take priority over locals needs, otherwise funding may be cut. (**Note:** This is less likely here as funding is mainly driven by population size.)

Measurement issues

For an organisation like DDD, once shareholders have been prioritised, all decisions can be evaluated by reference to financial measures such as profitability. While non-financial targets will be incorporated as well, the 'bottom line' will be seen as key. Thus financial targets can be set for most objectives.

For CCC it is much more difficult to measure whether it is achieving its stated aims and hence to set targets.

For example, how do you assess whether somewhere is an 'attractive place to live and work' or whether health and education provision is 'excellent'?

Other issues

All organisations need to ensure that objectives set relate to controllable factors to ensure staff are motivated to meet them.

All organisations need to differentiate between cause and effect and have objectives for both. For example, DDD may have an objective of customer satisfaction, which will need to be translated into objectives for quality, cost, etc.

Answer to the second task:

As described above, companies make decisions with the primary objective of maximising shareholder wealth.

Investment decisions

Potential investments should thus be assessed using NPV or SVA, rather than ROCE to ensure that shareholder wealth is increased.

This should be the case for both MS and DDD, though the former will have more difficulty determining a suitable discount rate as it is unquoted.

Dividend decisions

Once shareholder value has been created, the firm needs to decide how to return those gains to shareholders – either as dividends or reinvested to enhance the share price further.

Modigliani and Miller argued that, given certain assumptions, dividend policy was irrelevant to shareholder wealth. If a dividend were cut, for example, shareholders could manufacture dividends by selling shares without any overall loss of wealth. Central to their theory was the idea that shareholders had perfect information and would understand why a dividend policy was changed.

In the case of MS, shareholders are also employees so will have full information regarding any change in dividend policy and will not thus perceive any information content in the dividends themselves. However, should the dividend be cut, shareholders who require income will not be able to sell shares to generate cash as the company is unquoted. MS should thus try to continue the stable dividend policy it has adopted to date, even though historical dividend cover is lower than the 'rule of thumb' of two.

In the case of DDD, major institutional shareholders will have good information from the company but may have tax preferences regarding income and capital gains so DDD should adopt a consistent dividend policy to meet their requirements. DDD will probably have attracted a certain clientele of shareholder based on previous policies.

Financing decisions

Both firms need to raise finance in order to undertake new investments to increase shareholder wealth. The issue here is whether the finance used ultimately affects shareholder wealth as well.

From a theoretical point of view, Modigliani and Miller argued that, in the absence of taxation and certain other assumptions, the choice between debt or equity finance was irrelevant. With corporation tax they concluded that debt finance was preferable, due to the benefits of the tax shield.

With personal taxes the conclusions depend on the specific circumstances of the company and its shareholders. Incorporating real world factors, many analysts argue that there is an optimal gearing level for each company.

DDD is already at the typical gearing ratio for its industry so it would reasonable to assume that this is its optimal gearing level. Future financing should involve a mixture of debt and equity to maintain this ratio.

MS is all-equity financed at present so it should seek to raise at least some of the $15 million required using debt finance to take advantage of the tax relief and low costs involved.

Inter-relationships

All three types of decisions are interrelated, thus the financing decision will affect the cost of capital and, as a consequence, the net benefits obtainable from a particular project, thereby influencing the investment decision, while the financing decision concerning gearing will affect both the other decisions.

The dividend decision, in determining the level of retentions, will affect the cash available for investment, and the extent to which external sources of funds need to be sought in financing to optimise operations.

4

Financing – Equity finance

Chapter learning objectives

Lead outcome	Component outcome
B3: Evaluate equity finance	(a) Evaluate methods of flotation
	(b) Discuss rights issues

Topics to be covered

- Methods of flotation and implications for management and shareholders

- Rights issues, choice of discount rates and impact on shareholders

- Calculation of theoretical ex-rights price (TERP) and yield adjusted TERP

1 Overview of chapter

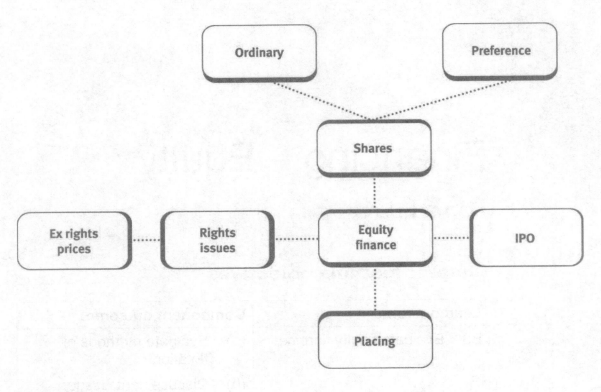

Introduction

In Chapter 3: 'Development of financial strategy', the financing decision was identified as one of the three key decisions of financial strategy (along with the investment decision and the dividend decision).

This chapter and the next two look at the financing decision of an entity in more detail.

First, this chapter introduces the factors to consider when making the fundamental financing decision i.e. should equity finance or debt finance be used?

Then, this chapter covers the main sources of equity finance and the next chapter looks at debt finance.

Finally, Chapter 6: 'Financing – Capital structure' considers the theoretical and practical implications of changing the entity's capital structure (i.e. the mix of long-term debt and equity finance).

2   General introduction to financing

Sources of finance

If a company has a large cash surplus, it may be able to afford to undertake new investment projects without having to resort to external sources of finance.

However, if external funds are required, the company might raise finance from the following sources:

1   The capital markets:

–   new share issues, for example by companies acquiring a stock market listing for the first time;

–   rights issues;

–   issues of marketable debt (e.g. bonds).

A company must be quoted/listed on a recognised stock exchange in order to be able to raise finance from the capital markets.

2   Bank borrowings – long-term loans or short-term loans, including bank facilities such as revolving credit facilities (RCFs) and money market lines.

3   Venture capital funds.

This is high risk finance provided by specialist organisations. The main problem is that the providers of venture capital funding tend to demand significant equity participation in a company and will also want to influence the policy of the company.

4   Government and similar sources.

In general, finance can be raised from Equity or Debt sources.

 Criteria for selecting sources of finance

To decide whether debt or equity should be used to fund a new investment, the following factors will be considered:

•   cost of the different sources of finance

•   duration – for how long is finance required?

•   lending restrictions – for example security and debt covenants

•   gearing level (also called capital structure – covered in detail in the next chapter).

•   liquidity implications – the ability of the business to service the new debt, allocating sufficient cash resources to meet interest and capital repayment obligations

•   the currency of the cash flows associated with the new project

•   impact of different financing options on the financial statements, tax position and financial stakeholders of the entity

- availability – availability of finance depends on the creditworthiness of the borrower and also the willingness of lenders to extend credit (for bank borrowings) or liquidity of the capital markets (for equity and bonds).

In an exam, you will need to identify how these general factors apply to the specific circumstances of the entity in the question, in order to identify the preferred choice of finance in a particular situation.

More details on financing criteria

Cost

Each source of finance has a different cost. With debt capital, a company must pay interest on the debt, and to raise new debt finance it must pay a current rate of interest to persuade investors to provide capital. The cost of interest is an allowable expense for tax purposes, so the cost of debt capital to a company is the interest cost less the tax relief on the interest. This fact, and the fact that the providers of debt finance have lower risk than the providers of equity finance tend to make debt finance cheaper than equity.

The cost of equity capital is the return that ordinary shareholders expect on their investment, in the form of current dividends and expectations of dividend and share price growth in the future. Although a company does not have a legal obligation to pay dividends to its shareholders, it must provide a satisfactory return to support the share price. Without the prospect of good returns, investors will not subscribe for new equity when the company needs to raise new capital.

It is important here to appreciate that debt finance tends to be cheaper than equity. This is because providers of debt take lower risks than providers of equity and therefore earn less return. Interest on debt finance is also normally corporation tax deductible, returns to equity are not. The period of the finance will also affect the cost as long-term finance tends to be more expensive than short-term finance.

Duration

Equity capital is long-term 'permanent' capital. Most debt capital, on the other hand, is obtained for a fixed term. The length of borrowing can range from very short term (overdraft facility) to long-term. Bank loans are generally for no longer than the medium term (say, five to seven years) whereas debt finance raised by issuing bonds can be for a much longer term.

When a company is deciding whether to obtain long-term or short-term capital, it should apply the rule: 'Long-term assets should be financed by long-term funds'. Short-term assets, such as inventories and receivables, should normally be financed by a mixture of short-term and long-term funds.

Thus we would expect to see working capital financed partly by short-term facilities such as trade payables and a bank overdraft, whilst non-current assets should be funded by long-term sources of finance. This rule might be broken to gain access to cheap short-term funds, particularly short- term trade payables (which have no obvious cost) but the risks involved should be appreciated.

Lending restrictions

Security is often required for debt finance. This could be derived from existing assets or new assets to be acquired. Assets such as land and buildings hold their value better and are easier for a lender to sell than, say, plant and machinery.

Debt covenants are clauses written into existing debt agreements which protect the lender's interests by requiring the borrower to satisfy certain criteria.

Examples of debt covenants are:

- the interest cover must not fall below 5, and

- the ratio of non-current liabilities to equity must not increase beyond 0.75:1.

The lender will be reassured that the risk associated with the borrower will not change dramatically as long as such covenants are not breached.

Gearing

Gearing is the ratio of debt to equity finance. A high gearing ratio can be very risky. Although high gearing involves the use of cheap debt finance, high levels of debt also create an obligation to meet interest payments and debt principal repayment schedules. If these are not met the company could end up in liquidation. A company should try to achieve a satisfactory balance between equity finance and medium- and long-term debt for its long-term funding, to benefit from the lower cost of debt finance without exposing itself to the risks arising from excessive debt obligations.

The currency of the cash flows associated with the new project

If the cash flows from the investment project are expected to be denominated in a foreign currency, the entity may decide to raise finance denominated in the same foreign currency, to reduce the risk of exchange rate movements by matching the receipts from the project with the servicing costs of the finance.

> ## The impact of different financing options on the financial statements, tax position and financial stakeholders of the entity
>
> Investors (both debt holders and shareholders) will use ratio analysis to assess the performance of the business. It is therefore important that management consider the impact of any new financing on the financial statements of the business. For example, raising debt finance will affect the Return on Equity of the business, as well as the interest cover and gearing ratios.
>
> Also, raising debt finance will give rise to interest payments which are tax deductible, so impacting the tax position of the business.
>
> The existing financial stakeholders of the business (debt holders and shareholders) will be constantly monitoring the business's performance, so it will be important for management to clearly explain the rationale for any new financing method which impacts the financial statements or the tax position.
>
> ### Availability
>
> Not all companies have access to all sources of finance. Small companies traditionally have problems in raising both equity and long-term debt finance. Remember that many firms do not have an unlimited choice of funding arrangements.
>
> The availability of debt finance is enhanced if an entity has a good credit rating. The more creditworthy a borrower is assessed as being, the more likely it is that funds will be relatively easy to raise.

3 Equity finance

Equity is another name for shares or ownership rights in a business.

Important terminology

Share – a fixed identifiable unit of capital in an entity which normally has a fixed nominal value, which may be quite different from its market value. (CIMA Official Terminology, 2005)

Shareholders receive returns from their investment in shares in the form of dividends, and also capital growth in the share price.

Ordinary shares

Ordinary shares pay dividends at the discretion of the entity's directors. The ordinary shareholders of a company are the owners of the company and they have the right to attend meetings and vote on any important matters.

On a winding-up of a company, the ordinary shareholders are subordinate to all other finance providers (i.e. they receive their money last, if there is any left after all other finance providers have been paid).

Preference shares

Preference shares are a form of equity that pays a fixed dividend, which is paid in preference to (before) ordinary share dividends, hence the name.

Also, on a winding-up of a company, the preference shareholders are subordinate to all the debt holders and creditors, but receive their payout before ordinary shareholders.

 More details on preference shares

Comparison of preference shares with debt and with ordinary shares

Preference shares pay a fixed proportion of the share's nominal value each year as a dividend. This is why they are often considered to behave in a way which is more similar to debt finance (fixed annual returns) rather than ordinary shares (variable dividend at the discretion of the directors).

However, unlike interest on debt finance, preference share dividends are paid out of post-tax profits, so there is no tax benefit to a company of paying preference share dividends.

Also, there are certain circumstances (e.g. where a company has insufficient distributable profits) when the company will be allowed to skip its preference share dividends in a year. This is not the case with debt interest, which is an obligation every year, whether or not the company can afford to make the payment.

The lack of tax relief on dividends mentioned above explains why preference shares are relatively unattractive to companies compared with bank borrowings and other forms of fixed rate security such as bonds.

However, they do have some appeal to risk-averse investors looking for a relatively reliable income stream.

Different types of preference shares

There are four types of preference shares:

- cumulative preference shares, for which dividends must be paid including skipped dividends i.e. if a dividend is skipped one year, the skipped dividend has to be paid the following year along with the 'normal' dividend;

- non-cumulative preference shares, for which skipped dividends do not have to be paid later;

- participating preference shares, which give the holder fixed dividends plus extra earnings based on certain conditions (in a similar way to ordinary shares); and

- convertible preference shares, which can be exchanged for a specified number of ordinary shares on some given future date.

Also, note that some preference shares are redeemable, meaning that holders will be repaid their capital (usually at par) on some future date.

Example of convertible preference shares

Convertible preference shares are fixed-income securities that the investor can choose to turn into a certain number of ordinary shares after a predetermined time span or on a specific date.

The fixed-income component offers a steady income stream and some protection of the investor's capital. However, the option to convert these securities into ordinary shares gives the investor the opportunity to gain from a rise in the share price.

Convertibles are particularly attractive to those investors who want to participate in the rise of hot growth companies while being insulated from a drop in price should the ordinary share price growth not live up to expectations.

If a company were to issue some 5% $10 nominal value preference shares, convertible to ordinary shares in five years' time, the investor would receive a fixed amount of $5 each year for the first five years.

In five years' time though, the investor would have the choice to keep the preference shares or convert to a number of ordinary shares. The conversion ratio would have been set when the preference shares were first issued. For example it could be 3, i.e. each preference share could be converted into 3 ordinary shares.

In this example, the investor would be keen to convert if the ordinary shares on the conversion date were worth more than ($10/3 =) $3.33.

For example, if the ordinary share price growth has been impressive and the shares are actually worth $4.50 each on the conversion date, and investor could trade a single preference share (value $10) for 3 ordinary shares worth $13.50 in total.

Preference shares, especially convertible preference shares, are often used in the context of Management Buyouts (MBOs) – see details in the later chapter on 'Financial and strategic implications of mergers and acquisitions'.

The shares in a listed, or quoted, company will be traded on a capital market.

Capital markets

Capital markets (or stock markets) must fulfil both primary and secondary functions.

Primary function:

The primary function of a stock market is to enable companies to raise new finance (either equity or debt). Through the stock market, a company can communicate with a large pool of potential investors, so it is much easier for a company to raise finance in this way, rather than contacting investors individually.

Note that in the UK, a company must be a plc before it is allowed to raise finance from the public on the stock market.

Secondary function:

The secondary function of a stock market is to enable investors to sell their investments to other investors. A listed company's shares are therefore more marketable than an unlisted company's, which means that they tend to be more attractive to investors.

 Listed v private companies

Private limited company (Ltd in UK terminology)

A private company limited by shares, usually called a private limited company, has shareholders with limited liability and its shares may not be offered to the general public, unlike those of a public limited company (see details below).

'Limited by shares' means that the company has shareholders, and that the liability of the shareholders to creditors of the company is limited to the capital originally invested, i.e. the nominal value of the shares and any premium paid in return for the issue of the shares by the company. A shareholder's personal assets are thereby protected in the event of the company's insolvency, but money invested in the company will be lost.

A limited company may be 'private' or 'public'. A private limited company's disclosure requirements are lighter, but for this reason its shares may not be offered to the general public (and therefore cannot be traded on a public stock exchange). This is the major distinguishing feature between a private limited company and a public limited company. Most companies, particularly small companies, are private.

Public limited company (plc in UK terminology)

A public limited company is a limited liability company that may sell shares to the public. It can be either an unlisted company, or a listed company on the stock exchange.

A stock exchange listing

When an entity obtains a listing (or quotation) for its shares on a stock exchange this is referred to as a flotation or an Initial Public Offering (IPO).

Advantages of a listing

- Once listed, the market will provide a more accurate valuation of the entity than had been previously possible.

- Realisation of paper profits, and mechanism for buying and selling shares in the future at will.

- Raise profile of entity, which may have an impact on revenues, credibility with suppliers and long-term providers of finance.

- Raise capital for future investment.

- Makes employee share schemes more accessible.

Disadvantages of a listing

- Costly for a small entity (flotation, underwriting costs, etc.)

- Making enough shares available to allow a market, and hence loss of at least some control of the original owners.

- Reporting requirements are more onerous.

- Stock exchange rules for obtaining a quotation can be stringent.

Impact of a listing on key stakeholders

Shareholders will normally benefit from a listing, in that their shares become more marketable. The listing can have a positive impact on the reputation of the company, so consequently the share price may rise.

The improvement in the company's reputation and profile that results from a listing can also benefit the managers and the employees of a company. Listed companies tend to be larger and less likely to fail, so can afford to offer better pay and career progression opportunities.

The better reputation of a listed company also impacts its credit rating and therefore reduces the risk of non-payment to suppliers and lenders. Listed companies are more likely to be viewed favourably by lenders, and to be granted generous credit terms by suppliers.

UK capital markets

There are two important capital markets in the UK:

- the full Stock Exchange – a market for larger companies. Entry costs are high and scrutiny is very high for companies listed on the 'full list', but the profile of a Stock Exchange listed company's shares is very high, so the shares are extremely marketable.

- the Alternative Investment Market (AIM) – a market for smaller companies, with lower associated costs and less stringent entry criteria.

Many other countries have a similar set up, including Japan, Germany and the USA.

The operation of stock exchanges

Prices of shares on the stock exchange are determined by the forces of supply and demand in the market. For example, if a company performs well, its shares become attractive to investors. This creates demand which drives up the price of the shares.

Conversely, investors who hold shares in an underperforming company will try to sell those shares, creating supply in the market. This drives down the price of the shares.

Methods of issuing new shares

The three most commonly used methods of issuing shares are:

A   **IPO (initial public offering), or flotation**

B   **Placing**

C   **Rights issue**

If a company already has a listing on a stock market then the company will either raise new funds by means of a rights issue, or by means of a placing. An IPO is more suitable when a company seeks a listing on the stock exchange for the first time.

These three methods will now be covered in turn below.

A   An IPO (or flotation)

Shares are offered for sale to investors, through an issuing house. The offer could be made at a fixed price set by the company, or in a tender offer investors are invited to tender for new shares issued at their own suggested price. All shares being offered are subsequently sold at the best price at which they would be taken up.

B   Placing

Shares are placed directly with certain investors (normally institutions) on a pre-arranged basis.

 More details on IPOs and placings

Initial Public Offerings (IPOs)

These offers may be of completely new shares or they may derive from the transfer to the public of some or all of the shares already held privately. An issuing house, normally a merchant bank, acquires the shares and then offers them to the public at a fixed price.

The offers are usually made in the form of a prospectus detailed in newspapers, sometimes in an abbreviated form. Buying new issues through the prospectus in the newspaper avoids dealing charges.

Other examples of such issues include:

- government privatisations; and

- privately held shares transferred to the public.

It is easier for prospective purchasers to form a judgement about such entities where there is some track record, rather than with offers for a completely new entity.

Stagging

Some investors apply for new issues in the hope of selling immediately and reaping a quick profit. For this to succeed the number of shares purchased must be sufficiently high to cover selling charges. For oversubscribed issues, the allocation may be scaled down and the applicant may receive only a small number of shares. The strategy of selling immediately is called stagging (and investors who do it are called stags).

This is often successful since companies typically price new issues conservatively in order to ensure the shares are sold and the required finance raised. This can often lead to an immediate share price rise post issue.

There have been some notable successes for stags, particularly in some of the privatisation issues, but there have also been cases where the initial dealing price has been substantially below the offer price.

An IPO lock-up period

An IPO lock-up period is a contractual restriction that prevents insiders who are holding a company's shares, before it goes public, from selling the shares for a period usually lasting 90 to 180 days after the company goes public. Insiders include company founders, owners, managers, employees and venture capitalists.

The purpose of an IPO lock-up period is to prevent the market from being flooded with a large number of shares, which would depress the share price.

Insiders' selling activities can have a particularly strong impact on a company's share price when the company has recently gone public because these shareholders typically own a relatively large percentage of the company's shares, while only a small percentage of shares are sold to the public.

Tender offers

A tender offer is an alternative to a fixed price offer.

Under a tender offer, subscribers tender for the shares at, or above, a minimum fixed price. Once all offers have been received from prospective investors, the company sets a 'strike price' and allocates shares to all bidders who have offered the strike price or more.

The strike price is set to make sure that the company raises the required amount of finance from the share issue.

Once the strike price has been set, all bidders who offered the strike price or more are allocated shares, and they all pay the strike price irrespective of what their original bid was.

Example of a tender offer

Bragg Co needs to raise $20 million to invest in a new project. The company has asked investors for tender offers and the following offers have been received:

Maximum price offered ($ per share)	No. of shares requested at this price (million)
2.00	5.0
2.20	4.1
2.40	1.9
2.60	3.2

The strike will be set at the highest possible level that generates the required amount of finance. This is to make sure that the company does not issue more shares than it has to, so that the dilution of the existing shareholders' holdings is kept to a minimum.

If Bragg Co sets the strike price at $2.60, only 3.2 million shares will be issued, raising $8.32 million in total ($2.60 × 3.2 million). This is not acceptable, since $20 million is needed.

If Bragg Co sets the strike price at $2.40, 5.1 million shares will be issued (being 1.9 million to the people who bid $2.40 and 3.2 million to the people who bid $2.60). Therefore, the total finance raised will be $2.40 × 5.1 million = $12.24 million, which again is not sufficient.

If Bragg Co sets the strike price at $2.20, 9.2 million shares will be issued (being 4.1 million to the people who bid $2.20, 1.9 million to the people who bid $2.40 and 3.2 million to the people who bid $2.60).

Therefore, the total finance raised will be $2.20 × 9.2 million = $20.24 million, which now is sufficient.

Hence, to ensure that $20 million is raised from the tender offer, the strike price would be set at $2.20, and any investor who bid $2.20 or more would be allocated shares at the strike price of $2.20.

Placings

A placing (sometimes called a 'placement' or 'private placement') is the sale of securities to a relatively small number of select investors as a way of raising capital.

Investors involved in private placements are usually large banks, mutual funds, insurance companies and pension funds.

Private placement is the opposite of a public issue, in which securities are made available for sale on the open market. Since a private placement is offered to a few, select individuals, the placement does not have to be registered or publicly announced. In many cases, detailed financial information is not disclosed and the need for a prospectus is waived. Finally, since the placements are private rather than public, the average investor is only made aware of the placement after it has occurred.

This method is very popular, being cheaper and quicker to arrange than most other methods. However, it does not normally lead to a very active market for the shares after flotation.

Private equity

Private equity firms are taking an increasingly important role as equity investors.

Private equity is equity capital that is not quoted on a public exchange. It consists of investors and funds that make investments directly into private companies or conduct buyouts of public companies that result in a delisting of public equity.

Capital for private equity is raised from retail and institutional investors, and can be used to fund new technologies, expand working capital within an owned company, make acquisitions, or to strengthen a balance sheet.

The majority of private equity consists of institutional investors and accredited investors who can commit large sums of money for long periods of time. Private equity investments often demand long holding periods to allow for a turnaround of a distressed company or a liquidity event such as an IPO or sale to a public company.

The size of the private equity market has grown steadily since the 1970s. Private equity firms will sometimes pool funds together to take very large public companies private. Many private equity firms conduct leveraged buyouts (LBOs), where large amounts of debt are issued to fund a large purchase.

Private equity firms will then try to improve the financial results and prospects of the company in the hope of reselling the company to another firm or cashing out via an IPO.

Advisors to an IPO

Investment banks usually take the lead role in an IPO and will advise on:

- the appointment of other specialists (e.g. lawyers);
- stock exchange requirements;
- forms of any new capital to be made available;
- the number of shares to be issued and the issue price;
- arrangements for underwriting;
- publishing the offer.

Stockbrokers provide advice on the various methods of obtaining a listing. They may work with investment banks on identifying institutional investors, but usually they are involved with smaller issues and placings.

Institutional investors have little direct involvement other than as investors, agreeing to buy a certain number of shares. They may also be used by the entity and its advisors to provide an indication of the likely take up and acceptable offer price for the shares. Once the shares are in issue institutional investors have a major influence on the evaluation and the market for the shares.

C   Rights issue

A rights issue is where new shares are offered for sale to existing shareholders, in proportion to the size of their shareholding.

The right to buy new shares ahead of outside investors is known as the 'pre-emption rights' of shareholders. Note that the purpose of pre-emption rights is to ensure that shareholders have an opportunity to prevent their stake being diluted by new issues. Pre-emption rights are protected by law, and can only be waived with the consent of shareholders.

Rights issues are far cheaper to organise than a public share issue, but may be more expensive than a placing.

An issue price must be set which is:

- low enough to secure acceptance of shareholders; but
- not too low, so as to avoid excessive dilution of the earnings per share.

More details on rights issues

Definition

A rights issue may be defined as: "Raising of new capital by giving existing shareholders the right to subscribe to new shares in proportion to their current holdings. These shares are usually issued at a discount to market price." (CIMA Official Terminology, 2005)

Explanation

In a rights issue, the entity sets out to raise additional funds from its existing shareholders.

It does this by giving them the opportunity to purchase additional shares. These shares are normally offered at a price lower than the current share price quoted, otherwise shareholders will not be prepared to buy, since they could have purchased more shares at the existing price anyway. The entity cannot offer an unlimited supply at this lower price, otherwise the market price would fall to this value. Accordingly the offer they make to the existing shareholders is limited. For example they may offer one new share for every four held.

Selection of an issue price

In theory, there is no upper limit to an issue price but in practice it would never be set higher than the prevailing market price (MPS) of the shares, otherwise shareholders will not be prepared to buy as they could have purchased more shares at the existing market price anyway. Indeed, the issue price is normally set at a discount on MPS. This discount is usually in the region of 20%. In theory, there is no lower limit to an issue price but in practice it can never be lower than the nominal value of the shares. Subject to these practical limitations, any price may be selected within these values. However, as the issue price selected is reduced, the quantity of shares that has to be issued to raise a required sum will be increased.

Underwriting

Underwriting avoids the possibility that the entity will not sell all of the shares it is issuing, and so receive less funds than it expects.

Underwriters are normally financial institutions such as merchant banks. In return for a fee, they agree to buy any shares that are not subscribed for in the issue. Underwriters receive their fee whether or not they are required to take up any unsubscribed shares.

The underwriting costs could potentially be avoided through a deep-discounted rights issue. In such an issue, the issue price is set at a large discount to the current market price so reducing the possibility of shareholders not taking up their rights.

Selection of an issue quantity

It is normal for the issue price to be selected first and then the quantity of shares to be issued becomes a passive decision. The effect of the additional shares on earnings per share, dividend per share and dividend cover should be considered. The selected additional issue quantity will then be related to the existing share quantity for the issue terms to be calculated. The proportion is normally stated in its simplest form, for example, 1 for 4, meaning that shareholders may subscribe to purchase one new share for every four they currently hold.

Terms of a rights issue

The issue price for a rights issue can be set by the company.

For example, if Lauchlan Co wanted to raise $2m for a new investment project, it could issue 1m shares at $2 each, or 500,000 shares at $4 each, or 250,000 shares at $8 each, etc.

To decide on the final terms of the issue, the current share price needs to be considered.

Assume that in this example, Lauchlan Co currently has 2m $1 ordinary shares in issue, with a current market price of $5 per share.

Issuing new shares at anything greater than the existing share price of $5 per share would not help to encourage investors to take up their rights. In order to attract investors, a discount on current market value is usually offered.

However, note that if the new shares were issued at (say) $2 each, this would require 1m new shares to be issued, and so many new shares would have a big impact on the company's earnings per share.

In this case, it would seem sensible to balance the various requirements by offering the new shares to investors at $4 per share. This is sufficiently below current market price to give an incentive to the shareholders to take up their rights, while at the same time only requiring 500,000 new shares to be issued, so restricting the impact on earnings per share.

If the new shares were offered to existing shareholders at $4 per share, 500,000 new shares would need to be issued. Given that there are 2m shares currently in issue, the new issue would be announced as a '1 for 4 rights issue at $4 per share'. (2m/500,000 = 4).

Market price after issue

- After the announcement of a rights issue there is a tendency for share prices to fall.

- The temporary fall is due to uncertainty about:
    - consequences of the issue;
    - future profits; and
    - future dividends.

- After the actual issue the market price will normally fall again because:
    - there are more shares in issue (adverse effect on earnings per share); and
    - new shares were issued at market price discount.

 ### 'Cum rights'

When rights issue is announced, all existing shareholders have the right to subscribe for new shares, and so there are rights ('cum rights') attached to the shares, and the shares are traded 'cum rights'.

'Ex rights'

On the first day of dealings in the newly issued shares, the rights no longer exist and the old shares are now traded 'ex rights' (without rights attached).

 ### Theoretical prices/values

(a) Theoretical 'ex rights' price is the theoretical price that the class of shares will trade at on the first trading day after issue. It is calculated as follows:

$$\frac{(N \times \text{cum rights price}) + \text{Issue price}}{N + 1}$$

(b) Theoretical 'value of rights' per share is calculated as:

$$(\text{Theoretical ex rights price} - \text{issue price})/N$$

where N = no of rights required to buy 1 share

Rights issue illustration

TERP

Using the figures for Lauchlan Co (in the section 'Terms of a rights issue' above), where:

Cum rights price = $5

Issue price = $4

N = 4

Therefore, TERP = [(4 × $5) + $4]/5 = $4.80

Value of the rights

Also, the value of the rights = (4.80 − 4) = $0.80 per new share, or 0.80/4 = $0.20 per old share.

Test your understanding 1 (Integration question)

(a)   Plover Co has 1 million GBP1 ordinary shares quoted at GBP4.50 ex div. It is considering a 1 for 5 rights issue at GBP4.20 per share.

Required:

Calculate the theoretical ex rights share price.

(b)   Assume that Plover Co intends to use the funds raised to finance a project with an NPV of GBP300,000.

Note: The NPV method has been covered earlier in the CIMA syllabus.

Required:

Calculate the theoretical ex rights share price if the project is undertaken.

Yield adjusted ex-rights price

The calculations of theoretical ex-rights price above assume that the additional funds raised will generate a return at the same rate as existing funds. If an entity expects (and the market agrees) that the new funds will earn a different return than is currently being earned on the existing capital then a 'yield-adjusted' TERP should be calculated.

Yield adjusted TERP

= [Cum rights price × $N/(N + 1)$] + [(Issue price/N + 1) × (Y_n/Y_0)]

where

Y_0 = Yield on 'old' capital

Y_n = Yield on 'new' capital

Using the figures for Lauchlan Co (in the section 'Terms of a rights issue' above), where:

Cum rights price = $5

Issue price = $4

and the rights issue was a 1 for 4 issue,

and also assuming:

- the rate of return (yield) on the new funds = 15%

- the rate of return on the existing funds = 12%

The yield-adjusted ex-rights price becomes:

Yield adjusted TERP = (5 × 4/5) + [(4/5) × (15/12)] = $5

Alternatively, this is 1 new share at $4 × (15/12), plus 4 old shares at $5 each i.e. $25 in total, or $5 per share.

Notice that if the new funds are expected to earn a return above the rate generated by existing funds, there will be less dilution of the market price than suggested by the original TERP calculation.

Note: If you are given the NPV of the new project which the rights issue has funded (as in the Test your understanding question above), the yield adjusted TERP is calculated as:

(Original company market capitalisation + NPV of project + rights issue proceeds)/New total number of shares

Courses of action open to a shareholder

Possible actions for a shareholder are:

- do nothing. (Shareholders may be protected from the consequences of inaction by the company selling the rights on behalf of inactive shareholders);

- renounce the rights and sell them on the market;

- exercise the rights (that is buy all the shares at the rights price);

- renounce part of the rights and take up the remainder.

Illustration of actions open to a shareholder

A shareholder receiving notification of a rights issue from an entity has a number of options available.

Consider the position of a shareholder in Lauchlan Co (from the above example in the 'Terms of a rights issue' section.

If the shareholder owns 1,200 shares (worth $5 each), in the 1 for 4 rights issue he will be offered 300 new shares at $4 each.

Option 1 – Do nothing.

In this situation, the market value of the investment could be expected to fall by $240 from $6,000 to $5,760 (1,200 shares at $4.80).

The company would normally reserve the right to sell any 'unaccepted' shares for the best price available in the market. After having deducted any expenses and, of course, $4 per share, the balance would be sent to the shareholder. This cash balance could fully or partially compensate the shareholder for the reduction in market value. The shareholder's percentage share of the entity would reduce.

Option 2 – Sell the rights.

In this situation, the shareholder decides to sell the right to buy the shares at $4 each to another investor. A rational investor would not be expected to pay more than 80 cents per share (TERP – $4) for such a right. The existing shareholder might receive $240 (300 at 80 cents) less any dealing costs incurred. The shareholder's percentage share of the entity would be reduced.

Option 3 – Fully subscribe for the new shares.

In this situation, the shareholder will have to increase the value of the shareholding by paying the entity $1,200 for the 300 new shares. The shareholder will then own 1,500 shares which, using TERP, will be valued at $7,200. The shareholder's percentage share of the entity will be maintained.

> ### Option 4 – Sell some rights to buy some new shares.
>
> In this situation, the shareholder may be unable or unwilling to invest more funds in the entity. Since the rights can normally be sold in the market, the shareholder could sell sufficient of the rights to purchase the balance. In the Lauchlan Co example, each block of 5 rights sold at 80 cents raises sufficient cash to purchase one new share at $4. The shareholder could sell 250 at 80 cents to raise $200 which would be sufficient to purchase 50 at $4. The value of the investment will be maintained at $6,000 but the shareholder's percentage share of the entity will be reduced.

Implications of a rights issue

(a)   From the viewpoint of the shareholders:

– they have the option of buying shares at preferential price;

– they have the option of withdrawing cash by selling their rights;

– they are able to maintain their existing relative voting position (by exercising the rights).

(b)   From the viewpoint of the company:

– it is simple and cheap to implement;

– it is usually successful ('fully subscribed');

– it often provides favourable publicity.

Test your understanding 2 (Integration question)

Molson Co has a paid-up ordinary share capital of EUR2,000,000 represented by 4 m shares of 50 cents each.

Earnings after tax in the most recent year were EUR750,000 of which EUR250,000 was distributed as dividend. The current price/earnings ratio of these shares, as reported in the financial press, is 8.

The entity is planning a major investment that will cost EUR2,025,000 and is expected to produce a positive NPV of EUR402,400.

The necessary finance is to be raised by a rights issue to the existing shareholders at a price 25% below the current market price of the entity's shares.

Required:

(a)   Calculate:

(i)   the current market price of the shares already in issue;

(ii)   the price at which the rights issue will be made;

(iii)   the number of new shares that will be issued;

> (iv) the price at which the shares of the entity should theoretically be quoted on completion of the rights issue (i.e. the 'ex-rights price'), ignoring incidental costs and assuming that the market accepts the entity's forecast of project NPV.
>
> (b) It has been said that, provided the required amount of money is raised and that the market is made aware of the earning power of the new investment, the financial position of existing shareholders should be the same whether or not they decide to subscribe for the rights they are offered.
>
> **Required:**
>
> Illustrate and comment on this statement.

4 End of chapter objective test questions

Test your understanding 3 (Objective test question)

A company, whose shares currently sell at $75 each, plans to make a rights issue of one share at $60 for every four existing shares.

What is the theoretical ex-rights price of the shares after the issue?

A $75.00

B $72.00

C $67.50

D $63.00

Test your understanding 4 (Objective test question)

Park Co is hoping to raise $460,000 through a rights issue to fund a new project.

Currently it has 1 million $1 shares in issue, trading at $1.45. The directors think that a discount of 20% will be required to encourage investors to take up their rights.

What should the terms of the rights issue be?

A   1 for 2

B   2 for 5

C   1 for 1

D   2 for 3

Test your understanding 5 (Objective test question)

Lambchop Co has 1 million shares in issue and it wants to raise some new finance by undertaking a 1 for 5 rights issue at $4.40 per share.

The theoretical ex rights price is $4.90.

What was the share price before the rights issue (to two decimal places)?

A $4.40

B $4.82

C $4.90

D $5.00

Test your understanding 6 (Objective test question)

Which of the following statements regarding preference shares are true?

A   Preference shares pay a dividend each year, being a fixed percentage of market value

B   Preference share dividends are tax deductible, just like debt interest

C   The cost of preference shares is generally higher than the cost of debt, but lower than the cost of ordinary shares

D   Preference shares are sometimes convertible and sometimes cumulative, but they are never redeemable

Test your understanding 7 (Objective test question)

DCD is a manufacturer of heavy construction equipment. It has manufacturing facilities around the world.

DCD's Ordinary Share Capital has a nominal value of $70 million ($0.50 shares) and the current market price per share is $6.00.

Proposed new manufacturing facility

The Board is planning to build a new manufacturing facility and has already identified a suitable site and prepared a schedule of forecast cash flows arising from the project.

It is expected that the proposed new facility would be fully operational within a year of the initial investment and that the project would generate a rate of return on funds invested of 20%. This is greater than the return on existing funds of 15% due to the greater efficiency of the new manufacturing facility.

Rights issue

The Board has decided to use a rights issue to finance the initial investment of $250 million. The new shares will be issued at a discount of 40% on current market price.

What is the approximate yield adjusted theoretical ex-rights price of the DCD shares?

A $4.90

B $5.20

C $5.60

D $6.93

Test your understanding 8 (Objective test question)

Alan Jones owns 2,000 shares in Bifold Co, a listed company with an issued share capital of 10m ordinary $1 shares with a current market price of $1.80 per share.

The company has just publicly announced its intention to pursue a 1-for-2 rights issue at $1.00 per share to raise funds for a new project with a net present value of $2m.

What will be the change in the overall wealth of Alan Jones (compared to his current wealth) if he chooses to subscribe for his rights?

A $267 loss

B   No change

C $200 gain

D $400 gain

Test your understanding 9 (Objective test question)

Audrey Co needs to raise $4 million to invest in a new project. The company has asked investors for tender offers and the following offers have been received:

Maximum price offered ($ per share)	No. of shares requested at this price (million)
1.00	4.2
1.10	3.7
1.20	2.2
1.30	1.2

At what price would the strike price be set, and how much finance would be raised in total?

A   Strike price: $1.00, Total funds raised $4.20 million

B   Strike price: $1.10, Total funds raised $4.07 million

C   Strike price: $1.20, Total funds raised $4.08 million

D   Strike price: $1.20, Total funds raised $4.20 million

Test your understanding 10 (Objective test question)

Maximo Co has some $1, 8% preference shares in issue. The shares are currently trading at $1.10.

The preference shares are redeemable at a 4% premium in three years' time, or alternatively they will be convertible into two ordinary shares on that date.

Maximo Co's ordinary shares have a nominal value of $0.25 and they are trading at $0.48. The ordinary share values have grown at 3% per year in recent years, and this level of growth is expected to continue.

What value (per preference share) is the rational investor likely to receive in three years' time if he chooses the better of the conversion or the redemption option?

A $0.99

B $1.04

C $1.05

D $1.14

Test your understanding 11 (Objective test question)

JJ Co has in issue 1.2 million shares, currently valued at $3 each, and a rights issue is being considered.

The rights issue will be either:

- 1 for 4 at $2.50 per share, or

- 1 for 3 at $1.875 per share.

Assuming that all shareholders take up their rights, and that there are no issue costs, what will be the effect of the rights issue on each shareholder's total wealth before taking account of any positive NPV generated by investing the new capital?

A   Total wealth increases more under the 1 for 4 scheme

B   Total wealth increases more under the 1 for 3 scheme

C   Total wealth is unchanged under both schemes

D   Total wealth decreases under both schemes

Test your understanding 12 (Objective test question)

MNO is planning a rights issue at a 30% discount to the current share price, in order to raise $7 million.

It currently has 10 million shares in issue, trading at $2.00 per share.

The directors are trying to calculate the theoretical value of a right per existing share, so that they can inform shareholders what the likely proceeds will be if shareholders decide to sell their rights rather than take them up.

What is the theoretical value of a right per existing share in these circumstances? Enter your answer in the box below, in $ and to two decimal places.

$

5   End of chapter case style question

Test your understanding 13 (Case style question)

KB has a paid-up ordinary share capital of $1,500,000 represented by 6m shares of 25 cents each. It has no debt finance. Earnings after tax in the most recent year were $1,200,000. The P/E ratio of the entity is 12.

The company is planning to make a large new investment which will cost $5,040,000 and is considering raising the necessary finance through a rights issue at 192 cents.

Required:

(i)   Calculate the current market price of KB's ordinary shares.

(ii)   Calculate the theoretical ex-rights price, and state what factors in practice might invalidate your calculation.

(iii) Briefly explain what is meant by a deep-discounted rights issue, identifying the main reasons why an entity might raise finance by this method.

(30 minutes)

Test your understanding answers

Test your understanding 1 (Integration question)

(a)   The theoretical ex rights price (TERP) is:

$$\frac{(N \times \text{cum rights price}) + \text{Issue price}}{N + 1}$$

$= [(5 \times 4.50) + 4.20]/6 = \text{GBP4.45}$

Alternatively, TERP can be calculated by looking at the total value of all the shares as follows:

$$= \left(\frac{(1m \times £4.50) + (\frac{1}{5} \times 1m \times £4.20)}{1m + \frac{1}{5} \times 1m} \right)$$

$= \text{GBP4.45}$

(b)   The NPV of the project is GBP300,000, so in an efficient market, this will be the gain in wealth of the shareholders if the project is undertaken.

The total number of shares in issue is now

1 million + (1/5 × 1 million) = 1.2 million

Thus, the theoretical share price after the rights issue, and after undertaking the project is

4.45 + (300,000/1.2 million) = GBP4.70

Test your understanding 2 (Integration question)

(a)   (i)   Current market price of shares already in issue: EPS = 750,000/4m = EUR 0.1875

Therefore, since the P/E ratio is 8, the price per share is 8 × 0.1875 = EUR 1.50

(ii)   Price at which rights issue will be made: EUR1.50 × 75% = EUR1.125

(iii)   Number of new shares that will be issued: EUR2,025,000/EUR 1.125 = 1.8 million

(iv)   1.8m new shares are being issued at EUR1.125 per share, 4m existing shares are in issue with a market price of EUR 1.50 per share, and the new project will have an NPV of EUR 402,400.

Hence, the TERP is

[(4m × 1.50) + (1.8m × 1.125) + 402,400]/5.8m = EUR 1.453

Alternatively: Ignoring the project initially, and using the formula from the formula sheet,

$$\text{TERP} = \frac{(N \times \text{cum rights price}) + \text{Issue price}}{N + 1}$$

= [(4m/1.8m) × 1.50 + 1.125]/(4m/1.8m) + 1 = EUR 1.384

and with the new project worth NPV = EUR402,400, this increases to 1.384 + (402,400/5.8m) = EUR 1.453 as before

(b)   This statement can be illustrated as follows:

For every 20 shares held, the rights issue means another 9 shares.

At least in theory, the selling price of the right to purchase one share will be EUR 1.453 less EUR 1.125, that is, EUR 0.328.

A shareholder with 20 shares taking up the rights will have wealth of

	EUR
Market value of 29 shares at EUR1.453 each	42.137
Less: Cost of taking up rights of nine new shares at EUR1.125 each	(10.125)
	32.012

A shareholder with 20 shares selling the rights will have wealth of:

EUR Market value of 20 shares at EUR1.453 each	29.060
Add: Sale of nine rights at EUR0.328 each	2.952
	32.012

The above calculations, however, assume no transaction costs.

Furthermore, the market may read a particular message into the rights issue that would affect the calculations.

Test your understanding 3 (Objective test question)

The answer is (B).

[(4 × $75) + $60]/5 = $72

Test your understanding 4 (Objective test question)

The answer is (B).

A discount of 20% on the shares that are trading at $1.45 means an issue price of $1.16.

To raise $460,000 by issuing shares at $1.16 means that (460,000/1.16 =) 396,552 shares need to be issued (i.e. approximately 400,000).

400,000 new shares compared to 1 million existing shares is a ratio of 2 to 5.

Test your understanding 5 (Objective test question)

The answer is (D).

The TERP is:

$$\frac{(N \times \text{cum rights price}) + \text{Issue price}}{N + 1}$$

Therefore:

4.90 = [(5 × share price) + $4.40]/(5 + 1)

So the share price was $5.00 before the rights issue.

Test your understanding 6 (Objective test question)

The answer is (C) only.

Preference share dividends are a fixed percentage of NOMINAL value (A) and they are NOT tax deductible (B). Preference shares are sometimes redeemable (D).

Because the risk to a preference share investor is lower than that of an ordinary shareholder but higher than that of a debt holder, the cost of preference shares does tend to lie between the costs of the other two types of finance (C).

Test your understanding 7 (Objective test question)

The answer is (C).

A 40% discount to current market price is 60% × $6 = $3.60

Therefore, to raise $250m, 69.44 million shares will have to be issued ($250m/$3.60). With 140m shares currently in issue, this amounts to (approximately) a 1 for 2 rights issue.

Yield adjusted TERP

= [Cum rights price × N/(N + 1)] + [(Issue price/N + 1) × (Yn / Y0)]

= [$6 × 2/3] + [($3.60/3) × (20/15)]

= $5.60

Test your understanding 8 (Objective test question)

The answer is (D).

Current wealth is 2,000 × $1.80 = $3,600

Ex rights price incorporating the $2m NPV project will be

[(10m × $1.80) + (5m × $1.00) + $2m]/15m shares = $1.6667

Therefore, if he subscribes for his rights (1,000 extra shares) his total share value will increase to (3,000 × $1.6667) = $5,000

The cost of taking the rights was 1,000 × $1.00 = $1,000

Hence his total wealth will be $5,000 – $1,000 = $4,000 (a gain of $400)

Test your understanding 9 (Objective test question)

The answer is (C).

The strike will be set at the highest possible level that generates the required amount of finance. This is to make sure that the company does not issue more shares than it has to, so that the dilution of the existing shareholders' holdings is kept to a minimum.

If Audrey Co sets the strike price at $1.20, 3.4 million shares will be issued (being 1.2 million to the people who bid $1.30 and 2.2 million to the people who bid $1.20).

Therefore, the total finance raised will be $1.20 × 3.4 million = $4.08 million.

Test your understanding 10 (Objective test question)

The answer is (C).

The redemption option will be worth $1 × 1.04 = $1.04

The conversion option will be worth (assuming 3% per year growth continues):

$(1.03)^3 × $0.48 × 2 = 1.05

The rational investor would choose the higher amount.

Test your understanding 11 (Objective test question)

The answer is (C).

Total wealth is always unaffected by the rights issue itself. Wealth only changes as a consequence of the NPV generated by any project invested in.

Test your understanding 12 (Objective test question)

The answer is **$0.20**.

An issue price at a 30% discount means $2.00 × (1 – 0.30) = $1.40

To raise $7 million using an issue price of $1.40, we need to issue 5 million shares (i.e. $7m/$1.40). Therefore this rights issue is a 1 for 2 issue (5 million new shares being issued and 10 million existing shares).

TERP is:

$$\frac{(N × \text{cum rights price}) + \text{Issue price}}{N + 1}$$

i.e. [(2 × $2.00) + $1.40]/(2 + 1) = $1.80

and so the value of a right per existing share is (Theoretical ex-rights price – issue price)/N ($1.80 – $1.40)/2 = $0.20

Test your understanding 13 (Case style question)

(i)   Earnings per share (EPS) = Profit after taxation/No of shares = 1,200,000/6m = $0.20

Market price = EPS × P/E = 0.20 × 12 = $2.40

(ii) Number of shares issued in rights issue = 5,040,000/$1.92 = 2,625,000

Therefore, TERP = [(6m × $2.40) + (2.625m × $1.92)]/ (6m + 2.625m) = $2.254

Factors that may invalidate this calculation in practice include:

–   adverse factors affecting the value of KB's shares between setting the terms of the rights issue and the issue date (e.g. a market crash);

–   whether the market considers the forecast return from the new funds to be realistic;

–   the increased number of shares in issue may affect their marketability, causing a further reduction in the ex-rights share price;

–   if shareholders do not take up their rights, shares will be left with the underwriters, which will depress the share price;

–   the new project may be seen by investors as more risky than existing projects, with no corresponding increase in return;

–   investors' expectations of future dividends per share may change as a consequence of the increase in the share capital.

(iii) A deep-discounted rights issue is an issue where the issue price is set well below the current market price of the shares. In some cases, the discount has been as much as 40% on the pre-issue price. The issue price must still, however, be above the nominal value to comply with company law. If share prices are volatile, there is a risk that the market price will fall below the rights issue price, which would lead to undersubscription. A deep-discounted rights issue should avoid this potential problem.

The lower issue price does mean that more shares will need to be issued to raise the same level of finance, with a consequent impact on future dividends per share and earnings per share.

Financing – Debt finance

Chapter learning objectives

Lead outcome	Component outcome
B2: Analyse long term debt finance	Analyse: (a) Selecting debt instruments (b) Target debt profile (c) Issuing debt securities (d) Debt covenants (e) Tax considerations

Topics to be covered

- Types of debt instruments and criteria for selecting them
- Managing interest, currency and refinancing risks with target debt profile
- Private placements and capital market issuance of debt
- Features of debt covenants

1 Overview of chapter

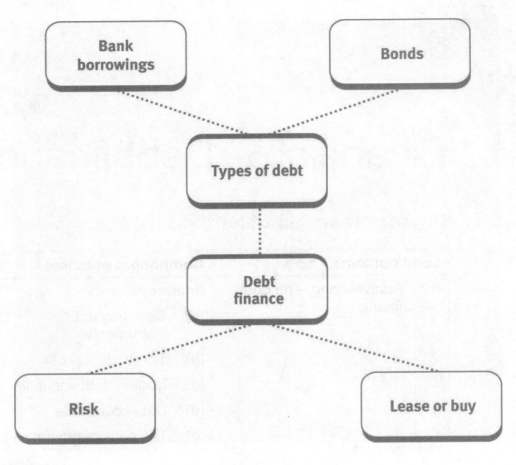

Introduction

The previous chapter considered different sources of equity finance. Now we move on to look at the different sources of debt finance.

This chapter looks at the different sources of debt finance, and the criteria to consider when trying to manage the risk associated with an entity's debt finance.

It concludes by introducing the important 'lease v buy' decision.

2 Debt finance

Debt finance is the loan of funds to a business without conferring ownership rights.

If the borrower does not make the interest and principal payments when they fall due, the lender can apply to the courts to have the borrower liquidated (or "wound up").

Tax considerations

Debt is a tax-efficient form of financing.

Interest is paid out of pre-tax profits as an expense of the business. Therefore, paying interest reduces the taxable profits of the business and hence the tax payable.

This means that the cost of servicing the debt (from the company's point of view) is cheaper than the stated rate of interest on the borrowing.

For example, if a company borrows money from the bank at an interest rate of 5% per year, and if the tax rate is 20%, the post-tax cost of debt from the company's point of view is only 4% (5% × (1 − 0.20)).

(See the later Chapter 6: 'Financing – capital structure' for more details on this.)

Security – charges

The lender of funds will normally require some form of security against which the funds are advanced. This means that, in the event of default, the lender will be able to take assets in exchange of the amounts owing. There are two types of 'charge' or security that may be offered/required:

1   **Fixed charge** – The debt is secured against a specific asset, normally land or buildings. This form of security is preferred because, in the event of liquidation, it puts the lender at the 'front of the queue' of creditors.

2   **Floating charge** – The debt is secured against the general assets of the business. This form of security is not as strong; again it confers a measure of security on liquidation as a 'preferred creditor', meaning the lender is higher in the list of creditors than otherwise.

Covenants

A further means of limiting the risk to the lender is to restrict the actions of the directors through the means of covenants. These are specific requirements or limitations laid down as a condition of taking on debt financing. They may include:

1   **Dividend restrictions** – Limitations on the level of dividends a company is permitted to pay. This is designed to prevent excessive dividend payments which may seriously weaken the company's future cash flows and thereby place the lender at greater risk.

2   **Financial ratios** – Specified levels which certain ratios may not breech, e.g. minimum interest cover, maximum gearing ratio, minimum EBITDA / finance cost.

3   **Financial reports** – Regular accounts and financial reports to be provided to the lender to monitor progress.

4   **Issue of further debt** – The amount and type of debt that can be issued may be restricted. Subordinated debt (i.e. debt ranking below the existing unsecured debt) can usually still be issued.

More details on covenants

Introduction

Covenants are put in place by lenders to protect themselves from borrowers defaulting on their obligations due to financial actions detrimental to themselves or the business.

Covenants are most often represented in terms of financial ratios which must be maintained for businesses which lend, such as a maximum debt-to-asset ratio or other such ratios. Covenants can cover everything from minimum dividend payments to levels that must be maintained in working capital to key employees remaining with the firm. Once a covenant is breached, the lender will typically have the right to call back the obligation from the borrower.

Impact on lender and borrower

Debt covenants benefit both the lender and the borrower:

- debt restrictions could protect the lender by requiring or prohibiting certain activities of the lender: in other words, debt covenants should restrict the borrower from making decisions that would be detrimental to the lender; and

- debt restrictions could benefit the borrower by reducing the cost of borrowing (e.g. through lower interest rates and higher credit ratings).

Debt covenants do not aim to place a burden on the borrower. Debt covenants are used to solve the agency problems among the management (i.e. of the borrowing company), debt holders, and shareholders that arise due to the differences in the objectives of the borrower and the lender.

Positive and negative debt covenants

Debt covenants can be either positive or negative.

Negative debt covenants state what the borrower cannot do and may include the following:

- Incur additional long-term debt (or require that additional borrowing be subordinated to the original borrowing)

- Pay cash dividends exceeding certain threshold

- Sell certain assets (e.g. sell accounts receivable)

- Enter into leases

- Combine in any way with another firm (e.g. takeover, merger)

- Compensate or increase salaries of certain employees

Positive debt covenants state what the borrower must do and may include the following:

- Maintain certain minimum financial ratios

- Maintain accounting records in accordance with generally accepted accounting principles

- Provide audited financial statements (normally within a specified amount of time after the year-end)

- Perform regular maintenance of assets used as security

- Maintain all facilities in good working condition

- Maintain life insurance policies on certain key employees

- Pay taxes and other liabilities when due

Examples of covenants

The most common financial ratios used in debt covenants include the following: net debt to cash flow, net debt to EBITDA, interest cover, tangible net worth, net worth, gearing ratio, current ratio, cash interest cover, debt to equity, etc.

In the above listed ratios, the same term can have different meanings in different debt agreements. For example:

Debt: total debt, funded debt, funded debt less cash, etc.

Cash flow: cash from operations, EBIT, EBITDA, etc.

According to research, covenants that most commonly lead to technical default include net worth (or tangible net worth) and current ratio.

Breach of a covenant

When a debt covenant is breached by the borrower, the lender has a range of alternative responses, including the following (non-exhaustive list):

- Waive the breach and continue the loan

- Waive the breach and impose additional constraints

- Require penalty payment

- Increase interest rate

- Demand immediate repayment of the loan

- Increase security needed

- Terminate debt agreement

It is usually better for the borrower to approach the lender if they suspect a breech is likely to occur. Early negotiations can be started to minimise any penalties. This may include giving the lender details of a recovery plan, additional security or parent company guarantees.

> A debt covenant breach represents a breach of contract. Lender's response to the breach of contract usually depends on the severity of the breach as well as the terms of the debt agreement. When a debt covenant breach is not severe, usually lenders either waive the breach or impose additional constraints on the borrower.

 ## Types of debt finance

Debt may be raised from two general sources – banks or capital markets.

Bank finance

For companies that are unlisted, and for many listed companies, the first port of call for borrowing money would be the banks.

These could be the high street banks or, more likely for larger companies, merchant banks.

Terms and conditions are negotiable dependent on the term of the borrowing, the amount borrowed, and the credit rating of the company wishing to make the borrowing.

Capital markets

As an alternative to borrowing funds from a bank, a listed company may issue (long term) bonds or (short term) commercial paper in the capital markets.

Criteria for selecting debt instruments

Most companies can borrow from banks, but view direct borrowing from a bank as more restrictive and expensive than selling bonds on the capital market.

Entities deciding whether issue a bond or borrow from a bank to finance a particular investment should consider

- liquidity,
- timescale and
- cost

as determining factors.

Detailed considerations: Criteria to consider

Entities use bonds and bank borrowings to finance investment projects. These range from short-term to long-term investments and cover a variety of reasons including infrastructure development and corporate expansions. Generally speaking, a bond is meant to finance a long-term investment, whereas a bank borrowing is more suitable for short-term needs. But that is not always the case. In recent years, financial managers have shifted their attention to the bond market as it offers liquidity, lower overall costs and the flexibility entities need to run their businesses.

Accessibility to the market is a key feature that differentiates the bond market from bank borrowings. While the latter is open for most corporate entities, the bond market implies costly and cumbersome hurdles for the aspiring company. Only those that have overcome the process can operate in the bond market.

There is a tendency for small and medium sized enterprises (SMEs) to use bank borrowings. Clearly, local banks provide financial support, satisfy liquidity needs and a range of other banking services on a daily basis. Eventually, banks engage in a long relationship with SMEs that benefits the entity whenever the need for capital arises. This relationship provides flexibility when it comes to agree on the terms and conditions of the lending. A bank borrowing often allows borrowers to pay off the borrowing partly or totally, at any time, with little or no warning. A downside, however, is that repayment charges are typically linked to regional interest rates and other admin fees subject to the whim of the bank. Lenders are also capable of substantially changing the terms of the deal, but borrowers can take their accounts elsewhere assuming there is another lender available.

On the bond market, entities need to build up a reputation. They need to communicate their credit quality, which should determine the interest rate on the bond. Bonds have highly standardised terms and conditions. Standardisation plays an important role for entities. It enables the entity to reach a wider range of investors and creates liquidity.

Both types of funding entail operational costs, but there are differences between them. Entering the bond market might be rather difficult and expensive, but once in, the costs reduce significantly. This is because the lending agreement is based on the standardised terms defined by the issuer.

Borrowing from a bank, as discussed earlier, implies submission to the terms set out by the bank as well as dealing with sometimes uncertain conditions.

Examples of long-term debt finance: Terminology

Bank finance

Money market borrowings

The money market consists of financial institutions and dealers in money or credit who wish to either borrow or lend.

The money market is used by participants as a means for borrowing and lending in the short-term, from several days to just under a year. This contrasts with the capital market for longer-term funding, for example bonds and equity.

The core of the money market consists of interbank lending – banks borrowing from, and lending to, each other. However, large profit-making entities will also borrow and lend on the money market.

Revolving credit facilities (RCFs)

Under a RCF the borrower may use or withdraw funds up to a pre-approved credit limit. The amount of available credit decreases and increases as funds are borrowed and then repaid.

The borrower makes payments based only on the amount they've actually used or withdrawn, plus interest and the borrower may repay the borrowing over time or in full at any time.

RCFs are very flexible debt financing options, and they enable a company to minimise interest payments because the amount of funds borrowed fluctuates over time and is never more than the company needs.

Often the RCF will be offered by a single bank, or in the case of a large amount of finance required, a syndicate (group) of banks may offer the RCF to reduce the risk to any one lender.

Capital markets

Bonds

A bond is a debt security, in which the issuer owes the holders a debt and, depending on the terms of the bond, is obliged to pay interest (the coupon) and/or to repay the principal at a later date. i.e. a bond is a formal contract to repay borrowed money with interest at fixed intervals.

Thus a bond is like a loan: the issuer is the borrower (debtor), the holder is the lender (creditor) and more commonly referred to as the investor, and the coupon is the interest. Bonds provide the borrower with external funds to satisfy long-term funding requirements.

Bonds and shares are both securities which can be traded in the capital markets, but the major difference between the two is that shareholders have an equity stake in the company (i.e. they are owners), whereas bondholders have a creditor stake in the company (i.e. they are lenders). Another difference is that bonds usually have a defined term, or maturity, after which the bond is redeemed, whereas shares may be outstanding indefinitely.

Commercial paper

Large, well-established listed companies with good credit ratings may issue short-term unsecured money market securities, referred to as commercial paper.

This commercial paper will generally mature within 9 months, typically between a week and 3 months. However, 3 month commercial paper is often "rolled over", with a new issue every 3 months, so the company can increase or decrease the amount issued regularly.

This can be risky if used for longer term finance, because there may be insufficient investor interest at one of these issue dates. Therefore, the company would need to arrange back-up, stand-by facilities.

Commercial paper can be traded at any time before the maturity date.

 More details on the capital market (bond market)

Issuing debt finance (bonds) in the capital markets enables an entity to borrow a large amount of finance from (potentially) a wide range of potential investors.

The bond market can essentially be broken down into three main groups: issuers, underwriters and purchasers.

Issuers

The issuers sell bonds in the capital markets to fund the operations of their organisations. This area of the market is mostly made up of governments, banks and corporations.

The biggest of these issuers is the government, which uses the bond market to help fund a country's operations. Banks are also key issuers in the bond market, and they can range from local banks up to supranational banks such as the European Investment Bank. The final major issuer is corporates, which issue bonds to finance operations.

Underwriters

The underwriting segment of the bond market is traditionally made up of investment banks and other financial institutions that help the issuer to sell the bonds in the market.

In most cases, huge amounts of finance are transacted in one offering. As a result, a lot of work needs to be done to prepare for the offering, such as creating a prospectus and other legal documents. In general, the need for underwriters is greatest for the corporate debt market because there are more risks associated with this type of debt.

The underwriters sometimes place the bonds with specific investors ('bond placement'), or they can attempt to sell the bonds more widely in the market. Alternatively, under a medium term note (MTN) programme, the issuer (via the underwriter) can issue debt securities on a regular and/or continuous basis.

Purchasers

The final players in the bond market are those who buy the bonds. Buyers basically include every group mentioned as well as any other type of investor, including the individual.

Governments play one of the largest roles in the market because they borrow and lend money to other governments and banks. Furthermore, governments often invest in bonds issued by other countries if they have excess reserves of that country's money as a result of trade between countries. For example, Japan is a major holder of U.S. government debt, such as U.S. gilts.

How to issue bonds on the market

Listing and admission to the London stock exchange

The admission process in the UK is made up of two stages; listing and admission to trading.

Listing

If the bond issuer is not already a listed company, it must first apply to become listed on the London stock exchange.

Admission of companies to the Official List is controlled by the UK Listing Authority (UKLA), a division of the Financial Conduct Authority (FCA).

The FCA retains responsibility for the approval of prospectuses, however issuers seeking admission to the Official List will also need to submit listing particulars to the UKLA.

A debt issuer seeking a London listing for its securities must apply for admission to the Official List (a 'listing') through the UKLA. The listing is dependent on the securities gaining admission to trading on the Main Market through satisfying the Exchange's admission and disclosure standards.

The listing process can take as little as three days depending on the complexity of the transaction and the completeness of the listing document submitted for approval. Appointing advisers with extensive experience of listing and agreeing the timetable well in advance should help shorten the process.

Admission to trading

In February 2010 London Stock Exchange launched an electronic, order-driven trading service for UK government, corporate and supranational bonds, called the Order book for Retail Bonds (ORB). This aims to offer retail investor's efficient access to an on-screen secondary market in retail denominated London listed debt instruments. This new trading service was introduced in response to demand from private investors in the UK for a cost effective and transparent mechanism for gaining access to fixed income securities and to develop the market for retail denominated bonds in the UK.

For admission to the ORB, the Admissions team at London Stock Exchange require documentation to be submitted at least 11 days prior to the admission date. This documentation should include an electronic copy of the base prospectus and the relevant pricing supplement/final terms document, a copy of the relevant board minutes relating to the issue, confirmation of the market maker who will be supporting the security, and an indicative opening price for the security.

Market making

To ensure that all instruments available on the ORB are tradable and have prices available throughout the day it is a requirement for all bonds admitted to the ORB to have at least one registered market maker.

The issuer can act as market maker to their own securities or can engage the services of a third party broker, however the market maker must be a member firm of London Stock Exchange and be authorised to deal.

The market maker will be required to quote two-way prices (buy and sell) in the security throughout the continuous trading period.

The prices must be within a maximum spread requirement which is determined by the trading segment and trading sector of the security. There is also a minimum volume (equivalent to nominal value) of securities which must be quoted on either side.

To register in a security the market maker must complete and submit a registration information form. The market maker has no obligation to quote in more than one security and there is no fee payable to register in ORB securities.

International debt finance

Large companies can borrow money in foreign currencies as well as their own domestic currency from banks at home or abroad.

The main reason for wanting to borrow in a foreign currency is to fund a foreign investment project or foreign subsidiary.

The foreign currency borrowing provides a hedge of the value of the project or subsidiary to protect against changes in value due to currency movements. The foreign currency borrowing can be serviced from cash flows arising from the foreign currency investment.

More detail on foreign currency borrowings

The choice of currency for debt finance

In the developed countries of the world, companies can choose which currency they prefer for both bank borrowings and bonds. In most developing countries, companies will need to raise finance in an international currency such as US dollars.

Eurobond markets

Eurobonds are bonds issued on the international capital markets. They can be denominated in any major international currency (i.e. not necessarily denominated in euro). Eurocurrency bonds may be listed on the domestic currency stock exchange but cannot be traded through that exchange. They are usually bearer instruments and pay interest annually, gross of tax.

This is in contrast to domestic bonds which are both listed and traded on the local stock exchange, and are usually registered bonds, that is, registered to a named holder.

The Eurobond market is a self-regulated off-shore market. Self-regulation is promoted by the International Capital Market Association (ICMA) who set rules for members to follow in areas such as processing transactions and payment of commission.

3 Target debt profile

The next chapter ('Financing – Capital structure') discusses the factors an entity will have to consider when choosing what its overall capital structure (mix of debt and equity finance) should be.

Once an entity has decided how much debt finance is needed, several issues need to be considered as the entity aims to achieve its target debt profile. In particular, the following questions need to be answered:

- Should the entity borrow at a fixed or a floating (variable) rate?

- Should the debt have a short-term or a long-term repayment date?

- Should domestic currency or foreign currency borrowings be used?

The answers to these questions will determine the level of interest rate, refinancing and currency risk that the entity will face.

Interest rate risk

Interest rate risk is the risk of gains or losses on assets and liabilities due to changes in interest rates. It will occur for any organisation which has assets or liabilities on which interest is payable or receivable.

The exposure to interest risk will depend on the amount of interest bearing assets or liabilities that an entity holds and the type that these are (floating or fixed rate).

Refinancing risk

Refinancing risk is associated with interest rate risk because it looks at the risk that borrowings will not be refinanced or will not be refinanced at the same rates.

The reasons for this could include:

- Lenders are unwilling to lend or only prepared to lend at higher rates.

- The credit rating of the company has reduced making it a more unattractive lending option.

- The company may need to refinance quickly and therefore have difficulty in obtaining the best rates.

The use of longer-term debt finance reduces the refinancing risk. Short-term debt finance has to be regularly repaid and then renegotiated if additional finance is needed, so the refinancing risk is higher.

Currency risk

Currency risk is the risk that arises from possible future movements in an exchange rate. It is a two-way risk, since exchange rates can move either adversely or favourably.

Currency risk affects any organisation with:

- assets and/or liabilities in a foreign currency

- regular income and/or expenditures in a foreign currency

- no assets, liabilities or transactions that are denominated in a foreign currency. Even if a company does not deal in any currencies, it will still face a risk since its competitors may be faring better due to favourable exchange rates on their transactions.

Currency risk and interest rate risk are covered in more detail in Chapter 8: 'Financial risk', and several risk management techniques are covered in Chapter 9: 'Currency risk management' and Chapter 10: 'Interest rate risk management'.

 ## 4   Other sources of finance

Retained earnings/existing cash balances

There is a common misconception that a company with a large amount of retained earnings in its balance sheet (statement of financial position) can fund its new investment projects using these retained earnings. This is not the case.

A company can only use internal sources of finance to fund new projects if it has enough cash in hand.

The level of retained earnings reflects the amount of profit accumulated over the company's life. It is not the same as cash.

Sale and leaseback

This means selling good quality fixed assets such as high street buildings and leasing them back over many years (25+). Funds are released without any loss of use of assets.

Any potential capital gain on assets is forgone.

Sale and leaseback is a popular means of funding for retail organisations with substantial high street property e.g. Tesco, Marks and Spencer.

Grants

These are often related to technology, job creation or regional policy. They are of particular importance to small and medium-sized businesses (i.e. unlisted). Their key advantage is that they do not need to be paid back.

Grants can be provided by local governments, national governments, and other larger bodies such as the European Union.

Debt with warrants attached

A warrant is an option to buy shares at a specified point in the future for a specified (exercise) price. Warrants are often issued with a bond as a sweetener to encourage investors to purchase the bonds.

The warrant offers a potential capital gain where the share price may rise above the exercise price.

The holder has the option to buy the share on the exercise date but can also choose to sell the warrant before that date.

Convertible debt

This is similar in effect to attaching a warrant to a debt instrument except that the warrant cannot be detached and traded separately. The convertible debt is where the debt itself can be converted into shares at a predetermined price at a date or range of dates in the future.

This has the effect of giving the debt holder a potential capital gain over and above the return from the debt interest. If the value of the shares is greater than that of the debt on the exercise date, then conversion will be made by the investor. If, however, the share value is lower than the debt value, the investor may retain the debt to maturity.

Venture capital

This is finance provided to young, unquoted profit-making entities to help them to expand. It is usually provided in the form of equity finance, but may be a mix of equity and debt.

Venture capitalists generally accept low levels of dividends and expect to make most of their returns as capital gains on exit. A typical exit route is an IPO or flotation, which enables the venture capitalist to sell his stake in the entity on the stock market.

Venture capital is covered in more detail in the later chapter on 'Financial and strategic implications of mergers and acquisitions'.

Business angels

Business angels are similar to venture capitalists. Venture capitalists are rarely interested in investing in very small businesses, on the grounds that monitoring progress is uneconomic.

Business angels are wealthy investors who provide equity finance to small businesses.

Government assistance

Governments will often have a number of schemes, aimed at providing assistance to:

- small- and medium-sized profit-making entities;

- entities wanting to expand or relocate in particular regions;

- promote innovation and technology;

- projects that will create new jobs or protect existing ones.

You do not need to have knowledge of any specific scheme, but relevant discussion of methods of government assistance in your own country will earn credit in the examination.

 ## 5 The lease v buy decision

If a new project requires the use of an asset, such as a machine, a business often has the choice of whether to buy the asset outright, or whether to lease it.

 ## Terminology

Lease

A lease is a commercial arrangement where an equipment owner (the lessor) conveys the right to use the equipment in return for payment by the equipment user (the lessee) of a specified rental over a pre-agreed period of time.

Reasons for leasing

- It is a readily available form of finance, especially for plant and equipment or motor vehicles. It is therefore very convenient for companies to enter into such arrangements.

- It removes the need for a significant capital outlay at the beginning of a project's life i.e. it avoids the need to find the capital at the outset.

- It may be cheaper in financial terms than conventional debt financing i.e. the effective interest rate on leasing may be less than the interest payable on a loan. This is because a lease is asset-backed finance and so is less risky for the lender. Consequently, lenders may therefore be prepared to offer a lower rate of interest than on a standard borrowing.

The lease v buy decision

Lease-or-buy decisions

The evaluation of the lease-or-buy decision is not a pure financing decision as it also involves interactions with the investment decision.

The decision to lease or buy an asset is a financing decision that will be made only once the decision to invest in the asset has been taken. The decision to invest in the asset would be determined by discounting the operational costs and benefits from using the asset at the cost of capital normally used by the entity to evaluate projects, typically its weighted average cost of capital. Investing in the asset would be justified if a positive NPV is obtained.

The financing decision is then concerned with identifying the least-cost financing option.

In evaluating the financing decision, it is usually assumed that the entity would have to borrow funds in order to purchase the asset.

 ### Lease v buy evaluation

If an asset is needed for a major new investment, and the asset can be leased, then a critical decision is:

- should the asset be leased?; or

- should the asset be purchased and the purchase cost financed by debt issue?

In the exam you may need to evaluate the lease against the borrowing to buy option to determine which would be better in financial terms.

The traditional approach to the evaluation is to use the NPV method i.e. determine the present value cost of leasing and compare this to the present value cost of borrowing to buy.

 Note: The NPV method (Net Present Value) was covered earlier in the CIMA syllabus.

 ### Note on discount rate

In the lease v buy evaluation, it is considered that the risk associated with the lease option is comparable to the risk associated with the borrow to buy option. Hence the same discount rate should be used for both NPV calculations.

The discount rate to use is the **post-tax cost of debt finance** – clearly this rate applies to the borrow to buy option, and it is considered to be appropriate to the leasing option too, since the post-tax cost of debt is effectively the opportunity cost of leasing.

Test your understanding 1 (Integration question)

Penny Co wishes to invest in a new lorry costing $130,000. The lorry has a life of four years and no scrap proceeds are expected to be available after this period. Tax allowable depreciation is available at 25% on a reducing balance basis. The company can borrow at 12% pre-tax.

The lorry could alternatively be leased for a cost of $40,000 per year payable in arrears for four years. Assume for now that the full lease payment is a tax deductible expense and that no tax allowable depreciation can be claimed on a leased asset. Corporation tax is 33% payable one year in arrears.

Required:

Determine whether the company should lease or purchase the asset.

Further calculations on lease interest

In the above example, to simplify the calculations, we were told specifically that the full lease payment was to be treated as a tax deductible expense.

In reality, it will usually be just the interest element of the lease payment which is tax deductible. In this case, the first step is to calculate the interest element, using either the actuarial method, or the sum of digits method.

The following illustration shows how both methods work.

Illustration 1

Assume that KL Co has the option to buy an asset for USD100,000, or to lease it by paying USD29,500 per year in arrears for 4 years.

Clearly, the interest element in the lease amounts to (4 × USD29,500) – USD100,000 = USD18,000 in total.

This interest can be allocated to years using either the actuarial method, or the sum of digits method.

Actuarial method

Here the implied interest rate is found by using an IRR approach. As a short cut, the 4 year annuity factor at the IRR can be found by dividing the cost of the asset by the annual interest payment (i.e. 100,000/29,500).

This gives a 4 year annuity factor of 3.390, which (from tables) is very close to the 7% factor. Hence, the implied interest rate in the lease is (approximately) 7%.

Now, the interest can be allocated to individual years using the following table:

USD	Year 1	Year 2	Year 3	Year 4
Opening balance	100,000	77,500	53,425	27,665
+ Interest (7% × Op Bal)	7,000	5,425	3,740	1,937
– Lease payment	(29,500)	(29,500)	(29,500)	(29,500)
Closing balance	77,500	53,425	27,665	102

Note: The closing balance at the end of year 4 should be zero. The difference is due to rounding.

The lease interest payments have now been allocated to years, so can be used to calculate the tax relief each year.

Sum of digits method

This is a simpler way of allocating interest, based on the sum of digits formula:

$$n(n+1)/2$$

In this example, the lease payments are to be made over 4 periods, so the sum of digits is 10 (working: 4 × 5 /2 = 10)

Hence, the interest allocation is:

Year 1	4/10 × 18,000	USD7,200
Year 2	3/10 × 18,000	USD5,400
Year 3	2/10 × 18,000	USD3,600
Year 4	1/10 × 18,000	USD1,800

Once again, the tax relief on the lease interest can now be calculated easily.

Note: The sum of digits method is an allowable and quick approximation of the actuarial method.

Test your understanding 2 (Integration question)

Following on from the information in the Illustration above:

Assume that KL Co has the option to buy an asset immediately for USD100,000, or to lease it by paying USD29,500 per year in arrears for 4 years.

Other information

- KL Co is liable to corporate tax at a marginal rate of 30% which is settled at the end of the year in which it arises.

- KL Co accounts for depreciation on a straight-line basis at the end of each year

- Under the buy option, tax depreciation allowances on the full capital cost are available in equal instalments over the first four years of operation.

- Under the lease option, both the accounting depreciation and the interest element of the lease payments are tax deductible.

Required:

Advise KL Co whether the asset should be leased or bought, assuming that the interest on the lease should be allocated using the actuarial method. Use a discount rate of 5% in your evaluation.

6 End of chapter objective test questions

Test your understanding 3 (Objective test question)

A company is evaluating the decision whether to lease an asset or to buy it outright using newly borrowed funds.

Which of the following is the BEST discount rate to use for the evaluation, assuming that the decision has already been taken to acquire the asset?

A   Post tax cost of debt

B   WACC

C   Cost of equity

D   Pre-tax cost of debt

Test your understanding 4 (Objective test question)

Which THREE of the following statements about eurobonds are correct?

A   Entities that issue eurobonds keep a register of their eurobond holders

B   Eurobonds are traded on the international capital markets

C   They are sometimes denominated in euros

D   They are sometimes denominated in US dollars

E   Eurobond interest is normally paid semi-annually (every six months)

Test your understanding 5 (Objective test question)

The following information relates to an asset which a company is considering leasing or buying.

- Life of asset 10 years

- Cost if purchased $28,000

- Residual value $3,000

- Lease details: Ten annual repayments of $3,800 to begin at start of lease

The shareholders view the adoption of the lease as being an equivalent risk to borrowing at an after-tax cost of 10% per annum.

The first lease payment (or the purchase price) would be due on 1 January 20X2. The purchase price would not be eligible for tax depreciation allowances but lease payments would be allowed as a deduction from profit for tax purposes.

The firm has a 31 December year end and pays corporation tax at 35% one year after the year end in which profits are earned.

It makes sufficient profits to obtain tax relief on lease payments as soon as they arise.

What (to the nearest $100) is the net after-tax benefit of leasing the asset as opposed to buying it?

A $1,200

B $4,200

C $8,600

D $18,300

Test your understanding 6 (Objective test question)

Reef Co needs to raise some debt finance and the directors want to limit the entity's exposure to refinancing risk and interest rate risk.

Although the overall debt profile of an entity should be considered to fully assess the overall risk, as a general rule

- refinancing risk is likely to be greater with _____ **(long term / short term)** debt, and

- interest rate risk is likely to be greater with _____ **(fixed rate / floating rate)** debt

(Enter the correct phrase from the choice given.)

Test your understanding 7 (Objective test question)

An entity may issue convertible unsecured loan stock because

A   it is cheaper to service than ordinary debt

B   sales and earnings are expected to fall over the next few years

C   if conversion takes place, it will not disturb the firm's gearing ratio

D   if conversion takes place, it will generate additional capital funds for the firm

7 End of chapter case style question

> ### Test your understanding 8 (Case style question)
>
> XTA plc is the parent entity of a transport and distribution group based in the United Kingdom. The group owns and operates a network of distribution centres and a fleet of trucks (large delivery vehicles) in the United Kingdom. It is currently planning to expand into Continental Europe, operating through a new subsidiary entity in Germany. The subsidiary will purchase distribution centres in Germany and invest in a new fleet of trucks to be based at those centres. The German subsidiary will be operationally independent of the UK parent.
>
> Alternative proposals have been put forward by Messrs A, B and C, Board members of XTA plc on how best to structure the financing of the new German operation as follows:
>
> - **Mr A:** 'I would feel much more comfortable if we were to borrow in our base currency, British pounds (GBP), where we already have long-standing banking relationships and a good reputation in the capital markets. Surely it would be much more complicated for us to borrow in euros (EUR)?'
>
> - **Mr B:** 'I am concerned about the exposure of our consolidated statement of financial position and investor ratios to GBP/EUR exchange rate movements. How will we be able to explain large fluctuations to our shareholders? If we were to raise long-term euro borrowings, wouldn't this avoid exchange rate risk altogether? We would also benefit from euro interest rates which have been historically lower than UK rates.'
>
> - **Mr C:** We know from our market research that we will be facing stiff competition in Germany from local distribution companies. This is a high-risk project with a lot of capital at stake and we should finance this new venture by XTA plc raising new equity finance to reflect this high risk.'
>
> Assume that today is Saturday 1 October 20X5. A summary of the latest forecast consolidated statement of financial position (balance sheet) for the XTA Group at 31 December 20X5 is given below. It has been prepared BEFORE taking into account the proposed German investment:

	GBP million
Assets	
Total assets	450
Equity and liabilities	
Equity	250
Long term borrowings (there were no other non-current liabilities)	150
Current liabilities	50
Total equity and liabilities	450

The proposed investment in Germany is scheduled for the final quarter of 20X5 at a cost of GBP 60m for the distribution centres, and GBP 20m for the fleet of trucks when translated from euros at today's exchange rate of GBP/EUR1.50 (that is GBP1 = EUR 1.50). There is a possibility that the euro could weaken against GBP to GBP/EUR 2.00 by 31 December 20X5, but it can be assumed that this will not occur until after the investment has been made. The subsidiary's statement of financial position at 31 December 20X5 will only contain the new distribution centres and fleet of trucks matched by an equal equity investment by XTA plc and will only become operationally active from 1 January 20X6.

Required:

(a) Write a memorandum to the Board of XTA plc to explain the advantages and disadvantages of using each of the following sources of finance:

– a rights issue versus a placing (assuming UK equity finance is chosen to fund the new German subsidiary); and

– a euro bank borrowing versus a euro-denominated Eurobond (assuming euro borrowings are chosen). **(15 minutes)**

(b) Evaluate EACH of the alternative proposals of Messrs A, B and C for financing the new German subsidiary and recommend the most appropriate form of financing for the group. Support your discussion of each proposal with

– a summary forecast consolidated statement of financial position for the XTA group at 31 December 20X5 incorporating the new investment; and

– calculations of gearing using book values

using year end exchange rates of both GBP/EUR 1.50 and GBP/EUR 2.00. **(30 minutes)**

Test your understanding answers

Test your understanding 1 (Integration question)

The discount rate is the post-tax cost of debt ∴12% (1 – 0.33) = 8.04% ≈ 8%.

Assumptions:

1   Asset is purchased on first day of year 1.

2   Tax is delayed by 1 year.

Buy asset

Tax allowable depreciation

		Tax @ 33%	Date
0	130,000		
1 TAD	32,500/97,500	10,725	2
2 TAD	24,375/73,125	8,044	3
3 TAD	18,281/54,844	6,033	4
4 SCRAP	0		
Balancing allowance	54,844	18,099	5

Year	Cash flow	PVF @ 8%	PV
0	(130,000)	1	(130,000)
1	–	–	–
2	10,725	0.857	9,191
3	8,044	0.794	6,387
4	6,033	0.735	4,434
5	18,099	0.681	12,325
			(97,663)

Lease asset

Year	Lease	Tax	Net	PVF @ 8%	PV
1	(40,000)		(40,000)	(0.926)	(37,040)
2	(40,000)	13,200	(26,800)	0.857	(22,968)
3	(40,000)	13,200	(26,800)	0.794	(21,279)
4	(40,000)	13,200	(26,800)	0.735	(19,698)
5		13,200	13,200	0.681	8,989
					(91,996)

Decision:

On purely financial grounds it is better to lease rather than buy the asset.

Test your understanding 2 (Integration question)

Buy option

	T₀	T₁–T₄
Purchase cost	(100,000)	
Tax relief on tax depreciation (30% × 100,000/4)		7,500
Discount factor (5%)	1	3.546
Present value	(100,000)	26,595
Net present value	(73,405)	

i.e. Buying the asset to undertake the project will cost USD 73,405 in present value terms.

Lease option

	T₁	T₂	T₃	T₄
Lease payment	(29,500)	(29,500)	(29,500)	(29,500)
Tax relief on depreciation and lease interest **(W1)**	9,600	9,128	8,622	8,081
	(19,900)	(20,372)	(20,878)	(21,419)
Discount factors (5%)	0.952	0.907	0.864	0.823
Present value	(18,945)	(18,477)	(18,039)	(17,627)
Net present value	(73,088)			

i.e. Leasing the asset to undertake the project will cost USD 73,088 in present value terms.

(W1) Tax relief calculation

	T_1	T_2	T_3	T_4
Implied interest (from Illustration 3 earlier in the chapter)	7,000	5,425	3,740	1,937
Depreciation	25,000	25,000	25,000	25,000
	32,000	30,425	28,740	26,937
Tax relief (30%)	9,600	9,128	8,622	8,081

Note: The tax relief on the lease interest is included in the evaluation as a relevant cash flow, but the lease interest itself is not a cash flow, so is not included.

Conclusion:

The lease option is cheaper so should be undertaken on financial grounds. However, the difference is so marginal that it will be important to undertake sensitivity analysis, and to consider other non-financial factors before a final decision is made.

Note that we are assuming that the positive NPV of any cash flows arising from the new project must exceed the negative NPV associated with the cost of the asset, to give an overall positive NPV.

Test your understanding 3 (Objective test question)

The answer is (A).

Test your understanding 4 (Objective test question)

The answer is (B), (C) and (D).

Eurobonds are bearer instruments, so no register of bond holders is kept (A). Interest is normally paid annually (E).

They are traded on international capital markets (B) and can be denominated in any major global currency – (C) and (D).

Test your understanding 5 (Objective test question)

The answer is (C).

PV of buying = $28,000 – ($3,000 × 0.386) = $26,842

PV of lease payments (years 0-9) = $3,800 × (1 + 5.759) = $25,684

PV of lease tax relief (years 2-11) = $3,800 × 0.35 × 5.586 = $7,429

So the benefit of leasing is 26,842 – 25,684 + 7,429 = $8,587

Test your understanding 6 (Objective test question)

As a general rule

- refinancing risk is likely to be greater with **short term** debt, and

- interest rate risk is likely to be greater with **floating rate** debt.

Test your understanding 7 (Objective test question)

The answer is (A).

One of the main advantages of issuing CULS is the lower return that it demands due to the attraction of the option of conversion to equity, i.e. it is cheaper to service than ordinary debt.

If sales and earnings are expected to rise (not fall), it may be beneficial to issue CULS rather than to issue effectively underpriced equity (B).

If conversion takes place the firm's gearing ratio will change (C). No extra capital is generated on conversion (D).

Test your understanding 8 (Case style question)

(a) **Rights issue versus placing**

Advantages of a rights issue

- no dilution of ownership by current shareholders

- reliable (can be underwritten)

Disadvantages of a rights issue

- limits potential investors to current shareholder base (placements can be marketed to a wider selection of institutional investors)

- more complex and more expensive than a placing

- takes longer to arrange than a placing

Euro bank borrowing versus euro-denominated eurobond

Advantages of a euro bank borrowing

–   direct contact with lender

–   flexible terms

–   promotes good bank relationship

–   access to a wider source of funds via syndicated credit from a panel of banks

–   not dependent on a good rating

–   relatively quick and cheap to arrange

Disadvantages of a euro bank borrowing

–   does not give access to large, deep international capital markets which may support larger issues

–   better rates possible from Eurobonds

–   longer maturities may be harder to obtain from a bank (for example 20 years)

Examiner's note:

The answer to (a) above has been given in list form as a study aid, but in a case study examination, candidates would be expected to provide a memorandum, with short paragraphs (which could be in bullet point form) for each point.

(b) **Revised statements of financial position (balance sheets)**

The balance sheet of the German subsidiary is translated at closing rate since the company is operationally independent of the UK parent.

Table A: Mr A's proposal – long term borrowings in GBP

	Ex rate GBP/EUR1.50 GBP million	Ex rate GBP/EUR2.00 GBP million
Total assets	530	510
	(450 + 120/1.50)	(450 + 120/2.00)
Equity and liabilities		
Equity (balancing figure)	250	230
Long term borrowings	230	230
Current liabilities	50	50
Total equity and liabilities	530	510

Table B: Mr B's proposal – long term EUR borrowings

	Ex rate GBP/EUR1.50	Ex rate GBP/EUR2.00
	GBP million	GBP million
Total assets	530	510
	(450 + 120/1.50)	(450 + 120/2.00)
Equity and liabilities		
Equity (balancing figure)	250	250
Long term borrowings	230	210
	(150 + 120/1.50)	(150 + 120/2.00)
Current liabilities	50	50
Total equity and liabilities	530	510

Table C: Mr C's proposal – UK (GBP) equity funding

	Ex rate GBP/EUR1.50	Ex rate GBP/EUR2.00
	GBP million	GBP million
Total assets	530	510
	(450 + 120/1.50)	(450 + 120/2.00)
Equity and liabilities		
Equity (balancing figure)	330	310
Long term borrowings	150	150
Current liabilities	50	50
Total equity and liabilities	530	510

Table D: Gearing levels

Current position (debt to debt plus equity) = 150/(150 + 250) = 37.5%

Scenario:	Ex rate GBP/EUR1.50	Ex rate GBP/EUR2.00
Mr A	48%	50%
Mr B	48%	46%
Mr C	31%	33%

Evaluation of Board members' comments

Mr A: GBP-denominated borrowings

Reputation in the UK markets: Mr A's comment on the advantage of GBP borrowings due to reputation in the UK capital markets is not valid since banks providing GBP loans should be equally willing to provide euro loans and a good reputation in the capital markets will extend beyond the United Kingdom.

Foreign exchange risk: There is, however, a major exchange risk arising from funding euro-based assets with GBP borrowings, arising mainly from the retranslation of the net investment in the subsidiary at the year end and the effect this has on equity values and gearing levels. This is illustrated in Table A, where the value of equity has fallen from GBP 250m to GBP 230m as a result of the weakening of the euro against GBP from a rate of GBP/EUR 1.50 to GBP/EUR 2.00.

The effect on gearing is seen in Table D where a fall in the value of the euro leads to deterioration in gearing levels from 48% to 50%.

Impact on gearing: The use of borrowings has a major impact on gearing level, with debt/equity deteriorating from 37.5% to 48% (at GBP/EUR 1.50). Euro-denominated borrowings have a similar impact at current exchange rates.

Other exchange risk: There is also an exchange risk on the GBP value of the repatriation of euro profits to the United Kingdom via dividends, interest and management charges.

Mr B: euro-denominated borrowings

Lower euro interest rates: This is not a valid argument since, under interest rate parity, spot rates are expected to move to compensate for lower euro interest rates and so any gain on interest payments is likely to be offset by a loss on the capital value of the borrowing when it is repaid.

Exchange risk and equity values: Euro borrowings provide a natural hedge by matching the currency of the assets with that of the funding used to finance those assets. At the statement of financial position date, the exchange gain or loss on retranslating the net investment in the German subsidiary will be substantially matched by an equal and opposite gain or loss on retranslating the euro borrowings. This is illustrated in Table B, where a weakening of the euro borrowings against GBP is seen to have no impact on the value of equity.

Note: It could be noted that the hedge accounting provisions of IFRS 9 can be applied to avoid volatility in reported profit figures. Without hedge accounting, gains and losses on the borrowing would be recognised in profit for the year whereas gains and losses on the investment in the German subsidiary would be recognised as part of equity under IAS 21. If hedge accounting is permitted, the hedge provided by the borrowing can be designated as such and exchange rate movements on both the investment and the borrowing recognised as changes in the value of equity.

Exchange risk and gearing levels: The gearing ratio has again deteriorated markedly as a result of increased borrowing. In addition, gearing levels are exposed to exchange rate changes. In this case, gearing has improved from 48% to 46% as a result of a fall in the value of the euro, but a negative impact would have resulted from a strengthening of the euro against GBP.

Mr C: UK equity

Risk profile: Mr C is correct in his assertion that equity finance is more suitable than long-term borrowings for a high risk project, since dividends can be cut or reduced if profits are lower than expected, whereas the interest on borrowings always has to be paid in full at each due date.

Exchange risk: However, with equity finance denominated in GBP and the investment being linked to the value of the euro, there is no natural hedge of exchange rate risk arising on the revaluation of the net investment in Germany. Table C shows that the value of equity would fall from GBP 330m to GBP 310m as a result of a fall in the value of the euro from GBP/EUR 1.50 to GBP/EUR 2.00 and there would be a deterioration in gearing from 31% to 33%.

Gearing levels: These are at a much more acceptable level of around 31%. Indeed, additional long-term borrowings may not be practical if lenders are concerned about the already high gearing levels in the group and/or if the new venture has a high risk profile. In this case, the company may have no choice but to raise new equity finance.

Recommendation

The German distribution centre and transport fleet should be financed by long-term euro borrowings (which would be designated as a hedge under IFRS 9 and hedge accounting provisions applied, as noted above) in order to match the currency and maturity of the assets to be funded and remove exposure of equity and reported profit to exchange rate gains and losses.

It would be preferable for such euro borrowings to be raised by the German subsidiary so that the euro borrowing interest can be paid out of euro earnings. This also provides the opportunity for reducing the cost of funding by securing the borrowings on the euro assets.

The proportion of new long-term borrowings may be restricted by the following:

- German tax authority regulations on minimum capitalisation levels.

- Value of assets in the German subsidiary that can be used for security.

- Level of parent company loan guarantees offered (where additional security is required).

- Debt capacity of the group (that is acceptable gearing level).

To the extent that long-term borrowings are not possible, the group should consider a rights issue or placing to raise additional equity finance.

Financing – Capital structure

Chapter learning objectives

Lead outcome	Component outcome
B1: Evaluate the capital structure of a firm	Evaluate: (a) Choice of capital structure (b) Changes in capital structure

Topics to be covered

- Capital structure theories (traditional theory and Miller and Modigliani (MM) theories)
- Calculation of cost of equity and weighted cost of capital to reflect changes in capital structure
- Impact of choice of capital structure on financial statements
- Structuring debt/equity profiles of companies in a group

1 Overview of chapter

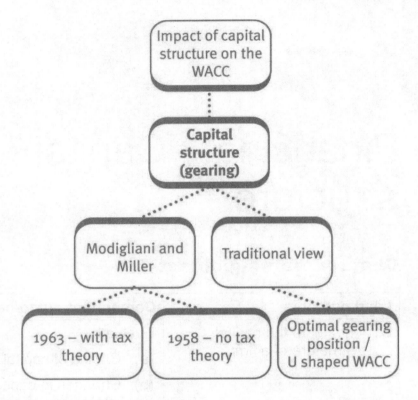

Introduction to capital structure

An analysis of capital structure, using the gearing ratio and interest cover, is important when trying to assess the risk associated with a business.

This chapter looks at capital structure in detail. In particular we shall consider the implications for the business of a change in capital structure.

When a business changes its capital structure, there will be an impact on its financial ratios and an impact on its weighted average cost of capital (WACC).

The impact on financial ratios is covered later in the chapter, but we start with a detailed analysis of the impact on WACC of a change in capital structure.

2 The impact on WACC of a change in capital structure

The WACC formula was introduced earlier in the CIMA syllabus:

$$k_o = k_{eg}\left[\frac{V_E}{V_E + V_D}\right] + k_d(1-t)\left[\frac{V_D}{V_E + V_D}\right]$$

It is clear that if a company changes its capital structure (gearing level), the WACC will change, since the ratio of debt to equity is a key variable in the formula.

Also, since the value of an entire company (debt plus equity) can be calculated as the present value of its post-tax operating cash flows (before financing) discounted at the WACC, when the WACC changes so does the value. (See the later Chapter 12: 'Business valuation' for more details on this.)

Several studies have focused on this link between capital structure and company value. The key question is:

> "What capital structure should the company aim for in order to maximise the company's value?"

The main studies are:

- the traditional view;

- the Modigliani-Miller view, ignoring taxation;

- the Modigliani-Miller view, taking into account the tax relief on debt interest payments.

These studies are based on different assumptions and come to different conclusions. They are covered below.

In order to understand the different views, it is vital to understand the two opposing forces which impact on the WACC as capital structure changes.

 The two opposing forces which impact WACC

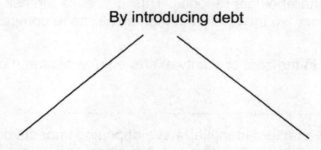

By introducing debt

Downward force on WACC

- Debt is cheaper than equity and would cause the WACC to fall

Upward force on WACC

- Ke increases because of financial risk and would cause the WACC to rise

Impact on WACC of an increase in gearing

As an entity increases the amount of debt in its capital structure, two opposing forces impact on the weighted average cost of capital:

Downward force on the WACC

In general, the entity's cost of debt finance is cheaper than its cost of equity finance, for two reasons:

- Interest is an obligation which has to be paid out each year, whereas dividends are paid only if the company can afford them. This means that debt holders face less risk, so accept lower returns.

- Interest is a tax deductible expense, whereas dividends are paid out of post-tax profits. This further reduces the cost of debt for the company.

Therefore, as the entity increases its gearing by raising more debt finance, the greater proportion of (cheaper) debt in the capital structure exerts a downward force on the WACC.

Upward force on the WACC

As the gearing level increases, the extra interest payments to debt holders mean that the likelihood of the entity being able to afford to pay dividends to shareholders reduces. This increases the risk perception of the shareholders, so they demand higher returns to compensate for the increased risk.

This increase in the cost of equity exerts an upward force on the WACC.

Net effect

Clearly, the two factors identified have opposing impacts on the weighted average cost of capital. The key questions are:

Which of the two forces is stronger?

What is the net effect of these two factors?

There is no simple answer to these questions. In fact, the different gearing theories propose different answers to the questions, based on different assumptions.

However, an understanding of these two factors, and these key questions, is crucial to a sound understanding of the capital structure theories covered in this chapter.

Impact of capital structure on the equity investor

High gearing exists when an entity has a large proportion of prior charge capital in relation to equity and low gearing exists when there is a small proportion of prior charge capital. High gearing increases the financial risk of the equity investor but the reward can be in the form of increased dividends when profits rise. If, however, profits falter, the equity investor can expect to be the first to feel the effect of the reduction in profits.

Low gearing or no gearing may not necessarily be in the equity investor's best interests because the entity might then be failing to exploit the benefits which borrowing can bring.

Provided that the return generated from borrowed funds is greater than the cost of those funds, capital gearing could be increased. The extent to which it is prudent for an entity to increase its capital gearing will depend upon many variables such as the type of industry within which the entity operates, the cost of funds in the market, the availability of investment opportunities and the extent to which the company can continue to benefit from the 'tax shield'.

The ordinary share price of highly geared entities will tend to be depressed in times of rising interest rates.

3 Traditional view

According to the 'traditional' view of gearing and the cost of capital, as an organisation introduces debt into its capital structure the weighted average cost of capital will fall because initially the benefit of cheap debt finance more than outweighs any increases in the cost of equity required to compensate equity holders for higher financial risk.

As gearing continues to increase the equity holders will ask for increasingly higher returns. The cost of equity therefore rises as gearing increases. Eventually this increase in the cost of equity will start to outweigh the benefit of cheap debt finance, and the weighted average cost of capital will rise. At extreme levels of gearing the cost of debt will also start to rise (as debt holders become worried about the security of their loans) and this will also contribute to an increasing weighted average cost of capital.

The diagram below demonstrates this position in which:

- k_e is the cost of equity;

- k_d is the cost of debt;

- k_o is the overall or weighted average cost of capital.

Traditional view of gearing and the cost of capital

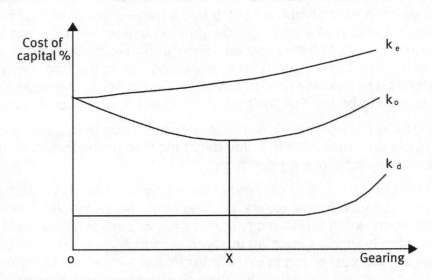

X = optimal level of gearing, where ko is at a minimum.

The traditional view therefore claims that there is an optimal capital structure where the weighted average cost of capital is at a minimum. This is at point X in the above diagram.

At point X the overall return required by investors (debt and equity) is minimised.

It follows that at this point the combined market value of the entity's debt and equity securities will also be maximised (because the value of the entity's debt and equity and the WACC are inversely related – discounting the future operating cash flows at a lower cost of capital will give a higher value.)

Optimal capital structure

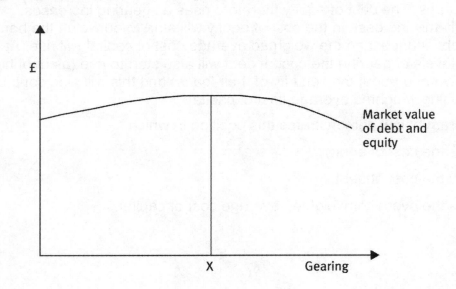

4   Capital structure: Modigliani and Miller's view

In 1958, the two American economists, Professors Modigliani and Miller, challenged the traditional view of gearing and the cost of capital. Over a 20-year period they put forward a number of propositions as to why the traditional view of gearing might be wrong.

They began by assuming that the effect of tax relief on debt interest could be ignored.

Modigliani and Miller without tax (1958)

The 1958 proposition was that companies which operate in the same type of business and which have similar operating risks must have the same total value, irrespective of their capital structures.

Their view is based on the belief that the value of a company depends solely upon the future post tax (pre financing) operating income generated by its assets.

The way in which the funding is split between debt and equity should make no difference to the total value of the company (equity plus debt). In fact, one of M & M's assumptions is that the investors are indifferent between personal and corporate gearing.

Thus, the total value of the company will not change with gearing. This means that its weighted average cost of capital will not change with gearing, and will be the same at all levels of gearing.

Their view is represented in the following diagrams.

Modigliani and Miller view (no taxation)

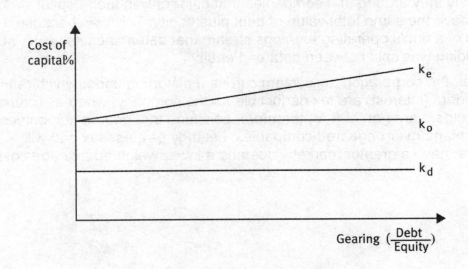

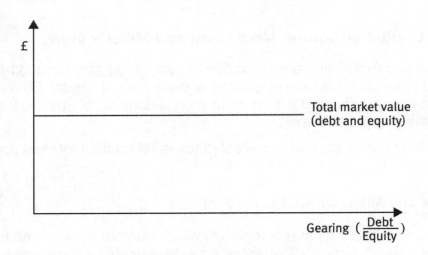

If the weighted average cost of capital is to remain constant at all levels of gearing, it follows that any benefit from the increased proportion of cheaper debt finance (downward force on the WACC) must be exactly offset by the increase in the cost of equity (upward force on the WACC).

The essential point made by M & M is that, ignoring taxation, a company should be indifferent between all possible capital structures. This is at odds with the beliefs of the traditionalists.

M & M support their case by demonstrating that market pressures will ensure that two companies identical in every aspect apart from their gearing level will have the same overall market value.

Modigliani and Miller with tax (1963)

In 1963, M & M amended their model to include the impact of corporation tax. This alteration changes the results of their analysis significantly.

Previously they argued that companies that differ only in their capital structure should have the same total value of debt plus equity. This was because it was the size of a firm's operating earnings stream that determines its value, not the way funding was split between debt and equity.

However, the corporation tax system carries a distortion under which returns to debt holders (interest) are tax deductible for the company, whereas returns to equity holders are not. M & M, therefore, conclude that geared companies have an advantage over ungeared companies, i.e. they pay less tax and will, therefore, have a greater market value and a lower weighted average cost of capital.

Graph of M & M model with tax

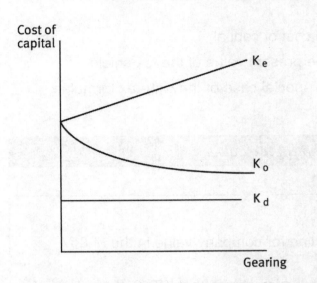

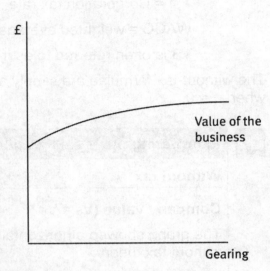

As gearing increases, the WACC steadily decreases, and hence the value of the company (debt plus equity) increases.

In the presence of tax, the downward force on the WACC (the impact of the greater proportion of debt finance) is stronger than the upward force (the increase in cost of equity).

If the other implications of the M & M view are accepted, the introduction of taxation suggests that the higher the level of taxation, the lower the combined cost of capital.

 ## Modigliani and Miller (M & M) formulae

M & M developed the following formulae that can be applied to finding the value, cost of equity or WACC of companies that have a given level of business risk, but changing capital structure.

	With tax
Value of the company (debt+equity)	$V_g = V_u + TB$
Cost of equity	$k_{eg} = k_{eu} + (k_{eu} - k_d) V_D(1 - t) / V_E$
WACC	$k_{adj} = k_{eu} [1 - (V_D t / (V_E + V_D))]$

where V = Value of company (V_g = value of geared company, V_u = value of ungeared company)

k_e = Cost of equity (k_{eg} = cost of equity in geared co, k_{eu} = cost of equity in ungeared co)

k_d = Cost of debt (must be gross of tax)

k_{adj} = the weighted average cost of capital in a geared company

B, V_D = MV of debt

V_E = MV of geared company's equity

T, t = Corporation tax rate

WACC = weighted average cost of capital

TB is often referred to as the present value of the tax shield

The without-tax formulae are simply a special case of the with-tax formulae, where t = 0.

Interpreting the M & M graphs and formulae

Without tax

Company value ($V_g = V_u$)

The graph showed a horizontal line for company value in the M & M without tax theory.

This is backed up by the formula, which shows that if T=0, the values of an ungeared company and an equivalent ungeared company are the same.

WACC ($k_{adj} = k_{eu}$)

The graph also showed a horizontal line for WACC in the M & M without tax theory.

Again, the formula backs this up. If t=0, the formula reduces to $k_{adj} = k_{eu}$. This shows that the WACC of the geared company is always the same as the WACC of an equivalent ungeared company, irrespective of the level of gearing.

With tax

Company value ($V_g = V_u + TB$)

The graph showed an upward sloping line for company value in the M & M with tax theory.

This is backed up by the formula, which shows that the higher the value of B (value of debt), the greater the value of the entire company should be.

As the company increases its gearing, the value of the entire company (debt plus equity) increases.

Cost of equity ($k_{eg} = k_{eu} + (k_{eu} - k_d) V_D (1 - t) / V_E$)

The cost of equity slopes upwards as gearing increases under M & M's assumptions, because shareholders face higher risk so demand higher returns.

We can see from the formula that the k_{eg} increases as the amount of debt (V_D) increases relative to the value of equity (V_E).

Note that the inclusion of $(1 - t)$ in the formula has the impact of reducing the slope of the line if the tax rate increases. Most importantly, this means that the cost of equity in the M & M with tax theory will always increase less steeply than in the without tax theory. This helps to explain why the upward force on WACC is smaller in the with tax theory, and hence why the downward force on the WACC caused by the (net of tax) cheap debt finance is the net stronger force in the with tax theory.

WACC $[k_{adj} = k_{eu} (1 - V_D t / (V_E + V_D))]$

The formula shows that WACC will reduce as gearing (measured by debt divided by (debt + equity)) increases. This is seen on the graph as a downward sloping line.

Test your understanding 1 (Integration question) – no tax

X Co is identical in all operating and risk characteristics to Y Co, except that X Co is all equity financed and Y Co is financed by equity valued at $2.1m and debt valued at $0.9m based on market values. **X Co and Y Co operate in a country where no tax is payable.**

The interest paid on Y Co's debt is $72,000 per annum, and it pays a dividend to shareholders of $378,000 per annum. X Co pays an annual dividend of $450,000.

Required:

(a)   Calculate the value of X Co.

(b)   Calculate the cost of capital for X Co.

(c)   Calculate the cost of equity for Y Co, and the cost of debt for Y Co.

(d)   Calculate the weighted average cost of capital for Y Co.

Test your understanding 2 (Integration question) – with tax

X Co is identical in all operating and risk characteristics to Y Co, except that X Co is financed only by equity valued at $3m whereas Y Co has debt valued at $0.9m (based on market value) as part of its capital structure. **X Co and Y Co operate in a country where tax is payable at 33%.**

The interest paid on Y Co's debt is $72,000 per annum, and it pays a dividend to shareholders of $401,760 per annum. X Co pays an annual dividend of $450,000.

Required:

(a)   Calculate the value of the equity of Y Co.

(b)   Calculate the cost of capital for X Co.

(c)   Calculate the cost of equity for Y Co, and the cost of debt for Y Co.

(d)   Calculate the weighted average cost of capital for Y Co.

M & M's assumptions

- There exists a perfect capital market in which there are no information costs or transaction costs.

- Debt is risk free and k_d remains constant at all levels of gearing.

- Investors are indifferent between personal and corporate gearing.

- Investors and companies can borrow at the same rate of interest.

M & M's key belief was that the market would not reward companies for something that could be achieved at zero cost and zero risk. If the market believes that a company has made too little use of gearing, then investors can correct that by borrowing, and using the borrowed funds to buy more shares. This would give exactly the same effect as the company borrowing more, but only if the assumptions listed above are valid.

 5   Capital structure in the real world

Introduction

We need to adjust M & M's theories to also take into account real life factors.

The most unrealistic of M & M's key assumptions is that debt is risk free.

In reality, there is a greater risk to both the lenders and shareholders with very high levels of gearing. This is the risk that the company is unable to service the debt and end up in financial distress or even insolvent.

In reality, lenders will ask for higher interest if they perceive that there is a greater risk of default.

Practical considerations

This then leaves the problem of how companies determine their capital structures in the real world.

The main practical considerations are:

- The company's ability to borrow money (the company's 'debt capacity')

- Existing debt covenants

- Increasing costs of debt finance as gearing rises

- Views of other stakeholders and rating agencies

- Tax exhaustion

More detail on practical considerations

The company's ability to borrow money (the company's 'debt capacity')

- The maximum level of borrowing that a company can comfortably support is referred to as its debt capacity. (**Definition** of debt capacity from CIMA Official Terminology, 2005 is the "extent to which an entity can support and/or obtain loan finance.")

- A company can only increase its gearing if it can find a lender who will provide it with debt finance. In recessionary times, this should not be taken for granted.

- A company's capacity to borrow is increased if it is able to offer good quality, valuable assets as collateral.

- Debt capacity is function of a company's credit-worthiness (introduced in an earlier chapter) and credit scoring. (**Definition** of credit scoring from CIMA Official Terminology, 2005 is the "assessment of the credit-worthiness of an individual or company by rating numerically a number of both financial and non-financial aspects of the target's present position and performance.")

Existing debt covenants

- Debt covenants reduce the flexibility of management. Existing debt covenants may even prevent the company from borrowing more.

- Management must keep the company well within the terms of the existing covenants (keeping plenty of 'leeway' or 'headroom') to ensure that the flexibility of the company is maximised.

Increasing costs of debt finance as gearing rises

- M & M assumed that debt was risk free, and that kd would be constant at all levels of gearing. In reality, an increased level of gearing is likely to be perceived as risky by lenders, so the interest rates on borrowings generally increase as gearing increases.

Views of other stakeholders and rating agencies

- The gearing theories focus on the position of the shareholders and the lenders at different levels of gearing. In reality, the views of other stakeholders should also be considered. In particular, many stakeholders perceive high levels of gearing to be risky. This could impact on the credit score or credit worthiness of the company. A reduction in credit worthiness may be evidenced by a credit rating downgrade by one of the credit rating agencies.

- For example,
  - customers may be concerned about buying goods from companies that have poor credit worthiness (due to concerns about warranties and guarantees being honoured)
  - suppliers might not want to supply, or advance credit (due to the risk of default)
  - employees and managers might choose to leave if they fear for their job security.
- All these factors will damage the company's prospects and reputation.

Tax exhaustion

- M & M's with tax theory suggests that the benefits of tax relief on debt interest will help to reduce the company's cost of capital at all levels of gearing. This is not the case in practice.

- At some level of gearing the interest payable will be so high that taxable profit will be reduced to zero. Beyond this point, there will be no further benefit of raising debt finance.

- However, in order for tax exhaustion to apply, the company must be making a loss and will have breached any interest cover covenants. The company is therefore likely to have much greater problems to contend with than the loss of tax relief.

6 The impact on financial ratios of a change in capital structure

When an entity changes its financing (capital structure), there will be an impact on ratio analysis (especially the gearing ratio).

The impact of a change in financing on ratio analysis – the gearing ratio

The two key measures of gearing are:

$$\text{Capital gearing} = \frac{\text{Debt}}{\text{Debt + Equity}} \times 100$$

$$\text{OR} \quad \frac{\text{Debt}}{\text{Equity}} \times 100$$

Note: Both of these measures are used in practice, but the first one is more commonly used.

Clearly if an entity changes its capital structure by raising new finance as either debt or equity, these gearing ratios will change.

Exam questions often test the calculation of gearing ratios before and after a change in capital structure.

Test your understanding 3 (Objective test question)

Statement of financial position for X Co

	USDm
Non-current assets (total)	23.0
Current assets (total)	15.0
TOTAL ASSETS	**38.0**
Equity and Liabilities	
Ordinary share capital	10.0
Ordinary share premium	4.0
Preference share capital (irredeemable)	1.5
Reserves	1.5
Non-current liabilities	
10% bonds	8.0
Current liabilities	
Trade creditors	8.0
Bank overdraft	5.0
TOTAL EQUITY & LIABILITIES	**38.0**

X Co statement of profit or loss extract

	USDm
Operating profit (PBIT)	4.0
Finance Charges	(1.0)
Profit before tax (PBT)	3.0
Tax @ 30%	(0.9)
Net profit	2.1

X Co is considering raising additional debt finance of USD 6m. The interest rate on the new debt will be 12% per annum. Operating profit is expected to stay constant after the new finance has been raised.

What will be the interest cover and the capital gearing ratio (measured as debt / (debt + equity) at book value, and including the bank overdraft as part of debt) for X Co after the new finance has been raised?

A   Interest cover 2.33, gearing 52.8%

B   Interest cover 2.33, gearing 56.9%

C   Interest cover 1.22, gearing 52.8%

D   Interest cover 1.22, gearing 56.9%

Illustration 1 – More complex gearing ratio calculation

PPP is considering raising $250 million new finance to fund the acquisition of QQQ. QQQ is considered to have a value to PPP of $270 million.

Extracts from PPP's statement of financial position show:

	$m
Long term borrowings	950
Share capital ($1 shares)	500
Retained reserves	400

The directors of PPP haven't yet decided whether debt or equity finance should be used to fund the takeover. However, if equity is to be used, the new shares will be issued at a price of $2.60 per share. The current market share price is $2.90 per share.

Required:

Calculate the gearing ratio measured as (debt/(debt + equity)):

(a) before the acquisition of QQQ,

(b) after the acquisition, assuming that debt finance is used to fund the takeover,

(c) after the acquisition, assuming that equity finance is used to fund the takeover.

In all cases, present your calculations using both book values and market values.

Solution:

Gearing based on book values

Pre-acquisition	950/[950 + (500 + 400)] = **51.4%**
Post-acquisition – using debt	(950 + 250)/[(950 + 250) + (500 + 400 + 20 (W1))] = **56.6%**
Post-acquisition – using equity	950/[950 + (500 + 400 + 250 + 20 (W1))] = **44.8%**

(W1) Since QQQ is worth $270m to PPP but the purchase price is $250m, the value of PPP's equity will increase by $20m irrespective of how the purchase is financed.

> ### Gearing based on market values (W2)
>
> | | |
> |---|---|
> | Pre-acquisition | 950/[950 + 1,450] = **39.6%** |
> | Post-acquisition – using debt | (950 + 250)/[(950 + 250) + (1,450 + 20)] = **44.9%** |
> | Post-acquisition – using equity | 950/[950 + (1,450 + 250 + 20)] = **35.6%** |
>
> **(W2)** Market value of existing shares = $2.90 × 500m = $1,450m
>
> **Note:** The issue price of the new shares ($2.60) is irrelevant when calculating the gearing ratios. Of course the issue price does affect the number of shares issued and therefore other ratios such as EPS (see further examples below), but gearing ratios are calculated based on total values of equity and debt so the issue price is not relevant here.

Debt covenants

A useful application of the impact of financing decisions on ratio analysis is in the context of debt covenants.

For example, the gearing ratio is often used in debt covenants – an entity might have to keep its gearing ratio below a given percentage to comply with its debt covenants.

If you are asked in the exam to assess the impact of a decision on a given debt covenant, you should calculate the necessary ratio assuming the decision has been made and then compare the result to the given target.

For example, if the covenant requires that gearing should not exceed 30% (measured as (debt/(debt + equity))) you should calculate the ratio (assuming the decision has been made) using the formula given, and see if the result remains below 30%.

Test your understanding 4 (Objective test question)

Grass Co has a debt covenant that requires its gearing ratio (measured as debt/(debt + equity) using book values) to be less than 50%, and its interest cover to be greater than 2.

Extracts from its recent financial statements show that it has 100,000 $1 shares in issue and it has a 10% interest bank borrowing of $60,000. It made a profit before interest and tax last year of $15,000, and overall accumulated retained earnings are $25,000.

The current share price is $1.40 per share.

The directors of Grass Co are considering borrowing an extra $20,000 from the bank as a secured borrowing at an interest rate of 6% per annum.

Annual profits are expected to stay constant, but the share price is expected to fall to $1.35 per share to reflect the shareholders' perception of increased financial risk.

Assuming the new finance is raised, which of the following shows Grass Co's position with regard to its debt covenant:

A   Gearing: MET, Interest cover: MET

B   Gearing: FAILED, Interest cover: MET

C   Gearing: FAILED, Interest cover: FAILED

D   Gearing: MET, Interest cover: FAILED

7   Structuring the debt/equity profile of group companies

Introduction

Individual companies and groups of companies both have to decide on an appropriate capital structure by considering the various theoretical and practical points covered earlier in this chapter.

However, there are additional considerations for groups of companies.

General considerations for groups of companies

Tax issues

Within a group of companies, it makes sense to maximise borrowings in regimes with the highest tax rate, to increase the amount of tax relief available. Tax relief can be limited though, by transfer pricing issues and by thin capitalisation rules – see below for details.

Country risk

There will be less exposure to risk if an entity borrows funds in the country where it generates its net income. Any servicing costs for the finance can then be paid out of the income generated without worrying about exchange rate movements.

Type of finance provided by the parent

Note that if debt and equity are both supplied by the parent company, the choice between debt and equity finance for a subsidiary has no cash implications in the context of groups, unlike the situation for a single company.

This is because both are financed in cash by the parent and therefore can be funded by the parent by either debt or equity.

The choice of capital structure for a subsidiary is therefore independent of the decision regarding the appropriate group capital structure.

Transfer pricing

Transfer pricing adjustments may be necessary for transactions between connected companies, to ensure that companies cannot reduce their tax liabilities by using a transfer price that is below or above an arm's length price.

In the context of capital structure, this means that if one company in a group has borrowed money from another company in a group, an adjustment will be necessary if it is deemed that the interest rate charged is not set at a market rate.

Illustration 2 (Objective test question)

Vulture Co is a wholly owned subsidiary of Red Co.

It has borrowed $100,000 from Red Co, at an annual interest rate of 2%. The market rate of interest is 5% per annum.

What is the annual interest payment from Vulture Co to Red Co, and what is the adjustment needed for tax purposes?

A   Interest $5,000, tax purposes adjustment $3,000

B   Interest $2,000, tax purposes adjustment $3,000

C   Interest $5,000, tax purposes adjustment $2,000

D   Interest $2,000, tax purposes adjustment $5,000

Solution:

The answer is (B).

Annual interest payment = $100,000 × 2% = $2,000

However, at market rate of interest (5%) the interest paid would have been $100,000 × 5% = $5,000.

Therefore an adjustment of $3,000 (5,000 – 2,000) will be made to Vulture Co and Red Co's accounts for tax purposes. Vulture Co will reduce its profits for tax purposes and Red Co will increase its profits by the same amount.

Thin capitalisation rules

When a company pays a dividend, there is no tax relief for the payment. When it pays interest on borrowings, the interest is tax allowable. This means that companies would prefer to be financed through borrowings (debt) rather than through shares (equity).

The thin capitalisation rules aim to stop companies from getting excessive tax relief on interest.

This occurs (usually) because they have entered into a borrowing with a related party that exceeds the amount a third party lender would be prepared to lend. (Note that the additional borrowing is most likely to be provided by the parent company within a group structure.)

The rules ensure that

- interest on the part of the borrowing that an independent third party would be prepared to lend the company is allowable

- the excess is disallowed

- the borrowing capacity of the individual company and its subsidiaries is considered (but not the rest of the group).

Factors determining thin capitalisation

The tax authorities will usually look at two areas to determine whether they believe a company is thinly capitalised:

- *Gearing*

    - This is measured as the ratio of debt to equity.

    - A higher proportion of debt could cause thin capitalisation problems.

    - In the UK a limit of around 50:50 is considered by the tax authorities to be reasonable.

- *Interest cover*

    - This is the ratio of earnings before tax and interest to interest on borrowings.

    - It measures how risky the loan is for the lender.

    - Many commercial lenders will look for a ratio of around 3, so this is the figure considered by the tax authorities to be reasonable.

Illustration 3 (Integration question)

Archer plc is UK company, which is a wholly owned subsidiary of Berry Inc, a company resident in Babylonia.

Archer borrows GBP100,000 from Berry Inc paying a market rate of interest of 8%. Archer had to borrow from Berry Inc as its UK bankers were not prepared to lend it more than GBP60,000.

Required:

Advise Archer plc of how much interest on borrowings it is likely to have relieved for tax purposes.

Solution:

A third party was only prepared to lend Archer plc GBP60,000.

As it has borrowed GBP100,000 from its parent company, it is likely that interest on the excess GBP40,000 will be disallowed for tax purposes.

Therefore, of the GBP8,000 interest Archer plc pays to Berry Inc, only GBP4,800 is likely to be allowed for tax.

Test your understanding 5 (Integration question)

Eagle Co is a wholly owned subsidiary of White Co.

Extracts from Eagle Co's financial statements for the last accounting period are shown below:

	$m
Share capital	10.0
Reserves	15.6
Bank borrowing	8.5
Borrowing from parent company	20.0

The annual interest rate payable on both the bank borrowing and the borrowing from the parent company is 4%. The borrowing from the parent company was 25% more than Eagle Co could have raised from the bank at that time.

The tax authorities consider a company to be thinly capitalised if its gearing ratio (debt : equity) is above 50:50.

Required:

Calculate the amount of Eagle Co's interest payable on the parent company borrowing that will be allowable for tax relief.

8 End of chapter objective test questions

Test your understanding 6 (Objective test question)

Modigliani and Miller's 1958 'without tax' gearing theory concludes that:

A   There is an optimum gearing level at which the value of the company is minimised

B   There is an optimum gearing level at which the value of the company is maximised

C   The value of the company is unaffected by the gearing level

D   The value of the company reduces as the gearing level increases

E   The value of the company increases as the gearing level increases

Test your understanding 7 (Objective test question)

A company has:

- Current cost of equity of 12%
- Ungeared cost of equity of 10%
- WACC of 9.25%
- Market value of equity of $210 million
- Market value of debt of $70 million
- Tax rate of 30%

The company plans to raise $20 million of debt and use these funds to repurchase shares.

According to Modigliani and Miller's theory with tax, WACC would move to:

A   8.62%

B   10.35%

C   9.06%

D   10.87%

Test your understanding 8 (Objective test question)

The traditional view of gearing concludes that:

A   There is an optimum gearing level at which the cost of capital is minimised

B   There is an optimum gearing level at which the cost of capital is maximised

C   The cost of capital continually reduces as the gearing level increases

D   The cost of capital continually increases as the gearing level increases

E   The cost of capital is unaffected by the gearing level

Test your understanding 9 (Objective test question)

Ghost Co's most recent statement of financial position shows long term borrowings of $12.4 million, share capital ($1 shares) of $6.8 million and accumulated reserves of $5.2 million.

Ghost Co is considering raising $4 million of new long term debt finance to fund the acquisition of Face Co.

Face Co is considered to have a value to Ghost Co of $4.5 million. The current market share price for Ghost Co is $2.90 per share.

What will be the gearing ratio – measured as (debt/(debt + equity)) at book value – after the acquisition?

A   69.2%

B   59.2%

C   56.7%

D   49.8%

Test your understanding 10 (Objective test question)

Until recently, VV was an ungeared company with a cost of equity of 13%. It recently issued some debt finance and its cost of equity increased to 14%.

If VV pays tax at a rate of 20%, and if the yield required by VV's lenders is 8%, what is the gearing level (measured as (debt/equity)) of VV according to Modigliani and Miller's theory with tax:

A   0.25

B   0.20

C   0.33

D   0.30

Test your understanding 11 (Objective test question)

BB is an all-equity financed company with a cost of equity of 10%.

The directors of BB are proposing to raise $200 million to invest in a new project. This investment will carry similar risk to BB's current business. It is proposed that the investment will be financed by either

- a rights issue of shares, or

- an issue of an undated bond carrying 5% interest pre-tax (this rate is deemed to reflect the returns required by the market for the risk and duration of the bond).

Earnings before interest and tax for BB are forecast to be $100 million in the first year after the new investment. Subsequently, earnings are expected to remain at a constant level each year. The corporate income tax rate is 20%. This is not expected to change.

According to Modigliani and Miller's theory with tax, BB's value if it issues the bond and undertakes this project will be:

A $ 840 million

B $1,000 million

C $1,040 million

D $1,200 million

Test your understanding 12 (Objective test question)

Which THREE of the following are key assumptions of Modigliani and Miller's 1963 gearing theory?

A   The capital market is strongly efficient

B   Debt is risk free

C   Cost of equity stays constant at all levels of gearing

D   Companies do not pay tax

E   Investors and companies can borrow at the same rate of interest

Test your understanding 13 (Objective test question)

The following information relates to Present Co, a geared company that pays tax at 25%:

- Current cost of equity 14%
- Ungeared cost of equity 12%
- WACC 11.4%

Market value of equity is $400 million and market value of debt is $100 million. Present Co plans to raise $50 million of debt and use these funds to repurchase shares.

According to Modigliani and Miller's theory with tax, WACC would move to:

A   12.55%

B   10.76%

C   12.98%

D   11.12%

Test your understanding 14 (Objective test question)

Modigliani and Miller's 1963 Theory of Capital Structure with Tax assumes that

A   The cost of equity remains constant regardless of gearing level

B   A company is liable to tax, but not its shareholders

C   Companies can borrow at zero cost

D   Financial distress does not carry any cost

Test your understanding 15 (Objective test question)

Which THREE of the following reasons are most likely to result in an entity using equity (rather than debt) finance to fund a new investment project?

A   the project is a short-term project

B   the entity has a very low level of gearing

C   the banks are unwilling to lend, having just downgraded the entity's credit rating

D   the project's cash flows are likely to be variable, and might even be negative in the first year

E   the entity is a service business with very few tangible assets

9 End of chapter case style questions

Test your understanding 16 (Case style question)

The finance director of Netra plc, a company listed on the UK's AIM (Alternative Investment Market), wishes to estimate what impact the introduction of debt finance is likely to have on the company's overall cost of capital. The company is currently financed only by equity.

Netra plc Summarised capital structure

	£000
Ordinary shares (25 pence par value)	500
Reserves	1,100
	1,600

The company's current share price is 420 pence, and up to £4 million of fixed rate irredeemable debt could be raised at an interest rate of 10% per annum. The corporate tax rate is 33%.

Netra's current earnings before interest and tax are £2.5 million. These earnings are not expected to change significantly for the foreseeable future.

The company is considering raising either:

(i)   £2 million in debt finance;

(ii)   £4 million in debt finance

In either case the debt finance will be used to repurchase ordinary shares.

Required:

(a)   Using Miller and Modigliani's model in a world with corporate tax, estimate the impact on Netra's cost of capital of raising:

(i)   £2 million; and

(ii)   £4 million in debt finance.

State clearly any assumptions that you make.

(b)   Briefly discuss whether or not the estimates produced in part (a) are likely to be accurate.   **(30 minutes)**

Test your understanding 17 (Case style question)

Canalot Co is an all equity company with an equilibrium market value of GBP32.5 million and a cost of capital of 18% per year.

The company proposes to re-purchase GBP5 million of equity and to replace it with 13% irredeemable bonds.

Canalot's earnings before interest and tax are expected to be constant for the foreseeable future. Corporate tax is at the rate of 35%. All profits are paid out as dividends.

Required:

Explain and demonstrate how this change in capital structure will affect:

1   the market value;

2   the cost of equity; and

3   the cost of capital

of Canalot Co, using the assumptions of Modigliani and Miller.

(15 minutes)

Explain any weaknesses of both the traditional and Modigliani and Miller theories and discuss how useful they might be in the determination of the appropriate capital structure for a company.

(15 minutes)

Test your understanding answers

Test your understanding 1 (Integration question) – no tax

(a) $V_g = V_u + TB$

so given that T = 0,

$V_g = V_u$

so the value of X Co is the same as the value of Y Co, ($2.1m + $0.9m) $3m

(b) Assuming no growth in dividends, using the dividend valuation model,

k_{eu} = Dividend/V_E = 450,000/3,000,000 = 15%

(c) **Cost of debt for Y Co** (assuming debt is irredeemable)

k_d = Interest/V_D = 72,000/900,000 = 8%

Cost of equity for Y Co:

Using M & M's formula:

$k_{eg} = k_{eu} + (k_{eu} - k_d) V_D(1 - t)/V_E$

k_{eg} = 15% + (15% – 8%) × 0.9/2.1 = 18%

(Alternatively, using the dividend valuation model,

k_{eg} = Dividend/V_E = 378,000/2,100,000 = 18%)

As shown on the graphs, the geared company has a higher cost of equity.

(d) Weighted average cost of capital:

WACC = (18% × 2.1/3) + (8% × 0.9 /3) = 15%

Again, notice that this corresponds to the graphs seen above. In the no tax case, the WACC is constant irrespective of capital structure.

Test your understanding 2 (Integration question) – with tax

(a) $V_g = V_u + TB$

so given that T = 0.33,

V_g = 3,000,000 + (33% × 900,000) = $3,297,000

so the value of the equity = 3,297,000 – 900,000 (value of debt) = $2,397,000

(b) Assuming no growth in dividends, using the dividend valuation model,

k_{eu} = Dividend/V_E = 450,000/3,000,000 = 15%

(c) **Cost of debt for Y Co** (assuming debt is irredeemable)

k_d = Interest/V_D = 72,000/900,000 = 8%

Cost of equity for Y Co:

Using M & M's formula:

$k_{eg} = k_{eu} + (k_{eu} - k_d)\,V_D(1 - t)/V_E$

k_{eg} = 15% + (15% − 8%) × 900,000 × (1 − 0.33)/2,397,000 = 16.76%

As shown on the graphs, the geared company has a higher cost of equity.

(d) Weighted average cost of capital:

WACC = (16.76% × 2,397/3,297) + (8% × (1 − 0.33) 900/3,297) = 13.65%

Alternatively, using M & M's formula:

$k_{adj} = k_{eu}\,(1 - tL)$ = 15% (1 − 33% × 900/3,297) = 13.65%

Again, notice that this corresponds to the graphs seen above. In the with tax case, the WACC reduces as the level of debt in the capital structure increases.

Test your understanding 3 (Objective test question)

The answer is (A).

Interest cover = 4m/(1m + (12% × 6m)) = 2.33 times

Capital gearing ratio

Debt	=	5m + 8m + 6m	= USD19m
Equity	=	10m + 4m + 1.5m + 1.5m	= USD17m
D/(D+E)	=	19m/(19m + 17m) × 100	= 52.8%

Test your understanding 4 (Objective test question)

The answer is (A). Both covenant terms will still be met after the finance is raised.

Before the finance is raised:

Gearing (BOOK VALUES) = 60,000/(60,000 + (100,000 + 25,000)) = 32%

Interest cover = 15,000/(10% × 60,000) = 2.5

After the finance is raised:

Gearing (BOOK VALUES) = (60,000 + 20,000)/(60,000 + 20,000 + (100,000 + 25,000)) = 39%

Interest cover = 15,000/[(10% × 60,000) + (6% × 20,000)] = 2.1

Test your understanding 5 (Integration question)

Interest payable on the parent company borrowing and charged through the accounts is ($20m × 4%) = $0.8m

Current gearing (debt : equity) is (20m + 8.5m)/(10.0m + 15.6m) i.e. $28.5m/$25.6m

Accordingly the company is considered to be too thinly capitalised by the tax authorities, and the thin capitalisation rules apply.

The amount of interest on the parent company borrowing disallowed for tax purposes will be ($20m × 25/125 × 4%) = $0.16m

Therefore the amount of interest on the parent company borrowing that is tax allowable is (0.8m − 0.16m) = $0.64m

Test your understanding 6 (Objective test question)

The answer is (C).

Modigliani and Miller's 1958 gearing theory is the 'no tax' theory. It concludes that the value of the company is unaffected by the gearing level.

Test your understanding 7 (Objective test question)

The answer is (C).

WACC = k_{eu} (1 − tL)

where k_{eu} is given as 10%, t is 30% and L is the gearing level measured as (debt/debt+equity)).

Gearing working:

The value of the company was $280 million (210 equity and 70 debt).

Therefore, using the equation $V_g = V_u + TB$,

280 = V_u + (30% × 70)

so V_u = $259 million

Hence, with the new gearing level,

V_g = 259 + (30% × 90) = $286 million

and therefore, WACC = 0.10 × [1 − (30% × 90/286)] = 9.06%

Test your understanding 8 (Objective test question)

The answer is (A).

The traditional view of gearing concludes that the cost of capital follows a U shaped curve, and therefore that there is an optimum gearing level at which the cost of capital is minimised.

Test your understanding 9 (Objective test question)

The answer is (C).

Debt will rise to $12.4m + $4m = $16.4m.

Equity will rise (because of the extra value generated by the takeover) to $6.8m + $5.2m + $0.5m = $12.5m

Therefore, $[D/(D+E)] = 16.4/(16.4 + 12.5) = 56.7\%$

Test your understanding 10 (Objective test question)

The answer is (A).

M & M's formula is:

$k_{eg} = k_{eu} + (k_{eu} - k_d)\, V_D(1 - t)/V_E$

where k_d is the yield to the debt holders. Plugging the given numbers in shows:

$0.14 = 0.13 + [(0.13-0.08)\, VD(1 - 0.20)/V_E]$

So rearranging the equation gives $V_D/V_E = 0.25$

Test your understanding 11 (Objective test question)

The answer is (A).

Modigliani and Miller's formula is:

$V_g = V_u + TB$

Therefore, the value of the company if it funds the project using the bond is V_u (the value if the company continued to be all equity financed) plus 20% × $200 million (i.e. $40 million).

V_u can be found by discounting the earnings figure as a perpetuity.

So $V_u = \$100m\ (1 - 0.20)/0.10 = \$800$ million

Therefore, $V_g = \$800$ million $+ \$40$ million $= \$840$ million

Test your understanding 12 (Objective test question)

The answer is (A), (B) and (E).

The key assumptions of Modigliani and Miller's 1963 gearing theory are:

- Companies do pay tax
- The capital market is strongly efficient
- There are no transaction costs
- Debt is risk free
- Cost of debt stays constant at all levels of gearing
- Investors are indifferent between personal and corporate gearing
- Investors and companies can borrow at the same rate of interest

So the correct three points were (A), (B) and (E) (i.e. the capital market is strongly efficient, debt is risk free and investors and companies can borrow at the same rate of interest).

Test your understanding 13 (Objective test question)

The answer is (D).

$$\text{WACC} = k_{eu} (1 - tL)$$

where k_{eu} is given as 12%, t is 25% and L is the gearing level measured as (debt/debt+equity)).

Gearing working:

The value of the company was $500 million (400 equity and 100 debt). Therefore, using the equation $V_g = V_u + TB$,

$500 = V_u + (25\% \times 100)$

so $V_u = \$475$ million

Hence, with the new gearing level,

$V_g = 475 + (25\% \times 150) = \$512.5$ million

and therefore, WACC $= 0.12 \times [1 - (25\% \times 150/512.5)] = 11.12\%$

Test your understanding 14 (Objective test question)

The answer is (D).

Under M & M's theory, the cost of equity rises as gearing increases (A) and the risk of debt is nil so companies can borrow at low cost (but not zero cost) (C).

Both shareholders and companies are assumed to pay tax in the 1963 theory (B).

In their 1963 theory, M & M assumed that there were no costs to financial distress and liquidation (D).

Test your understanding 15 (Objective test question)

The answer is (C), (D) and (E).

Short term projects (A) should not be funded by long term equity finance.

A low level of gearing would generally mean that the entity is not fully benefitting from the tax advantages of debt finance (B).

Few tangible assets (E) and a poor credit rating (C) would make raising debt finance more difficult. For a project with variable cash flows (D), the necessity of making interest payments each year could cause financial distress.

Test your understanding 16 (Case style question)

(a) Assuming that all earnings are paid out as dividends, the current cost of equity (and overall cost of capital) is total earnings divided by the market value of the company's shares:

	£000
Earnings before finance charges and tax	2,500
Taxation	825
Earnings = dividends	1,675

The market value of equity is two million shares × 420 pence per share = £8.4 million.

$$K_e = \frac{£1,675,000}{£8,400,000} = 19.94\%$$

If equity is replaced by debt the value of the company will increase.

V geared = V ungeared + TB (tax rate × amount of debt)

With £2 million debt

V geared = 8,400 + (2,000 × 0.33) = 9,060.

	£000
Total value of the company	9,060
Market value of debt	2,000
Value of equity	7,060

With £4 million debt

V geared = 8,400 + (4,000 × 0.33) = 9,720

	£000
Total value of the company	9,720
Market value of debt	4,000
Value of equity	5,720

Cost of equity	£2 million debt	£4 million debt
	£000	£000
Earnings before f.charges and tax	2,500	2,500
Finance charges	(200)	(400)
	2,300	2,100
Taxation (33%)	(759)	(693)
Earnings/dividends	1,541	1,407
Cost of equity K_e =	1,541/7,060 = 21.83%	1,407/5,720 = 24.60%

WACC

£2 million debt:

$$WACC = 21.83 \times \frac{7,060}{9,060} + 10\,(1 - 0.33)\ \frac{2,000}{9,060} = 18.49\%$$

£4 million debt:

$$WACC = 24.60 \times \frac{5,720}{9,720} + 10\,(1 - 0.33)\ \frac{4,000}{9,720} = 17.23\%$$

Alternative method of calculation

Or alternatively using WACC = $K_{eu}\left(1 - \dfrac{D_t}{E + D}\right)$

£2 million debt:

WACC = $19.94\left(1 - \dfrac{2,000 \times 0.33}{7,060 + 2,000}\right)$ = 18.49%

£4 million debt:

WACC = $19.94\left(1 - \dfrac{4,000 \times 0.33}{5,720 + 4,000}\right)$ = 17.23%

The higher the level of gearing, the lower the cost of capital becomes, due to the benefit from tax relief on finance charges.

(b)   As debt is introduced into the capital structure it is likely that the cost of capital will initially fall. However, the estimates produced in (a) may not be accurate because:

(i)   They rely on the assumptions of the Modigliani and Miller (M & M) model, many of which are unrealistic such as the capital market is perfectly efficient, debt is risk free, information is costless and readily available, there are no transaction costs, investors are rational and make the same forecasts about the performance of companies, and investors and companies can borrow at the risk-free rate.

(ii)   Only corporate taxation is considered and not the impact of other forms of taxation including personal taxation.

(iii)   M & M assumed that debt is permanent.

(iv)   The estimates ignore possible costs that might be incurred as gearing increases, which would reduce share price and increase the cost of equity (and possibly debt). These include bankruptcy costs, agency costs and tax exhaustion.

(v)   Inaccuracies exist in the measurement of the data required for the model.

Test your understanding 17 (Case style question)

Answer to the first task:

Market value

Modigliani and Miller's hypothesis including the effects of corporation tax suggests that:

$$V_g = V_u + TB$$

Where V_g is the value of the geared company

V_u is the value of an equivalent ungeared company

B is the market value of debt

T is the rate of corporation tax

In the case of Canalot:

V_u = GBP32.5 million

B = GBP5 million

T= 35%

$\therefore V_g$ = 32.5m + 5m × 35% = GBP34.25m

The original value was GBP32.5 million.

This therefore represents an increase of GBP1.75 million.

Cost of equity

Modigliani and Miller propose the following formula for calculating the cost of equity of a geared company:

$$K_{eg} = K_{eu} + (K_{eu} - K_d) \times \frac{V_d(1-t)}{V_e}$$

Where K_{eg} is the cost of equity of the geared company

K_{eu} is the cost of equity of an equivalent ungeared company

K_d is the cost of debt before tax

V_d is the market value of debt

V_e is the market value of equity

t is the rate of corporation tax

K_{eu} = 18% (given)

K_d = 13%

V_d= 5m

$V_e = V_g - D$ = 34.25m – 5m = 29.25m

$$\therefore K_e = 18\% + (18\% - 13\%)\frac{5}{29.25} \times (1 - 0.35)$$

$$= 18.56\%.$$

The cost of equity has increased by 0.56%, reflecting the increase in financial risk as a result of gearing.

Cost of capital

Using Modigliani and Miller's formula:

$$WACC = K_{eu}\left[1 - \frac{D_t}{D + V_e}\right]$$

$$= 18\%\left[1 - \frac{5 \times 0.35}{34.25}\right]$$

$$= 17.08\%$$

Alternatively the traditional weighted average cost of capital formula may be used, i.e.

$$WACC = 18.56\% \times \frac{29.25}{34.25} + 13\%(1 - 0.35) \times \frac{5}{34.25}$$

$$= 17.08\%$$

The previous WACC was equal to Keu, i.e. 18%. It has therefore decreased by 0.92%, reflecting the tax benefits of increased gearing.

Answer to the second task:

The traditional view of capital structure theory is intuitive only; it is not based on any empirical evidence or computation and therein lies its major weakness.

It argues that there exists an optimal capital structure where the overall cost of capital is minimised and thus the company value is maximised. This is based on the following propositions:

- as gearing increases the cost of equity rises due to the increase in financial risk, but this is outweighed by the lower cost of debt and so the overall cost of capital decreases;

- as gearing continues to increase the cost of equity rises more sharply, such that this effect is greater than the effect of the lower cost of debt and the cost of capital rises;

- therefore there exists a minimum optimal cost of capital

The theory is useful in as much as it highlights the fact that financing and capital structure may affect a company's value but it gives no suggestion as to where that optimal level lies.

Modigliani and Miller's theory, however, was initially based on empirical evidence and followed by quantification. Their hypothesis which includes the effects of corporate taxes (an adjustment to their original model) suggests that the optimal capital structure comprises 99.9% debt. Since this policy is not adopted by companies there must be certain flaws in this theory, the most important of which was later corrected by Miller himself, i.e. the effect of personal taxes.

Other common criticisms of the model include the following:

- the use of unrealistic assumptions, for instance:
  - there are no transaction costs;
  - information is freely available;
  - individuals can borrow on the same terms as companies;
  - individuals are prepared to exchange personal gearing for corporate gearing;

- costs associated with high levels of gearing are not considered. These may include the following:

  1 **Bankruptcy costs**

     As gearing reaches high levels the probability of bankruptcy increases and if bankruptcy occurs there will be associated costs. These include the liquidation fees and the loss on the disposal of assets in a forced sales situation.

  2 **Tax exhaustion**

     The benefit derived from increasing the level of gearing relates to the tax relief obtained by companies on returns paid to debt, i.e. interest. However, at very high levels of gearing there is the possibility that the company will not have sufficient taxable profits from which to deduct the debt interest. In this situation the advantage of gearing up will be lost.

  3 **Agency costs**

     These relate to constraints imposed on the company by providers of finance through restrictive covenants contained within terms of agreement. Such constraints are aimed to protect the interest of (primarily) the debt holders when a company finds itself in a potentially difficult situation close to bankruptcy.

     As a result of the above and the effect of personal taxes, it is clear that benefits related to increased gearing do not continue indefinitely. The final position is not well defined, but it may be possible that there exists a point where the cost of capital is minimised before the additional costs of high gearing outweigh the benefits. Thus, if managers are able to quantify such costs and benefits, this adapted theory may be of use to them in identifying an appropriate level of gearing to adopt.

Dividend policy

Chapter learning objectives

Lead outcome	Component outcome
B4: Evaluate dividend policy	Evaluate policy in the following areas: (a) Cash dividends (b) Scrip dividends (c) Share repurchase programmes

Topics to be covered

- Features and criteria
- Impact on shareholder value and entity value, financial statements and performance

1 Overview of chapter

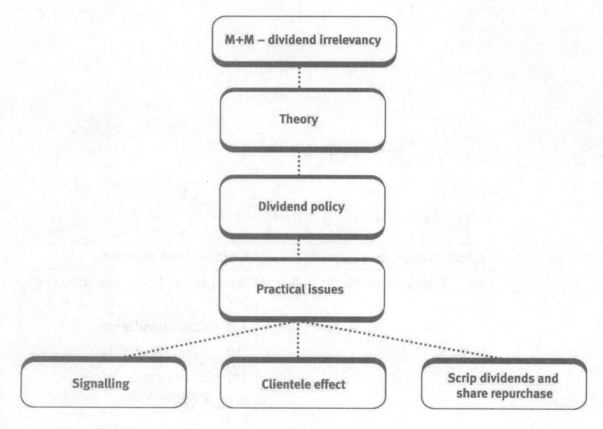

2 Dividend policy

One long-standing question in corporate finance is: Is shareholders' wealth affected by a company's dividend policy?

Notice that the question is not asking whether dividends matter – of course they do (as we know from the dividend valuation model) – what the question asks is whether the chosen policy matters. Examples of such policies may include:

(i)   paying a constant annual dividend;

(ii) paying out a constant proportion of annual earnings;

(iii) increasing dividends in line with the annual rate of inflation, etc;

(iv) paying out what's left after financing all future investment – the residual policy.

The key factors to consider in relation to the payment of dividends are:

1   Modigliani and Miller's (M & M) dividend irrelevancy argument

2   The interests of shareholders (the clientele effect and the bird-in-the- hand argument)

3   The signalling effect or information content of dividends

4   The cash needs of the entity

Dividend irrelevancy: Modigliani and Miller's theory

M & M's dividend irrelevancy theory says that the pattern of dividend payout should be irrelevant. As long as companies continue to invest in positive NPV projects, the wealth of the shareholders should increase whether or not the company makes a dividend payment this year.

M & M's Dividend Irrelevancy Theory

M & M's argument here is built up as follows:

(i)   The return on a share is determined by the share's (systematic) risk.

(ii)   The return itself is delivered to shareholders in two parts: one part is the dividend paid and the other is the capital gain/loss in the share price.

(iii)   The dividend decision that a company makes is a decision as to how the return is delivered: how much of the annual earnings should be paid out as dividends and how much of the annual earnings should be retained and re-invested within the company – and so flow through to shareholders in the form of a capital gain on the share price.

(iv)   As the dividend decision does not affect the risk of the shares, it does not affect their return. All the dividend decision therefore does is to determine how the return is to be split up between dividends and capital gains.

(v)   Do shareholders mind how their returns are split between dividends and capital gains? The answer according to M & M is: no, they do not if we assume:

(a)   There are no taxes (really, there are no differences between the taxation on dividends and on capital gains).

(b)   Shares can be bought and sold free of any transaction costs (such as stock-brokers' commission).

M & M argue that shareholders can 'manufacture' a dividend policy irrespective of the company policy. For instance, if a person is holding shares for income but the company withholds a dividend, the shareholder can sell some of the shares to replace the lost income.

The assumptions that M & M make play a key role. Obviously, if dividends were taxed and capital gains were tax free, shareholders would mind how their return was delivered – they would strongly prefer it to be delivered in the form of capital gains rather than dividends.

Similarly, investors who were holding shares for the income they generated would mind how their return was delivered if they had to incur transaction costs when realising their capital gains so as to turn them into income – such investors would strongly prefer if the return were delivered in the form of dividends, rather than capital gains.

> However, given their assumptions hold good, M & M could claim that shareholders are indifferent between dividends and capital gains and so the dividend decision/the dividend policy that the company pursues is irrelevant.

The interests of shareholders

It is critical that a business satisfies the needs of its shareholders with its dividend policy. If the shareholders don't feel that the business's dividend policy meets their expectations, they will sell their shares, perhaps causing the share price to fall.

Two important considerations in the context of shareholders' interests are the clientele effect and the bird-in-the-hand argument:

Clientele effect

In the real world, there are differential tax treatments of dividends and capital gains, and there are transaction costs on share dealings.

As a result, shareholders are concerned as to how their return is delivered to them by the company. Thus companies should follow a consistent dividend policy so as to ensure that they gather to them a clientele of shareholders who like that particular policy.

Thus the argument here is that the actual dividend policy that a company follows is unimportant but, having decided on a particular policy, it should then keep to it.

The bird-in-the-hand argument

This analysis puts forward a very simple argument.

Some investors may find capital gains more tax-efficient than dividends, and some investors will avoid transaction costs if their returns are delivered in the form of capital gains rather than dividends; despite all this, investors generally have a strong preference for dividends.

The reason given is that a dividend is certain and investors prefer a certain dividend now, to the promise of uncertain future dividends (arising out of retaining and re-investing earnings).

The signalling effect

Investors read 'signals' into the company's dividend decision and that these signals say as much about the company's future financial performance as they say about its past financial performance.

Thus management will not necessarily reduce the dividend per share just because last year's performance was poor, if they believe that next year's performance will be good.

If this analysis is correct, and investors do indeed read signals into the dividend decision, then the dividend decision becomes important: it becomes important for the company not to give the wrong signal.

More details on signalling

It is widely believed that there are two very strong dividend signals:

1   a reduction in the dividend per share signals that the company is in financial difficulties;

2   a failure to pay out any dividend at all signals that the company is very close to receivership.

Thus a company must take great care when settings dividend levels and ensure that the market is kept fully informed of future prospects.

These ideas are very widely held in practice and this view is supported by Lintner who discovered that dividend growth lagged two to three years behind earnings growth. This evidence can be interpreted to mean that managers are reluctant to increase the dividend per share until they are confident that they will be able to maintain that new level of dividends in the future (and will not be subsequently obliged to reduce the dividend per share).

However, there are exceptions to this interpretation. For many years, Apple Computers paid no dividends to its investors, preferring instead to reinvest the profits back into the business to fund new investments and to reduce the requirement to raise finance externally. Despite the absence of a dividend, the market responded positively to Apple throughout, and the share price rose strongly.

In conclusion, although paying dividends (or not paying dividends) can give investors a signal as to how successful the company is likely to be in future, it is not the only important indicator to investors. Other factors such as investment plans, gearing levels, strategy and quality of management are also important as investors assess the likely success of a business.

The cash needs of the entity

We saw in the earlier Chapter 3: 'Development of financial strategy' that the investment, financing and dividend decisions are all inter-linked.

Therefore, it is important to also consider the impact of investment and financing when considering dividend policy. Different types of business will have very different cash needs and will therefore have to set their dividend, investment and financing policies accordingly.

For example:

*   A small company, or a company with a poor credit rating, will often struggle to raise finance from external sources, so its cash needs might have to be met by restricting the amount of dividends it pays out.

*   A growing company will have many potential investment opportunities. The cash needs for these new investments will have to be met by balancing dividend policy alongside external finance sources.

- A well-established, stable company might well be cash rich, in which case it might be able to afford to pay out large dividends without compromising its internal cash needs.

🔑 How to reconcile these differing views of dividend policy in the real world

Given these contrasting views, how are managers to decide on the dividend policy that they should pursue?

The answer is that, in the real world, like so much else in corporate finance, managers have to make a judgement after taking many varying factors into account.

In this process they will consider:

1   What dividends are the shareholders expecting (e.g. the clientele effect)?

2   What are the cash needs of the company?

3   What dividend did the company pay last year? Consider the signal that a dividend announcement will give.

However they will also take into account a range of other factors, such as:

1   Is it legal to pay out a dividend?

2   Is the cash available to pay out a dividend?

3   Do we have a minimum gearing ratio imposed on the company as a financial covenant in a debt agreement?

4   What is the tax impact for shareholders of paying dividends?

5   What investment opportunities does the company face?

6   How difficult/expensive is it to raise external finance?

7   What has been the rate of inflation (and so what dividend increase is needed to maintain the purchasing power of last year's dividends)?

8   What has been the capital gain/loss in the share price over the last year?

3   Dividend policy in practice

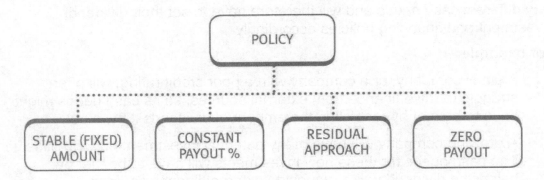

In practice, there are a number of commonly adopted dividend policies:

- stable dividend policy
- constant payout ratio
- zero dividend policy
- residual approach to dividends.

Stable dividend policy

Paying a constant or constantly growing dividend each year:

- offers investors a predictable cash flow
- reduces management opportunities to divert funds to non-profitable activities
- works well for mature firms with stable cash flows.

However, there is a risk that reduced earnings would force a dividend cut with all the associated difficulties.

Constant payout ratio

Paying out a constant proportion of equity earnings:

- maintains a link between earnings, reinvestment rate and dividend flow but
- cash flow is unpredictable for the investor
- gives no indication of management intention or expectation.

Zero dividend policy

All surplus earnings are invested back into the business. Such a policy:

- is common during the growth phase
- should be reflected in increased share price.

When growth opportunities are exhausted (no further positive NPV projects are available):

- cash will start to accumulate
- a new distribution policy will be required.

Residual dividend policy

A dividend is paid only if no further positive NPV projects available. This may be popular for firms:

- in the growth phase
- without easy access to alternative sources of funds.

However:

- cash flow is unpredictable for the investor
- gives constantly changing signals regarding management expectations.

Ratchet patterns

Most firms adopt a variant on the stable dividend policy – a ratchet pattern of payments. This involves paying out a stable, but rising dividend per share:

- Dividends lag behind earnings, but can then be maintained even when earnings fall below the dividend level.
- Avoids 'bad news' signals.
- Does not disturb the tax position of investors.

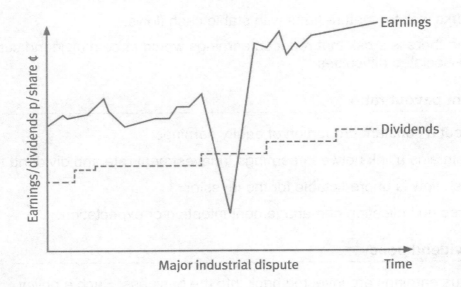

4 Scrip/bonus dividends and share repurchase

Scrip dividends

A scrip dividend (or bonus/scrip issue) is where shareholders are offered bonus shares free of charge as an alternative to a cash dividend.

They are useful where the company wishes to retain cash in the business or where shareholders wish to reinvest dividends in the company but avoid brokerage costs of buying shares. There may also be tax advantages of receiving shares rather than cash in some jurisdictions.

If all shareholders opt for bonus shares, the scrip issue has the effect of capitalising reserves. Reserves reduce and share capital increases.

The disadvantage to shareholders is that, unlike reserves, share capital is non-distributable in the future. In addition, both share price and earnings per share are likely to fall due to the greater number of shares in issue, although the overall value of each shareholder's shares and share in future earnings should, theoretically, remain unchanged.

However, it has the important advantage to the issuer of retaining cash in the business while still achieving a distribution of reserves.

Example of a scrip dividend

A recent issue by Santander bank in February 2011 was set up in a similar manner to a rights issue except that the rights were issued without charge.

Shareholders were given rights to receive additional Santander shares and three options for their allotment of rights:

1 Sell the rights off market to Santander and receive a fixed cash amount.

2 Sell the rights on market and receive cash.

3 Hold the rights and receive new Santander shares, 1 share for every 65 rights held.

Share repurchase

A share repurchase can be used to return surplus cash to shareholders.

It tends to be used when the company has no positive NPV projects to invest the cash in, so it returns the cash to shareholders so that they can make better use of it rather than it sitting idle (in cash investments) in the company.

Alternatively, a share repurchase can be used to privatise a company, by buying back a listed company's shares from a wide pool of investors. However, this is rare.

Share repurchase v one-off large dividend

As an alternative to a share repurchase, a company may decide to use a one-off large dividend to return surplus cash to shareholders.

If all shareholders agree to the repurchase, both a share repurchase and a one-off large dividend have the same impact on the cash, and the gearing of the company (they reduce the value of equity, so increase the gearing and hence financial risk and cost of equity). Although the impact on shareholder value is the same for any individual shareholder, the impact on the price per share will differ. A dividend results in a lower share price as the number of shares remains the same, but a share repurchase is unlikely to affect the individual share price but only the number of shares in issue.

The one-off dividend has the advantage of certainty of ultimate payout. However, a share repurchase has the following advantages:

- investors can choose whether or not to sell their shares back (they may prefer to keep the shares if they feel that future returns will be high)

- it avoids the risk of a false dividend signal – after a one-off large dividend, the shareholders may be disappointed when the higher level of dividend is not maintained in the future.

5 The impact of scrip dividends and share repurchase on financial ratios

Scrip dividends

The impact of a scrip dividend on shareholder wealth is nil. There are more shares in issue but the overall shareholder value stays the same, hence the share price decreases.

For example, if price per share is $11 and if a shareholder has 100 shares, then after the issue of a 10% scrip dividend, the number of shares increases to 110. Hence, price per share will decrease to $1100/110 = $10.

The impact of a scrip dividend on the entity's performance measures / ratios is:

- total shareholder's equity (in the statement of financial position) remains the same

- it doesn't change the capital structure (and gearing ratio) because the equity value stays the same.

Test your understanding 1 (Objective test question)

LL is a large listed company. Its $1 ordinary shares are quoted on the local stock exchange.

Equity comprises:

- Ordinary share capital ($1 shares) $1,500m
- Reserves $500m

LL's share price is $1.90 per share.

The Board of LL is aware that the market is expecting LL to pay a dividend of $200m to be paid at the year end, but in order to fund the investment in an important new project, the Board is considering offering a scrip dividend of 1 share for every 12 shares held instead of a cash dividend.

Profit after tax and interest is forecast to be $380 million in the current financial year.

What is the expected share price of LL after the scrip dividend has been issued? (to 2 decimal places)

A $0.16

B $1.75

C $1.90

D $2.03

Share repurchase

The impact of a share repurchase on shareholder wealth is the same as the impact of a cash dividend being paid.

The impact of a share repurchase on the entity's performance measures / ratios is different from the impact of a cash dividend though. After a share repurchase there will be fewer shares in issue, so the earnings per share of the entity will increase.

Illustration 1 (Integration question)

McGreggor Co has 10,000 shares in issue, trading at $50 per share. The Board is considering returning cash of $50,000 to shareholders either as a cash dividend or as a share repurchase.

Required:

Calculate the wealth of a shareholder who currently owns 100 shares in each case.

Solution:

Cash dividend

Dividend per share = ($50,000/10,000 shares) = $5

Therefore, ex-dividend share price = $50 – $5 = $45

So the shareholder who owns 100 shares will have wealth of:

Dividend received + Share value

= (100 × $5) + (100 × $45) = $5,000

Share repurchase

Number of shares repurchased in total will be ($50,000/$50) = 1,000 i.e. 10% of the total 10,000 shares.

Therefore there will now be (10,000 − 1,000 =) 9,000 shares in issue, with a value of

[(10,000 × $50) − $50,000]/[10,000 − 1,000] = $50 each

So the shareholder who owned 100 shares before the repurchase will now have wealth of:

Cash received in share repurchase + Share value

= (10 × $50) + (90 × $50) = $5,000

6 End of chapter objective test questions

Test your understanding 2 (Objective test question)

Mr Smith is an investor who is considering buying shares.

Mr Smith is retired, so does not receive a regular income from any source. He therefore pays little (if any) income tax. However, he does have several valuable assets that he could sell if he needed to.

Which TWO of the following companies have dividend policies that most closely match Mr Smith's requirements?

Company A – follows the residual dividend policy advocated by Modigliani and Miller

Company B – follows a zero dividend policy, preferring to reinvest all profits back into the business

Company C – follows a stable dividend policy where each year's dividend is 3% higher than the year before

Company D – pays out a dividend each year of 20% of earnings per share

Test your understanding 3 (Objective test question)

A company plans to return surplus cash to shareholders by paying a special dividend, making it clear to investors that this is a one-off event.

The company is funded by a mix of debt and equity and currently does not have any unused bank facilities available.

Which of the following is the MOST likely consequence of this plan?

A   The share price would rise due to the signalling effect of the special dividend

B   Shareholder wealth would decrease by the value of cash paid as a special dividend

C   The company would become less vulnerable to a hostile takeover bid

D   The company would become more able to respond promptly to new business opportunities

Test your understanding 4 (Objective test question)

A company has 10 million $0.50 shares in issue. The company is planning to repurchase 1 million of these shares at a price of $1.50 each.

Currently, the company's cash balance is $2 million and its earnings per share is $0.20.

What will be the cash balance and the earnings per share (EPS) after the share repurchase?

A   Cash: $1.5 million, EPS: $0.22

B   Cash: $0.5 million, EPS: $0.20

C   Cash: $1.5 million, EPS: $0.20

D   Cash: $0.5 million, EPS: $0.22

Test your understanding 5 (Objective test question)

Honeybear Co has 6 million shares in issue, trading at $5.20 per share.

The directors have decided to offer a 3 for 5 scrip dividend to shareholders.

What will be the company's share price after the scrip dividend has been issued?

A $1.95

B $3.12

C $3.25

D $8.67

Test your understanding 6 (Objective test question)

Redhead Co has 100 million $1 shares in issue, trading at $2.24. It also has $70 million of bonds in issue, trading at $106 per cent.

After several years of growth, the company has accumulated a cash pile of $20 million. The directors have decided to repurchase some of the company's shares at market value in order to return this cash pile to the shareholders.

What will be the gearing level of Redhead Co after the share repurchase? (measured as debt/(debt + equity) using market values)

A   24.9%

B   26.7%

C   41.2%

D   46.7%

Test your understanding 7 (Objective test question)

Which THREE of the following strategies are most likely to enhance shareholder wealth?

A   Increasing cash for bonuses

B   Increasing the dividend payout ratio

C   Increasing brand reputation and recognition

D   Investing in projects with a positive NPV

E   Moving profitable operations to low tax regimes

Test your understanding 8 (Objective test question)

P Co is considering paying out a large one-off special dividend to return a large amount of cash to its shareholders.

Which TWO of the following are valid arguments in favour of such a policy?

A   If P Co has no foreseeable use for the cash, it should be returned to investors so that they can put it to better use

B   It sends a positive signal to the market, unlike a share repurchase

C   A large payment in a single year reduces the risk of a misleading signalling effect

D   It is likely to increase shareholder wealth

E   Paying the cash out is likely to provide protection against hostile take-over

Test your understanding 9 (Objective test question)

Mr Jones is an investor who is considering buying shares.

Mr Jones is a chartered management accountant who works for a large listed company. He earns a large salary from his employment and pays income tax at the highest marginal rate. However, he has few valuable assets and has never previously made any taxable capital gains.

Which TWO of the following companies have dividend policies that most closely match Mr Jones's requirements?

Company A – follows the residual dividend policy advocated by Modigliani and Miller

Company B – follows a zero dividend policy, preferring to reinvest all profits back into the business

Company C – follows a stable dividend policy where each year's dividend is 3% higher than the year before

Company D – pays out a dividend each year of 20% of earnings per share

Test your understanding 10 (Objective test question)

Which of the following statements is consistent with Modigliani and Miller's dividend irrelevancy theory?

A   A policy of steady growth in dividends is preferable to a residual dividend policy

B   Shareholder wealth can be maximised by retaining a high percentage of earnings

C   The share price is NOT affected by a dividend payment

D   Shareholder return can be measured as the aggregate of dividends plus growth in share price

7 End of chapter case style questions

Test your understanding 11 (Case style question)

KK is a listed manufacturing company that is wholly equity financed. 25% of the shares are held by members of an extended family group. KK has adopted 31 December as its financial year end.

Dividend decision

In previous years, KK has maintained a dividend pay-out rate of 80% of earnings. However, some board members have recently questioned whether such a policy is appropriate. Some board members support the 80% pay-out but others have suggested that a lower dividend is necessary in order to help finance expansion in manufacturing capacity to take advantage of new markets that are opening up in Asia.

It is too late to change the dividend for the current financial year, 20X3, since the dividend for the year is about to be paid. The first time that a change in dividend policy could be adopted is in 20X4.

Additional financial information for KK:

- It is standard practice for KK to pay dividends once a year based on forecast earnings for that year.

- Dividends are paid at or shortly before the end of the year.

- A dividend of $ 0.50 in respect of the current financial year (20X3) has already been declared. This was based on the historical pay-out rate of 80% of forecast earnings for 20X3 of $ 12.5 million.

- Historically, KK has achieved a return on reinvested funds of 16%.

- KK has a cost of equity of 14.7%.

- There are currently 20 million shares in issue.

- Today's share price is $ 5.00 (cum div).

Possible reduction in dividend pay-out

The board of KK is considering cutting the regular dividend pay-out rate from 80% to 50% of earnings with effect from 20X4. If agreed, this would be made public by an announcement on 1 January 20X4.

The board is aware that there would be a delay of 12 months between cutting the dividend pay-out rate and realising any benefit in terms of higher earnings as a result of the higher level of reinvested funds. Discussions regarding a possible change in the dividend pay-out rate have so far been internal and only known by the management team at KK. No announcement has yet been made about a possible change in dividend policy and the share price does not yet reflect the possibility of a cut in pay-out rate.

Growth formula

$g = r \times b$

- Where g = annual growth

- r = return on reinvested funds

- b = proportion of funds retained

Required:

Calculate the following performance measures for KK for both years 20X4 and 20X5 assuming a reduction in KK's dividend pay-out to 50% of earnings from 20X4 onwards:

- Growth rate using the growth formula provided.

- Earnings.

- Dividend per share.

(20 minutes)

Test your understanding 12 (Case style question)

DIVS plc is a large international company with widespread interests in advertising, media and various consultancy activities associated with sales promotion and marketing. In recent years the company's earnings and dividend payments, in real terms, have grown on average by 15% and 12% per year respectively. The company is likely to have substantial cash surpluses in the coming year, but a number of investment opportunities are being considered for the subsequent two years. The senior managers of the company are reviewing their likely funding requirements for the next two to three years and the possible consequences for dividend policy.

At present the company has a debt : equity ratio of 1 : 5, measured in market value terms. It does not want to increase this ratio at the present time but might need to borrow to pay a maintained dividend in the future.

The senior managers of the company are discussing a range of issues concerning financial strategy in general and dividend policy in particular.

Required:

Assume you are an independent financial advisor to the board of DIVS plc. Write a report to the board which discusses the following issues:

(i)   The re-purchase of some of the company's shares in the coming year using the forecast surplus cash, the aim being to reduce the amount of cash needed to pay dividends in subsequent years. Other implications of share repurchase for the company's financial strategy should also be considered.

(ii) The advisability of borrowing money to pay dividends in years 2 and 3.

(iii) The likely effect on the company's cost of equity if the company decides on share repurchase and / or further borrowing.

(45 minutes)

Test your understanding 13 (Case style question)

STR is a well-established marketing consultancy in a country with a low interest rate. STR is a successful business which has experienced rapid growth in recent years. There are 20 million $1 ordinary shares in issue. These ordinary shares are quoted on a recognised stock exchange and 40% are owned by the founders of the business. Dividends were 40 cents per share in 20X3 and grew by 5% per annum between 20X3 and 20X6. This pattern is expected to continue beyond 20X6. Dividends are paid in the year in which they are declared.

Extracts from the financial statements for the past three years are as follows:

	20X4 $million	20X5 $million	20X6 $million
Profit before tax	21.6	24.4	26.7
Tax expense	7.7	2.6	4.3
Net cash generated after deducting interest, tax and net capital expenditure, but excluding ordinary dividends	19.2	(7.1)	18.8

Additional information:

- The opening cash balance in 20X4 for cash and cash equivalents was $6 million;

- The opening book value of equity in 20X4 was $60 million;

- Long-term borrowings remained at $50 million throughout the three years and the annual gross interest cost on the borrowings was $1 million;

- There were a number of disposals of non-current assets in 20X4 and an exceptionally high level of capital expenditure in 20X5.

The directors have noticed the build-up of cash and cash equivalents. They are concerned that this might not be in the best interest of the shareholders and could have an adverse effect on the share price. Various proposals have been made to reduce the level of cash and cash equivalents.

Required:

(a) Calculate the following financial information for STR for each of the years 20X4 to 20X6:

- Closing cash balance;

- Closing book value of equity.

(10 minutes)

(b) Analyse and discuss the financial performance of the entity from the viewpoint of both the lenders and shareholders, referring to the information calculated in part (a) above and making appropriate additional calculations. Up to 6 marks are available for calculations.

(20 minutes)

(c) (i) Discuss the comparative advantages and disadvantages of a share repurchase versus a one-off dividend payment.

(15 minutes)

(ii) Advise the directors of STR on alternative financial strategies that they could consider that would reduce the level of surplus cash.

(15 minutes)

Test your understanding answers

Test your understanding 1 (Objective test question)

The answer is (B).

In theory, shareholder wealth is unaffected by a scrip dividend.

Consider a typical shareholder with 120 shares. Under the terms of the scrip dividend, this shareholder would receive an entitlement to one new share for every 12 held. That is, the right to acquire 10 new shares (where 10 = 120/12).

This may give the shareholder the illusion of increased 'value' as he now holds 130 shares. However, the company itself has not changed in value and so the total value that those shares represent is unchanged.

Therefore, the value of each share after the scrip issue will be ($1.90 × 120)/130 = $1.75

Test your understanding 2 (Objective test question)

The answer is (C) and (D).

Mr Smith has no other regular income, so he would prefer to invest in a company that pays out a dividend each year.

Company C would be his preferred choice – it gives a predictable payout.

Company D would be his second choice – a dividend will be paid each year, although the amounts could be variable.

Companies A and B would not give Mr Smith the income he needs. Selling shares to manufacture dividends would not be appealing to Mr Smith because he has capital gains already but pays very little income tax, so he would prefer dividends to capital gains.

Test your understanding 3 (Objective test question)

The answer is (C).

Having paid out a large amount of cash as a dividend there would be much less chance of a predator wanting to take over the company.

Test your understanding 4 (Objective test question)

The answer is (D).

The amount of cash required for the repurchase is 1 million shares at $1.50 each, so $1.5 million in total. Hence, cash will fall from $2 million to $0.5 million.

The new number of shares in issue will be (10 million – 1 million =) 9 million, so assuming that earnings stay constant, the EPS will be (total earnings/9 million).

Currently, earnings are $0.20 × 10 million = $0.20 million. Therefore, EPS will be $0.20 million/9 million = $0.22 after the repurchase.

Test your understanding 5 (Objective test question)

The answer is (C).

A scrip dividend does not change the value of the overall company, therefore the total company value will still be:

6 million × $5.20 = $31.2 million.

After the 3 for 5 scrip issue, the number of shares in issue will be:

6 million + (6 million × 3/5) = 9.6 million.

Therefore, the share price will be $31.2 million/9.6 million = $3.25.

Test your understanding 6 (Objective test question)

The answer is (B).

Market value of debt is $70m × 1.06 = $74.2m

Current market value of equity is 100m × $2.24 = $224m, so after the share repurchase it will be $204m.

Therefore (D/(D+E)) = 74.2/(74.2 + 204) = 26.7%

Test your understanding 7 (Objective test question)

The answer is (C), (D), and (E).

Cash for bonuses (A) would cause more money to be paid out of the business, leaving less for reinvestment.

Increasing the dividend payout ratio (B) without any underlying increase in positive NPVs generated would make no difference to shareholder wealth.

Test your understanding 8 (Objective test question)

The answer is (A) and (E).

Paying a dividend of any sort should not impact shareholder wealth - only undertaking a positive NPV project can enhance shareholder wealth (D).

A large payment in a single year would increase the risk of a misleading signalling effect (C).

Both special dividends and share repurchases can send positive signals to the market (B).

Test your understanding 9 (Objective test question)

The answer is (A) and (B).

Mr Jones has a large regular income, so he would prefer to invest in a company that pays out as little as possible in dividends. If Mr Jones ever does need an income from his investments, selling shares to create capital gains would be the most tax efficient approach.

Test your understanding 10 (Objective test question)

The answer is (D).

M & M's theory said that the pattern of dividends is irrelevant. The key point is that any positive NPV projects should be undertaken. Hence (A) and (B) are incorrect.

Although shareholder wealth will not be affected by a dividend payment, the share price will be under M & M's theory. A large dividend will convert shareholder wealth from share value to cash, so the share price will fall even though overall shareholder wealth stays the same. Therefore (C) is incorrect.

Test your understanding 11 (Case style question)

Performance measure	20X3	20X4	Workings	20X5	Workings
Earnings growth (%)	3.2	3.2	No change as reinvestment of additional retained earnings not actioned until this year	8	g = r × b = 16% × 50% = 8%
Earnings ($m)	12.5	12.9	= $ 12.5 million × 1.032	13.932	= $ 12.9 million × 1.08
Dividend per share ($)	0.50	0.3225	= 12.9m × 50%/20m	0.3483	= (13.932 × 50%)/20m

where 3.2% = r × b = 16% × 20%

Test your understanding 12 (Case style question)

Report

To: Board of Directors, DIVS plc

From: Independent financial advisor

Date: XX/XX/XX

Re: Dividend policy and other financing issues

You are currently considering the current and future position of the company as regards dividend payments and financing over the next two to three years, in the light of your current cash surplus and the investment opportunities available to you from next year.

This report addresses the following issues:

- the implications of share re-purchase to reduce future dividend payments;

- borrowing funds to finance dividends;

- the possible effects on cost of equity if either or both of the above actions are taken.

(i) *Share re-purchase*

You are likely to have substantial cash surpluses in the coming year. Your first decision is to decide how much to distribute, bearing in mind both your investment financing requirements in the future and the possible reactions of shareholders and other market players. In the current climate, it is expected that 'spare' cash, in excess of that required for specific profitable investment opportunities, should be returned to the shareholders to do with as they wish.

You have some investment opportunities open to you in the near future. Whether or not you have to retain some of the current surplus cash to fund these will depend upon the extent to which you expect there to be spare funds generated in the next two or three years.

Once the amount to be distributed (if any) has been decided upon, you then need to decide whether to return it to all the shareholders as a dividend, or to some of them in the form of a share re-purchase. The latter option will result in only a small number of shareholders – likely to be the large institutional investors – receiving cash, although their proportionate holding, and therefore entitlement to future dividends, will be reduced.

Other shareholders will have to sell shares, incurring transaction costs, to 'manufacture' dividends should they need them.

It should be noted that a share re-purchase is administratively more complex in that it requires prior approval from a general meeting of shareholders (assuming the Articles of Association provide that it can happen at all). It is also no longer possible for institutions to reclaim tax on the distribution in the UK.

The two types of distribution will also affect share prices differently. When a dividend is declared, the value of the shares falls from cum-div to ex-div, the shareholders having had some of their capital investment realised as cash.

In theory, if the share re-purchase is made at current market price, a share re-purchase should leave the individual share price unchanged – there has been a reduction in total market value in proportion to the total number of shares in issue.

It should also be noted that a share re-purchase would result in a higher future EPS figure than if a normal dividend had been paid. However this should not affect the market's perception of the health of the company, as it is purely a result of the same earnings being spread over a smaller number of shares.

Overall, it would appear that there is no particularly strong argument for a share re-purchase in preference to a dividend payment to all shareholders. Whilst you may see this as a means of reducing future dividend payments, it is likely that the remaining shareholders, who would be holding a greater proportion of shares than previously, would expect a higher dividend per share. If this expectation is not met, share prices may be affected adversely.

(ii) *Borrowing to pay dividends*

If it is decided to distribute an amount in the current year that cannot be maintained (with planned growth) in future years out of operational cash flows, then additional funds will need to be borrowed.

This will raise the company's gearing level above the current 1:5 debt:equity ratio, with two consequences. First, the company will be funded by a greater proportion of cheap finance, particularly as debt interest is tax deductible. Second, shareholders may perceive a greater risk as being attached to their dividends, as more of the earnings are attributed to fixed interest payments. It is a question of finding the optimum balance between these two effects.

(iii) *Effect on cost of equity*

The probable effect of increasing the gearing level will be, as discussed in (ii) above, to increase the required return by (cost of) equity. Borrowing will directly affect the gearing level, by increasing the debt element.

The payment of a dividend or a share repurchase will also increase the gearing level, by lowering the value of the equity (as discussed in (i) above, a dividend results in a lower share price with the number of shares being maintained; a share repurchase results in a maintained share price with a lower number of shares).

Thus both actions may result in a higher cost of equity.

Overall recommendations

It is advised that any surplus cash over and above the needs of all positive NPV investments should be paid out in the form of a dividend. This 'residual' dividend policy may lead to fluctuating dividends, however, and institutional investors generally prefer a steady dividend pattern; you will need to keep a careful eye on your share price to ensure it is not being adversely affected in the long term.

Should you need to borrow in the future, you should find this to your advantage, as your current gearing level is quite low, and the benefits of cheaper debt should outweigh any increase in cost of equity.

Test your understanding 13 (Case style question)

Key answer tips

In part (a) ensure that your workings are clearly set out. In part (b) it is vital that you discuss any ratios calculated rather than simply presenting the examiner with a set of numbers. Part (c) is bookwork and a good reminder that you need to be familiar with all aspects of the syllabus.

(a) **Cash balances**

	20X4 $m	20X5 $m	20X6 $m
Net cash flow before dividends	19.2	(7.1)	18.8
Dividends **(W1)**	(8.4)	(8.8)	(9.3)
Net cash flow	10.8	(15.9)	9.5
Cash b/f	6	16.8	0.9
Cash c/f	16.8	0.9	10.4

Book value of equity

	20X4 $m	20X5 $m	20X6 $m
Profit before interest and tax (bal)	22.6	25.4	27.7
Interest	(1.0)	(1.0)	(1.0)
Profit before tax	21.6	24.4	26.7
Tax expense	(7.7)	(2.6)	(4.3)
Profit after tax	13.9	21.8	22.4
Dividends (W1)	(8.4)	(8.8)	(9.3)
Retained profit	5.5	13.0	13.1
Book value of equity b/f	60	65.5	78.5
Book value of equity c/f	65.5	78.5	91.6

(W1) *Dividends*

20X4: dividend = 20 million × $0.40 × 1.05 = $8.4 million

20X5: dividend = $8.4 million × 1.05 = $8.82 million

20X6: dividend = $8.82 million × 1.05 = $9.261 million

(b) **Additional calculations**

	20X4	20X5	20X6
Interest cover	22.6×	25.4×	27.7×
Dividend cover	1.65×	2.48×	2.41×
Earnings per share (cents)	69.5	109	112

Gearing = debt net of cash/(debt + equity)

	20X4	20X5	20X6
Debt	50	50	50
Cash	16.8	0.9	10.4
Debt net of cash	33.2	49.1	39.6
Equity	65.5	78.5	91.6
Debt (net) + equity	98.7	127.6	131.2
Gearing	33.6%	38.5%	30.2%

Return on equity

	20X4	20X5	20X6
Profit after tax	13.9	21.8	22.4
Equity	65.5	78.5	91.6
Profit before tax	21.2%	27.8%	24.5%

Return on capital employed, using net debt + equity

	20X4	20X5	20X6
Profit before interest and tax (bal)	22.6	25.4	27.7
Debt (net) + equity	98.7	127.6	131.2
Return on capital	22.9%	19.9%	21.1%

Comments

The financial performance from the shareholders' point of view has generally been encouraging:

–   Both earnings per share and the book value of equity have been increasing.

–   Dividends have increased.

–   Return on equity has consistently been above 20%.

–   Financial gearing has fallen in 20X6 and dividend cover is now over two, indicating lower risk attached to the dividends.

The only area of worry, however, is that return on equity fell from 20X5 to 20X6.

The financial performance from the lenders' point of view has been less convincing. On a positive note:

–   Interest cover is very high and rising, suggesting a low default risk.

–   Gearing fell in 20X6, again suggesting less risk for lenders.

However,

–   STR had poor cash flow in 20X5. Lenders may wish to see more detailed analysis of cash flow to determine if any underlying problems persist.

(c) (i) The relative advantages of a share repurchase verses a one-off dividend are as follows:

Share repurchase	One-off dividend
• A repurchase may be more tax efficient than a dividend for some shareholders.	• A dividend may be more tax advantageous for some shareholders.
• A reduction in the number of shares should boost EPS.	• All shareholders are treated fairly.
• Increased gearing as equity is reduced. This is only an advantage if STR is moved closer to its optimal gearing level.	• The amount of cash paid is more certain – with a repurchase it will not be known in advance how many shareholders will choose to sell.
• Does not create an expectation of higher future dividends. On the contrary, less cash will be needed for future dividends due to fewer shares.	

(ii) Alternative strategies for reducing a cash surplus include the following:

- increase the growth rate of dividends

- long-term equity investments – e.g. acquire other firms and/or buy stakes in rivals, customers, etc.

- reduce debt by repaying borrowings

- increase capital expenditure

- increase investment in research and development – e.g. to enter new markets.

Financial risk

Chapter learning objectives

Lead outcome	Component outcome
C1: Discuss the sources and types of financial risks	Discuss: (a) Sources of financial risk (b) Types of financial risk
C2: Evaluate financial risks	(a) Evaluate how financial risks are quantified
C3: Recommend ways of managing financial risks	(a) Recommend ways to manage economic and political risks

Topics to be covered

- Economic risk
- Political risk
- Currency risk
- Interest rate risk
- Responses to economic, transaction and translation risks
- Value at risk

1   Overview of chapter

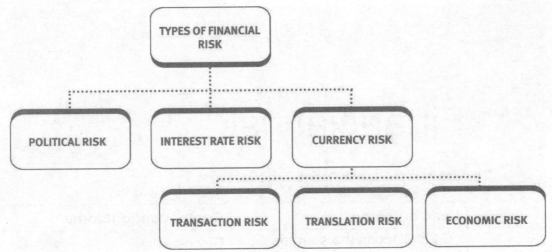

Introduction – definition of financial risk

Financial risk is 'a risk of a change in a financial condition such as an exchange rate, interest rate, credit rating of a customer, or price of a good'.

Political risk is not necessarily a financial risk but is included here because often financial risk is from the perspective of foreign business activities. Political risk is essentially to do with the wider risks of foreign direct investment.

2   Political risk

Political risk is the risk faced by an overseas investor, that the host country government take adverse action against, after the company has invested.

It can take different forms and the threats (financial and non-financial) can include:

- Risk of confiscation or destruction of overseas assets
- Commercial risks because foreign governments discriminate against overseas firms e.g. quotas, tariffs, other taxes
- Restricted access to local borrowings
- Insisting on resident investors or a joint venture with a local company
- Restrictions on repatriating cash (capital or dividends)
- Restrictions on conversion of the currency
- Rationing the supply of foreign currency
- Exchange rate volatility due to political actions
- A minimum number of local nationals to be employed
- Price fixing by the government
- Minimum percentage of local components to be used
- Invalidating patents
- Claiming compensation for past actions

More on sources of political risk

Whilst governments want to encourage development and growth they are also anxious to prevent the exploitation of their countries by multinationals.

Whilst at one extreme, assets might be destroyed as the result of war or expropriation, the most likely problems concern changes to the rules on the remittance of cash out of the host country to the holding company.

Exchange control regulations, which are generally more restrictive in less developed countries. For example:

- rationing the supply of foreign currencies which restricts residents from buying goods abroad

- banning the payment of dividends to foreign shareholders such as holding companies in multinationals, who will then have the problem of blocked funds.

Import quotas to limit the quantity of goods that subsidiaries can buy from its holding company to sell in its domestic market.

Import tariffs could make imports (from the holding company) more expensive than domestically produced goods.

Insist on a minimum shareholding, i.e. that some equity in the company is offered to resident investors.

Company structure may be dictated by the host government – requiring, for example, all investments to be in the form of joint ventures with host country companies.

Discriminatory actions

- **Supertaxes** imposed on foreign firms, set higher than those imposed on local businesses with the aim of giving local firms an advantage. They may even be deliberately set at such a high level as to prevent the business from being profitable.

- **Restricted access to local borrowings** by restricting or even barring foreign owned enterprises from the cheapest forms of finance from local banks and development funds. Some countries ration all access for foreign investments to local sources of funds, to force the company to import foreign currency into the country.

- **Expropriating assets** whereby the host country government seizes foreign property in the national interest. It is recognised in international law as the right of sovereign states provided that prompt consideration at fair market value in a convertible currency is given. Problems arise over the exact meaning of the terms prompt and fair, the choice of currency, and the action available to a company not happy with the compensation offered.

Management of political risk

Companies cannot prevent political risk, but they should seek to minimise it whenever the risk appears significant.

Before undertaking a foreign direct investment, a company needs to assess its exposure to political risk by:

- Using political ranking tables such as Euromoney magazine tables;
- Evaluating the country's macro-economic situation – balance of payments, unemployment levels, per capita income, inflation, exchange rate policy, rate of economic growth;
- Evaluating the current government's popularity, stability and attitude to foreign investment, together with the attitude of opposition parties;
- Looking at the historical stability of the political system;
- Looking at changing religious and cultural attitudes;
- Taking advice from the company's bank (if there is a representative office in the overseas country) and the company's home embassy in the overseas country.

Some methods of minimising risks are as follows:

- Prior negotiation (concession agreements and planned divestment)
- Structuring investment (local sourcing of materials and labour)
- Entering into foreign joint ventures
- Obtaining agreements and contracts with overseas government
- Using local financing
- Plans for eventual ownership/part-ownership by foreign country's investors.

More on managing political risk

Joint ventures. A company might go into a joint venture with one or more partners. A joint venture can reduce risk because:

- if each joint venture partner contributes a share of the funding for the venture, the investment at risk for each partner is restricted to their share of the total investment (although, the upside is reduced because each party has less invested in this potentially lucrative venture)
- if a local company is selected as a joint venture partner, the likelihood of winning major contracts in the country might be much greater. Some governments have made the involvement of a local company in a joint venture a condition of awarding contracts to consortia involving a foreign company
- the local venture partner has a better understanding of the local political risks and can manage them more effectively than a foreigner would be able to. Also the government might be less inclined to act against the interests of the local venture partner.

Pre-trading agreements. Prior to making the investment, agreements should be secured if possible with the local government regarding rights, remittance of funds and local equity investments and (where appropriate) the award of government contracts to businesses.

Gaining government funding. In some situations, it might be possible to gain government funding for a project or contract, with the government being either a customer, a backer or a partner for the deal. If government funding can be obtained:

- the government will have an interest in the transaction reaching a successful conclusion

- there should be little or no risk of exchange control regulations preventing the withdrawal of profits from the country.

Local finance. A company might try to obtain local finance for an investment in a particular country. The availability of local finance might depend on the state of the banking and capital markets in the country concerned. The major advantage of local finance is that it creates liabilities in the foreign currency, and so reduces:

- translation exposures: assets in the foreign currency can be offset against liabilities in the same currency

- transaction exposures, in the sense that interest costs will be payable in the foreign currency and can be paid from income in the same currency.

Raising finance locally might also help to maintain the interest of the local government in the success of the business, and there is less risk that the assets will be confiscated.

Planning for the eventual part-ownership or full ownership of the business by locals. Target dates might be set in advance of making the investment for the eventual part-ownership or full ownership of the business by local people. The transfer of ownership should be extended over a long-term, partly to ensure that a satisfactory return on investment is obtained but also to encourage the local government to understand the long-term benefits of foreign investment.

Test your understanding 1 – Political risk (Integration question)

A UK company is planning to build and operate a factory in West Africa.

Required:

Discuss the potential political risks that may arise and recommend risk mitigation strategies that could be implemented to bring these risks to a satisfactory level.

3 Interest rate risk

As defined in the earlier Chapter 5: 'Financing - Debt finance', interest rate risk is the risk of gains or losses on assets and liabilities due to changes in interest rates. It will occur for any organisation which has assets or liabilities on which interest is payable or receivable.

> ### Interest rates and LIBOR
>
> Non-financial organisations normally have many more interest-bearing liabilities than interest-bearing assets. These include bank loans and overdrafts, and issues of bonds or debentures. As a general rule:
>
> - interest on bank loans and overdrafts is payable at a **variable rate** or **floating rate**, with the interest set at a margin above a benchmark rate such as the base rate or the London Inter Bank Offer Rate (LIBOR)
>
> - interest on most bonds, debentures or loan stock is at a **fixed rate**.
>
> When interest is at a floating rate, the amount of interest payable in each period is set by reference to the benchmark interest rate on a specific date, such as the starting date for the interest period. For example, suppose that a company has a bank loan on which it pays interest every six months at 50 basis points above LIBOR. (100 basis points = 1%, therefore 50 basis points = 0.50%.) At the start of an interest period, the six-month LIBOR rate might be, say, 4.75%: if so, the company would pay interest at the end of the six months at 5.25% for the six-month period. If LIBOR moves up or down, the interest rate payable every six months will go up or down accordingly.
>
> (**Note:** LIBOR is the London Interbank Offered Rate. It is a money market rate at which top-rated banks are able to borrow short-term in the London sterling or eurocurrency markets. There are LIBOR rates for major traded currencies, including the US dollar, euro and yen, as well as sterling (British pounds).)

Exposure to interest rate risk

The exposure to interest risk will depend on the amount of interest bearing assets or liabilities that it holds and the type that these are (floating or fixed rate).

Types of interest rate risk exposure

- **Floating rate loans:** If a company has floating rate loans, changes in interest rates alter the amount of interest payable or receivable. This directly affects cash flows and profits and the risk therefore is quite obvious.

- **Fixed rate loans:** If a company has fixed rate loans interest rate risk still exists. Even though interest charges themselves will not change, a fixed rate can make a company uncompetitive if its costs are higher than those with a floating rate and interest rates fall. (Remember interest rate risk can be about assets or liabilities – an asset that pays a fixed rate of interest will be worth less if interest rates rise.)

More on fixed rate exposure

Companies with fixed rate borrowings are also exposed to interest rate risk, because by paying a fixed rate of interest on its liabilities, a company runs the risk that:

- if interest rates fall, it will be unable to benefit from the lower rates available in the market, because it is committed to paying fixed rates, and

- competitor organisations might have floating rate liabilities, and so will benefit from lower interest costs, and so improve their profitability and competitive strength.

The same, of course, is true in reverse for a company that has fixed or floating rate deposits/investments.

Measuring exposure to interest rate risk

Floating rate loans

Interest risk exposure is the total amount of floating rate assets and liabilities. The higher the value of loans the greater the exposure to changes in interest rates.

Fixed rate loans

This is measured by the total amount of fixed rate assets or liabilities together with average time to maturity and average interest rate. Longer periods of tie-in at fixed rates could be beneficial, or more costly, to businesses depending on what market rates are and also what the future expectations of interest rate changes are. It is expectations that determine risks.

Illustration of interest rate risk exposure

Block has the following liabilities at 1 January Year 1:

- Bank loans $400 million, interest at LIBOR + 50 basis points
- $50 million floating rate bonds, interest at LIBOR + 25 basis points
- $200 million 6.5% bonds, redeemable 30 June Year 3
- $350 million 6% bonds, redeemable 30 September Year 4

Interest rate exposure:

The company has floating rate liabilities of $450 million and fixed rate liabilities of $550 million.

Average interest rate of fixed rate liabilities:

$200m × 6.5%	$13m
$350m × 6%	$21m
$550m of loans with	$34m of interest = 6.18% average rate

The average interest rate would be compared to other companies in the same industry to ascertain whether it was higher or lower, whilst bearing in mind the general expectation of movement in the base rate. For example, if Block's average rate is higher than the competitors and the base rate is expected to fall, then it will be deemed more risky because Block will pay more interest in the future compared to its competitors.

Average time to maturity of fixed rate liabilities:

$200m × 2.50 years	500.00
$350m × 3.75 years	1,312.50
	1,812.50
1,812.50/$550m	3.30 years average remaining life

Time to maturity creates a separate measure of exposure. Again Block's average time to maturity will be compared to its competitors. If the time to maturity is longer than the competitors and rates are expected to fall then Block is more risky since it has tied itself in to longer term fixed rate borrowings, paying out too much interest and possibly incurring a redemption penalty if it tried to restructure its debt.

Refinancing risk

Refinancing risk is associated with interest rate risk because it looks at the risk that loans will not be refinanced or will not be refinanced at the same rates.

The reasons for this could include:

- Lenders are unwilling to lend or only prepared to lend at higher rates.
- The credit rating of the company has reduced making them a more unattractive lending option.
- The company may need to refinance quickly and therefore have difficulty in obtaining the best rates.

4 Currency risk

 Currency risk is the risk that arises from possible future movements in an exchange rate. It is a two-way risk, since exchange rates can move either adversely or favourably.

Currency risk affects any organisation with:

- assets and/or liabilities in a foreign currency
- regular income and/or expenditures in a foreign currency
- no assets, liabilities or transactions that are denominated in a foreign currency. Even if a company does not deal in any currencies, it will still face economic risk since its competitors may be faring better due to favourable exchange rates on their transactions.

 Currency risk can be categorised into three types: economic, transaction and translation exposure.

Economic risk

Economic risk is any change in the economy, home or abroad, which can affect the value of a transaction before a commitment is made i.e. payment or receipt.

A company may not have any transactions in a foreign currency i.e. it buys and sells in its home currency, but it is still affected by economic risk.

This can be due to several factors:

- Competitive position – even if a company trades wholly in its own currency, other companies can cause it to lose money in the form of reduced sales. For example, if a competitor company trades (either buys or sells) abroad where the currency is more favourable – cheaper for supplies, or allows a higher price for sales, then the competitor will be more profitable. Conversely, if the exchange rates are adverse for the competitor, they would be less profitable.

- Elasticity of demand – exchange rates can make a company's products more or less expensive. When an exchange rate makes the product more expensive, say, the demand for that product will probably fall. However, if the product is available at a lower price from another company, who perhaps trades in a different currency which enables the product to be made and sold more cheaply, then demand does not fall but transfers to that other company. Therefore the home company has lost sales, is less profitable and shareholder returns will fall.

- Pricing – currency movements can affect pricing decisions, even if an entity has no foreign operations and does not trade internationally. For example, a Scottish sheep farm could sell lamb exclusively to local supermarkets and have no imports or exports whatsoever. The farmer must still be aware of exchange rates because a strengthening of the British Pound against, say, the New Zealand Dollar will make it cheaper for farmers to import New Zealand lamb and the farmer may have to reduce his prices in response.

  In effect, economic risk is the variation in the value of the business (i.e. the present value of future cash flows) due to unexpected changes in the economy.

Management of economic risk

One way the risk can be reduced is to diversify globally, meaning that a company can reduce its risk by having operations located all over the world or by doing business with other companies located in other parts of the world. This is portfolio theory – the idea of reducing risk by 'not having all your eggs in one basket'. This can be broken down into:

Diversification of production and sales

If a firm manufactures all its products in one country and that country's exchange rate strengthens, then the firm will find it increasingly difficult to export to the rest of the world. Its future cash flows and therefore its present value would diminish. However, if it had established production plants worldwide and bought its components worldwide (a policy which is practised by many multinationals, e.g. Ford) it is unlikely that the currencies of all its operations would revalue at the same time. It would therefore find that, although it was losing on exports from some of its manufacturing locations, this would not be the case in all of them. Also if it had arranged to buy its raw materials worldwide it would find that a strengthening home currency would result in a fall in its input costs and this would compensate for lost sales.

Diversification of suppliers and customers

Similarly a company could diversify its supplier and customer base so that if the currency of, say, one supplier strengthens, purchasing could be switched to a cheaper supplier.

Diversification of financing

When borrowing internationally, firms must be aware of foreign exchange risk. When, for example, a firm borrows in Swiss francs it must pay back in the same currency. If the Swiss franc then strengthens against the home currency this can make interest and principal repayments far more expensive. However, if borrowing is spread across many currencies it is unlikely they will all strengthen at the same time and therefore risks can be reduced.

Borrowing in foreign currency is only truly justified if returns will then be earned in that currency to finance repayment and interest. International borrowing can also be used to hedge the adverse economic effects of local currency devaluations. If a firm expects to lose from devaluations of the currencies in which its subsidiaries operate it can hedge this exposure by arranging to borrow in the weakening currency. Any losses on operations will then be offset by cheaper financing costs.

Note that diversification (of any type) will not necessarily help in extreme circumstances e.g. during a global recession.

Marketing

A way of managing economic risk is quite simply to have a very good marketing ploy that enables you to convince your customers that your product is the one to buy despite it being more expensive!

More on economic risk

Economic risk is the possibility that the value of the company (the present value of all future post tax cash flows) will change due to unexpected changes in future economies (which includes exchange rates). The size of the risk is difficult to measure as economies can change significantly and unexpectedly. Such changes can affect firms in many ways:

- Imagine a UK company had an investment in South East Asia during the late 1990s. They would have suffered some economic risk due to the economic downturn in that part of the world at that time. An economic downturn can reduce trade and have an impact on foreign currency exchange rates. This means that the UK company's investment might be worth less upon first glance. However, the wider implications might include the fact that the factory makes goods for export. Then the downturn might reduce costs. Meanwhile if the competition are manufacturing in the 'booming' West and costs are higher (material and wage inflation) then the Asian subsidiary may have the competitive advantage. Therefore, the economic downturn may not be wholly downside risk.

- Suppose a UK company invests in a subsidiary in Africa. The currency of the African country depreciates each year for several years. The cash flows remitted to the UK are worth less in GBP terms each year, causing a reduction in the investment value.

- A French company buys raw materials that are priced in US dollars. It converts the raw materials into a finished product which it exports to Japan. Over several years the euro appreciates against the dollar but depreciates against the yen. The euro value of the French company's income increases while the US dollar cost of its materials decreases, resulting in an increase in value of the company's cash flows.

- Insisting on dealing in only the home currency may affect the foreign demand for its products if the pound appreciates or their relationship with suppliers if the pound weakens.

- Consider a UK company exporting goods or services to Spain, in competition with (say) US companies. In this case, if the US dollar weakens relative to the euro (even if the pound remains unchanged against the euro), it will become cheaper for the Spanish customers to import those goods and services from the US supplier if the order is denominated in the foreign currency. Even if the order is denominated in euros (the Spanish currency) the euro price from the US supplier might not convert into enough GBP to make it worthwhile for the UK company.

- Deciding to acquire resources, say equipment in Italy, with a view to supplying goods or services to the UK market. In this case the company's costs are in euros with expected revenues in GBP. If the GBP were to weaken against the euro, the costs of the operation could become uneconomic.

However, many of the above examples are not as straightforward as they might first seem, due to the compensating actions of economic forces. For example, if the exchange rate of a South American country depreciates significantly, it is probably due to high inflation. If the South American subsidiary of a UK company increases its prices in line with inflation in South America, its cash flows in the local currency will increase. However, these will be converted at a depreciating exchange rate to produce (theoretically) a constant GBP value of cash flows. Alternatively, if the subsidiary does not increase its prices, it may increase its sales volume by selling at a lower price. Therefore the subsidiary / group has not 'lost out'.

Measurement of economic exposure

Although economic exposure is difficult to measure it is of vital importance to firms as it concerns their long-run viability. Economic exposure cannot be ignored as it could lead to reductions in the firm's future cash flows or an increase in the systematic risk of the firm, resulting in a fall in shareholder wealth.

There are a very limited number of factors that can be observed to attempt to quantify economic exposure, which include the price elasticity of demand for products. For example, as prices rise demand usually falls, but the rate at which it falls and the resulting cash flows will impact on the value of a company. The price rise could be due to a change in the exchange rate.

Economic risk example

Imagine a fictitious airport, XL, in country X with the British pound (GBP) as its currency.

XL services passengers that live in its own country (20%) and passengers that travel from other countries (80%).

90% of the travellers passing through XL are holiday makers while the other 10% travel for business purposes.

The fuel bought by the airlines passing through XL is mainly bought in the US where the currency is the USD.

Why is the company exposed to currency risk?

Passenger numbers will be affected by the strength of the GBP:

- Only 20% of passengers live in the UK and travel within the country on internal flights. The other 80% will be exposed to foreign currency movements making their trips more or less expensive. For example, a holiday maker from the UK will find a holiday in the US more expensive if the GBP weakens against the USD and may choose not to travel. Similarly passengers from outside the UK may choose other destinations if the GBP strengthens against their home currency.

- Most passengers are travelling on holiday so they have a much wider choice of destinations than business travellers. A business person may have to go to a particular country because that is where the customer or supplier is based. In theory, 90% of XL's customers could change their travel plans and that could reduce demand for XL's routes.

- Movements in the value of the GBP could affect interest rates and that may also prevent holiday makers from travelling due to the increase in the cost of their mortgage.

- If the GBP weakens against the USD, say, then fuel, for example, may become more expensive. This could force the airlines to raise prices which might reduce passenger numbers or the number of flights.

How can the risks you have identified be managed?

The first step is to always consider whether there are any natural hedges. For example, a strong GBP would give holiday makers from country X more spending money when they travel abroad. However, that will also increase the airlines' costs when converted to their home currency and so fares may increase. These factors might offset each other.

Once the airport has established the overall impact of the strengthening or weakening of the GBP the next step would be to hedge that risk. For example, if the strengthening was discovered to be bad then the airport might borrow in USD to create a hedge.

It would also be worth diversifying the routes covered by the airlines. It might be worth offering airlines that travel to popular destinations a discount for flying from XL. The cost of the discount could be viewed as an investment in managing currency risk.

Test your understanding 2 (Objective test question)

Which of the following can reduce economic risk for a UK company?

A   Diversifying activities across the UK

B   Diversifying production and sales

C   Diversifying suppliers and customers

D   Diversification of financing

Transaction risk

This is the risk related to buying or selling on credit in foreign currencies. There is a danger that, between the time of the transaction and the date of the cash flow, exchange rates will have moved adversely. This risk, unlike the translation risk, actually affects the cash flows of the business.

Illustration of transaction risk

A UK company purchases goods on six months' credit from a US supplier for USD150,000. At the time of the transaction, the exchange rate was GBP 1/USD1.8000 and the expected payment for the purchase was GBP 83,333 (USD150,000/1.8000).

However, suppose that the exchange rate changes in the next six months, and the dollar strengthens in value to GBP 1/USD1.5000. The company must acquire the USD150,000 to make the payment, and if it buys this dollar currency at the exchange rate when the date of the payment is due, the actual cost will be GBP 100,000. This is GBP 16,667 more than originally expected. The UK company has been exposed to a transaction liability in US dollars for six months, and as a result of the dollar increasing in value during that time, an unexpected 'loss' of GBP 16,667 arose.

The exchange rate might have moved the other way. If the exchange rate when the payment was due had changed to GBP 1/USD2.0000, with the dollar falling in value, it would cost only GBP 75,000 to acquire the dollars to make the payment. This is GBP 8,333 less than originally expected, therefore there would be a 'profit' of GBP 8,333 on the favourable exchange rate movement.

Test your understanding 3 (Objective test question)

A UK company has just despatched a shipment of goods to Sweden. The sale will be invoiced in Swedish kronor, and payment is to be made in three months' time.

Neither the UK exporter nor the Swedish importer uses the forward foreign exchange market to cover exchange risk.

If the British pound were to weaken substantially against the Swedish kronor, what would be the foreign exchange gain or loss effects upon the UK exporter and the Swedish importer?

A   UK exporter: Gain/Swedish importer: No effect

B   UK exporter: No effect/Swedish importer: Gain

C   UK exporter: Loss/Swedish importer: No effect

D   UK exporter: Gain/Swedish importer: Gain

Test your understanding 4 – H Co (Integration question)

H Co (a UK company) expects to make the following transaction in six months' time:

- USD100,000 purchases from US suppliers.

Exchange rates are as follows:

Rate today USD1/GBP 0.5556

Rate in six months USD1/GBP 0.5420

Required:

Calculate the payment required in GBP if H Co makes the payment now or in six months' time.

Management of transaction risk

This will be covered in detail in the next chapter.

Translation risk

This arises when a company has assets or liabilities denominated in foreign currencies. The risk is that exchange rate volatility will cause the value of assets to fall or liabilities to increase resulting in losses to the company.

More on translation risk

The financial statements of overseas subsidiaries are usually translated into the home currency in order that they can be consolidated into the group's financial statements. Note that this is purely a paper-based exercise – it is the translation not the conversion of real money from one currency to another.

Settled transactions

When a company enters into a transaction denominated in a currency other than its functional currency (which could be the home currency or that of its parent), that transaction must be translated into the functional currency before it is recorded. The transaction will initially be recorded by applying the spot rate. However when cash settlement occurs the settled amount will be translated using the spot rate on the settlement date. If this amount differs from that used when the transaction occurred, there will be an exchange difference which is taken to the income statement in the period in which it arises.

Unsettled transactions

The treatment of any 'foreign' items remaining on the statement of financial position at the year end will depend on whether they are classified as monetary or non-monetary.

Monetary items include cash, receivables, payables and loans, and they are re-translated at the closing rate (year-end spot).

Non-monetary items include non-current assets, inventory and investments, and are not re-translated but left at historic cost.

For example, if a company has a foreign subsidiary which includes property, plant and equipment this will be valued at the date it was acquired (or revalued). However, if these assets were acquired using a loan, then the loan is translated at the closing rate (current spot) which could be very different to the spot when the assets were bought. This gives rise to currency risk because the assets and liabilities no longer offset each other. (This is covered by the 'temporal method' in International Accounting Standard (IAS) 21.)

The reported performance of an overseas subsidiary in home-based currency terms can be severely distorted if there has been a significant foreign exchange movement.

Any foreign exchange gains or losses are recorded in equity. They are unrealised and will only become realised when the subsidiary is sold.

Unless managers believe that the company's share price will fall as a result of showing a translation exposure loss in the company's accounts, translation exposure should not normally be hedged. (The company's share price, in an efficient market, should only react to exposure that is likely to have an impact on cash flows.)

However, research shows that company directors do spend (in some people's opinion – waste) money hedging translation risk. The management of translation risk is often considered to be dysfunctional behaviour.

Management of translation risk

Any change in parity will affect reported profits (and hence earnings per share), total assets, borrowings, net worth (and hence gearing) but – to repeat – it will not have affected the measured cash flow in the period being reported on.

Academic theory argues that translation risk, of itself, need not concern financial managers, but in practice, there are two strong arguments in favour of the relevance of translation risk:

1   Although it does not affect the value of the entity as a whole, it can affect the attribution of that value between the different stakeholders. Higher gearing may lead to higher interest rates being charged on bank loans, either directly in accordance with clauses in borrowing agreements or indirectly as a result of the company's credit rating being reduced. The banks benefit at the expense of the equity investors in the business. If the treasurer is pursuing an objective of maximising shareholder wealth, he will want to manage this risk.

2   If the accounts are being used 'beyond their design specification', for example as the basis for calculating bonus payments for directors and senior managers, then there is a temptation to protect the current year's figures, even though it is known that doing so has a long-term cost. This is comparable to pulling profit into the current year, knowing that it will both reduce next year's profit and result in tax being paid earlier than necessary.

The former is a good reason, but the latter is often the real reason for managing translation risk

Test your understanding 5 (Objective test question)

The risk that exchange rates will cause assets to fall in value, or liabilities to increase in value, resulting in losses to a company is called:

A   Transaction risk

B   Translation risk

C   Economic risk

D   Currency risk

5 Using financing packages to split risks

As discussed in the earlier chapters on financing, different finance options carry differing levels of risk and return for the investors concerned. The two extremes are:

- Equity (ordinary share capital) usually carries the highest risk (unsecured, uncertain dividend, share price may fall, last in line in the event of a liquidation) but potentially the highest return.

- Loan capital is usually lower risk (secured, specified interest) but has a lower typical return.

In between these extremes are a wide range of alternatives with differing risk/return profiles.

For example, venture capitalists often like to invest in unquoted companies via convertible loan stock to skew their risk exposure:

- If the company concerned performs moderately then the risk exposure effectively amounts to getting interest paid and the loan redeemed at some future point (usually within 5 years).

- If the investment performs badly then the downside exposure is limited to getting some interest paid and perhaps their investment back in the event of a winding up.

- If the investment performs well, then the company is usually prepared for flotation when the VC will convert the debt into equity to sell a large number of shares at a high profit.

Any financing package can be assessed by how it shares risks and returns out between different investors.

Test your understanding 6 – MacDonald Farm (Case style question)

Context

The entire share capital of MacDonald Farm Ltd is owned by Ken MacDonald and his wife, Jane. Its business is owning and running a 1,200 acre farm, growing a range of fruit and vegetables.

Due to changes in farm subsidies and increasing customer pressure from large supermarket chains, MacDonald Farm Ltd faces a sharp decline in its annual trading profits, which in recent years have averaged $180,000.

Ken MacDonald is therefore investigating using 200 acres to set up a new exclusive 18-hole golf course. Preliminary research suggest that planning permission will be forthcoming and demand projections are encouraging, given that membership waiting lists at the two existing golf clubs in the area exceed 350. If the project goes ahead, the new golf club is expected to be much better appointed than the two existing courses nearby.

Further information

The golf club company

It is proposed that MacDonald Farm Ltd will sign a 100-year lease with a new company, Calum Golf Club Ltd, which will pay an annual rent of $50,000 to MacDonald Farm Ltd for use of the land.

The issued capital of the golf club company will be two $1 shares, owned by Mr and Mrs MacDonald, and the remainder of its initial funding will be $2 million in the form of 15% per annum irredeemable loan stock. Fifty local business men, including Mr MacDonald, have each agreed to purchase $40,000 of this stock. The terms of the debenture loan stock issue prohibit a dividend being paid on the two ordinary shares so that any surplus is applied for the benefit of the club and its members.

Of the funds thus raised, $450,000 will be spent on converting the arable land to become a landscaped golf course. A further $50,000 will provide working capital.

The club house company

The remaining $150,000 will be used to purchase a 25% stake in a separate company, Tarpon Club House Ltd, that will develop and operate a club house. This will have conference facilities, a sports hall, two bars and a restaurant. A local property company will subscribe the other 75% of the share capital of Tarpon Club House Ltd.

Calum Golf Club Ltd will pay an annual rent of $50,000 for the use of the club house, but Tarpon Club House Ltd will manage and run all facilities offered there, taking the profits that will be earned.

When ready to commence business in January 20X6, the new golf club will be much better appointed than the two existing Norbridge courses, and the only serious competition for comparable leisure facilities will come from three hotels in Norbridge itself and a country house four miles away.

Costs and revenues

Annual operating expenses of Calum Golf Club Ltd are budgeted at $900,000.

On the revenue side, Calum Golf Club Ltd's share of profits on the investment in Tarpon Club House Ltd is expected to total $200,000 in 20X6, the first year of operations. Green fees, chargeable to non-members using the golf course, are expected to amount to an additional $100,000 a year.

On the assumption that target membership levels are achieved, annual subscriptions are initially to be set at $1,000 for each member. This will be $200 less than for full membership at the two rival golf clubs in the area. In addition, no joining fees will be payable in the first year of operation, but thereafter (as with the other two clubs) they will be equal to one year's subscription.

Breakeven analysis

Based on the above data the break-even point for Calum Golf Club Ltd has been estimated at 600 members:

Expected fixed costs	$900,000
Income from Club House	$200,000
Green Fees Income	$100,000
Net costs to be covered	$600,000
Membership fee	$1,000
Break-even membership	600

Required:

Write a brief report to Mr and Mrs MacDonald regarding the proposed golf club explaining their risk/return profile under different possible scenarios.

(30 minutes)

6 Value at risk

Value at Risk (VaR) allows investors to assess the scale of the likely loss in their portfolio at a defined level of probability. It is becoming the most widely used measure of financial risk and is also enshrined in both financial and accounting regulations.

VaR is based on the assumption that investors care mainly about the probability of a large loss. The VaR of a portfolio is the maximum loss on a portfolio occurring within a given period of time with a given probability (usually small).

- Calculating VaR involves using three components: a time period, a confidence level and a loss amount or percentage loss.

- Statistical methods are used to calculate a standard deviation for the possible variations in the value of the total portfolio of assets over a specific period of time.

- Making an assumption that possible variations in total market value of the portfolio are normally distributed, it is then possible to predict at a given level of probability the maximum loss that the bank might suffer on its portfolio in the time period.

- A bank can try to control the risk in its asset portfolio by setting target maximum limits for value at risk over different time periods (one day, one week, one month, three months, and so on).

- VaR may be calculated as standard deviation × Z-score (where the Z-score can be found from the normal distribution tables).

Normal distribution

Normal distributions can be seen when we measure things such as:

- Exam results
- Staff performance gradings
- The heights of a group of people etc.

A normal distribution has the following characteristics:

The mean is shown in the centre of the diagram and the curve is symmetrical about the mean. This means that 50% of the values will be below the mean and 50% of the values will be above the mean.

Note: The mean, median and mode will all be the same for a normal distribution.

How far the values spread out from the mean is the standard deviation. This can be seen in the following diagram:

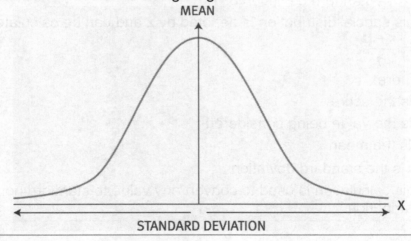

The total area under the curve is equal to 1.

If we can think of a standard normal distribution curve with three standard deviations as follows:

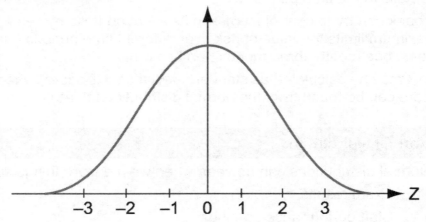

In general 68% of values are within one deviation (between -1 and 1), 95% of values are within two standard deviations (between -2 and 2) and 99.7% of values are within three standard deviations (between -3 and 3).

From this we can see that if we look at a set of data which fits a normal distribution the majority of values will occur closer to the mean, with fewer and fewer occurring the further from the mean we move.

A standard normal distribution has:

- a mean of 0
- a standard deviation of 1.

This special distribution is denoted by z and can be calculated as:

$$z = \frac{x - \mu}{\sigma}$$

Where:

z is the score

x is the value being considered

μ is the mean

σ is the standard deviation

This calculation is used to convert any value to standard normal distribution.

Looking up the normal distribution tables

Once we have calculated our 'z score' we can look this up on the normal distribution table to find the area under the curve, which equates to the percentage chance (probability) of that value occurring.

So if we calculated a z score of 1.00. From the table the value is 0.3413.

This means that $(0.3413 \div 1.0)$ or 34.13% is the area shown from 0 - 1 on the diagram

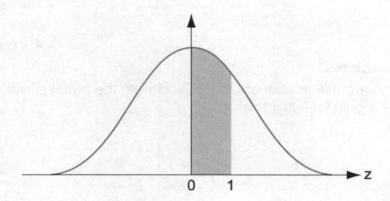

From this we can deduce that 34.13% would be the area shown from 0 -1 on the diagram. So we can say that 68.26% of values will fall within one standard deviation (-1 to 1).

VaR calculation

For VaR , there are two types of calculation to consider:

1   The confidence level that the result will be above a particular figure – this is referred to as a one tail test.

2   The confidence level that a figure will be within a particular range – this is referred to as a two tail test.

In both cases we are working backwards from the percentage to find the value of x.

One tail test

If you are asked to calculate the 95% VaR, this is a one tail test. As we are looking at risk, it is usually about being 95% certain that the outcome will be above a particular value.

50% of the distribution is on one side of the mean, so within the tables we are looking for the value as close as possible to 0.4500 (45%).

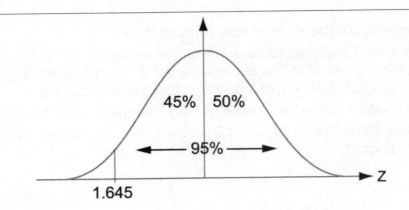

Two tail test

If you are asked about being 95% certain the result is within a range, the area would look like this:

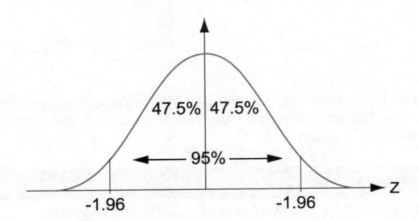

We would be looking for 0.4750 in the tables, 47.5% above and below the mean.

One tail test example

Z is a bank. The management accountant of Z has estimated that the value of its asset portfolio at year end will be $1,500 million, with a standard deviation of $300 million.

Required:

Calculate the value at risk of the portfolio, at a 97.5% confidence level. (Express your answer in $, rounded to the nearest million.)

Solution:

The Z value for a one-tail 97.5% confidence level is 1.96 (from the Normal Distribution tables).

VaR = standard deviation × Z value, so the

VaR = $300 million × 1.96 = $588 million

This means there is a 2.5% chance that the value of the portfolio will be (1,500 - 588) $912 million or below.

Two tail test example

AL, a UK based company is expecting to receive USD 10 million from a US customer. The value in GBP is dependent on the exchange rate between the USD and the GBP.

The mean exchange rate is USD 1.25/GBP 1 and the daily volatility of the USD/GBP exchange rate is 0.25%.

Required:

What is the range of values that AL will be 95% confident of receiving in 1 day?

Solution:

The mean value of the USD 10 million is GBP 8 million (USD 10 million ÷ USD 1.25/GBP 1) The daily standard deviation is (0.25% × GBP 8 million =) GBP 20,000

As we are looking at a range, this is a two tail test, to be 95% confident this will be within 47.5% of the mean on either side.

First find 0.4750 in the normal tables, this is a z value of 1.96.

VaR = Z × Std deviation = 1.96 × 20,000 = GBP 39,200

This means that AL is 95% confident that the value will be within GBP 39,200 of the mean.

Therefore AL is 95% confident the amount received will be between GBP 7,960,800 and GBP 8,039,200.

Given the 1 day VaR, we can easily calculate the VaR for longer holding periods as:

n day VaR = 1 day VaR × $\sqrt{n}$

The VaR increases with the holding period. Thus, the longer the holding period, the greater the VaR.

Further examples of VaR

Suppose a UK company expects to receive USD 14 million from a US customer. The value in GBP to the UK company will depend on the exchange rate between the USD and the GBP resulting in gains or losses as the exchange rate changes. Assume that the exchange rate today is USD 1.75/GBP 1 and that the daily volatility of the USD/GBP exchange rate is 0.5%.

Required:

Calculate the

(a)   1-day 95% VaR

(b)   1-day 99% VaR

(c)   5-day 95% VaR

(d)   30-day 99% VaR

Solution:

The value of the USD 14 million today is GBP 8 million (USD 14 million ÷ USD 1.75/GBP 1) with a daily standard deviation of GBP 40,000 (0.5% × GBP 8 million).

(a)   The standard normal value (Z) associated with the one-tail 95% confidence level is 1.645 (see Normal Distribution tables). Hence, the 1-day 95% VaR is 1.645 × GBP 40,000 = GBP 65,800. This means that we are 95% confident that the maximum daily loss will not exceed GBP 65,800. Alternatively, we could also say that there is a 5% (1 out of 20) chance that the loss would exceed GBP 65,800.

(b)   The standard normal value (Z) associated with the one-tail 99% confidence level is 2.33 (see Normal Distribution tables). Hence, the 1-day 99% VaR is 2.33 × GBP 40,000 = GBP 93,200. Thus, there is a 1% (1 out of 100) chance that the loss would exceed GBP 93,200.

(c)   If we wanted to calculate the VaR for a longer period of 5 days, at the 95% level the calculation would be:

5 day 95% VaR = 1 day 95% VaR × $\sqrt{5}$ = GBP 65,800 × 2.236 = GBP 147,133

There is a 5% chance that the company's foreign exchange loss would exceed GBP 147,133 over the next 5 days.

(d)   Similarly, the 30-day 99% VaR would be:

1 day 99% VaR × $\sqrt{30}$ = GBP 93,200 × 5.477 = GBP 510,477

This illustrates the longer the holding period, the greater the VaR.

More on value at risk (VaR)

The Basel committee established international standards for banking laws and regulations aimed at protecting the international financial system from the results of the collapse of major banks. Basel II established rigorous risk and capital management requirements to ensure each bank holds reserves sufficient to guard against its risk exposure given its lending and investment practices. Regulators require banks to measure their market risk using a risk measurement model which is used to calculate the Value at Risk (VaR).

However, the global financial crisis has identified substantial problems with banks' governance procedures in terms of understanding operational risk and applying risk measurement models like VaR. This has been emphasised by the number of banks that have failed or required government support – Northern Rock and Bradford and Bingley in the UK; Bear Sterns and Washington Mutual in the US amongst others.

The problem is that VaR is based on historical observations, which means that it cannot allow for the possibility of an extreme event that is not predicted by past trends. For example, in the lead up to the Credit Crunch, banks evaluated the value of their mortgage portfolios (and made lending decisions) on the basis that house prices had risen consistently for years. The banks assumed that this trend would continue, but unfortunately it didn't.

Test your understanding 7 (Integration question)

A company expects to receive USD 10 million from a US customer. The value in GBP will depend on the exchange rate changing. Assume that the exchange rate today is USD 1.6667 / GBP 1 and that the daily volatility of the USD/GBP exchange rate is 0.5%.

Required:

What is the 10-day 95% VaR?

Test your understanding 8 – Value at risk (Integration question)

A bank has estimated that the expected value of its portfolio in two weeks' time will be $50 million, with a standard deviation of $4.85 million.

Required:

Calculate and comment upon the value at risk of the portfolio, assuming a 95% confidence level.

7 End of chapter objective test questions

Test your understanding 9 (Objective test question)

Sadie Co trades regularly with suppliers and customers in foreign countries. Three months ago the company agreed to buy a large shipment of raw materials on credit from a foreign supplier.

By the time Sadie Co paid for the shipment last week, the exchange rate had moved significantly, causing the cost of the raw materials to be 10% more than originally expected.

What type of risk is this an example of?

A   Translation risk

B   Economic risk

C   Political risk

D   Transaction risk

Test your understanding 10 (Objective test question)

A UK company has just despatched a shipment of goods to Sweden. The sale will be invoiced in British pounds, and payment is to be made in three months' time.

Neither the UK exporter nor the Swedish importer uses the forward foreign exchange market to cover exchange risk.

If the British pound were to weaken substantially against the Swedish kronor, what would be the foreign exchange gain or loss effects upon the UK exporter and the Swedish importer?

A   UK exporter: No effect/Swedish importer: Gain

B   UK exporter: No effect/Swedish importer: Loss

C   UK exporter: Loss/Swedish importer: No effect

D   UK exporter: Gain/Swedish importer: Gain

Test your understanding 11 (Objective test question)

The management accountant of Sweep Bank has estimated that the value of its asset portfolio at the coming year end will be $1,000 million, with a standard deviation of $350 million.

What is the value at risk of the portfolio, at a 95% confidence level?

A $424 million

B $576 million

C $950 million

D $1,576 million

Test your understanding 12 (Objective test question)

A UK based company expects to receive EUR 5 million from a French customer. The value in GBP will depend on the exchange rate changing. Assume that the exchange rate today is EUR 1.2500 / GBP 1 and that the daily volatility of the EUR/GBP exchange rate is 0.3%.

What is the 5-day value at risk, at a 90% confidence level? (rounded to the nearest GBP'000)

A   GBP 15,000

B   GBP 34,000

C   GBP 44,000

D   GBP 77,000

Test your understanding 13 (Objective test question)

A UK based company expects to receive EUR 5 million from a French customer. The value in GBP will depend on the exchange rate changing. Assume that the exchange rate today is EUR 1.2500 / GBP 1 and that the daily volatility of the EUR/GBP exchange rate is 0.3%.

What is the upper limit of the range of values that the company will be 95% confident of receiving in 1 day? (rounded to the nearest GBP'000)

A   GBP 4,024,000

B   GBP 4,020,000

C   GBP 3,976,000

D   GBP 3,980,000

8 End of chapter case style questions

Test your understanding 14 – Equip (Case style question)

Equip is a UK company that is a major exporter of agricultural equipment to Australia, New Zealand and throughout Europe. All production facilities are in the United Kingdom. The majority of raw materials and tools are also sourced in the United Kingdom, with a few imports from Eire, priced in British pounds. Major competitors are based in the United States and Germany. There are plans to set up a manufacturing subsidiary in Australia, funded in part by an Australian dollar loan to be taken out by Equip. The new manufacturing facility would be used to source the Australian and New Zealand markets.

Required:

(a) Describe the potential currency exposures faced by this company before setting up the manufacturing subsidiary.

(10 minutes)

(b) Consider the effects of setting up the new manufacturing subsidiary in Australia with respect to the following:

(i) Will any of the exposures identified in (a) above be reduced?

(ii) What new currency exposures will the group face?

(15 minutes)

Test your understanding 15 – Economic risk (Case style question)

Scenario

R is a large retail organisation that imports goods from Australia for sale in its home market, where the currency is the R$. The directors of R are aware that the company is subject to significant economic exposure to movements on the AUS $ because any appreciation of the AUS $ will increase the cost of goods for resale. R has attempted to create a partial hedge against this by placing all of its cash reserves in an AUS $ bank account. That way the losses associated with any increase in cost prices will be partially offset by a gain on the bank account.

Trigger

The directors are concerned that the translation gains and losses on the AUS$ bank balance are visible to shareholders, whereas the offsetting of economic exposure is not and so their hedging policy may be misunderstood. The AUS bank account has a balance of AUS$30m. The exchange rate is presently R$3 to AUS$1.

Required:

(a) Prepare a briefing note advising the directors on the matters that they would have to consider in order to determine the extent of R's economic exposure.

(10 minutes)

(b) Evaluate the validity of the directors' concern that "the translation gains and losses on the AUS$ bank balance are visible to shareholders, whereas the offsetting of economic exposure is not and so their hedging policy may be misunderstood".

(15 minutes)

Test your understanding answers

Test your understanding 1 – Political risk (Integration question)

By entering into another country, the UK company is exposing itself to significant political risk.

Political risk arises due to political interference in either the company's own country of operation, or any country it chooses to expand into.

It can also be generated by neighbouring countries if West Africa could be affected. If, for example, the UK company intends to ship goods from WA then these ships may become a target by the pirates with a cost in the form of lost goods in transit and delays in production.

West Africa's political risk can be viewed from different levels of government:

Local government

Local political risk arises from the influence of local councils or state governments. It manifests itself in the decisions made by local government that may negatively affect the factory (such as business rates increases, or indirect taxation). Ideally, the UK company should try to source a representative from the local government on to the factory project.

National government

Government decisions will also impact upon the factory. For example, the National government may have offered tax incentives for the first few years of the project but might increase taxes or even introduce new streams of taxation such as green taxes in later years. They may also take punitive measures such as penalising businesses they see as operating incorrectly (e.g. low wages), or businesses operating at odds with their specified aims and objectives.

International government

International bodies such as the UN can also be a source of political risk for businesses if they find out about activities of which they disagree e.g. low wages.

Although the new factory might serve both parties aims and objectives now, there may come a point in time in the future where the respective governments of the UK & West Africa disagree on an issue, which could have serious repercussions for the UK company in the long run.

In addition, if West Africa had a relatively new government this would also be a concern, insofar that if their term in office was short any future government may reverse the decisions taken by their predecessors.

Political risk also covers legal and compliance risk to an extent. The UK company should ascertain whether there are any additional laws in West Africa of which they should be aware. The use of local lawyers should help.

Mitigation strategies

Mitigating political risk is never easy, as governments tend to be far more powerful than individual companies. However, there are some methods of reducing the risk. One such method would be for the UK company to invite locals (employees, local government) to become part owners in the factory.

Another option is for it to provide the foreign government with details of an eventual exit strategy that will leave the business in the hands of locals.

Neither of these strategies may be acceptable to the UK company.

Test your understanding 2 (Objective test question)

The answer is (B), (C) and (D).

Diversifying globally would be better than diversifying across the UK. Having operations across the world will reduce risk – portfolio theory.

Test your understanding 3 (Objective test question)

The answer is (A).

*   The Swedish importer is unaffected as he is invoiced in his local currency
*   The UK exporter will gain as the kronor received can be converted into more pounds.

Test your understanding 4 – H Co (Integration question)

Value of transaction at original rates

                                                    GBP
    USD 100,000 purchases @ 0.5556 55,560 payment

Value of transaction at future rates

    USD 100,000 purchases @ 0.5420 54,200 payment

The amount saved by paying in six months' time is GBP1,360. This saving arises due to the exchange rate moving in your favour.

Do not forget that you would have had approximately GBP55,000 in the bank for six months longer, earning interest which makes this an even better option.

Test your understanding 5 (Objective test question)

The answer is (B).

Transaction risk is the risk of buying or selling on credit.

Economic risk is any change in the economy, home or abroad, which can affect the value of a transaction before a commitment is made.

Currency risk is the risk that arises from possible future movements in an exchange rate.

Test your understanding 6 – MacDonald Farm (Case style question)

Report

To: Mr and Mrs MacDonald

From: An advisor

Date: Today

The risk/return profile of the proposed golf club investment

Introduction

This report has been prepared to analyse the risk/return profile of Mr and Mrs MacDonald if they undertake the proposed development of Calum Golf Club.

Risk appetite/objectives

Given increasing pressure on farm income we have assumed that the primary objective with the golf club investment is to provide a low risk source of income to compensate for anticipated falls in profit.

Risk exposure

We have analysed your risk exposure under the following scenarios:

Scenario 1: the golf club is extremely successful:

- You will receive an annual rent of $50,000 and interest of $6,000 on the debentures.

- No dividends can be paid on profits.

- Presumably you will also have a 100% share in a successful golf company, although no information has been given as to the possibility of selling this. Also the value of the shares will be limited by the restriction on dividends.

Scenario 2: the golf club just hits its BEP of 600 members:

- You will receive an annual rent of $50,000 and interest of $6,000 on the debentures.

- No dividends can be paid on profits.

Scenario 3: the golf club fails to hit its BEP

- In the short term the club could borrow funds if required to be able to meet its cost commitments so it is likely that you will still receive an annual rent of $50,000 and interest of $6,000 on the debentures.

- Given your investment via limited shares, you will not face any further liability for club losses.

- However, if faced with the prospect of making an ongoing loss, the golf club may decide to start trying to cut costs. The choices are not attractive – it could cut salary and maintenance costs but this would undermine its competitive strategy of differentiation, making the situation worse.

Scenario 4: the golf club cannot pay interest on the debentures

- If the interest is not paid, then the debenture holders may insist on the appointment of a receiver to liquidate their investment.

- In such a scenario it is unlikely that any rent will be paid. If this occurs, then it is not clear if the farm can reclaim the land and sell the club house, perhaps even returning the land to arable use.

Conclusion and preliminary recommendations

Unless the golf club does very badly, you should receive a steady income of $56,000 per annum, equating to around $280 per acre, considerably higher than the $150 per acre earned on arable land historically. The investment gives a higher return than arable farming and at a lower risk, and is thus recommended on financial grounds.

However, before proceeding, we recommend that you seek to clarify/address the following risk areas:

- What is the legal position concerning the land and club house should rent not be paid?

- What assets are the debentures secured on, if any, as this will affect possible outcomes should interest not be paid?

Test your understanding 7 (Integration question)

The value of USD 10 million today is GBP 6 million (USD 10 m/1.6667) with a standard deviation of GBP 30,000 (0.5% × GBP 6 million).

The one-tail 95% confidence level is 1.645.

Hence a ten day 95% VaR is 1.645 × GBP 30,000 × $\sqrt{10}$ = GBP 156,058

Test your understanding 8 – Value at risk (Integration question)

At the 95% confidence level the value at risk = 1.645 × 4.85 = $8 million (1.645 is the normal distribution value for a one-tailed 5% probability level – this can be taken from the normal distribution tables).

As the information is for the 2 week period, and not a daily mean or standard deviation, there is no need to use the n day VaR adjustment.

There is thus a 5% probability that the portfolio value will fall to $42 million or below.

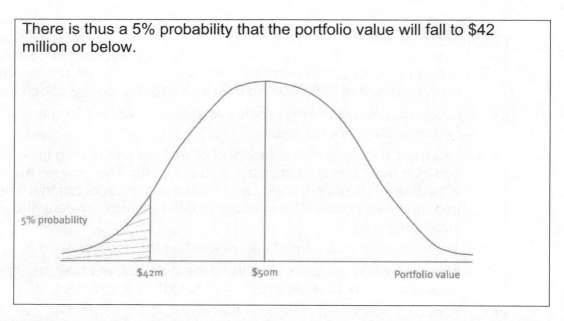

Test your understanding 9 (Objective test question)

The answer is (D).

Test your understanding 10 (Objective test question)

The answer is (A).

- The UK exporter will be unaffected as he receives his own currency.
- The Swedish importer will gain because he'll be able to buy more of the (weak) pounds with his (strong) Swedish currency.

Test your understanding 11 (Objective test question)

The answer is (B).

At a 95% confidence level the value at risk = 1.645 × $350 million = $576 million (1.645 is the normal distribution value for a one-tailed 5% probability level – this can be taken from the normal distribution tables).

As the information is for the 2 week period, and not a daily mean or standard deviation, there is no need to use the n day VaR adjustment.

There is thus a 5% probability that the portfolio value will fall to $424 million or below ($1,000 million - $576 million).

Test your understanding 12 (Objective test question)

The answer is (B).

The value of EUR 5 million today is GBP 4 million (EUR 5 m/1.2000) with a standard deviation of GBP 12,000 (0.3% × GBP 4 million).

The one-tail 90% confidence level is (approximately) 1.28.

Hence a five day 90% VaR is 1.28 × GBP 12,000 × $\sqrt{5}$ = GBP 34,346

Test your understanding 13 (Objective test question)

The answer is (A).

The mean value of the EUR 5 million is GBP 4 million (EUR 5 million ÷ EUR 1.2500/GBP 1).

The daily standard deviation is (0.3% × GBP 4 million =) GBP 12,000

As we are looking at a range, this is a two tail test, to be 95% confident this will be within 47.5% of the mean on either side.

First find 0.4750 in the normal tables, this is a z value of 1.96.

VaR = Z × Std deviation = 1.96 × 12,000 = GBP 23,520

This means that AL is 95% confident that the value will be within GBP 23,520 of the mean.

Therefore AL is 95% confident the amount received will be between GBP 3,976,480 and GBP 4,023,520.

Test your understanding 14 – Equip (Case style question)

(a) **Transaction risk:**

Sales revenue denominated in Australian dollars, New Zealand dollars euros, other.

Economic risk:

Purchase costs denominated in British pounds but sourced from Eire.

Price pressure from competitors in the United States and Germany (this will be affected by the currency cost base of these companies).

Translation risk:

Minor as Equip has no foreign subsidiaries – just retranslation of year-end currency debtors.

Overall assessment:

Mismatch of British pounds cost base versus exposed sales revenue.

(b) (i) Reduction in exposure:

- Australian dollar transaction risk.
- Australian dollar economic risk.
- Exposure from competitors is not eliminated.

(ii) New exposures, to the extent that they do not net out:

- Translation risk from incorporating subsidiary accounts.
- Translation risk arising from the Australian dollar debt.
- Transaction risk as a result of the Australian dollar dividend payments to the UK.

The end result will depend on the success of the Australian operation, the actual figures involved and any increase in local sales that may naturally result from a greater presence in Australia. For example, exposure to New Zealand dollars could increase if sales to New Zealand were to increase

Test your understanding 15 – Economic risk (Case style question)

(a)   **Briefing note**

To: The Board

From: A.N. Accountant

Date: Today

Subject: Determining the extent of R's economic exposure

Dear Sirs,

Economic exposure is generally difficult to measure, but an understanding can be obtained by identifying the factors that will lead to economic exposure. Generally, these boil down to identifying the effects of changes to cost prices and selling prices, both for the entity itself and for its competitors. R's purchase prices may be affected by movements in the AUS$. The actual effects may not be linear because R's Australian suppliers may not pass on the full effects of the currency movement. The suppliers may believe that the market for these products is sensitive to price rises and so the suppliers may choose to absorb some of the increased cost themselves. The likelihood of that happening will be determined in part by the availability of similar goods from economies that are not bound by the AUS$.

Currency movements may force R to raise its selling prices to customers. That makes the elasticity of demand for R's products important. It may be that prices are inelastic and that consumers are willing to buy just as much even if the price rises slightly. R's competitors may also buy products priced in AUS$ and that will reduce R's problem to an extent because all competing products will be affected in the same manner.

(b)   The financial statements will show the gains and losses arising on R's currency holdings. The shareholders may be concerned that the company's assets are exposed in this way and that they are risking a serious loss if the AUS$ declines against the R$. The economic exposure that is being hedged will be apparent from the fact that the company will generate less revenue and make less profit when the AUS$ is high. This will not appear anywhere as a single, visible item or disclosure in the financial statements.

The shareholders could be forgiven for believing that the only exposure is with respect to the AUS$ balance. There is nothing to prevent the directors from explaining their strategy to the shareholders. It does not matter that there is a lack of symmetry in accounting for the different currency exposures provided the shareholders accept this explanation. This is, however, a complicated area and it would be legitimate for the directors to worry that the shareholders will misunderstand. If the shareholders believe that the directors' policy is misguided then it could undermine their confidence in the board. Technically, the directors are supposed to pursue the maximisation of shareholder wealth and so they should always act in accordance with the shareholders" best interests. It would be dishonest to leave the company exposed to a manageable risk for no good reason simply because the shareholders may misinterpret the directors' behaviour.

Currency risk management

Chapter learning objectives

Lead outcome	Component outcome
C2: Evaluate financial risks	(a) Evaluate how financial risks are quantified
C3: Recommend ways of managing financial risks	(b) Discuss currency risk instruments

Topics to be covered

- Theory and forecasting of exchange rates (e.g. interest rate parity, purchasing power parity and the Fisher effect)
- Operations and features of swaps, forward contracts, money market hedges, futures and options
- Internal hedging techniques

1 Overview of chapter

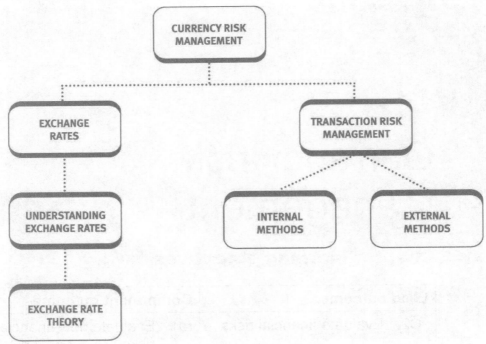

Understanding exchange rates

The foreign exchange, or forex, market is an international market in national currencies. It is highly competitive and virtually no difference exists between the prices in one market (e.g. New York) and another (e.g. London).

Exchange rates

 An exchange rate is expressed in terms of the quantity of one currency that can be exchanged for one unit of the other currency – it can be thought of as the price of a currency. For example:

1 USD = 0.6667 GBP

This means that 0.6667 GBP will buy 1 USD, i.e. the price of a USD is 0.6667 GBP. Hence:

- to convert from USDs to GBPs you must multiply by 0.6667
- to convert from GBPs to USDs you must divide by 0.6667.

(**Note:** This could also be stated as USD1 = GBP 0.6667, or USD1: GBP 0.6667. You may see any of these expressions in exam questions. By convention exchange rates are expressed (and rounded) to four decimal places, though this may not always be the case for information provided in questions.)

Spot rate

This is the rate given for a transaction with immediate delivery. In practice this means it will be settled within two working days.

Inverting exchange rates

Exchange rates may also be expressed the other way round, i.e. the USDs are expressed in terms of GBPs instead of vice versa.

e.g. the above spot rate 1 USD = 0.6667 GBP

may be expressed in terms of USDs to GBPs by dividing the rate into 1,

i.e. 1 ÷ 0.6667 = 1.5000

Therefore an equivalent illustration of the rate is:

1 GBP = 1.5000 USD

 Spread

Banks do not operate wholly for the greater good; in fact they wish to make a profit out of the deal. This means that they need to earn a **margin** or **spread** on the deal, as well as commission and fees.

e.g. 1 GBP = 1.5500 – 1.4500 USD

- the rate at which the bank will sell the variable currency (USDs) in exchange for the base currency (GBPs) is 1.4500 USD. (i.e. the rate at which it will buy GBPs).

- the rate at which the bank will buy USDs in exchange for GBPs is 1.5500 USD. (i.e. the rate at which it will sell GBPs).

The key to understanding our (the company's) position is to identify that the bank always wins, hence in the example above the bank buys GBP LOW and sells GBP HIGH.

 Illustration of spread prices

The rate quoted is 1 GBP = 1.4330 – 1.4325 USD.

- Company A wants to buy 100,000 USD in exchange for GBP.
- Company B wants to sell 200,000 USD in exchange for GBP.

Required:

Identify which rate the bank will offer each company.

Company A wants to buy USD100,000 in exchange for GBP (so that the bank will be selling USDs and buying GBPs):

- If we used the lower rate of 1.4325, the bank would sell dollars for GBP69,808

- If we used the higher rate of 1.4330, the bank would sell dollars for GBP69,784.

Clearly the bank would be better off selling dollars (and buying GBP) at the lower rate of 1.4325.

Company B wants to sell USD200,000 in exchange for GBP (so the bank would be buying USDs and selling GBPs):

- If we used the lower rate of 1.4325, the bank would buy dollars for GBP139,616

- If we used the higher rate of 1.4330, the bank would buy dollars for GBP139,567

The bank will make more money buying dollars (and selling GBP) at the higher rate of 1.4330

Test your understanding 1 – Spread (Integration question)

Assume that the spread is GBP 1 = USD 1.5500 – 1.4500. Consider the situations of three UK-based companies:

(a)   A Ltd imports goods from Texas to the value of USD100,000. Payment is cash on delivery; what is the cost in GBP of this purchase?

(b)   B plc exports goods to California valued at USD50,000. Receipt of payment is immediate on delivery of the goods; what is the value of GBP received?

(c)   C Ltd wishes to buy a product from US that is for sale in the UK at GBP12 each; at what dollar price must it purchase the product?

Cross rates

You may not be given the exchange rate you need for a particular currency, but instead be given the relationship it has with a different currency. You will then need to calculate a **cross rate.**

For example, if you have a rate in GBP1/USD and a rate in GBP1/EUR, you can derive a cross rate for EUR1/USD by dividing the GBP1/USD rate by the GBP1/EUR rate.

Illustration of cross rate calculation

A French company is to purchase materials costing USD100,000. You have the following information:

GBP1/USD   1.9000
GBP1/EUR   1.4500

Required:

Calculate the value of the purchase in euros.

Solution:

The solution could be calculated in two stages:

1   Convert the purchase into GBP:
     USD100,000/1.9000 = GBP52,632

2   Convert the GBP value into euros
     GBP52,632 × 1.4500 = EUR76,316

However, an easier alternative, particularly if there are a number of transactions to convert, is to calculate a cross rate:

The EUR1/USD rate will be 1.9000/1.4500 = 1.3103

The value of the transaction is therefore:

USD100,000/1.3103 = EUR76,318

Test your understanding 2 (Integration question)

The exchange rate for USD/GBP is USD1.4417/GBP1 and the exchange rate for EUR/GBP is 1.1250.

Required:

How many US dollars are there to the Euro?

Test your understanding 3 – Cross rates (Integration question)

A US company has to pay EUR100,000 for a machine. You have the following information:

GBP1/EUR1.5300
GBP1/USD1.8700

Required:

What is the cost of the machine in dollars?

2   Exchange rate theory

Forecasting exchange rates

A company may wish to forecast exchange rates for a number of short-term and long-term reasons. These may include:

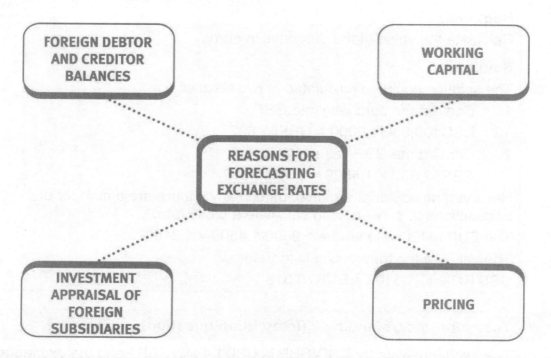

📖 **More on forecasting exchange rates**

- **Foreign debtor and creditor balances** – Our balances in other currencies may change dramatically over the short-term in terms of our domestic currency. If we are unable to forecast with some degree of certainty we open ourselves up to potentially very damaging exchange rate losses.

- **Working capital** – For a company with subsidiaries overseas it is important to be able to forecast movements in exchange rates over the medium-term to better facilitate the funding of those balances.

- **Pricing** – Movements in exchange rates may force the company to revise its pricing strategy in an individual country. This may be in response to a movement in the exchange rates between the country of manufacture and that of sale. Alternatively it is possible that an exchange rate movement favouring a competitor may also lead to a revision of prices.

- **Investment appraisal of foreign subsidiaries** – A longer-term forecast of exchange rate movements will be needed to identify the impact on a NPV analysis of the economic risks of a project.

- In the short-term rates may fluctuate due to market sentiment and **speculation** which are not easily explained theoretically, over the longer-term more fundamental factors take effect.
- If we could forecast exchange rates with some degree of accuracy this would reduce the transaction risk faced by a company, and may allow it to minimise hedging costs.

Why exchange rates fluctuate

Changes in exchange rates result from changes in the demand for and supply of the currency. These changes may occur for a variety of reasons including:

Speculation

Speculators enter into foreign exchange transactions with a view to making a profit from their expectations of the currency's future movements. If they expect a currency to devalue, they will short sell the currency with the hope of buying it back cheaply at a future date.

Balance of payments

Since currencies are required to finance international trade, changes in trade may lead to changes in exchange rates. In principle:

- demand for imports in the US represents a demand for foreign currency or a supply of dollars
- overseas demand for US exports represents a demand for dollars or a supply of the currency.

Thus a country with a current account deficit where imports exceed exports may expect to see its exchange rate depreciate, since the supply of the currency (imports) will exceed the demand for the currency (exports).

Any factors which are likely to alter the state of the current account of the balance of payments may ultimately affect the exchange rate.

Government policy

Governments may wish to change the value of their currency. This can be achieved directly by devaluation / revaluation, or via the foreign exchange markets (buying of selling their currency onto the markets).

> ## Capital movements between economies
>
> There are also **capital movements between economies**. These transactions are effectively switching bank deposits from one currency to another. These flows are now more important than the volume of trade in goods and services.
>
> Thus supply/demand for a currency may reflect events on the capital account. Several factors may lead to inflows or outflows of capital:
>
> - changes in *interest rates*: rising (falling) interest rates will attract a capital inflow (outflow) and a demand (supply) for the currency
>
> - *inflation rates:* asset holders will not wish to hold financial assets in a currency whose value is falling because of inflation.
>
> These forces which affect the demand and supply of currencies, and hence exchange rates, have been incorporated into a number of formal models.

We shall consider three related theories that together should give some insight into exchange rate movements:

1 Purchasing power parity theory (PPPT)
2 Interest rate parity theory (IRPT)
3 The International Fisher Effect

Purchasing power parity theory (PPPT)

This theory suggests the rate of exchange will be directly determined by the relative rates of inflation suffered by each currency. If one country suffers a greater rate of inflation than another its currency should be worth less in comparative terms.

The basis of PPPT is the 'Law of One Price':

- identical goods must cost the same regardless of the currency in which they are sold.

- if this is not the case then **arbitrage** (buying at the lower price, selling at the higher price) will take place until a single price is charged. Remember this is where a commodity that appears cheap is bought by many traders. The sellers then realise that they can put up their price due to the commodities popularity. Demand will then fall at this higher price and potential profits have been competed away. However, imagine that this commodity has to cross a countries border – it would be easy to cross the border from, say Switzerland to France to buy cheaper groceries. If many Swiss did this it might affect the Swiss Franc/Euro exchange rate. However it is much more difficult to make the same saving if you live in the UK even if you believe that the GBP/Euro is out of line.

PPPT

A company is going to buy a non-current asset at a cost of USD30 million. If the current rate is GBP1/USD1.5000 this would mean that in GBP terms it would cost **GBP20 million.**

What would be the prices in one year in each country given that the inflation rate in the US is 8% and in the UK is 5%?

	The US market	The UK market	
Year 0 (now)	USD30m	GBP1/USD1.5000	GBP20m
Inflation	8%		5%
Year 1	USD32.4m		GBP21m

What is the effective exchange rate in one year's time?

We can divide the US price by the UK price to calculate the revised exchange rate:

$$Rate = \frac{32.4}{21.0} = 1.5429$$

 Rule: The country with the higher inflation will suffer a fall (depreciation) in their currency.

The PPPT formula gives

$$Future\ spot\ rate = Current\ spot\ rate \times \frac{1 + i_f}{1 + i_h}$$

i_f rate of inflation in the foreign country

i_h rate of inflation in the home country spot rate in terms of 1 unit of home currency/foreign currency (e.g. GBP1/USD....)

In the above illustration, the future spot rate would be calculated by

$$1.500 \times = \frac{1.08}{1.05} = 1.5429$$

Test your understanding 4 (Integration question)

The USD and GBP are currently trading at GBP1/USD1.7200.

Inflation in the US is expected to grow at 3% pa, but at 4% pa in the UK.

Required:

What will be the future spot rate in a year's time? (Give your answer to 4 decimal places)

Problems with PPPT in practice

- Is the law of one price justified? In many markets it is apparent that the suppliers or manufacturers charge what the market will bear, this differing from one market to another.

- The costs of physically moving some products from one place to another mean that there will always be a premium in some markets in relation to another.

- Differing taxation regimes may dramatically affect the costs of a product in one market to that in another.

- Manufacturers may be able to successfully differentiate products in each market to limit the amount of arbitrage that occurs.

Is PPPT a good predictor of future spot rate?

PPPT certainly does explain the reasoning behind much of the movements in exchange rates but is not a very good predictor of exchange rates in the short- to medium-term.

Reasons for this include:

- Future inflation rates are only an estimate and often cannot be relied upon to be accurate.

- The market is dominated by speculation and currency investment rather than trade in physical goods.

- Government intervention in both direct (e.g. management of exchange rates) and indirect ways (e.g. taxation policies) can nullify the impact of PPPT.

Interest rate parity theory (IRPT)

This theory is based on very similar principles to that of PPPT.

The IRPT claims that the difference between the spot and the forward exchange rates is equal to the differential between interest rates available in the two currencies.

The **forward rate** is a future exchange rate, agreed now, for buying or selling an amount of currency on an agreed future date.

IRPT

An investor has USD 5 million to invest over one year in either dollars (USD) or sterling (GBP). His options are to:

- Invest in dollars at the prevailing dollar interest rate of 10.16% or,
- Convert the dollars to GBP at the prevailing spot rate (GBP1/USD1.5000) and invest in GBP at 7.1%.

The one-year forward rate is GBP1/USD1.5429.

Analysing the options open to this investor:

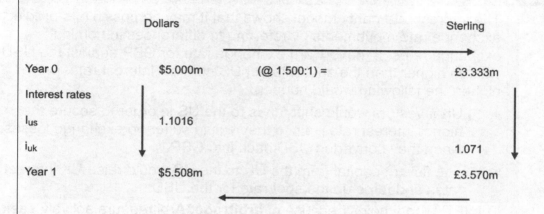

In one year USD 5.508 million must equate to GBP 3.570 million, so what you gain in extra interest you lose in an adverse movement in exchange rates. The effective exchange rate is

$$\text{Exchange rate} = \frac{5.508}{3.570} = 1.5429$$

which equals the forward rate for one year. The forward rate moves to bring about interest rate parity between the currencies.

Rule: IRPT predicts that the country with the higher interest rate will see the forward rate for its currency subject to a depreciation

The IRPT formula gives:

$$\text{Forward rate} = \text{Current spot rate} \times \frac{1 + ints_f}{1 + ints_h}$$

Where

$ints_f$ money risk-free rate of interest for the foreign currency

$ints_h$ money risk-free rate of interest for the home currency spot rate in terms of 1 unit of home currency/foreign currency (e.g. GBP1/USD)

Test your understanding 5 (Integration question)

A treasurer can borrow in Swiss francs (CHF) at a rate of 3% pa or in the UK at a rate of 7% p.a. The current rate of exchange is GBP1/CHF 10.

Required:

What is the likely rate of exchange in a year's time? (Give your answer to 4 decimal places)

More on IRPT

The interest rate parity model shows that it may be possible to predict exchange rate movements by referring to differences in nominal exchange rates. If the forward exchange rate for GBP against the USD was no higher than the spot rate but US nominal interest rates were higher, the following would happen:

- UK investors would shift funds to the US in order to secure the higher interest rates, since they would suffer no exchange losses when they converted USD back into GBP.

- The flow of capital from the UK to the US would raise UK interest rates and force up the spot rate for the USD.

The IRP theory holds because of **arbitrage**. Arbitrageurs actively seek out anomalies in the exchange rate market. They buy and sell currency to make a profit (buy at a low price and sell at a high price, as with any commodity). If many arbitrageurs do this, the exchange rate alters (differences in supply and demand will alter the price), the exchange rate moves and the anomaly then disappears. Arbitrage is discussed more fully later in this chapter.

Is IRPT applicable to determining forward rates?

The only limitation on the universal applicability of this relationship will be due to government intervention. These may arise in a number of ways including the following:

- **Controls on capital markets** – The government may limit the range and type of markets within their financial services system.

- **Controls on currency trading** – These may be in the form of a limit on the amount of currency that may be taken out of a country or the use of an 'official' exchange rate that does not bear any relation to the 'effective' rate at which the markets wish to trade.

- **Government intervention in the market** – The government may attempt to control or manipulate the exchange rate by buying or selling their own currency.

The International Fisher Effect

The International Fisher Effect claims that the interest rate differentials between two countries provide an unbiased predictor of future changes in the spot rate of exchange.

- The International Fisher Effect assumes that all countries will have the same real interest rate, although nominal or money rates may differ due to expected inflation rates.

- Thus the interest rate differential between two countries should be equal to the expected inflation differential.

- Therefore, countries with higher expected inflation rates will have higher nominal interest rates, and vice versa.

 The Fisher effect

As seen in your earlier studies, the Fisher effect looks at the relationship between interest rates and inflation. Inflation is the difference between the real return on investment (real interest) and the nominal return (nominal interest rate). The relationship between the nominal rate of interest, the real rate of interest and inflation can be expressed by the formula:

[1 + nominal rate] = [1 + real rate] × [1 + inflation rate]

Example

One-year money market interest rates in the UK are 5.06%. Inflation in the UK is currently running at 3% per annum.

The real one-year interest rate in the UK can be calculated as follows:

[1.0506] = [1 + real rate] × [1.03]

[1 + real rate] = 1.0506/1.03 = 1.02

Real rate = 0.02 or 2% per year.

The nominal or market interest rates in any country must be sufficient to reward investors with a suitable real return plus an additional return to allow for the effects of inflation.

Test your understanding 6 – Parity (Integration question)

Spot USD1/EUR0.9050

Interest rates p.a. on short-term government securities

US treasury	6.0%
Eurozone	4.5%

Inflation rates

US	2.0%
Eurozone	1.3%

Required:

Calculate using the parity relationships (PPPT and IRPT) the theoretically correct forward rates. Determine the reasons for a difference between the two, if one arises.

Test your understanding 7 – G clothing (Case style question)

Background

G is a major clothing retailer, specialising in fashionable clothes for young people. G has shops in every major town and city in its home country. G's customers are extremely conscious of brand names and G must stock the latest products from the biggest and most popular manufacturers in order to remain competitive.

Most of G's most popular brands are imported from the USA. The clothes are expensive to import because the Government in G's country imposes a tariff, which requires G (and all other importers) to pay a tax on all clothing imports. The Government's reason for imposing this tariff is to protect local manufacturers from foreign competition. G is located in a relatively prosperous country and wages are fairly high.

G has been losing sales to a major competitor, which is based in G's home country and has shops in the same towns and cities as G, which sells the same range of clothing but at a lower price. G attempted to compete on price, but stopped doing so when it became apparent that the competitor could undercut any price that G set.

G has investigated the competitor's trading strategy. It appears that the competitor is able to exploit anomalies in the market by buying its inventory in a neighbouring country and bringing it across the border. Two of the countries that adjoin G's home country are not particularly prosperous. Many foreign suppliers, including G's suppliers, supply goods to distributers (and also directly to retailers) in those countries at lower prices than they do in G's home country because they are aware that the final consumers there have low incomes and are not able to pay high prices for brand name clothing. Furthermore, those neighbouring countries do not charge tariffs on clothing imports.

Trigger

G's home country is part of a trading bloc which includes the neighbouring country from which the competitor is suspected of buying its inventory. There are no physical barriers to regulate the borders between countries within that bloc. Legally, any goods imported from a neighbouring country are subject to tariffs, but G suspects that the competitor has not been declaring these imports to the Government department responsible for collecting tax and so the competitor has benefitted from both cheaper purchase prices and the evasion of the tariff.

Some of G's senior managers have recommended that G should copy its competitor by cancelling all contracts with the major US manufacturers and buying all goods from intermediaries in a neighbouring country. Others recommend reporting their suspicions to the manufacturers and to the Government.

Required:

As G's management accountant, prepare a briefing note for the Board:

(a) Discussing the argument that purchasing power parity theory should prevent exporters from charging different prices in different countries.

(b) Discussing the potential risks and benefits to G of buying its inventory from intermediaries in the neighbouring countries

(c) Recommending actions that the Government in G's home country could take in order to determine whether G's competitor had been evading the tariff on imported clothing.

(45 minutes)

Arbitrage

Arbitrage is the simultaneous purchase and sale of a security in different markets with the aim of making a risk-free profit through the exploitation of any price differences between the two markets. (CIMA Official Terminology)

(The purchase and sale does not necessarily have to be a security. It could be as simple as buying apples in one market and selling them in another at a higher price.)

Arbitrage is mainly used by **speculators** rather than as a hedging tool.

Arbitrage differences are short-term. When other traders see differences in the price of a commodity they will exploit them and the prices will converge. The differences will disappear as equilibrium is reached.

Some kinds of arbitrage are completely risk-free – this is pure arbitrage. For instance, if Euros are available more cheaply in London than in New York, arbitrageurs can make a risk-free profit by buying euros in London and selling an identical amount in New York. Opportunities for pure arbitrage have become rare in recent years, partly because of the globalisation of financial markets and immediate access to information via the use of the internet. This enables almost anyone, who understands what they are doing, to trade and potentially make a profit (although it costs a great deal to buy immediate access to the real-time market prices and the anomalies are usually so small that arbitrageurs have to invest heavily in order to make the deals worthwhile after dealing costs).

 More on arbitrage

For example, imagine you bought and sold fruit and vegetables on a market stall. One day a customer asks for a kilo of apples.

You don't have any apples but you know where you can get some. Having ascertained that the customer will pay up to GBP1 per kilo, you contact a competitor who has apples on another market stall. They are selling at GBP0.90 per kilo. You offer to buy the kilo of apples at GBP0.90, collect them from the other market stall, and sell them for GBP1 making GBP0.10 profit.

If enough customers ask for apples, eventually the competitor will realise that there is an increased demand for apples, which appear to be in short supply, and they will increase their price.

This effectively eliminates the opportunity for arbitrage profits.

The same principle can be applied to any commodity. It is commonly used by 'day-traders' with exchange rates.

Day-trading on exchange rates

A day-trader is someone who believes she can spot short term speculative movements and benefit from them. She looks for an apparently 'cheap' currency and then sells it quickly, at a profit, to someone who needs it.

Example of day-trading

Margaret is a day-trader (based in the UK) looking for arbitrage opportunities on the currency market. On 1st June she thinks she has spotted a difference in the market for USD.

She can buy USD 2 for EUR1.50. She can buy one euro for GBP0.80. She can sell dollars for USD 1.50/GBP1. She has GBP100,000 available to invest for the purpose of making a profit.

Margaret converts her GBP in to EUR: GBP100,000/0.80 = EUR125,000

Margaret then converts her EUR into USD: (EUR125,000/1.5) × 2 = USD166,667

Margaret now sells the USD: USD166,667/1.50 = GBP111,111

Margaret has made a risk-free profit of GBP11,111.

Conclusion on day-trading

Unfortunately it is difficult to judge whether day-traders are successful, because they would lose their advantage if they admitted to being able to spot mispriced assets!

Test your understanding 8 (Integration question)

A speculator can buy USD2 for GBP1, sell one EUR for GBP0.80 and can sell USD for USD1.50/EUR1. There is GBP1,000,000 available to invest for the purpose of making a profit.

Required:

What is the possible profit using arbitrage opportunities? (Give your answer in GBP to the nearest GBP 100).

Test your understanding 9 – U company (Case style question)

U is an administrative assistant in the treasury department of a multinational company. U was checking some current market valuations when she noticed an anomaly in the rates associated with the USD/GBP exchange rates.

The spot rate for converting GBP to USD was 1.556 USD to the GBP. The three month forward rate for converting USD back to GBP was 1.499 USD to the GBP.

U's bank was prepared to lend GBP at a fixed rate of 5.08% per annum. The bank was also prepared to offer a fixed rate for USD deposits of 5.12%.

U printed these figures out and spoke to the company treasurer because she believed that there was an arbitrage opportunity. The treasurer agreed that U's figures indicated that an opportunity existed, but said that the opportunity would have disappeared in the time that it had taken her to walk across the office.

U asked why the multinational company did not pay greater attention to the possibility of arbitrage opportunities. The treasurer replied that "Arbitrage is a full-time occupation and it is a rather risky commercial venture. I am happy to leave the potential profits to the arbitrageurs who have made it their business to trade in that way". The treasurer also stated that the company's treasury department is a cost centre and that he had no desire to make it into a profit centre.

Required:

(a) Calculate the potential gain that could have been made by the company if it had borrowed GBP 10m in order to exploit the anomaly that she had identified.

(b) (i) Evaluate U's argument that the company could profit from this opportunity.

(ii) Evaluate the treasurer's argument that arbitrage is a risky commercial venture.

(c) Evaluate the treasurer's view that it is better for the company's treasury department to operate as a cost centre rather than as a profit centre.

(45 minutes)

3 Financial risk management

The stages in the financial risk management process are essentially the same as in any risk management process:

1 identify risk exposures

2 quantify exposures

3 decide whether or not to hedge

4 implement and monitor hedging program.

Hedge or not?

Hedging can involve the reduction or elimination of financial risk by passing that risk onto someone else. Or internal hedging techniques involve reducing risk by creating an offsetting position that has a tendency to cancel any risks.

Benefits of hedging

- hedging can provide certainty of cash flows which will assist in the budgeting process

- risk will be reduced, and hence management may be more inclined to undertake investment projects

- reduction in the probability of financial collapse (bankruptcy)

- managers are often risk-averse since their job is at risk. If a company has a policy of hedging it may be perceived as a more attractive employer to risk-averse managers.

Arguments against hedging

- shareholders have diversified their own portfolio, thus further hedging by the business may harm shareholders' interests
- transaction costs associated with hedging can be significant
- lack of expertise within the business, particularly with regards to use of derivative instruments
- complexity of accounting and tax issues associated with the use of derivatives.

Derivatives

A derivative is a financial instrument whose value depends on the price of some other financial asset or underlying factor (such as oil, gold, interest rates or currencies).

The directors of an organisation will decide how to use derivatives to meet their goals and to align with their risk appetite.

Derivatives have the following uses:

- **Hedging:** used as a risk management tool to reduce / eliminate financial risk.
- **Speculation:** used to make a profit from predicting market movements.
- **Arbitrage:** used to exploit price differences between markets. (This will be short-term only. If a commodity appears to be cheap, demand will increase which will push up the price. Hence the price differential, where a gain could be made in the past, has now closed.)

For the purposes of this subject we are interested in the hedging use of derivatives.

Treasury function

The treasury function exists in every business, though in a small business it may be absorbed into the accounting or company secretarial work.

The main functions of treasury are:

- **managing relationships with the banks** – regarding the investment of surplus cash or making arrangements to allow deficits of cash, or to arrange hedging.
- **working capital and liquidity management** – to ensure that sufficient but not excessive amounts of cash are available on a daily basis to fund inventory, payables and receivables.
- **long-term funding management** – providing cash for longer term investments such as non-current assets or arranging mortgages / debentures.

- **currency management** – dealing with all currencies which will entail both internal and external hedging techniques, sourcing currencies, managing foreign currency bank accounts.

More on the treasury function

Organisational structure

The treasurer has the capacity to make large gains or losses in a short period of time, particularly when trading in financial derivatives. As a result it is important to define and carefully monitor the responsibility and authority associated with treasury.

There are a number of differing structures for the treasury activity within a business. The two key debates are discussed below.

Profit centre or cost centre

Should the treasury activities be accounted for simply as a cost centre, or as a profit centre in its own right (making profit out of trading activities)?

Advantages of operating as a profit centre, as opposed to cost centre include:

- a market rate is charged to business units throughout the entity, making operating costs realistic
- the treasurer is motivated to provide services as efficiently and economically as possible.

The main disadvantages are:

- the profit concept brings the temptation to speculate and take excessive risk
- management time can be wasted on discussions about internal charges for the treasury activities
- additional administrative costs will be incurred.

Centralised or decentralised

Many large companies operate a centralised treasury function, which has merits and limitations.

Risks associated with centralised treasury include:

- a lack of motivation towards managing cash in the subsidiaries, since any cash that is received is swept up to head office to be managed from the group's perspective.
- the risk that, should head office commit some error in their treasury operations, the financial health of the whole group could be placed in jeopardy.

Risks associated with decentralised activity are:

- that one company might pay large overdraft interest costs, while another has cash balances in hand earning low interest rates.

- the risk of not generating the profits for the group that would be earned if the group funds were actively managed by a treasury operation seeking profits rather than individual executives just seeking to minimise costs.

 Corporate treasury policies

A UK retailer

A well-known UK retailer 'operates a centralised treasury function to manage the Group's funding requirements and financial risks in line with the Board approved treasury policies and procedures, and delegated authorities. ... Group Treasury also enters into derivative transactions, principally interest rate and currency swaps and forward currency contracts. The purpose of these transactions is to manage the interest-rate and currency risks arising from the Group's operations and financing. It remains Group policy not to hold or issue financial instruments for trading purposes, except where financial constraints necessitate the need to liquidate any outstanding investments. The treasury function is managed as a cost centre and does not engage in speculative trading. The principal risks faced by the Group are liquidity/funding, interest rate, foreign currency risks and counterparty risks.

(a) **Liquidity/funding risk**

The risk that the Group could be unable to settle or meet its obligations as they fall due at a reasonable price.

The Group's funding strategy ensures a mix of funding sources offering flexibility and cost effectiveness to match the requirements.

(b) **Counterparty risk**

Counterparty risk exists where the Group can suffer financial loss through default or non-performance by financial institutions.

Exposures are managed through Group treasury policy which limits the value that can be placed with each approved counterparty to minimise the risk of loss. The counterparties are limited to the approved institutions with secure long-term credit ratings A+/A1 or better assigned by Moody's and Standard & Poor's respectively, unless approved on an exception basis by a Board director. Limits are reviewed regularly by senior management.

(c) **Foreign currency risk**

Transactional foreign currency exposures arise from both the export of goods from the UK to overseas subsidiaries, and from the import of materials and goods directly sourced from overseas suppliers.

Group treasury hedge these exposures principally using forward foreign exchange contracts progressively covering up to 100% out to 18 months. Where appropriate hedge cover can be taken out longer than 18 months, with Board approval. The Group is primarily exposed to foreign exchange risk in relation to GBP against movements in USD and EUR.

(d) **Interest rate risk**

The Group is exposed to interest rate risk in relation to the GBP, USD, EUR and Hong Kong dollar (HKD) variable rate financial assets and liabilities.

The Group's policy is to use derivative contracts where necessary to maintain a mix of fixed and floating rate borrowings to manage this risk. The structure and maturity of these derivatives correspond to the underlying borrowings and are accounted for as fair value or cash flow hedges as appropriate.

Capital policy

The Group's objectives when managing capital are to safeguard its ability to continue as a going concern in order to provide optimal returns for shareholders and to maintain an efficient capital structure to reduce the cost of capital.

In doing so the Group's strategy is to maintain a capital structure commensurate with an investment grade credit rating and to retain appropriate levels of liquidity headroom to ensure financial stability and flexibility. To achieve this strategy the Group regularly monitors key credit metrics such as the gearing ratio, cash flow to net debt see (note 29) and fixed charge cover to maintain this position. In addition the Group ensures a combination of appropriate committed short-term liquidity headroom with a diverse and smooth long-term debt maturity profile.

During the year the Group maintained an investment grade credit rating of Baa3 (stable) with Moody's and BBB-(stable) with Standard & Poor's, and through the successful tender of GBP200m of existing short-dated bonds in conjunction with a new GBP400m 10 year bond issue extended the average fixed debt maturity by one year to ten years and increased short-term liquidity by GBP200m.

In order to maintain or re-align the capital structure, the Group may adjust the number of dividends paid to shareholders, return capital to shareholders, issue new shares or sell assets to reduce debt.

Test your understanding 10 – J electronics (Case style question)

Scenario

J manufactures specialised electronic equipment in the UK.

All of J's directors come from an electronic engineering background and the small administrative staff provides basic clerical and book-keeping support.

Trigger

The company has just won its first export order and will receive payment of USD 15 million in three months. J's Chief Executive is concerned that the USD may decline against the GBP during the three months and has asked the company's bank to offer a guaranteed price for the currency when it is received.

The bank has offered to enter into a forward contract with J at a rate of GBP1 = USD 1.65.

J's Chief Executive is unhappy with this offer because the present exchange rate is GBP1 = USD 1.60. Given the size of the transaction, this constitutes a major additional cost that J had not budgeted for when setting its selling price. J's Chief Executive would rather wait until the payment is received in the hope that the spot rate at that time is better than the GBP1 = USD 1.65 offered by the bank.

J's Chief Executive is concerned that the differential rate being charged by the bank is unfair. He believes that global economics are so complicated that it is impossible to forecast exchange rate movements and the movements in the exchange rate are just as likely to be favourable as unfavourable to J over the next three months.

J's bank manager has pointed out that the rate offered is in line with market expectations and that it is unrealistic for the Chief Executive to ask the bank to commit itself to guaranteeing that today's exchange rate can be obtained on a transaction that will occur in three months.

The bank manager has recommended that J appoints a full-time corporate treasurer to take on the responsibility of the treasury function and relieve the Chief Executive of that burden.

Required:

Write a briefing note to the Board:

(a) Evaluating the bank manager's recommendation to appoint a corporate treasurer.

(b) Recommending, stating reasons, the steps that the directors of J should take in the selection of a suitable person for the role of corporate treasurer.

(30 minutes)

4 Transaction risk management

Transaction risk was identified in the previous chapter as one of the three types of currency risk. There are several methods of managing exposure to transaction risk. As a general rule the simplest and most convenient methods are used by any business.

The methods can be split as follows:

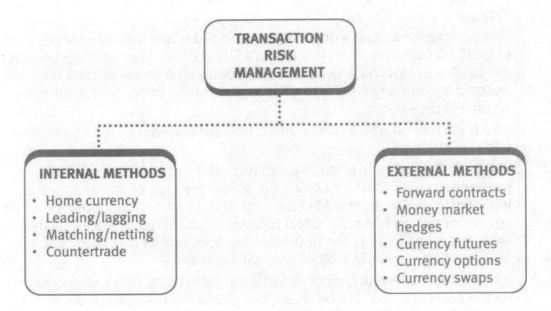

TRANSACTION RISK MANAGEMENT

INTERNAL METHODS
- Home currency
- Leading/lagging
- Matching/netting
- Countertrade

EXTERNAL METHODS
- Forward contracts
- Money market hedges
- Currency futures
- Currency options
- Currency swaps

The differences between internal and external hedging can be very significant:

- Internal hedging is often more effective for dealing with economic risk;
- Internal hedging is often cheaper and simpler to understand;
- External hedging is more complex, so it is usually undertaken by skilled staff in treasury departments.

5 Internal hedging

If a company wants to remove transaction risk, it is possible to hedge this internally in a number of ways, including:

- Invoice in home currency.
- Leading and lagging payments.
- Offsetting – matching, netting and pooling.
- Countertrade.

More on internal hedging techniques

Invoice in home currency

If a UK business invoices in GBP and only accepts invoices from suppliers in GBP then it partly removes currency risk. The currency risk is transferred to the customer or supplier. However economic risk is not removed – the value of the business will still fall if the overseas competition are 'winning' with their overseas trade in foreign currencies.

This method does give some very practical business issues:

- The customers and suppliers may not be prepared to accept all the currency risk and therefore they will not trade with the business.

- The other parties may not be prepared to accept the same prices and will require discounts on sales or premiums on purchases.

- There are other ways of hedging risks that mean that the risk of transacting in foreign currency is acceptable.

Leading and lagging

This is a method of trying to makes gains on foreign currency payments.

Leading is making a payment before it is due, and lagging is delaying a payment for as long as possible. This is effective if the company has a strong view about the future movements in the exchange rate.

For example, a company has to make a USD100,000 payment to a US supplier. The payment is due in two months' time but could be paid immediately or delayed until three months' time. Sterling is expected to depreciate in value against the US dollar over the next three months. In this case the company would want to pay as early as possible and therefore lead. To check this, consider that if the rate went from USD:GBP 2.0000 to USD:GBP 1.5000, the payment in GBP would go from GBP50,000 to GBP66,667. The company would obviously want to only pay GBP50,000.

Problems with leading and lagging include:

- Early payment will cost a company in interest foregone on the funds that have been disbursed early;

- The payee will not be happy that payment may become overdue, especially if the currency is expected to fall;

- It requires the company to take a view on exchange rates i.e. speculate. There is a risk that the company will be wrong.

Offsetting

Matching

This technique involves matching assets and liabilities in the same currency. Financing a foreign investment with a foreign loan would reduce the exposure to exchange risk since as the rate changes favourably on one it would move adversely on the other.

Netting

Netting normally involves the use of foreign currency bank accounts. If a company knows it will be both receiving and paying in foreign currency, it can reduce exchange risk by using the foreign receipts to cover the foreign payments. The netting will work best if the dates of the receipt and payment are as near together as possible.

In a group, netting can be done across the group by a treasury function. This would mean that if one subsidiary is making foreign payments and another subsidiary is taking foreign receipts, the group can net the two off.

Pooling

Pooling is a system of managing cash. When a business has several bank accounts in the same currency, it might be able to arrange a system with its bank(s) whereby the balances on each bank account in the same currency are swept up into a central account at the end of each day, leaving a zero balance on every account except the central account. Overdraft balances and positive cash balances are all swept up into the central account maximising interest earned and minimising any bank charges or interest payable.

This does not provide a system for hedging against FX risk, but can be an efficient system for cash management. It avoids overdraft costs on individual bank accounts, and it enables the treasury department to make more efficient use of any cash surpluses.

For an efficient system of cash pooling, there needs to be a centralised cash management system. The current organisation allows each subsidiary to operate their own cash management system. Pooling can be organised by each subsidiary. However, it might be even more efficient if subsidiaries operating in the same currencies shared the same pooling system, hence it is best operated by a central treasury function.

Countertrade

This involves parties exchanging goods and services of equivalent value. It is the old fashioned bartering and avoids any type of currency exchanges. However the tax authorities do not like this method – if cash does not change hands it is difficult to establish the value of the transaction and any related sales tax payable. For this reason, countertrade is not very common since it can lead to disputes with the tax authorities and take up management time.

Matching

A company wishes to fund a USD1m investment and uses a USD1m loan. The exchange rate is USD1.8:GBP1 on the date the investment is made, but the GBP strengthens to USD2:GBP1 six months later.

The company has matched its assets and liabilities:

Investment (asset)

At acquisition (USD1m/1.8) = GBP555.6k

Six months later (USD1m/2) = GBP500k

Loan (liability)

At acquisition (USD1m/1.8) = GBP555.6k

Six months later (USD1m/2) = GBP500k

Whether at acquisition or six months later, the asset and the loan are worth the same as each other.

Netting

Division A is due to receive USD1m on Friday. Division B has a payable of USD700,000 due on the same day.

Because the receipt is at the same time as the payment, the company should use the receipt of USD1m to pay their supplier USD700,000. This would minimise any transaction costs arising from buying USD700,000 from the bank.

The USD300,000 left could be kept in a USD bank account for later USD payments, saving on further transaction costs in later months, or it could be converted into the home currency (now, or at some time in the future when rates are more favourable).

6   External hedging

If a company wants to remove transaction risk it is also possible to hedge this externally in a number of ways including:

- Netting centres;
- Forward contracts;
- Money market hedges;
- Futures;
- Options;
- Swaps.

7 Netting centres

Multilateral netting is a treasury management technique used by large companies to manage their intercompany payment processes, usually involving many currencies. Netting can yield significant savings from reduced foreign exchange trading.

A netting centre collates batches of cash flows between a defined set of companies and offsets them against each other so that just a single cash flow to or from each company takes place to settle the net result of all cash flows.

The netting process takes place on a cyclical basis, typically monthly, and is managed by a central entity called the netting centre.

Although netting centres are occasionally used to net off cash flows in just one currency, it is more usual for a netting centre to manage cash flows in several currencies. In a multiple currency netting system, each company's cash flows are converted to an equivalent amount in the company's base currency, so that the company still has only a single net position to settle in that currency.

A netting centre is typically used by a multinational company that has many production and sales divisions in a number of countries. Direct billing in many currencies by each company can lead to excessive foreign exchange trading, in which individual companies may be both buying and selling the same currencies many times over. The objective of using a netting centre is to reduce the overall foreign exchange volume traded and thereby cut the amount of foreign exchange spread paid by the company to manage all the currency conversions.

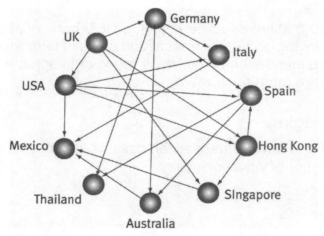

Without netting, each company settles its receipts and payments directly and individually with each of the other companies.

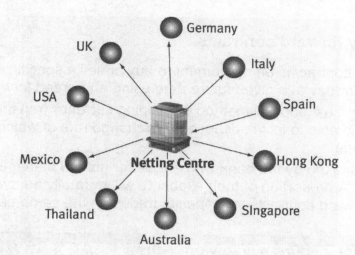

After using a netting centre, each company pays or receives a single local currency balance to or from the netting centre.

For netting to be successful participants must agree on a number of issues such as:

— Currencies – Which currencies will be used for invoicing? They may be the buyer's, the seller's or a third currency.

— Credit period – Ideally all participants should have the same credit periods but there may be variations for those participants who are long or short of funds.

— Settlement dates – The netting settlement dates and the netting cycle timetable must be known by all the participants and adhered to. Netting periods must also be decided e.g. weekly, monthly etc.

— Exchange rates – The exchange rates to be used in the netting must be agreed. Will it be spot or forward rates, mid at 11-00 am or some budgeted in-house rate? Rates should be 'arms length' as there would be potential tax issues otherwise.

— Conflict resolution – Multilateral netting may be payment driven, receivables driven or both. Either way disagreements will arise as to who owes what to whom so a process for sorting these issues out so that the items may be included in the netting will need to be in place. If not resolved then items may have to be pulled from the netting process.

— Management – will it be a bespoke system or bank managed.

8   Currency forward contracts

 A forward contract is an agreement to buy or sell a specific amount of foreign currency at a given future date using an agreed forward rate.

This is the most popular method of hedging currency transaction risk. The company is able to fix in advance an exchange rate at which a transaction will be made.

The risk is taken by the bank who are better able to manage their exposure. A proportion of their exposure will normally be avoided by writing forward contracts for opposite trades on the same day.

Illustration of currency forward contract

It is now 1 January and Y plc will receive USD10 million on 30 April.

It enters into a forward exchange contract to sell this amount on the forward date at a rate of GBP1/USD1.6000. On 30 April the company is guaranteed GBP6.25 million (USD10 million/1.6000).

The transaction risk has been removed (if the receipt arrives on time).

Features and operation

Forward contracts are a commitment, and as a result they have to be honoured even if the rate in the contract is worse than the rate in the market.

Forward contract rates are often quoted at a **premium** or **discount** to the current spot rate.

*   A discount means that the currency being quoted (e.g. USD) is expected to fall in value in relation to the other currency (e.g. GBP). If a currency falls in value then you need more of that currency to buy a single unit of the other, i.e. we need more dollars to buy a single pound.

*   A discount is often referred to as 'dis', a premium as 'prem'.

*   These can be quoted in cents (i.e. USD0.01) and shown as 'c' in the quote.

In most exam questions you can use the following rule for obtaining a forward rate from the spot rate:

*   add a forward discount to the spot rate (**'add:dis'**)

*   subtract a forward premium from the spot rate.

(**Note**: This rule is only applicable where the exchange rate is quoted as 'amount of foreign currency to a home currency unit'.)

(Also note that discounts and premiums derive from the interest rate parity formula, in theory.)

Remember that you will need to be aware of whether the premium or discount is quoted in, say, dollars or cents. It would usually be cents. There are 100 cents in a dollar. (Similarly there are 100 cents in a euro.) This affects how you add or deduct the discount or premium in terms of decimal places.

For example, if the dollar was currently 1.5000 and there was a premium of 0.5 c (c means cents, and there are 100 cents in a dollar so this is half a cent) this makes the forward rate 1.4950 (1.5000 − 0.0050).

Test your understanding 11 (Integration question)

Calculate the forward contract bid and offer prices in the following situation:

(i)   The current spot rate is   GBP1=USD1.5500 – 1.4500

and, one month forward rate is quoted at   0.55 – 0.50 c dis

(ii)   The current spot rate is   GBP1= EUR1.7150 – 1.6450

and, one month forward rate is quoted at   0.68 – 0.75 c pm

Test your understanding 12 (Integration question)

EEFS Ltd (a UK company) sold goods to the value of USD2.0 million. Receipt is due in 90 days.

The current spot rate is GBP1 = USD 1.5430 – 1.5150.

There is a three-month discount forward of 2.5 cents – 1.5 cents.

Required:

What is the amount of GBP that EEFS Ltd will receive under the forward contract? Give your answer in GBP to the nearest GBP 100.

Advantages and disadvantages

The advantages of forward contracts are that they:

*   Are simple, and so have low transaction costs;
*   Can be purchased from a high street bank;
*   Fix the exchange rate;
*   Are tailored, so are flexible to amount and delivery period.

The disadvantages are that there is:

*   A potential credit risk since the company is contractually bound to sell a currency, which it may not have received from its customer;
*   No upside potential.

More on disadvantages of forward contracts

There are two key disadvantages of forward contracts:

It is a **contractual commitment** which must be completed on the due date.

This means that if a payment from the overseas customer is late, the company receiving the payment and wishing to convert it using its forward exchange contract will have a problem. The existing forward exchange contract must be settled, although the bank will arrange a new forward exchange contract for the new date when the currency cash flow is due.

To help overcome this problem an **'option date' forward exchange contract** can be arranged. This is a forward exchange contract that allows the company to settle a forward contract at an agreed fixed rate of exchange, but at any time between two specified dates. If the currency cash flow occurs between these two dates, the forward exchange contract can be settled at the agreed fixed rate.

It is **inflexible**. It eliminates the downside risk of an adverse movement in the spot rate, but also prevents any participation in upside potential of any favourable movement in the spot rate. Whatever happens to the actual exchange rate, the forward contract must be honoured, even if it would be beneficial to exchange currencies at the spot rate prevailing at that time.

Test your understanding 13 – J electronics (Case style question)

J manufactures specialised electronic equipment in the UK. The company has just won its first export order and will receive payment of USD 15 million in three months. J's Chief Executive is concerned that the USD may decline against the GBP during the three months and has asked the company's bank to offer a guaranteed price for the currency when it is received.

The bank has offered to enter into a forward contract with J at a rate of GBP1 = USD 1.65.

J's Chief Executive is unhappy with this offer because the present exchange rate is GBP1 = USD 1.60. Given the size of the transaction, this constitutes a major additional cost that J had not budgeted for when setting its selling price. J's Chief Executive would rather wait until the payment is received in the hope that the spot rate at that time is better than the GBP1 = USD 1.65 offered by the bank.

J's Chief Executive is concerned that the differential rate being charged by the bank is unfair. He believes that global economics are so complicated that it is impossible to forecast exchange rate movements and the movements in the exchange rate are just as likely to be favourable as unfavourable to J over the next three months.

J's bank manager has pointed out that the rate offered is in line with market expectations and that it is unrealistic for the Chief Executive to ask the bank to commit itself to guaranteeing that today's exchange rate can be obtained on a transaction that will occur in three months.

The bank manager has recommended that J appoints a full-time corporate treasurer to take on the responsibility of the treasury function and relieve the Chief Executive of that burden.

All of J's directors come from an electronic engineering background and the small administrative staff provides basic clerical and book-keeping support.

Required:

Prepare a note to your finance director evaluating the respective arguments of J's Chief Executive and the bank manager about the rate offered by the bank on the forward contract.

(15 minutes)

9 Money market hedges (MMH)

 The money markets are markets for wholesale (large-scale) lending and borrowing, or trading in short-term financial instruments. Many companies are able to borrow or deposit funds through their bank in the money markets.

Instead of hedging a currency exposure with a forward contract, a company could use the money markets to lend or borrow, and achieve a similar result.

Since forward exchange rates are derived from spot rates and money market interest rates (see IRPT earlier in this chapter), the end result from hedging should be roughly the same by either method.

Features and operation

 The basic idea of an MMH is to create assets and liabilities that 'mirror' the future assets and liabilities.

Rule: The money required for the transaction is exchanged at today's spot rate, and is then deposited/borrowed on the money market to accrue to the amount required for the transaction in the future.

Note: Interest rates are used for the depositing / borrowing. The rates are usually quoted per annum. If you require a six monthly rate then you simply divide by 2. If you require a quarterly rate, then divide by 4.

Money market interest rates

Money market interest rates are available for any length of borrowing or deposit period, up to about one year. Banks quote rates for standard periods, such as overnight, one week, one month, three months, six months and one year.

Two rates are quoted:

- The **higher** rate is the interest rate that the bank will **charge on loans.**

- The **lower** rate is the interest rate that the bank will **pay on deposits**.

All rates are quoted on an annual basis.

Example

A London bank quotes the following interest rates on US dollars:

1 month

USD LIBOR 3¼ – 3 ⅛

In the above example, suppose that a company wanted to borrow US dollars for one month. The bank would charge 3¼% per annum.

For the purpose of your examination, you can assume that the rate for one month is one-twelfth of the rate for one year; therefore in this example, the actual interest for one month would be 3¼%/12 = 0.270833%. If the company borrowed, say, USD 1 million for one month, it would repay the loan plus interest of USD2,708.33 at the end of the loan period.

Characteristics

- The basic idea is to avoid future exchange rate uncertainty by making the exchange at today's spot rate instead.

- This is achieved by depositing/borrowing the foreign currency until the actual commercial transaction cash flows occur:

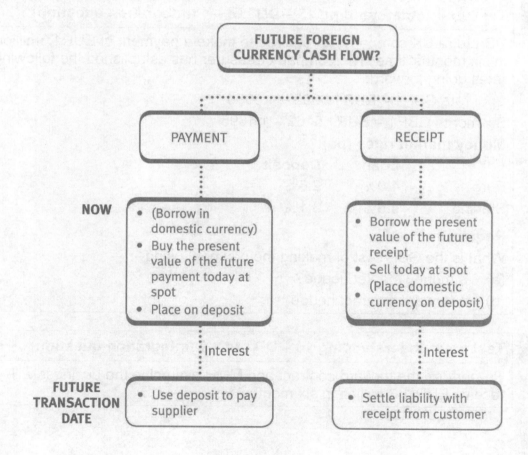

Test your understanding 14 (Integration question)

A UK company is due to receive USD12,000 in 6 months' time from a customer.

The USD/GBP forward rate is 1.9550 – 1.9600 and the spot rate is 1.9960 – 1.9990.

Interest rates in the US to borrow are 12% and to lend are 11%. In the UK interest rate to borrow are 11% and to lend are 10%.

Required:

If the company chooses to use a money market hedge, how much will it receive in GBPs in 6 months' time?

Test your understanding 15 – DD Ltd – 1 (Integration question)

DD Ltd (a UK company) is required to make a payment of EUR1.3million in six months' time. The company treasurer has established the following rates going forward:

Spot rate GBP1 = EUR1.5095 – 1.5050

Six month GBP1 = EUR1.5162 – 1.4895

Money market rates (pa):

	Loan	Deposit
Euro	4.0%	2.5%
Sterling	4.6%	3.1%

Required:

What is the GBP cost of making the payment using

(a)   a money market hedge?

(b)   a forward contract hedge?

Test your understanding 16 – DD Ltd – 2 (Integration question)

Re-perform the forward contract and MMH assuming the business will receive EUR 1.3 million in six months' time.

Advantages and disadvantages

The advantages of money market hedges are that they:

- Ensure there is no currency risk because exchange takes place today.
- Have fairly low transaction costs.
- Offer flexibility (especially if customer delays payment).

The disadvantages are that:

- They are complex.
- It may be difficult to get an overseas loan in the case of a foreign currency receipt.

Further comments

- Interest rate parity implies that a money market hedge should give the same result as a forward contract.
- This approach has obvious cash flow implications which may prevent a company from using this method, e.g. if a company has a considerable overdraft it may be impossible for it to borrow funds now.

10 Currency futures

 In essence this form of hedging is very similar to the use of a forward contract. The critical difference is that, whereas using a forward contract requires the preparation of a special financial instrument 'tailor-made' for the transaction, currency futures are standardised contracts for fixed amounts of money for a limited range of future dates.

Features and operation

Futures are derivatives contracts and as such can be traded on futures exchanges. The contract which guarantees the price (known as the futures contract) is separated from the transaction itself, allowing the contracts to be easily traded.

Denomination

Futures contracts are limited to a small range of currencies and are typically denominated in terms of dollars (USD). There are also markets in euro (EUR) denominated futures contracts but this is relatively new and much less common.

Given USD denominated currency futures, we would simply know them in terms of the other currency, i.e. the GBP1/USD future will be known as GBP contracts or EUR1/USD futures are known as EUR contracts.

Futures are standardised contracts for standardised amounts. For example, the Chicago Mercantile Exchange (CME) trades sterling futures contracts with a standard size of GBP62,500. Only whole number multiples of this amount can be bought or sold hence they rarely cover the exact foreign currency exposure.

Process

There is a three step process which can be followed to answer a futures question:

Step 1: Set up

Set up the hedge by addressing 3 key questions:

- Do we initially buy or sell futures?

To decide whether to buy or sell futures, the simplest way is to follow this rule: identify the currency of the futures contract (e.g. GBP) and then do the same to the futures that you intend to do to that currency (e.g. buy or sell).

- Which expiry date should be chosen?

Settlement takes place in three-monthly cycles (March, June, September or December). It is normal to choose the first contract to expiry after the required conversion date.

- How many contracts?

Step 2: Contact exchange

Pay the initial margin. Then wait until the transaction/settlement date.

Margin: The futures exchange requires all buyers and sellers of futures to pay a deposit to the exchange when they buy or sell. This deposit is called an initial margin. This margin is returned when the position is closed out.

Step 3: Closing out

At the end of the contract's term the position is closed out. This means that on expiry of the contract the trading position is automatically reversed. Any profit or loss is computed and cleared, and the underlying commodity is retained by the trader.

The margin is refunded by the exchange.

The value of the transaction is calculated using the spot rate on the transaction date.

 Concept

In essence we are hedging or speculating on the movement of the exchange rate on the futures market

More on futures contracts

When a futures contact is bought or sold, the buyer or seller must deposit an **initial margin** with the exchange. If losses are incurred, the buyer or seller may be called on to deposit additional funds **(variation margin)** with the exchange. Equally, profits are credited to the margin account on a daily basis as the contract is 'marked to market'.

Most futures contracts are closed out before their settlement dates by undertaking the opposite transaction to the initial futures transaction, i.e. if buying currency futures was the initial transaction, it is closed out by selling currency futures.

Effectively a future works like a bet. If a company expects a USD receipt in 3 months' time, it will lose out if the USD depreciates relative to GBP. Using a futures contract, the company 'bets' that the USD will depreciate. If it does, the win on the bet cancels out the loss on the transaction. If the USD strengthens, the gain on the transaction covers the loss on the bet.

Ultimately futures ensure a virtual no win/no loss position.

More on futures contracts

It is 15 October and a treasurer has identified the need to convert euros into dollars to pay a US supplier USD12 million on 20 November. The treasurer has decided to use December euro futures contracts to hedge with the following details:

- Contract size EUR 200,000.
- Prices given in USD per EUR (i.e. EUR1 = ...).
- Tick size USD 0.0001 or USD 20 per contract.

He opens a position on 15 October and closes it on 20 November. Spot and relevant futures prices are as follows:

Date	Spot	Futures price
15 October	1.3300	1.3350
20 November	1.3190	1.3240

Calculate the financial position using the hedge described.

Solution

Step 1	1 Buy or sell initially? 2 Which expiry date? 3 How many contracts?	1 We need to sell EUR (to buy USD), so sell futures now. 2 Transaction date is 20 November, so choose December futures (the first to expire after the transaction date). 3 Cover USD 12m/1.3350 = EUR 8.99 million, using EUR 200,000 contracts, hence 8.99m/0.2m = 44.9, which we will round to 45 contracts.
Step 2	Contact the exchange – state the hedge	Sell 45 December futures (at a futures price of EUR1/USD 1.3350)
Step 3	Calculate profit/loss in futures market by closing out the position.	Initially: Sell at 1.3350 Close out: Buy at 1.3240 Difference is USD0.011 per EUR1 profit 45 × EUR200,000 covered, so total profit is 0.011 × 45 × 200,000 = USD99,000
Step 3 continued	Transaction at spot rate on 20 November: Need to pay USD12m less profit = USD11.901m, needed at spot rate of EUR1/USD1.3190	Cost in EUR is EUR 9,022,744

Ticks

A tick is the minimum price movement for a futures contract.

Take for example a sterling futures contract for a standard amount of GBP 62,500 in sterling. The contracts are priced at the exchange rate, in US dollars, and the tick size (minimum price movement) is USD0.0001.

If the price of a sterling futures contract changes from, say, USD 1.7105 to USD 1.7120, the price has risen USD 0.0015 or 15 ticks.

The significance of a tick for futures trading is that every one tick movement in price has the same money value.

Take for example a sterling futures contract for a standard amount of GBP 62,500: every movement in the price of the contract by one tick is worth USD6.25, which is GBP 62,500 at USD0.0001 per GBP1.

Basis and basis risk

The current futures price is usually different from the current 'cash market' price of the underlying item. In the case of currency futures, the current market price of a currency future and the current spot rate will be different, and will only start to converge when the final settlement date for the futures contract approaches. This difference is known as the **'basis'**.

At final settlement date for the contract (in March, June, September or December) the futures price and the market price of the underlying item ought to be the same; otherwise speculators would be able to make an instant profit by trading between the futures market and the spot 'cash' market.

Most futures positions are closed out before the contract reaches final settlement. When this happens, there will inevitably be a difference between the futures price at close-out and the current spot market price of the underlying item. In other words, there will still be some basis.

Because basis exists, an estimate can be made when a hedge is created with futures about what the size of the basis will be when the futures position is closed.

Example

In February, a UK company wishes to hedge a currency exposure arising from a US dollar payment that will have to be made in May, in three months' time. The current spot exchange rate is USD1.5670 and the current June futures price is USD1.5530. The basis is therefore 140 points in February.

If it is assumed that the basis will decline from 140 points in February to 0 in June when the contract reaches final settlement (say four months later), we can predict that the basis will fall from 140 in February by 105 points (140 × 3 months/4 months) to 35 points in May, when it is intended to close the futures position.

Basis risk is the risk that when a hedge is constructed, the size of the basis when the futures position is closed out is different from the expectation, when the hedge was created, of what the basis ought to be.

In the example, when the futures position is closed in May, the actual basis might be, say 50 points, which is 15 points higher than expected when the hedge was constructed.

Advantages and disadvantages

The advantages of currency futures contracts are that they:

- Offer an effective 'fixing' of exchange rate;
- Have no transaction costs;
- Are tradable.

The disadvantages are that:

- A foreign futures market must be used for GBP futures;
- They require up front margin payments;
- They are not usually for the precise tailored amounts that are required.

Test your understanding 17 (Integration question)

A UK company sells goods to a US company to the value of USD 2,650,000 in August. It is now June and spot is USD 1.9800/GBP 1. A June futures contract is quoted as USD 1.9790. A September futures contract is quoted as USD 1.9000. Sterling futures are traded in contracts of GBP 62,500. The UK company always buys the minimum number of contracts, being prepared to leave un-hedged any small residual amount.

Required:

Calculate how many contracts should be bought.

11 Currency options

 A currency option is a right, but not an obligation, to buy or sell a currency at an exercise price on a future date.

If there is a favourable movement in rates the company will allow the option to **lapse**, to take advantage of the favourable movement. The right will only be **exercised** to protect against an adverse movement, i.e. the worst-case scenario.

Features and operation

As a result of this, options sound very attractive, BUT they have a cost. Because options limit downside risk but allow the holder to benefit from upside risk, the writer of the option will charge a non-refundable **premium** for writing the option.

It is possible for the holder of the option to calculate the gains and losses on using options:

The gain if the option is exercised: this is the difference between the exercise price (option strike price) and the market price of the underlying item	X
Less: The premium paid to purchase the option	(X)
	X

There are two types of option:

* A **call** option gives the holder the right to buy the underlying currency.
* A **put** option gives the holder the right to sell the underlying currency.

Test your understanding 18 – UK exporter (Integration question)

A UK exporter is due to receive USD 25 million in 3 months' time. Its bank offers a 3 month dollar put option on USD 25 million at an exercise price of GBP1/USD1.5000 at a premium cost of GBP 300,000.

Required:
Show the net GBP receipt if the future spot is either USD 1.6000 or USD 1.4000.

Illustration of currency options

A typical pricing schedule for the EUR currency option on the Philadelphia (US) exchange is as follows.

Strike price	CALLS			PUTS		
	Jun	Sept	Dec	Jun	Sept	Dec
115.00	1.99	2.25	2.47	0.64	1.32	2.12
116.00	1.39	2.03	2.28	1.00	1.56	–
117.00	0.87	1.55	1.81	1.43	2.22	–
118.00	0.54	1.08	1.30	–	–	–

- Here, the options are for a contract size of EUR 125,000 and prices (both strike price and premia) are quoted in USD (cents) per EUR 1.

- So to buy a call option on EUR 125,000 with an expiry date of September and at a strike price of EUR 1 = USD 1.1700 would cost 1.55 cents per euro, or USD 1,937.50.

- Similarly, the premium on a June put at a strike price of 115.00 (EUR 1 = USD 1.1500) would cost 0.64 cents per euro, or USD 800.

The decision as to which exercise price to choose will depend on cost, risk exposure and expectations.

- In the exam it is unlikely that you will be given such a wide range of values – it is more likely to have just one call and one put option price

Options hedging calculations

Step 1: Set up the hedge by addressing 4 key questions:

- Do we need call or put options?
- Which expiry date should be chosen?
- What is the strike price?
- How many contracts?

Step 2: Contact the exchange. Pay the up-front premium. Then wait until the transaction/settlement date.

Step 3: On the transaction date, compare the option price with the prevailing spot rate to determine whether the option should be exercised or allowed to lapse.

Step 4: Calculate the net cash flows – beware that if the number of contracts needed rounding, there will be some exchange at the prevailing spot rate even if the option is exercised.

In- and out-of-the money options

The strike price for an option might be higher or lower than the current market price of the underlying item.

For example, a call option might give its holder the right to buy GBP 125,000 in exchange for USD at USD 1.7900, and the current spot rate could be higher than USD 1.7900, below USD 1.7900 or possibly USD 1.7900 exactly.

- If the exercise price for an option is more favourable to the option holder than the current 'spot' market price, the option is said to be **in-the-money.**

- If the exercise price for an option is less favourable to the option holder than the current 'spot' market price, the option is said to be **out-of-the-money.**

- If the exercise price for the option is exactly the same as the current 'spot' market price, it is said to be **at-the-money.**

An option holder is not obliged to exercise the option, and will never do so if the option is out-of-the-money. **An option will only ever be exercised if it is in-the-money.**

However, when an option is first purchased, or during the period before the expiry date, an option might be out-of-the-money.

Options that start out-of-the-money might become in-the-money if the market price of the underlying item changes. On the other hand, an option that starts out-of-the-money might stay out-of-the-money until expiry, and so will lapse without being exercised

Advantages and disadvantages

The advantages of currency options are that:

- They offer the perfect hedge (downside risk covered, can participate in upside potential).

- There are many choices of strike price, dates, premiums, etc.

- The option can be allowed to lapse if the future transaction does not arise.

The disadvantages are that:

- Traded sterling currency options are only available in foreign markets.

- There are high up-front premium costs (non-refundable).

> ### Test your understanding 19 (Integration question)
>
> A company is due to receive USD 3 million in 3 months' time.
>
> The spot rate is USD 1.9500/GBP but the company is worried that the USD will weaken. They have been offered a three month put option on USD at USD 1.9700/GBP, costing USD 0.02 per GBP.
>
> **Required:**
>
> If the company chooses to buy and then exercise the option, what is its net receipt in GBP?

The Black-Scholes model

Writers of options have to decide what level of premium to set, and for this they use complex option pricing models. These models are also used to calculate the fair value of an option at any given date (useful for financial reporting purposes).

In the exam you will not be expected to calculate option values, but you are expected to be aware of the factors that affect the option price. The most common option pricing model used is the Black-Scholes model.

The basic principle of the Black-Scholes model is that the market value, or price, of a call option consists of two key elements:

– The intrinsic value of the option.

– The time value of the option.

Between these two elements there are five variables affecting the price of a call option.

Intrinsic value

This is the difference between the current price of the underlying asset and its option strike (exercise) price. For the market value of a call option to rise, one or both of the following variables must change:

1 Current price of the underlying asset must increase.

2 Strike price must fall (hence making it more likely that the option will be exercised, and so is worth something).

Time value

This reflects the uncertainty surrounding the intrinsic value, and is impacted by three variables:

1 Standard deviation in the daily value of the underlying asset. The more variability that is demonstrated, the higher the chance that the option will be 'in the money' and so will be exercised.

2 Time period to expiry of the option. A longer time period will increase the likelihood that the asset value increases and so the option is exercised.

3 Risk free interest rates. Having a call option means that the purchase can be deferred, so owning a call option becomes more valuable when interest rates are high, since the money left in the bank will be generating a higher return.

Limitations of the Black-Scholes model

The basic form of the Black-Scholes model has been illustrated above. It is widely used by traders in option markets to give an estimate of option values, and more expensive scientific calculators include the model in their functions so that the calculations can be carried out very quickly.

However, the model in its basic form does suffer from a number of limitations:

- It assumes that the risk-free interest rate is known and is constant throughout the option's life.

- The standard deviation of returns from the underlying security must be accurately estimated and has to be constant throughout the option's life. In practice standard deviation will vary depending on the period over which it is calculated; unfortunately the model is very sensitive to its value.

- It assumes that there are no transaction costs or tax effects involved in buying or selling the option or the underlying item.

Certain of these limitations can be removed by more sophisticated versions of the model, but the basic model is complicated enough for the purposes of this text.

The discussion of the value of options does not just relate to currency options but is relevant to interest rate options and other assets or liabilities.

For example, a company may wish to purchase an option to buy a factory which is under construction. The company might pay a premium to the builder of the factory which entitles them to first option to buy the completed factory (not a commitment to buy). If in the following months the council, say, change the planning guidelines and no further developments can be constructed, then the option becomes very valuable if another company then wishes to build a factory in the same location because it could be sold on (subject to the builder's agreement) at a profit.

Test your understanding 20 (Objective test question)

Which of the following is not a factor upon which an option value depends:

A   The current share price

B   The standard deviation of return on underlying share

C   The time to expiration of the option

D   The number of shares in issue

12   Swaps

A cross currency swap allows a company to swap a currency it currently holds for a different currency for a fixed period, and then swap back at the same rate at the end of the period.

The company's counterparty in a cross currency swap would generally be a bank.

A cross currency swap has two elements:

- An exchange of principals in different currencies, which are swapped back at the original spot rate.

- An exchange of interest rates – the timing of these depends on the individual contract.

It works in a very similar way to an interest rate swap, so is covered in detail straight after interest rate swaps in Chapter 10: 'Interest rate risk management'.

13   Chapter summary

This chapter has covered lots of different ways of reducing exposure to currency risks. The different hedging methods were categorised at the start of the chapter into internal methods and external methods.

Bear in mind that there are some risks that can be better covered by internal methods and some that can be better covered by external methods. It is really important for the exam to be able to identify what the risk is and to be able to match a suitable hedging method to the specific risk (rather than just suggesting forward contracts as a solution to every problem!)

For example, many students lose marks because they don't look beyond the financial instruments e.g. an economic risk arising from the fact that a UK company exports to the US and could suffer if the USD weakens could be hedged by matching its USD revenues with USD costs - ideally by importing materials priced in USD. A student in the exam would lose marks for trying to hedge this sort of exposure with (external) hedging instruments that have limited life spans.

14 End of chapter objective test questions

Test your understanding 21 (Objective test question)

If the interest rate on USD deposits is 8%, the interest rate on EUR deposits is 5%, and the spot rate is USD/EUR0.9200, what is the one year forward rate predicted to be if interest rate parity holds?

A   USD/EUR0.9463

B   USD/EUR1.0567

C   USD/EUR0.8944

D   USD/EUR1.1180

Test your understanding 22 (Objective test question)

The spot rate for Swiss francs is GBP1/CHF 1.6734 – 1.6802.

The three month forward premium is 0.0200 – 0.0250.

If you wanted to sell your CHF forward what exchange rate would you receive from the bank?

A   1.6552

B   1.6534

C   1.6934

D   1.7052

Test your understanding 23 – Option costs and premiums

Pricing schedule for Sterling currency options on the Philadelphia (US) exchange.

The contract size is GBP 31,250, all figures are quoted in USD (cents).

Strike price	CALLS			PUTS		
	Mar	Jun	Sept	Mar	Jun	Sept
145.00	1.41	2.57	3.82	–	0.42	0.87
146.00	1.21	2.34	3.41	0.15	0.81	1.27

A company wants to buy a call option at a strike price of 1.4600 with an expiry date of March; another company wants to set up a put option with a strike price of 1.4500 expiring in June.

Which of the following statements are correct?

A   The cost of each contract for the call option is USD 378.125

B   The cost of each contract for the call option is GBP 378.125

C   The cost of each contract for the call option is USD 131.25

D   The cost of each contract for the call option is GBP 131.25

E   The premium for each put option contract is USD 131.25

F   The premium for each put option contract is GBP 131.25

G   The premium for each put option contract is GBP 378.125

Test your understanding 24 (Objective test question)

Which of the following are characteristics of an 'over the counter option' as compared to an 'exchange traded option'?

A   Can be customised to meet the customer's needs in terms of amount and duration.

B   Settlement at maturity.

C   Easy to liquidate the position.

D   Potential to benefit from favourable exchange rate changes.

Test your understanding 25 (Objective test question)

Which of the following would decrease the intrinsic value of a put option? (Select ALL that apply)

A   An increase in the time to expiry

B   A decrease in the market value of the share

C   A decrease in the volatility value of the share

D   A decrease in the strike price

Test your understanding 26 (Objective test question)

Which of the following will increase the value of a call option? (Select ALL that apply)

A   An increase in the strike price

B   An increase in the time to expiry

C   A decrease in the volatility of the share

D   A decrease in the market value of the share

Test your understanding 27 (Objective test question)

Which of the following is an external hedging technique? (Select all that apply.)

A   A forward contract

B   A money market hedge

C   Pooling

D   A futures contract

Test your understanding 28 (Objective test question)

A UK company has sold goods to a Danish company and will receive 300,000 Danish Kroner in 3 months' time. Which of the following would hedge its position?

A   Selling a call option on Danish Kroner

B   Buying a put option on Danish Kroner

C   Using the forward market to buy Kroner at the 3 month forward rate

D   Buying Danish Kroner futures

15 End of chapter case style questions

Test your understanding 29 – L (Case style question)

L manufactures specialised paper products for sale in its home country, Country B. The market is very price sensitive. Some of L's competitors are based in its home country and others export to Country B.

The manufacturing process is not particularly skilled, but it is very labour intensive. L's largest costs are for wages and flax fibre (the basic raw material used in manufacturing L's products). Almost 60% of L's total manufacturing cost is for wages.

L's directors are considering moving production offshore to Country R, a developing country that has low wage rates. The products will then be transferred to Country B for sale.

L's home currency is the BND. Country R's currency is the RTD. At present, the exchange rate is 1.00 BND = 2.50 RTD.

L presently pays an hourly rate of 6.00 BND to its production staff. Workers with comparable skill levels would be paid 2.75 RTD per hour in Country R.

Flax fibre is sold as a commodity on the global markets. It is priced in US Dollars (USD). All of L's purchases of flax fibre are imported.

Shipping flax fibre to the new factory would be much cheaper than shipping it to L's home country. Those savings would pay for the cost of shipping the finished products to L's home country for sale.

L's directors are currently asking for information that will help them with an appraisal of the financial viability of the new factory. L's Chief Economist has reported that there are no credible long-term economic forecasts available. She has, however, obtained some basic economic indicators that could be used to predict future wage rates:

	Country B	Country R
Interest rates per annum	5.00%	9.00%
General inflation per annum	2.00%	4.70%

Required:

(a) (i) Produce a forecast of the hourly rate in BND that will be paid to employees in Country R in five years' time. You must explain the assumptions that you have made at each stage of your calculations.

(15 minutes)

(ii) Evaluate the assumptions that were made and explained in (a) (i) explaining why reality could differ from what you assumed.

(10 minutes)

(b) Discuss the Production Director's statement that the price of flax fibre is irrelevant to the decision to move production to Country R because flax fibre is priced in terms of USD.

(10 minutes)

(c) Advise L's board of the political risks that L will be taking in its home country if it proceeds with this project.

(10 minutes)

Test your understanding 30 – S (Case style question)

S has been studying some of the fundamental economic data relating to both the USA and the Eurozone. She believes that her understanding of economics gives her an advantage over many other market participants. She believes that she has spotted an anomaly in the pricing of futures for the EUR to USD exchange rate.

The contract value is USD 125,000.

The tick size is 0.0001, which gives a tick value of USD 12.50.

The current spot markets value 1 EUR = USD 1.3036.

The rate offered by the futures markets is USD 1.3004 for delivery in three months.

The interest rates offered on deposits are 3.000% per annum on EUR deposits and 2.000% per annum on USD deposits.

S notes that the markets expect the USD to strengthen against the EUR. However, S's own personal analysis of various economic and political indicators suggests that the USD will actually weaken to 1 EUR = USD 1.350. She intends to exploit this different view by entering into a futures contract that will require her to deliver USD in three months.

S has discussed this arrangement with a broker, who has advised her that it will be possible for her to enter into a contract which meets her requirements, but that she will have to make an initial margin payment of 15% of the EUR value of the future. In addition, she may be required to deposit further margin during the life of the contract. The broker will not pay any interest on the margin deposits.

S has personal savings of EUR 100,000 that she can use to invest in this venture. She does not believe that she will ever be asked to provide additional margin and so she intends to use as much of her funds as possible to invest in the initial margin.

Required:

(a) Calculate the gain S will make writing a futures contract, assuming that she invests the maximum possible amount that she can afford in the initial margin and that her expectations turn out to be accurate.

(b) Discuss the risks that S will be taking if she enters into this contract.

(c) Explain why S chose to use a futures contract as the basis for her speculation in the market.

(45 minutes)

Test your understanding 31 – Marcus (Integration question)

Marcus, based in France, has recently imported raw materials from the USA and has been invoiced for USD 240,000, payable in three months' time.

In addition, it has also exported finished goods to Japan and Australia.

The Japanese customer has been invoiced for USD 69,000, payable in three months' time, and the Australian customer has been invoiced for AUD 295,000, payable in four months' time.

Current spot and forward rates are as follows:

EUR1/USD

Spot	0.9850 – 0.9830
Three months' forward	0.9545 – 0.9520

AUD1/EUR

Spot:	1.8920 – 1.8890
Four months' forward:	1.9540 – 1.9510

Current money market rates (per annum) are as follows:

USD: 10.0% – 12.0%

AUD: 14.0% – 16.0%

EUR: 11.5% – 13.0%

Required:

Show how the company can hedge its exposure to FX risk using:

(i) the forward markets;

(ii) the money markets;

and in each case, determine which is the best hedging technique.

Test your understanding 32 – UK company (Integration question)

A UK company will receive USD 2.5 million from an American customer in three months' time in February.

Currently:

Futures	GBP contracts (GBP62,500)	December	GBP1/USD 1.5830
		March	GBP1/USD 1.5796

Margins are USD1,000 per contract.

GBP1/USD forward rates:

	Spot	1.5851 – 1.5842
	One month	0.53 – 0.56 c pm
	Three month	1.64 – 1.72 c pm

28 February:

   Assume that the spot rate moves to 1.6510 – 1.6490

   March futures have a price of 1.6513

Required:

Calculate the GBP receipt using a forward contract and a future.

Test your understanding answers

Test your understanding 1 – Spread (Integration question)

(a) A Ltd will need to sell GBP and buy USD and therefore the bank is buying GBP and selling USD. The bank always buys GBP low and sells GBP high and therefore the rate is GBP1 = USD1.4500.

Cost is therefore USD100,000 ÷ 1.4500 = GBP68,966.

(b) B plc is receiving USD and therefore the bank will buy USD and sell GBP. The rate is therefore GBP1 = USD1.5500.

Receipt is therefore USD50,000 ÷ 1.5500 = GBP32,258.

(c) C Ltd is importing goods and therefore needs to sell GBP and the bank needs to buy GBP. The rate is therefore GBP1 = USD1.4500.

The product must therefore cost GBP12 × 1.4500 = USD17.40.

Test your understanding 2 (Integration question)

The implied cross rate is USD/GBP divided by EUR/GBP = 1.4417/1.1250 = 1.2815

Test your understanding 3 – Cross rates (Integration question)

The USD1/EUR cross rate will be calculated as:

1.5300/1.8700 = 0.8182 i.e. USD1/EUR0.8182.

The cost of the machine is therefore:

EUR100,000/0.8182 = USD122,220

Test your understanding 4 (Integration question)

$$1.7200 \times \frac{1.03}{1.04} = USD1.7035$$

Test your understanding 5 (Integration question)

$$10 \times \frac{1.03}{1.07} = CHF9.6262 \text{ to GBP 1}$$

Test your understanding 6 (Integration question)

PPPT

Future spot rate $= 0.9050 \times \dfrac{1 + 0.013}{1 + 0.02}$

$ = $ EUR 0.8988

IRPT

Forward rate $= 0.9050 \times \dfrac{1 + 0.045}{1 + 0.06}$

$ = $ EUR 0.8922

The rates are similar, but not identical under the two different forecasting methods.

Using the Fisher Effect, the real rate of interest can be found in both US and Eurozone.

US:

$(1 + m) = (1 + r)(1 + i)$

$(1 + 0.06) = (1 + r)(1 + 0.02)$

Hence r = 3.9%

Eurozone:

$(1 + m) = (1 + r)(1 + i)$

$(1 + 0.045) = (1 + r)(1 + 0.013)$

Hence r = 3.2%

For the PPPT and the IRPT to give identical predicted rates, the International Fisher Effect must hold, which states that real rates of interest are identical in all countries. This is apparently not the case.

Other factors that may affect the prediction of exchange rates include:

- Transaction costs of shifting money and making investments.
- Lack of mobility of capital and goods, and the costs associated with this.
- Political intervention.
- Cultural differences between different countries.
- Central bank action.
- Trader activity.
- Key commodity prices (e.g. oil is priced in US dollars).

Test your understanding 7 – G clothing (Case style question)

Briefing note

To: The Board of G

From: Management accountant

Date: Today

Subject: Currency risk management

Dear Sirs,

Introduction

This briefing note covers three issues:

(a)   The argument that purchasing power parity theory should prevent exporters from charging different prices in different countries.

(b)   The potential risks and benefits to G of buying its inventory from intermediaries in the neighbouring countries.

(c)   Recommends actions that the Government in G's home country could take in order to determine whether G's competitor had been evading the tariff on imported clothing.

(a)   **Purchasing power parity theory (PPP)**

Purchasing power parity theory (PPP) suggests that a commodity will sell for the same amount across the world, regardless of the currency in which it is priced. That is because of arbitrage. It is illogical that customers will buy goods in their home country if they can buy them elsewhere and import them more cheaply.

There is considerable evidence that PPP does not hold in reality. There are some fairly obvious reasons for that. With very few exceptions, it is unlikely to be convenient to buy goods from across an international border. Travel and transportation costs will frequently exceed any savings.

There can be artificial factors, such as tariffs and differential pricing practices by suppliers.

(b)   **The potential risks and benefits to G of buying its inventory from intermediaries in the neighbouring countries**

The only benefit is the obvious one that G will possibly be able to reduce its costs. Those savings will make it easier to compete with other retailers who are using the same sources.

The fact that this behaviour is illegal in G's home country means that the company may be open to prosecution. The staff who are responsible for making the arrangements may also be held personally responsible, which will harm G's reputation if any of them are prosecuted. Staff may refuse to act illegally, which could undermine discipline in G and could lead to problems in processing partially completed transactions.

G's contract will be with foreign intermediaries, who may offer a lower standard of service than the manufacturer. Any disputes over quality or delivery may lead to G being unable to obtain an adequate resolution. The intermediaries may not offer the full range of new designs and may not be able to meet all of G's requirements for volume.

The manufacturers may be unwilling to encourage G to buy from intermediaries because they will lose the benefits of differential pricing in the two markets. They may report G to the authorities or take G to court to prevent it from stocking or selling these "grey imports". The manufacturers may then refuse to sell goods to G in the future in order to deter other retailers from copying this practice.

(c) **Actions that the Government in G's home country could take**

The government can inspect the retailer's books to determine where it obtains its goods. Given that most of the fashion clothes appear to be imported, there ought to have been duty paid on virtually all of the retailer's purchases. The total duty paid should be roughly equivalent to the total purchases multiplied by the rate of duty.

The retailer is unlikely to record all transactions accurately in its bookkeeping records if it is defrauding the revenue authorities. The government should check that the purchase records are accurate by going back to basic records, such as sales recorded by individual shops. There should be a realistic relationship between the level of sales and the level of purchases. If the gross profit percentage is very high then that would suggest that purchases are being understated.

The customs authorities should conduct spot checks of vehicles crossing into the country as a matter of routine anyway. Customs officers should be instructed to look out for goods despatched to the competitor by anyone other than the original manufacturer. Any such goods should be seized and the relevant paperwork investigated to determine whether duty has been paid.

The revenue authorities can conduct spot inspections of goods being delivered to the competitor's premises. Again, the origin of the goods should be investigated for unpaid duty. The authorities can always levy an estimated charge on the competitor and force the competitor to prove that such a payment is not appropriate.

Test your understanding 8 (Integration question)

GBP 66,700

The speculator should

1   Convert GBP into USD: 1,000,000 × 2 = USD2,000,000
2   Convert USD into EUR: 2,000,000/1.50 = EUR1,333,333
3   Now sell the EUR: 1,333,333 × 0.80 = GBP1,066,667

The speculator has made a risk-free profit of GBP66,667.

Test your understanding 9 (Integration/Case style question)

(a) Principle of borrowing, depositing and selling resulting balance forward

- Borrow GBP 10m
- Convert to USD at spot rate = GBP10m x 1.556 = USD 15.560m
- Deposit at 5.12% for three months. Interest = USD 15.560m × 5.12% × 3/12 = USD 0.1992m
- Total deposit by end of three months = USD 15.560m + 0.1992 = USD 15.7592m
- Sell USD forward = USD 15.7592m/1.499 = GBP 10.5131m
- Interest on GBP borrowings = GBP 10m × 5.08% × 3/12 = GBP 0.127m
- Total repayment = GBP 10.1270m
- Gain = GBP 10.5130 – 10.1271 = GBP 0.3861m

(i) U has clearly identified the possibility of an arbitrage profit that could be exploited without risk to the company. Interest rate parity suggests that if the USD is expected to strengthen against GBP then the interest rate offered for USD deposits should be lower than the rates on GBP. The fact that it wasn't made it possible to borrow in GBP, deposit in USD, sell the resulting USD forward, all in the knowledge that the resulting GBP balance would be more than enough to settle the GBP loan.

Any business opportunity that offers a positive return in absolute terms from zero investment with zero risk must be highly desirable. U has found such an opportunity through good luck. Simple economics suggest that markets will not offer positive returns to participants who do not invest anything and who do not take any risk and so such opportunities will either require great skill to identify or considerable good luck.

(ii) In practice, arbitrageurs draw attention to anomalies by moving funds to exploit them and the inconsistencies are quickly corrected to make further profits impossible. That explains why U's treasurer did not ask U to act on her discovery. Professional arbitrage companies use electronic trading to seek out these opportunities and exploit them. U discovered the opportunity by chance, but it is unlikely that she would have been able to put the various trades in place quickly enough to beat the professionals.

The very nature of arbitrage means that the trades themselves are risk free, but there are considerable costs associated with arbitrage operations. Arbitrageurs must pay a great deal for real-time market data, which is a substantial fixed cost. There is also substantial investment in the IT systems and other facilities. It is entirely possible that there will be too few opportunities offered by the market to generate an adequate return to cover those costs and provide a realistic return on investment.

The anomalies that arise tend to be far smaller than those discovered by U. Arbitrage requires very large transactions to generate sufficient profit in absolute terms to make the process worthwhile. Participants must be sufficiently liquid to meet margin requirements and to have the confidence of the institutions who have to accept the bids being made.

The financial institutions which create the markets have an incentive to avoid creating arbitrage opportunities and they are clearly going to use sophisticated systems of their own to avoid doing so. There will also be competition from other arbitrageurs, all of whom will be attempting to move more quickly than anybody else so that they enjoy all of the profit.

(c) Generally, the treasury department provides a service to the entity, by managing cash flows and dealing with banks and other sources of finance. The treasury aims to reduce the costs borne by the entity and the intention is that these savings will more than offset the cost of running the department.

The treasury can only become a profit centre if it develops a revenue stream. Normally that involves speculating in the financial markets in order to generate gains. There are two competing arguments relating to speculation:

One is that the treasury department has considerable expertise. Speculation is a zero sum game that involves being able to out-think the market and buy or sell mispriced financial instruments. The treasury department could use its natural advantage over other market participants, who have a lesser understanding and inferior data to trade at a profit.

The counter-argument is that active trading in the markets involves leaving positions exposed to loss and so there is a risk. Losses can arise when trades are unsuccessful. The entity would be bidding against counterparties who may be even more skilled and better informed.

It is generally difficult to make a consistent profit from speculation. Markets are generally efficient and most participants – even trained corporate treasurers – should accept that the market prices are correct. Active trading will increase costs and also increase risks for the entity.

Test your understanding 10 – J electronics (Case style question)

Briefing note

To: The Board

From: A.N. Accountant

Date: Today

Subject: Appointment of a corporate treasurer

Dear Sirs,

(a)   A corporate treasurer could strengthen J's management team. At present, there is nobody with any particular expertise in accountancy or finance in the company. The fact that J has secured an order of this magnitude suggests that the company is of a size where it requires more attention to be paid to financial management. The fact that the order was for export suggests that there is a need for support in this area, particularly given that the chief executive's discussion with the bank indicates a lack of understanding.

It could be argued that it would make more sense to appoint a qualified accountant to manage all aspects of the accounting function, including treasury matters. A qualified treasurer is trained in greater depth to manage the relationship with the bank and to manage receipts and payments. A professionally qualified accountant holding, say, the CIMA qualification should have sufficient skill in treasury matters to deal with the treasury needs of a medium-sized and growing company and should be able to contribute to other areas such as the development of management accounting and financial reporting.

There is a danger that the company's needs would not justify such an appointment and that the costs would outweigh the benefits. There is a danger that appointing an accountant or treasurer will prove a distraction from the basic business of manufacturing and selling electronics if the appointee feels it necessary to table reports and ask the board to fine-tune financial decisions.

It may be that J would be better advised to take on a part-time accountant rather than a full-time treasurer. That would strike a balance between the conflicting arguments for and against an appointment.

(b) The first step is to define the role clearly so that J can decide on the skills and experience that the treasurer will require.

It would be worth appointing a recruitment agency to assist with identifying suitable candidates. J's board has no experience to draw upon in identifying experts in this area and so it would make more sense for the company to ask a specialist agency to produce a shortlist.

The final interview should be conducted by J's directors. Even if the recruitment agency has shortlisted a suitable candidate it is important that the board is satisfied that it can work with this individual.

J should insist on seeing a detailed CV and checking up on all references. The board will not really be in a position to provide detailed oversight of this individual, which makes competence an issue, and the appointee will be in a significant position of trust with respect to J's bank balances, which makes honesty important too.

Test your understanding 11 (Integration question)

(i) **Add** a **discount** to get the forward rate.

Spot rate	1.5500	–	1.4500
	0.0055		0.0050
Forward rate	1.5555	–	1.4550

(ii) **Subtract** a **premium** to get the forward rate.

Spot rate	1.7150	–	1.6450
Subtract premium	(0.0068)		(0.0075)
Forward rate	1.7082	–	1.6375

Test your understanding 12 (Integration question)

GBP 1,275,500 (rounded)

EEFS Ltd is expecting a receipt of USD, and therefore wishes to buy GBP from the bank. The bank will sell GBP high and therefore the rate is 1.5430 (current spot). The discount of 2.5c must be added to the rate thus giving a rate of 1.5680.

The GBP receipt is therefore USD2m ÷ 1.5680 = GBP 1,275,510

Test your understanding 13 – J electronics (Case style question)

Note

To: Finance Director

From: A.N. Accountant

Date: Today

Subject: Forward contract offer rate

Dear Finance Director,

The Chief Executive is correct in stating that changes in the exchange rate cannot be predicted with any certainty, but that does not mean that today's rate is the best forecast of the rate that will prevail in three months' time. The capital markets use differences in interest rates to establish the anticipated rate between two currencies, which suggests that there will be an observable difference in the interest rates available on GBP versus USD which will explain the forward rate on offer. The interest rate on USD is, presumably, higher at present, which implies that the USD is expected to weaken against GBP and so it is perfectly realistic for the bank to offer an inferior rate for three months compared to spot.

The bank manager's argument seems to take the question of the differential rates for granted. The fact that the offer is consistent with market sentiments suggests that there is a rational basis to expect the USD to decline. If the market rate was unrealistic then there would be arbitrage opportunities that would enable market participants to exploit the market's pricing error and that market error would be corrected very quickly.

The Chief Executive's argument that J should leave this position unhedged suggests that it is illogical to pay a premium in return for a reduction in risk. There is clearly a possibility that J will enjoy an upside if the position if left unhedged and the USD weakens by less than the amount anticipated by the bank's forward rate. The question is whether the associated possibility of a loss outweighs the potential gain.

The fact that J has not taken the possibility of changing exchange rates into account in pricing this sale is irrelevant. J is going to receive USD 15m regardless of the fact that a higher price should have been charged to reflect anticipated changes in the exchange rate.

Test your understanding 14 (Integration question)

The company should borrow from the bank just enough to end up owing exactly USD12,000

- Amount borrowed = USD12,000/1.06 = USD 11,321.

They should convert this into GBP at spot

- Converted amount = 11,321/1.9990 = GBP 5,663.

They should then invest this for 6 months in the UK

- End up with 5,663 × 1.05 = GBP 5,946 (fixed, certain sum)

Test your understanding 15 – DD Ltd – 1 (Integration question)

DD Ltd

(a) The money market hedge to pay EUR in six months' time requires DD Ltd to borrow in GBP, translate to EUR and deposit in EUR.

A payment of EUR1.3 million in six months (only 1.25% interest) will require a EUR deposit now of (EUR1,300,000 ÷ 1.0125) EUR1,283,951. This means that with a spot rate of 1.5050 the GBP loan will need to be GBP853,124.

The loan of GBP853,124 will increase over the six months to the date of repayment by 2.3% and will therefore be GBP872,746.

The cost is therefore GBP872,746.

(b) The forward contract will use the six-month forward rate of 1.4895 for buying EUR.

The cost is therefore (EUR1,300,000 ÷ 1.4895) GBP872,776

There is virtually no difference between the two methods. This is expected because any significant difference would mean that profit could be made simply by converting one currency into another.

Test your understanding 16 – DD Ltd – 2 (Integration question)

Under an MMH the company would borrow EUR now, translate into GBP and deposit for six months.

The borrowing would be EUR1,300,000 ÷ 1.02	EUR 1,274,510
This would translate now into 1,274,510 ÷ 1.5095	GBP 844,326
By growth for interest for six months this becomes	GBP 857,413

Forward contract

The forward contract would give:

EUR 1,300,000 ÷ 1.5162 GBP 857,407

Test your understanding 17 (Integration question)

22

USD 2,650,000/(1.9000 × GBP 62,500) = 22.32 contracts

(rounded down to 22)

Test your understanding 18 – UK exporter (Integration question)

Dividing by the smallest GBP1/USD rate gives the highest GBP receipt – the premium is paid no matter what so it should be ignored for the purposes of determining whether to exercise the option.

Future spot USD 1.6000

- Exercise the option.
- USD 25m/USD1.5000 = GBP 16.67m less GBP300,000 premium gives a net receipt of GBP 16.37m

Future spot USD 1.4000

- Abandon the option.
- USD 25m/USD 1.4000 = GBP 17.86m less GBP 300,000 premium gives a net receipt of GBP 17.56m

Test your understanding 19 (Integration question)

The GBP received upon exercise will be 3,000,000/1.9700 = GBP 1,522,843.

The cost of the option will be 0.02 × 1,522,843 = USD 30,457.

At spot this cost in GBP is 30,457/1.9500 = GBP 15,619.

Therefore the net receipt will be 1,522,843 – 15,619 = GBP 1,507,224

Test your understanding 20 (Objective test question)

The answer is (D).

A, B and C are stated as factors affecting option prices in the Black – Scholes model

Test your understanding 21 (Objective test question)

The answer is (C).

$(1 + r_€)/(1 + r_\$) \times$ Spot $_{€/\$}$ = Forward $_{€/\$}$

$(1 + 0.05)/(1 + 0.08) \times 0.92 = 0.8944$

Test your understanding 22 (Objective test question)

The answer is (A).

A bank buys high and sells low so the appropriate spot rate is 1.6802.

A premium should be deducted. 1.6802 – 0.0250 = 1.6552

Test your understanding 23 – Option costs and premiums

Statements A and E are correct.

Call:

GBP 31,250 × USD 0.0121 = USD 378.125

Put:

GBP 31,250 × USD 0.0042 = USD 131.25

Test your understanding 24 (Objective test question)

The answer is (A) and (B).

Exchange traded options are easier to liquidate as there is an active, liquid secondary market. Both types of option allow the holder to benefit from favourable movements.

Test your understanding 25 (Objective test question)

The answer is (D).

A and B would increase the value of the option.

C would decrease the value of the option – but would not affect its intrinsic value (difference between the MV and the strike price)

Test your understanding 26 (Objective test question)

The answer is (B).

All the others would reduce the value

Test your understanding 27 (Objective test question)

The answer is (A), (B) and (D).

Pooling is where the balances of all subsidiaries are kept together when considering interest rates and overdraft limits. It should reduce interest payable, increase interest earned and prevent overdraft limits being breached.

Test your understanding 28 (Objective test question)

The answer is (B).

C and D would be used to hedge a Kroner payment.

A (selling options) is not a hedging method.

Test your understanding 29 – L (Case style question)

(a) (i) The forecast hourly rate is assumed to grow in line with the rate of inflation in the proposed host country. We assume that the inflation rate will remain constant for five years.

Over five years, the inflation rate will compound by $(1.047)^5 - 1$ = 25.8%. The forecast hourly rate is 2.75 RTD + 25.8% = 3.46 RTD.

We assume that the exchange rates will move in line with the differences in the interest rates. We assume that those rates will remain constant.

Over five years the rates will change as follows $(1.09/1.05)^5$ = 1.21.

The exchange rate will be 1 BND = 2.50 × 1.21 = 3.025 RTD.

The hourly rate in BND = 3.46/3.025 = 1.14 BND

(ii)   The first assumption is that wages will move in line with inflation in the host country. Given that prices are rising it seems likely that L will have to pay more for wages. The actual rises that will be granted will vary in accordance with the bargaining power of the employees and so it is unlikely that the actual rises will closely match the rate of inflation.

Given that L is a multinational operating in a developing country, it may have to pay rises that exceed the rate of inflation in order to avoid claims of exploitation.

Interest rate parity suggests that the expected exchange rates will move very closely in line with the differential interest rates. That does not mean that the actual rates will turn out in accordance with expectations. The governments of either country may decide to manage their interest rates in order to strengthen or weaken their exchange rates.

(b)   It could be argued that a kilo of fibre will cost a specific number of USD regardless of whether it is imported to the home country or the host. Basic costing suggests that the value is irrelevant, particularly when transportation does not affect pricing.

Unfortunately, things are more complicated because L will be importing finished paper, which contains flax fibre, rather than flax fibre itself. Transfer pricing arrangements will mean that the paper will have to be sold to L's trading subsidiary in the home country at the open market price for paper. Changes in the price of the underlying raw materials may not directly affect the market price in a linear manner and so the price of flax fibre could change the taxable profits in the two countries.

(c)   The most immediate problem is that L will make its present employees redundant. That will undermine the company's reputation. Customers may buy their paper from other suppliers rather than be associated with L. The home government may also be concerned that L has exported jobs and may take sanctions against the company. It could, for example, grant contracts to other companies.

L will also come under suspicion for operating in a developing country. Activists in the home country may feel that L is exploiting badly paid workers in the developing country.

Even if such accusations are unfounded L may suffer responses ranging from negative press comment to demonstrations at its remaining locations.

Test your understanding 30 – S (Case style question)

(a)   The margin requirement means that S can write forwards worth a maximum of EUR 100,000/15% = EUR 666,667.

The USD value = 666,667 × 1.3004 = USD 866,934.

S can write 866,934/125,000 = 6 contracts = USD 750,000.

S will have to pay a margin of USD 750,000/1.3004 × 15% = EUR 86,512.

If she deposited that sum for three months she would earn interest of EUR 86,512 × 3% /4 = EUR 649.

If her predictions prove accurate, the cost of closing out her position will be 750,000/1.350 = EUR 55 5,556 for the USD 750,000.

The counterparty's cost will be 750,000/1.3004 = EUR 576,746.

The overall position will be settled by a net payment of EUR 576,746 – 555,556 – 649 = EUR 20,541 in favour of S.

(b)   The most obvious risk is the upside risk that she will earn a significant return from her ability to identify an anomaly in the market. If she is confident then she must compare the possibility of a capital gain of EUR 576,746 – 555,556 = EUR 21,190 against the opportunity cost of interest foregone of EUR 649. This seems like a relatively small risk, provided S has not overstated the probability of success.

The downside risk is that the gain will not materialise and she will have tied up her finances needlessly. The market's expectation is that the spot rate will match the rate implied by her future contract. The currency markets for the USD and the EUR are both highly visible and are the subject of intense scrutiny. It would possibly be easier to develop better insights into smaller economies that do not attract the same degree of study. The financial loss is very limited in this case.

It is possible that the USD will strengthen further than the market's expectations, in which case she will be faced with the prospect of a loss when she closes out her position. For example, if the USD strengthens to 1.2 then closing out her position will cost a net EUR 576,746 – (750,000/1.2) = EUR 48,254. In theory, this speculative loss could be substantial. In practice, it is to be hoped that there will not be a massive movement of the EUR against the USD.

There could be a problem if the exchange rates move against her because S may be required to deposit additional margin. The fact that she could only write a whole contract would mean that she will have some of her EUR 100,000 left to meet such a contingency, but her position may be abandoned if she cannot keep up with margin requests.

The fact that the exchange requires margin deposits will indemnify S against any default by the counterparty.

(c) It would probably be difficult for S to exploit her expectations in any other way. She appears to be based in the eurozone. She could borrow USD in order to finance a EUR deposit, which would yield a profit when the USD loan was repaid using weakened currency. Doing so would almost certainly involve fairly disproportionate transaction costs.

Borrowing and investing directly would also limit her ability to profit from her insight. Using a derivative such as a future makes it possible to gear up her position. If she borrowed, say, EUR 100,000 worth of USD (to match her savings) then she would benefit from a position worth that amount. She can create a position with an exposure of USD 750,000 by investing only EUR 86,512 in margin.

Futures contracts make it possible for S to speculate via a regulated market, where the exchange will protect parties' interests. That would also make it relatively easy to close out her position in the event that she started to feel uneasy about the prospects of success.

Realistically, the downside is limited to the extent to which the USD could strengthen. If she invested in some other instruments, such as options, she could lose everything if the option expired out of the money

Test your understanding 31 – Marcus (Integration question)

USD Exposure

As Marcus has a USD receipt (USD 69,000) and payment (USD 240,000) maturing at the same time (three months), it can match them against each other to leave a net liability of USD 171,000 to be hedged.

(i) **Forward market hedge**

Buy USD 171,000 three months' forward at a cost of:

USD 171,000/0.9520 = EUR179,622 payable in three months' time.

(ii) **Money market hedge**

The money market hedge to pay USD in three months' time requires Marcus to borrow in EUR, translate to USD and deposit in USD.

A payment of USD 171,000 in three months (only 2.5% interest) will require a USD deposit now of (171,000 ÷ 1.025) USD166,829. This means that with a spot rate of 0.9830 the EUR loan will need to be EUR 169,714.

The loan of EUR 169,714 will increase over the three months to the date of repayment by 3.25% and will therefore be EUR 175,230.

The cost is therefore EUR 175,230.

In this case the money market hedge is a cheaper option.

AUD Receipt

Converting exchange rates to home currency

EUR1/AUD

Spot	0.5294 – 0.5285
Four months forward:	0.5126 – 0.5118

AUD 295,000 to be hedged.

(i) **Forward market hedge**

Sell AUD 295,000 four months' forward at a cost of:

AUD 295,000/0.5126 = EUR 575,497 receivable in four months' time

(ii) **Money market hedge**

The money market hedge to receive AUD in four months' time requires Marcus to borrow in AUD, translate to EUR and deposit in EUR.

A receipt of AUD 295,000 in four months (only 5.33% interest) will be balanced with a AUD loan now of (295,000 ÷ 1.0533) AUD 280,072. This means that with a spot rate of 0.5294 the EUR deposit will need to be EUR 529,037.

The deposit of EUR 529,037 will increase over the four months to the date of repayment by 3.83% and will therefore be EUR 549,299. In this case, more will be received in euros under the forward hedge.

Test your understanding 32 (Integration question)

Forward contract

$$\frac{2,500,000}{(1.5851 - 0.0164)} = GBP\ 1,593,676$$

Futures

Time line

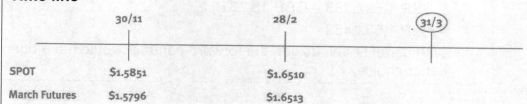

	30/11	28/2	31/3
SPOT	$1.5851	$1.6510	
March Futures	$1.5796	$1.6513	

Step 1: Set up – 30/11

- Downside risk will be if GBP rises in value.
- Bet that GBP will rise on futures market.
- Buy March GBP futures
- No. of contracts =

$$\frac{\dfrac{USD\ 2.5m}{USD\ 1.5796}}{GBP\ 62,500} = 25$$

Step 2: Contact exchange

- Buy 25 March futures contracts @ USD 1.5796
- Deposit margin $= \dfrac{25 \times USD\ 1,000}{USD\ 1.5842} = (GBP\ 15,781)$

Step 3: Close out – 28/2

- Futures profit:
  Difference = 1.6513 – 1.5796 = 0.0717.
  Profit = 0.0717 × 25 × 62,500 = USD 112,031
  + margin returned (USD 25,000) = USD 137,031

- Convert receipt & profit at spot = $\frac{USD\ 2.5m + USD\ 137,031}{USD\ 1.6510}$ = GBP 1,597,233

  Net futures position (net of initial margin payment)
  = GBP 1,597,233 – GBP 15,781
  = GBP 1,581,452
  With benefit of hindsight, the forward contract would have been a better choice.

Interest rate risk management

Chapter learning objectives

Lead outcome	Component outcome
C3: Recommend ways of managing financial risks	(c) Discuss interest rate risk instruments

Topics to be covered

- Operations and features of swaps, forward contracts, …. futures and options
- Techniques for combining options in order to achieve specific risk profile such as caps, collars and floors
- Internal hedging techniques

1 Overview of chapter

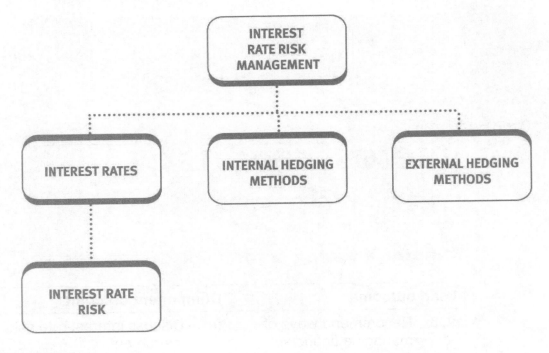

Interest rates

Lending and depositing rates

A bank will quote two interest rates to a customer – a lending rate and a depositing rate. The lending rate is always higher than the depositing rate because the bank wants to make a profit.

London Inter Bank Offer Rate (LIBOR)

This is the interest at which a major bank can borrow wholesale short-term funds from another bank in the London money markets.

- There are different LIBOR rates for different lengths of borrowing, typically from overnight to one year.
- Most variable rate loans are linked to LIBOR and therefore a loan at LIBOR + 2% (where LIBOR is 4.5%) would mean that the customer would pay interest at 6.5% on the loan.

 LIBOR, LIBID and basis points

LIBOR

Each top bank has its own LIBOR rates, but an 'official' average of LIBOR rates is calculated each day by the British Bankers Association. The LIBOR rates that it publishes, the BBA LIBOR rates, are used as benchmark rates for some financial instruments, such as short-term interest rate futures.

LIBOR is important because London is the world's major money market centre. However, other financial centres have similar benchmark interest rates in their money market. For example, the banks of the eurozone produce an alternative benchmark rate of interest for the euro. This is called euribor, but it is similar in concept to euro LIBOR, with the only difference that the average rate is calculated daily from data submitted by a completely different panel of banks.

Most floating rate loans for companies are linked to LIBOR. For example, a company might borrow at 1.25% above LIBOR. In the language of the financial markets, 1% = 100 **basis points**, so a loan at 1.25% above LIBOR might be called a loan at LIBOR plus 125 basis points. If it pays interest every six months, the interest payable at the end of each period will be set with reference to the LIBOR rate at the beginning of the period.

LIBID

LIBID stands for the London Interbank Bid Rate. It is less important than LIBOR, but you might come across it. LIBID is the rate of interest that a top-rated London bank could obtain on short-term wholesale deposits with another bank in the London money markets. LIBID is always lower than LIBOR.

2   Interest rate risk and its management

The concept of interest rate risk was discussed in Chapter 1: 'Objectives'. Along with the risk to cash flow and/or competitiveness, companies face the risk that interest rates might change in value (upside risk as well as downside risk), and between the point when the company identifies the need to borrow or invest and the actual date when they enter into the transaction. For example, a company might anticipate that they will need to borrow in the future but do not yet know exactly how much or when. If in the interim, interest rates rise the delayed decision will cause higher interest payments in the future.

 Compared to exchange rates, interest rates are less volatile, but changes in them can still be substantial.

The "term structure of interest rates" provides an implicit forecast (according to market expectations) that is not guaranteed to be correct but is the most accurate forecast available.

 Term structure of interest rates

The "term structure of interest rates" is the relationship between interest rates or bond yields and different terms or maturities. It is also known as a "yield curve", and it plays a central role in an economy.

The term structure reflects expectations of market participants about future changes in interest rates and their assessment of monetary policy conditions.

> In general terms, yields increase in line with maturity, giving rise to an upward-sloping yield curve i.e. bonds with longer maturity dates tend to have higher yields (interest rates).
>
> In theory, the shape of the yield curve reflects expectations of future interest rates. A borrower who requires a ten-year loan might be tempted by the possibility of taking out a succession of one-year loans if short-term debt is cheaper. The market's expectation is that the overall cost of the debt would be the same in either case (ignoring transaction costs). The one-year rates can be expected to increase in a manner that means the average interest would be the same as that on a ten-year loan.

Just like currency risk, interest rate risk management techniques can be split between internal and external methods.

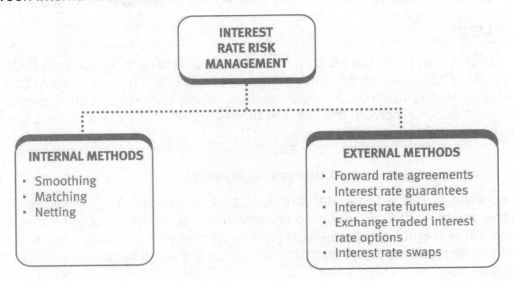

3   Internal hedging

Internal (or operating) hedging strategies for managing interest rate risk involve restructuring the company's assets and liabilities in a way that minimises interest rate exposure. These include:

- **Smoothing** – the company tries to maintain a certain balance between its fixed rate and floating rate borrowing. The portfolio of fixed and floating rate debts thus provide a natural hedge against changes in interest rates. There will be less exposure to the adverse effects of each but there will also be less exposure to favourable movements in the interest rate.

- **Matching** – the company matches its assets and liabilities to have a common interest rate (i.e. loan and investment both have floating rates).

- **Netting** – the company aggregates all positions, both assets and liabilities, to determine its net exposure.

Marks and Spencer's funding and interest rate hedging policy

The Group's funding strategy is to ensure a mix of financing methods offering flexibility and cost effectiveness to match the requirements of the Group … Interest rate risk primarily occurs with the movement of sterling interest rates in relation to the Group's floating rate financial assets and liabilities. Group policy for interest rate management is to maintain a mix of fixed and floating rate borrowings. Interest rate risk in respect of debt on the balance sheet is reviewed on a regular basis against forecast interest costs and covenants. A number of interest rate swaps have been entered into redesignate fixed and floating debt.

4 External hedging

To manage the risk of interest rates moving before an agreed loan or deposit date, the following techniques can be used:

	Over-the-counter (OTC) instruments	**Exchange traded instruments**
'Fixing' instruments	Forward rate agreements (FRAs)	Interest rate futures
'Insurance' instruments	Interest rate guarantees (IRGs), (sometimes called caps/floors or options)	Interest rate options

'Fixing' instruments lock a company into a particular interest rate providing certainty as to the future cash flow, whilst 'insurance' instruments allow some upside flexibility in the interest rate i.e. the company can benefit from favourable movements but are protected from adverse movements.

OTC instruments are bespoke, tailored products that fit the companies' needs exactly. Exchange traded instruments are ready-made and standardised.

These will be discussed in more detail in the following sections.

5 Forward rate agreements (FRAs)

 An FRA is a forward contract on an interest rate for a future short-term loan or deposit. An FRA can therefore be used to fix the interest rate on a loan or deposit starting at a date in the future.

It is a contract relating to the level of a short-term interest rate, such as three-month LIBOR or six-month LIBOR. FRAs are normally for amounts greater than GBP 1 million.

Features and operation

 An important feature of an FRA is that the agreement is independent of the loan or deposit itself.

- It is about the rate of interest on a **notional** amount of principal (loan or deposit) starting at a future date.

- The FRA does not replace taking out the loan (deposit) but rather the **combination** of the loan (deposit) and the FRA result in a fixed effective interest rate.

Settlement of FRAs

When an FRA reaches its settlement date, the buyer and seller must settle the contract.

- If the fixed rate in the agreement (the FRA rate) is higher than the reference rate (LIBOR), the buyer of the FRA makes a cash payment to the seller. The payment is for the amount by which the FRA rate exceeds the reference rate.

- If the fixed rate in the agreement (the FRA rate) is lower than the reference rate (LIBOR), the seller of the FRA makes a cash payment to the buyer. The payment is for the amount by which the FRA rate is less than the reference rate.

Setting up the hedge

Hedging is achieved by a combination of an FRA with the 'normal' loan or deposit.

- **Borrowing** (hence concerned about interest rate rises)

  The firm will borrow the required sum on the target date and will thus contract at the market interest rate on that date.

  Previously the firm will have **bought** a matching FRA from a bank or other market maker and thus receive compensation if rates rise.

- **Depositing** (hence concerned about a fall in interest rates)

  The firm will deposit the required sum on the target date and will thus contract at the market interest rate on that date.

  Previously the firm will have **sold** a matching FRA to a bank or other market maker and thus receive compensation if rates fall.

In each case this combination effectively fixes the rate.

Terminology

In the terminology of the markets, an FRA on a notional three-month loan/deposit starting in five months' time is called a '5–8 FRA' (or '5v8 FRA').

Pricing

FRA's will be priced according to the current bank base rate and future expectations of its movements. The bank will try to predict the interest rate at the date of inception of the borrowing and over its duration, and add on a profit margin. The bank will expect to make a profit for the risk they are taking in lending a company money and therefore any FRA will be priced at some amount above the base rate for a borrower. The amount above the base rate will depend on several factors including the banks attitude to their estimated interest rate (how sure they are in their prediction) and also the reputation of the company they are lending to.

Illustration of hedging using FRAs

A company wishes to borrow GBP 10 million in six months' time for a three-month period. It can normally borrow from its bank at LIBOR + 0.50%. The current three-month LIBOR rate is 5.25%, but the company is worried about the risk of a sharp rise in interest rates in the near future.

A bank quotes FRA rates of:

3 v 9:	5.45 – 5.40 %
6 v 9:	5.30 – 5.25%

Required:

(a) How should the company establish a hedge against its interest rate risk using an FRA?

(b) Suppose that at settlement date for the FRA, the LIBOR reference rate is fixed at 6.50%. What will be the effective borrowing rate for the company?

Solution:

(a) The company wants to fix a borrowing rate, so it should buy an FRA on a notional principal amount of GBP 10 million. The FRA rate is for a 6 v 9 FRA, and the FRA rate is therefore 5.30% (you will have to buy from the bank at the higher rate – remember the bank always wins!).

(b) At settlement date interest rates have risen and the reference rate is higher than the FRA rate. The FRA will therefore be settled by a payment to the FRA buyer of 1.20% (6.50% – 5.30%).

	%
Actual interest rate on three-month loan (LIBOR + 0.50%)	(7.00)
Gain on FRA	1.20
Effective interest cost	(5.80)

This effective interest cost is the FRA rate of 5.30% plus the 0.50% margin above LIBOR that the company must pay on its borrowing.

Test your understanding 1 (Integration question)

It is 30 June. A company needs a $10 million 6 month fixed rate loan from 1 October which it intends to hedge using a forward rate agreement (FRA). The relevant FRA rate is 6% on 30 June.

Required:

What would the net payment on the loan be if interest rates rose to 9% by 1 October?

Test your understanding 2 – Cooper Co – 1 (Integration question)

It is 31 October and Cooper Co is arranging a six-month $5 million loan commencing on 1 July, based on LIBOR. Cooper wants to hedge against an interest rate rise using an FRA. The current LIBOR is 8%.

Required:

(a)   evaluate the use of the FRA if LIBOR turned out to be 9% on 1 July.

(b)   re-evaluate the FRA if LIBOR on 1 July was 5%.

6   Interest rate guarantees (IRGs)

 Interest rate guarantees are options on FRAs so the treasurer has the choice whether to exercise or not.

IRGs are sometimes referred to as **interest rate options** or **interest rate caps/floors**.

Features and operation

They are over-the-counter instruments arranged directly with a bank and have a maximum maturity of one year.

A company wishing to **borrow** in the future could hedge by **buying** an FRA so would need an IRG that provides a **call** option on FRAs.

A company wishing to **deposit** in the future could hedge by **selling** an FRA so would need an IRG that provides a **put** option on FRAs.

The company would only exercise the option to protect against an adverse interest rate movement.

Decision rules

If there is an adverse movement   If there is an favourable movement

↓   ↓

Exercise the option to protect   Allow the option to lapse

IRGs are more expensive than the FRAs as one has to pay for the flexibility to be able to take advantage of a favourable movement.

 Test your understanding 3 – Cooper Co – 2 (Integration question)

It is 31 October and Cooper Co is arranging a six-month $5 million loan commencing on 1 July, based on LIBOR. Cooper wants to hedge against an interest rate rise using an IRG. The current LIBOR is 8%.

The IRG fee is 0.25% p.a. of the loan.

Required:

(a)   evaluate the use of the IRG if LIBOR turned out to be 9% on 1 July.

(b)   re-evaluate the IRG if LIBOR on 1 July was 5%.

---

7 Interest rate futures (IRFs)

 IRFs are similar in principle to forward rate agreements in that they give a commitment to an interest rate for a set period.

They are tradable contracts and operate for set periods of three months, and terminate in March, June, September and December.

As with currency futures, the futures position will normally be closed out for cash and the gain or loss will be used to offset changes in interest rates.

There are two types of IRFs

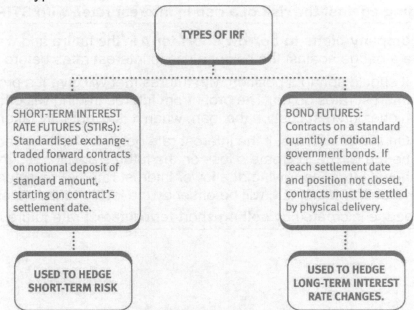

(**Note:** These notes concentrate on STIRs which are more common.)

Features and operation

The future operates by the customer making a commitment to effectively deposit or borrow a fixed amount of capital at a fixed interest rate. The notional sterling deposit/loan on the LIFFE (London futures exchange) is GBP 500,000.

Pricing

The future is priced by deducting the interest rate from 100.

- if the interest rate is 5% the future will be priced at 95.00.
- the reason for this is that if interest rates increase, the value of the future will fall and vice versa if interest rates reduce.

Gains and losses on STIRs are calculated by reference to the interest rate at the date of close out. The difference between the futures price at inception and close will be the gain or loss.

Futures hedging calculations

Companies can hedge using futures by buying or selling a number of futures contracts that cover a loan period and value.

- Most companies use futures to hedge **borrowings** and therefore hedge against an increase in the interest rate.
- To do this the company **sells** futures.

IRFs are complicated by a number of factors including:

- Contract sizes and standard contract lengths (3 months).
- Margins/deposits payable at the start of the hedge.
- Speculators – who dominate the market.

 More information on hedging with IRFs

Hedging against the risk of a rise in interest rates with STIRs

If a company plans to borrow short-term in the future and wants to create a hedge against the risk of a rise in interest rates before then:

- It should set up a position with futures that will give it a profit if interest rates go up. The profit from futures trading will offset the higher interest cost on the loan, when it is eventually taken out.
- On the other hand, if the interest rate goes down, the effect of the hedge will be to create a loss on the futures position, so that the benefit from borrowing at a lower interest rate on the actual loan, when it is taken out, will be offset by the loss on the futures position.

This hedge is created by **selling** short-term interest rate futures.

The **futures position should be closed** when the actual loan period begins, by buying an equal number of futures contracts for the same settlement date.

- **If interest rates have gone up, the market price of futures will have fallen.** A profit will be made from futures by having sold at one price to open the position and then buying at a lower price to close the position. The profit should offset the increased interest rate.

- **If interest rates have gone down, the price of futures will have risen.** A loss will be made from futures by having sold at one price to open the position and then buying at a higher price to close the position. The loss should offset the lower interest rate.

The company should have eliminated any downside or upside risk, and be paying the interest rate it wanted.

Test your understanding 4 (Integration question)

Global Inc wishes to borrow $9,000,000 for one month starting in 5 weeks' time. The base rate of interest is currently 3% and the treasurer of Global decides to fix the rate by selling interest rate futures at 96.90. The market rate subsequently rises by 25 basis points to 3.25%. As soon as the loan is agreed, the treasurer closes out Global's position by buying a matching number of contracts at 96.65.

Required:

(a) **Calculate the number of contracts required (Note: One 3-month contract is for $1,000,000).**

(b) **Demonstrate that, in this case, the gain on the futures contracts exactly matches the extra interest on the loan.**

Test your understanding 5 (Integration question)

Assume that today is the 31st of January.

A company is going to borrow $2,000,000 in two months' time for a period of three months. It fears that the current interest rate will rise from its current level of 5%, so it wants to use $500,000 3-month interest rate futures to hedge the position.

Data from the futures market:

   March futures price = 94.90
   June futures price = 94.65

Required:

Calculate the result of the relevant futures hedge on the assumption that interest rates have risen to 7% and the futures price has moved to 93.00 in two months' time.

Imperfect hedge with IRFs

One problem is that futures are for a **standard size** of contract, whereas the amount of the loan or deposit to be hedged might not be an exact multiple of the amount of the future contract's notional deposit.

For example, suppose that a company wishes to hedge against the risk of a rise in the three-month LIBOR rate for a three-month loan of USD 9,250,000. Futures could be sold to hedge the exposure, but the number of contracts sold would have to be either 9 or 10 (notional deposit = USD 1 million per contract). However, the unhedged amount is likely to be small (perhaps immaterial) in comparison to the hedged amount.

A second problem is the existence of **basis risk**: the future rate (as defined by the future prices) moves approximately but not precisely in line with the cash market rate.

The current futures price is usually different from the current 'cash market' price of the underlying item. In the case of interest rate futures, the current market price of an interest rate future and the current interest rate will be different, and will only start to converge when the final settlement date for the futures contract approaches. This difference is known as the '**basis**'.

At final settlement date for the contract (in March, June, September or December) the futures price and the market price of the underlying item ought to be the same; otherwise speculators would be able to make an instant profit by trading between the futures market and the spot 'cash' market (arbitrage).

Most futures positions are closed out before the contract reaches final settlement. When this happens, there will inevitably be a difference between the futures price at close-out and the current market price of the underlying item. In other words, there will still be some basis.

FRAs vs. STIRs

Short-term interest rate futures are an alternative method of hedging to FRAs. They have a number of similarities.

- Both are binding forward contracts on a short-term interest rate.
- Both are contracts on a notional amount of principal.
- Both are cash-settled at the start of the notional interest period.

FRAs have the advantage that they can be tailored to a company's exact requirements, in terms of amount of principal, length of notional interest period and settlement date.

However, futures are more flexible with regard to settlement, because a position can be closed quickly and easily at any time up to settlement date for the contract.

Given the efficiency of the financial markets, the difference between the two in terms of effective interest rate is unlikely to be large.

Hedging with bond futures

Bond futures might be used to hedge the risk of a change in the price of bonds over the next few months. They can be particularly useful to bond investors for hedging against the risk of a rise in long-term interest rates and a fall in bond prices.

Suppose that an investment institution has a quantity of UK government bonds and its financial year-end is approaching. It would like to secure the value of its bond portfolio and hedge against the risk of a rise in long-term interest rates and fall in bond prices over the next few months.

It can do this with bond futures. As with hedging with STIRs, a hedge is constructed so that if interest rates move adversely, an offsetting gain will be made on the bond futures position. For a bond investor, a hedge can be constructed whereby if interest rates go up and bond prices fall, there will be a loss on the bond portfolio but an offsetting gain on the bond futures position.

Bond futures fall in value when interest rates go up. **For a bond investor, the required hedge is therefore to sell bond futures**. If the interest rate goes up, both the bonds and the bond futures will fall in value. The futures position can be closed by buying futures at a lower price than the original sale price to open the position. The gain on the futures position should match the loss in the value of the bonds themselves.

8 Exchange traded interest rate options

The future and options market provides a product that can cap interest rates for borrowers like an IRG.

This option gives its buyer the right to buy or sell an interest rate future, at a specified future date at a fixed exercise rate, i.e. to effectively have the 'right to bet' on an interest rate increase as shown on the futures market.

Because they are an option as opposed to a commitment, they require the option holder to pay the writer of the option a **premium.**

Features and operation

The characteristics of an option are:

*   They can fix the interest amount, or can be allowed to lapse to take advantage of a favourable movement in interest rates.

*   They are for a given interest period (e.g. six months) starting on or before a date in the future.

(**Note:** Interest rate options are only options on interest rates and not an option to take a loan. The loan is taken quite independently of the option.)

Given that these are options to buy or sell futures, all the futures information is still valid, for example:

- The standard size of the contracts, i.e. GBP 500,000, USD 1,000,000, etc.
- The duration of the contract, i.e. 3 month contracts.
- Maturity dates end of March, June, September and December.

(Standard contracts are only for exchange traded options. It is possible to purchase a bespoke option – variable contract sizes and dates, provided a willing counterparty can be found.)

A **call** option gives the holder the right to **buy** the futures contract.

A **put** option gives the holder the right to **sell** the futures contract.

You always buy the option – buy the right to buy or buy the right to sell.

Cash market	Deposits	Loan
Futures market	Buy futures contracts	Self futures contracts
Options market	Buy calls	Buy puts

Test your understanding 6 (Objective test question)

It is 4 July. A company needs to deposit GBP 5 million for 6 months from 1 November and, to limit interest rate risk exposure, intends to hedge using options on short term interest rate futures (STIRs). The notional sterling deposit/loan for STIRs is GBP 500,000.

Which of the following statements is/are true? (Select all that apply)

A   The company will need 10 options contracts

B   The company will need 20 options contracts

C   The company will need 5 options contracts

D   The company will need put options

E   The company will need call options

Test your understanding 7 (Integration question)

It is now the 31st of August.

Tolhurst Co needs to borrow $10m in 1 month's time, for a 6 month period. The current market interest rate is 5%.

The following information is available regarding $500,000 3-month September interest rate options:

Exercise price	Call	Put
94.75	1.02	0.18

Premia are quoted in %.

Required:

Calculate the result of the options hedge if the interest rate has risen to 7.5% and if the September futures price has moved to 92.50 in one month's time.

Collars

- Premiums can be reduced by using a collar.
- Simultaneously buying a put and selling a call option creates a collar, hence a cap and floor is created but premium is saved.
- For example

	%
Cap at 5.75%, pay a premium	(0.77)
Floor at 5.25%, receive a premium	0.16
Net cost	(0.61)

- The premium saved comes at the expense of giving up the benefits of any interest rate falls below the floor value.

More on collars

- A company buys an option to protect against an adverse movement whilst allowing it to take advantage of a favourable movement in interest rates. The option will be more expensive than a futures hedge. The company must pay for the flexibility to take advantage of a favourable movement.

- A collar is a way of achieving some flexibility at a lower cost than a straight option.

- Under a collar arrangement, the company limits its ability to take advantage of a favourable movement. It buys a cap (or ceiling) by buying the right to sell (a put option) as normal but also sells a floor (by selling the right to buy - a call option) on the same futures contract to a counterparty, but with a different exercise price.

- The floor sets a minimum cost for the company. The counterparty is willing to pay the company for this guarantee of a minimum income. Thus the company gets paid for limiting its ability to take advance of a favourable movement if the interest rate falls below the floor rate. The company does not benefit therefore the counterparty does.

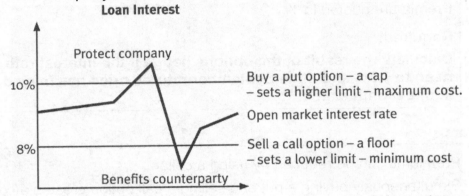

- It involves a company arranging both a minimum and a maximum limit on its interest rates payments or receipts. It enables a company to convert a floating rate of interest into a semi-fixed rate of interest.

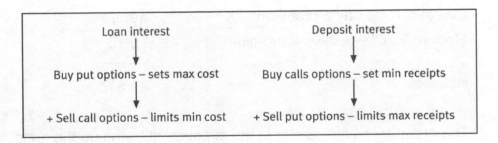

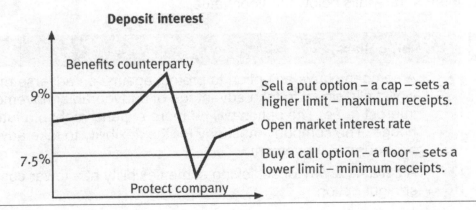

9 Swaps

Introduction to swaps

Swap – a contract to exchange payments of some sort in the future. (CIMA Official Terminology, 2005)

Swaps can be used to change the interest rate or currency profile of borrowings (e.g. fixed to floating and EUR to GBP borrowings) in line with capital structure targets and to manage risk.

When considering what kind of debt finance should be used, risk, cost and practicality will be key considerations.

Examples

- **Interest rate swap**
  - It might be cheaper for a company to issue a bond plus enter a swap to change the interest profile than raise floating rate bank borrowings directly. In this case an interest rate swap is being used to alter the interest rate profile of the borrowings from fixed to floating rates.

- **Cross currency swap**
  - In some cases where a company requires foreign currency borrowings, it may be easier and cheaper to raise funds in its own local currency and, at the same time, enter into a swap to change the currency profile to the required currency. In this case, the entity could use a borrowing in its own currency and a cross currency swap to access the foreign currency funds.
  - In other cases, it may be cheaper for a company to borrow in a global currency such as USD or EUR and then use a cross currency swap to change the currency profile to the home currency or a second foreign currency.
  - A common example of a cross currency swap is that of a parent company raising finance in a popular global currency (e.g. USD or EUR) and then swapping that into different currencies to lend on to foreign subsidiaries which require borrowings denominated in their own currencies. Even GBP companies may find it cheaper to issue bonds in EUR and then swap back into GBP.

Interest rate swaps

 An interest rate swap is an agreement whereby two parties agree to swap a floating stream of interest payments for a fixed stream of interest payments and vice versa. There is no exchange of principal.

Features and operation

- In practice interest rate swaps are probably the most common form of interest rate hedge used by companies because they can hedge borrowings of anywhere between a year and 30 years and therefore can be used for long-term borrowings.

- In our syllabus we only consider the 'plain vanilla' swap of fixed or floating rate (or vice versa) without any complications that can occur in practice.
- Banks act as swap counterparties.
- There is a large and liquid market in swaps in major currencies and banks will quote bid/offer rates against a reference rate such as 6 month LIBOR or 12 month LIBOR.

Note: LIBOR (the London Interbank Offered Rate) is the most widely used benchmark or reference rate for short-term interest rates worldwide, although the swap could relate to Euribor, say.

Calculations involving the bank's quoted swap rates

In practice a bank normally arranges the swap and will quote the following:

- The 'offer rate' at which the bank is willing to receive a fixed interest cash flow stream in exchange for paying LIBOR.
- The 'bid rate' that they are willing to pay in exchange for receiving LIBOR.
- The difference between these gives the bank's profit margin and is usually at least 2 basis points.

Alternatively, in an exam question you might be given the two rates (without any reference to the bid/offer terminology) as follows:

XX Bank's swap rates are 3.00% – 3.10% against 12 month LIBOR.

In order to decide which is the appropriate rate to use in a given situation, always remember that the bank will have set the swap rates to ensure that it makes a profit margin.

So in this example, if a company wanted to pay a fixed rate to the bank in exchange for a receipt of the LIBOR rate (to swap a floating rate into a fixed rate), 3.10% would be paid by the company to the bank.

Alternatively, if a company wanted to pay LIBOR rate in exchange for a fixed receipt (to swap a fixed rate into a floating rate), only 3.00% would be paid by the bank to the company.

Diagrammatic example

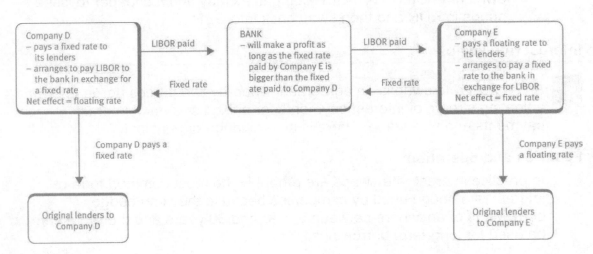

So, considering the numerical example above in the context of the diagram:

- Company D wants to swap a fixed rate to a floating rate, so would pay LIBOR to the bank in exchange for 3.00%

- Company E wants to swap a floating rate to a fixed rate, so would pay 3.10% to the bank in exchange for LIBOR

- The bank would make a profit by setting up swaps with both Company D and Company E, because the LIBOR payments net off, and the fixed rate received by the bank is bigger than the fixed rate paid.

Test your understanding 8 (Integration question)

Company A can borrow at a fixed rate of 5% or at a floating rate of LIBOR + 12 basis points.

Swap rates are 4.90 – 4.95 against 12-month LIBOR.

Required:

What is the cheapest way for the company to obtain floating rate finance?

The interest fixing date and the interest cash flows in an interest rate swap

In the above Illustration, we showed the net interest rate that would be paid by Company A in the swap arrangement, but exam questions might also ask you to calculate the interest cash flows.

In the case of Company A in the Illustration above, the net interest rate was LIBOR + 0.10%, so clearly the overall interest cash flow would be calculated by applying the actual LIBOR rate plus 0.10% to the value of Company A's borrowing.

However, it is important to note that the LIBOR rate will fluctuate daily, so in order to work out the interest cash flows in a swap, an 'interest fixing date' is agreed when the swap is set up, and it is the LIBOR on this fixing date that is used in the calculation.

Generally the interest fixing date is the start date of the swap period.

Test your understanding 9 (Objective test question)

Spray Co has a $10 million fixed rate borrowing. It has entered an interest rate swap to swap the interest to a floating rate for a three year period.

The bank has quoted a swap rate of 4.10% for LIBOR, with interest fixing dates on the start date of each year of the swap agreement.

Spray Co's fixed rate of interest is 4.40%.

LIBOR on the start date of year 2 of the three year swap agreement was 4.25%, but this had risen to 4.58% by the end of year 2 (12 months later).

What is the difference in Spray Co's overall net interest paid in the year (year 2 of the swap agreement) as a consequence of using the swap?

A	$15,000 saving
B	$15,000 extra cost
C	$18,000 extra cost
D	$48,000 extra cost

Advantages of using interest rate swaps

- To manage fixed and floating rate debt profiles without having to change underlying borrowing.

- To hedge against variations in interest on floating rate debt, or conversely to protect the fair value of fixed rate debt instruments.

- A swap can be used to obtain cheaper finance. For example, it may be cheaper to obtain floating rate finance by, say, issuing a bond and swapping into a floating rate rather than borrowing at floating rate directly from a bank.

Disadvantages of using interest rate swaps

- Interest rates may change in the future and the company might be locked into an unfavourable rate.

- Creditworthiness of the bank – the company and the bank arrange to make payments to each other for a fixed period. The company must therefore be confident about the creditworthiness of the bank before signing up to the swap.

Test your understanding 10 (Objective test question)

Ocean Co has a $5 million floating rate borrowing at a rate of LIBOR + 0.50%.

The directors have set up a swap, to fix the company's interest rate for a period of three years, from 1 January 20X0 to 31 December 20X2.

The bank's quoted swap rates are 3.80% – 4.00% for LIBOR, with interest fixing dates on the start date of each year of the swap agreement.

LIBOR information:

- LIBOR on 1 January 20X1 was 4.10%
- LIBOR on 1 July 20X1 was 4.05%
- LIBOR on 31 December 20X1 was 3.75%

What was the difference in Ocean Co's overall net interest paid in the year 20X1 as a consequence of using the swap?

A	$15,000 saving
B	$5,000 saving
C	$2,500 extra cost
D	$12,500 extra cost

Cross currency swaps

A cross currency swap allows a company to swap a currency it currently holds for a different currency for a fixed period, and then swap back at the same rate at the end of the period.

The company's counterparty in a cross currency swap would generally be a bank.

Characteristics of a cross currency swap

- In effect a cross currency swap has two elements:
    - An exchange of principals in different currencies, which are swapped back at the original spot rate.
    - An exchange of interest rates – the timing of these depends on the individual contract.
- The swap of interest rates could be 'fixed for fixed', 'floating for floating' or 'fixed for floating'
- The company entering the cross currency swap will end up with the currency it needs and also the type of interest rate it prefers (fixed or floating).

Test your understanding 11 (Integration question)

ABC Co is a US company that has issued a 100 million Swiss Francs (CHF) Eurobond on which it pays interest six-monthly at an annual fixed rate of 6%.

ABC Co has many operations in the USA, so wants to swap its CHF into US dollars (USD) using a fixed for fixed cross currency swap.

ABC Co's bank has quoted a cross currency swap exchange rate of CHF/USD 1.10 (that is, CHF 1 = USD 1.10), and fixed interest rates of 5.5% on USD in exchange for 6% on CHF, with interest payable semi-annually (that is, every six months).

Required:

Show how the fixed for fixed cross currency swap would work in the circumstances described, assuming the swap is only for one year and that interest is paid every six months.

Test your understanding 12 (Integration question)

Smiths Co is a UK based company that has borrowed 10 million British pounds (GBP) at a fixed interest rate of 5.25% per year, with interest paid annually.

The company is planning to expand into Europe so wants to swap GBP 10 million for Euros (EUR), and its fixed interest rate for a floating rate.

The bank has quoted a cross currency swap exchange rate of GBP/EUR 1.30 (that is, GBP 1 = EUR 1.30) and interest rates of LIBOR + 0.50% on EUR in exchange for 5.25% on GBP, with interest paid annually.

> Assume that LIBOR is 5% at the start date of the swap.
>
> **Required:**
>
> Show how the fixed for floating cross currency swap would work in the circumstances described, assuming the swap is only for one year and that interest is paid at the end of the year.

Advantages of using cross currency swaps

- A cross currency swap is a useful tool for changing the currency profile of debt.

- This may help reduce interest costs where debt can be raised more easily or at a competitive rate in a second currency and it proves to be cheaper or easier overall to borrow in one currency and simultaneously enter into a swap to change the currency profile into another currency or several different currencies as required.

- Cross currency swaps may also be used as part of a broader strategy for managing currency risk. For example, by obtaining foreign currency borrowings to on-lend to foreign subsidiaries denominated in their local currencies.

Disadvantages of using cross currency swaps

- The main disadvantage is that, as in an interest rate swap , there is a risk that the other party to the contract might default on the arrangement. This is an even greater risk for cross currency swaps because:

    - the cash flows are in different currencies (and hence there can be no agreement to net them as there could be for interest rate swaps), AND

    - final principals are exchanged (again, unlike interest rate swaps).

10 End of chapter objective test questions

> ### Test your understanding 13 (Objective test question)
>
> **Borrowers will wish to hedge against an interest rate rise by:**
>
> A   Selling futures now and selling futures on the day that the interest rate is fixed
>
> B   Selling futures now and buying futures on the day that the interest rate is fixed
>
> C   Buying futures now and selling futures on the day that the interest rate is fixed
>
> D   Buying futures now and buying futures on the day that the interest rate is fixed

Test your understanding 14 (Objective test question)

It is 24 May. A company needs to borrow GBP 20 million for 9 months from 1 December and, to limit interest rate risk exposure, intends to hedge using short term interest rate futures (STIRs). The notional sterling deposit/loan for STIRs is GBP 500,000.

Which of the following statements is/are true? (Select all that apply)

A   The company will need 240 futures contracts

B   The company will need 120 futures contracts

C   The company will need 40 futures contracts

D   The company will set up the hedge by buying futures

E   The company will set up the hedge by selling futures

F   The futures hedge will eliminate all interest rate risk for the company

Test your understanding 15 (Objective test question)

An option whereby the lender sets a maximum and minimum interest rate simultaneously is called:

A   A cap

B   A floor

C   A collar

D   An interest rate guarantee

Test your understanding 16 (Objective test question)

Company A can borrow at 6% fixed or LIBOR + 0.2% variable and would like a variable rate. Company B can borrow at 6.5% fixed or LIBOR + 0.4% variable and would like a fixed rate.

If the companies agree to share the differential equally, what is A's effective loan rate?

A   5.70%

B   5.85%

C   LIBOR + 0.35%

D   LIBOR + 0.05%

Test your understanding 17 (Objective test question)

Which of the following is an internal hedging technique? (Select all that apply.)

A   A forward contract

B   Netting

C   Smoothing

D   Matching

Test your understanding 18 (Objective test question)

An interest rate derivative characterised by being available for any amount, redeemable on any date, payment on settlement and traded over the counter, is called:

A   An interest rate swap

B   A forward rate agreement

C   An interest rate future

D   An interest rate option

Test your understanding 19 (Objective test question)

In relation to interest rate hedging, which of the following statements is correct? (Select all that are relevant)

A   The flexible nature of interest rate futures means that they can always be matched with a specific interest rate exposure

B   Interest rate options carry an obligation to the holder to complete the contract at maturity

C   Forward rate agreements are the interest rate equivalent of forward exchange contracts

D   Matching is where a balance is maintained between fixed rate and floating rate debt

Test your understanding 20 (Objective test question)

Brasil Co has a $10 million borrowing, on which it is currently paying a floating rate of LIBOR+0.55%. The directors are concerned that interest rates are going to rise, so they are considering an interest rate swap to manage the company's exposure to risk.

The bank has quoted Brasil Co a swap rate of 2.86% against LIBOR.

What is Brasil Co's net payment if it enters the swap?

A   LIBOR + 2.86%

B   2.31%

C   2.86%

D   3.41%

Test your understanding 21 (Objective test question)

Mouse Co has a $10 million borrowing on which it pays interest at a fixed rate of 4.35%.

The company's directors predict that interest rates will fall over the next 12 months, so they want to use an interest rate swap to enable them to benefit from this predicted movement.

The bank is quoting swap rates of 4.19% – 4.29% against 12 month LIBOR. 12 month LIBOR is currently 4.04%.

What will be Mouse Co's interest payment at the end of the year, assuming that the company uses the swap and that LIBOR has fallen to 3.90% by the year end?

A $396,000

B $406,000

C $410,000

D $420,000

11 End of chapter case style questions

Test your understanding 22 – IR hedging (Case style question)

Scenario

Assume you are the Treasurer of AB, a large UK based engineering company, and that it is now May 20X4.

Trigger

You have forecast that the company will need to borrow GBP 2 million by the end of September 20X4 for at least 6 months. The need for finance will arise because the company has extended its credit terms to selected customers over the summer period. The company's bank currently charges customers such as AB 7.5% per annum interest for short-term unsecured borrowing. However, you believe interest rates will rise by at least 1.5 percentage points over the next 6 months. You are considering using one of three alternative methods to hedge the risk:

- forward rate agreements; or

- interest rate futures; or

- an interest rate guarantee (a borrower's option or short-term cap).

You can purchase an interest rate cap at 7% per annum for the duration of the loan to be guaranteed. You would have to pay a premium of 0.1% of the amount of the loan. As part of the arrangement, the company will agree to pay a 'floor' rate of 6% per annum.

Required:

Prepare a briefing note to the Finance Director discussing the features of each of the three alternative methods of hedging the interest rate risk and advise on how each might be useful to AB, taking all relevant and known information into account.

(30 minutes)

Test your understanding 23 – Gymbob (Case style question)

Scenario

Gymbob plc is a national chain of gyms listed on the UK Stock Market. It was set up nearly twenty years ago, and has 40 branches nationwide each having essentially the same facilities – a dry side including a gym with running machines, cross trainers, rowing machines and weights, and a wet side including a swimming pool, sauna, spa pool, and steam room. There are daily classes for both the wet and dry side activities, held by various full-time and freelance instructors.

Trigger

The directors of Gymbob have heard of a rival gym chain being put up for sale for GBP 20 million. Gymbob would be very keen to acquire their competitor, since the gyms are well patronised and in locations that complement Gymbob's current portfolio. Gymbob would be able to raise most of the purchase price in cash or by liquidating investments, but would still need to borrow GBP 5 million. It is anticipated that, all going well, they would need to borrow the GBP 5 million in 3 months' time for only a one-year period. Current interest rates are 7% for this type of loan, and Gymbob's directors would not want to pay more than this since they have other commitments. They are considering the use of a forward rate agreement, interest rate future or an interest rate option.

Required:

Prepare an email to the finance director explaining how each of the three interest rate hedging alternatives might be useful to Gymbob.

(20 minutes)

Test your understanding 24 – Swaps (Case style question)

You are contacted by AB's bank and informed that another of the bank's clients, a smaller company in the same industry, is looking for a swap partner for a similar amount of borrowing for the same duration. The borrowing rates applicable to AB and RO are as follows:

	Floating	**Fixed**
AB	LIBOR + 0.3%	7.5%
R0	LIBOR + 0.5%	8.5%

Required:

Prepare a briefing note to the finance director:

(a) Commenting briefly on why swaps may be used.

(15 minutes)

(b) Recommending how the two companies could co-operate in a swap arrangement to their mutual benefit, including the option of changing the type of loan normally preferred. Support your recommendation with appropriate calculations.

(15 minutes)

(c) Discussing the advantages and disadvantages of arranging a swap through a bank rather than negotiating directly with a counterparty.

(15 minutes)

Test your understanding 25 – QW (Case style question)

Scenario

You are the treasurer of QW plc, a company with diversified, international interests. The company wishes to borrow GBP 10 million for a period of three years. Your company's credit rating is good, and current market data suggests that you could borrow at a fixed rate of interest of 8% per annum or at a floating rate of LIBOR + 0.2% per annum. You believe that interest rates are likely to fall over the next three years, and favour borrowing at a floating rate.

Trigger

Your company's bankers are currently working on raising a three-year loan for another of their customers, ER plc. This company is smaller and less well known than QW plc, and its credit rating is not as high. ER plc could borrow at a fixed rate of 9.5% per annum or a floating rate of LIBOR + 0.5%. ER plc has indicated to the bank that it would prefer a fixed-rate loan. Your bankers have suggested you engage in a swap which might benefit both companies. The bank's commission would be 0.2% of the benefits to the two parties. Your counterpart in ER plc suggests that the commission fees and swap benefits should be shared equally.

Assume that interest is paid at the end of each twelve-month period of the loan's duration and that the principal is repaid on maturity (i.e. at the end of three years).

Required:

Write a report to the board which:

(i) describes the characteristics and benefits of interest rate swaps compared with other forms of interest rate risk management, such as forward-rate agreements and interest rate futures.

(15 minutes)

(ii) explains the course of action necessary to implement the swap being considered with ER plc, and calculates and comments on the financial benefits to be gained from the operation.

(20 minutes)

Test your understanding answers

Test your understanding 1 (Integration question)

$300,000

- At 9% the company will pay $450,000 (9% × $10 million × 6/12).
- The FRA receipt will be $150,000 ($10 million × (9% − 6%) × 6/12)
- Net payment $450,000 − $150,000 = $300,000
- Or to simplify, the company will essentially pay 6% × $10 million × ½ year = $300,000.

Test your understanding 2 – Cooper Co – 1 (Integration question)

31 October:

Cooper would purchase FRA$_{8-14}$ @ 8%

1 July:

		% pa
(a)	**LIBOR = 9%**	
	Cooper will pay loan interest	(9.00)
	Claim on FRA	1.00
	Net interest	(8.00)
(b)	**LIBOR = 5%**	% pa
	Pay loan interest	(5.00)
	Pay out on FRA	(3.00)
	Net interest	(8.00)

Remember that the point of an FRA is to manage future risk. In reality there is no point in looking at the past to see whether rates rose or fell. Perhaps the only worthwhile reason for doing this would be to measure the ability of the Treasury department in guessing what will happen to interest rates.

Test your understanding 3 – Cooper Co – 2 (Integration question)

31 October:

Cooper would purchase IRG$_{8-14}$ @ 8%

1 July:

		% pa
(a)	**LIBOR = 9% (exercise option)**	
	Cooper will pay loan interest	(9.00)
	Pay fee	(0.25)
	Claim on IRG	1.00
	Net interest	(8.25)

		% pa
(b)	**LIBOR = 5% (allow option to lapse)**	
	Pay loan interest	(5.00)
	Pay fee	(0.25)
	Net interest	(5.25)

Note: When LIBOR has fallen the IRG allows Cooper to take advantage of the lower interest rates. BUT the fee is still paid!

Remember again that the point of an IRG is to manage future risk. In reality there is no point in looking at the past to see whether rates rose or fell. Perhaps the only worthwhile reason for doing this would be to measure the ability of the Treasury department in guessing what will happen to interest rates.

Test your understanding 4 (Integration question)

(a) Number of contracts = (9,000,000/1,000,000) × 1/3 = 3

(b) Extra interest cost on loan = 0.25% × 9,000,000 × 1/12 = $1,875

Gain on futures: Sell at 96.90 and close out by buying at 96.65, so gain is 0.25% per contract.

Total gain is 0.25% × 3 contracts × ($1,000,000 × 3/12) = $1,875

Test your understanding 5 (Integration question)

- Buy or sell futures? Sell, since we are borrowing
- Number of contracts = (2,000,000/500,000) × 3/3 = 4
- Which expiry date? March contracts – match the transaction date of 31st March.

Contact the exchange: We need to sell 4 March contracts at a price of 94.90

Two months later:

Transaction: Interest will be $2m × 3/12 × 7% = $35,000

Futures market:

- Gain per contract = (94.90 – 93.00) = 1.90%
- Total gain is 1.90% × 4 contracts × ($500,000 × 3/12) = $9.500

Hence, net cost = $35,000 – $9,500 = $25,500

(i.e. a net interest rate of 5.10%)

Test your understanding 6

The answer is (B) and (E).

STIRS are standardised for 3 month notional deposits or loans, so the number of contracts = (5 million/500,000) × (6 months/3 months) = **20**

The company wishes to deposit funds so would set up a hedge on the futures market by buying futures, so will need **call** options.

Test your understanding 7 (Integration question)

Set up hedge:

- Call or put options? Put here (option to sell futures), to cover a borrowing.
- How many contracts? ($10m/$500k) × (6/3) = 40

Contact exchange: We need to buy 40 September put options with an exercise price of 94.75.

Premium payable upfront = 0.18% × 40 × $500,000 × 3/12 = $9,000.

1 month later:

Transaction: Interest = 7.5% × $10m × 6/12 = $375,000

Futures/options market:

Exercise the put option i.e. sell at 94.75

Close out: Buy at futures price of 92.50

Gain is 2.25% × 40 contracts × $500,000 × 3/12 = $112,500

So, the net interest cost is $375,000 – $112,500 = $262,500 (plus the initial premium of $9,000).

Test your understanding 8 (Integration question)

Fixed rate borrowing	(5.00%)
Payment to bank under swap	(LIBOR)
Receipt from bank under swap (lower rate)	4.90%
Net interest rate after swap	(LIBOR + 0.10%)
Open market cost – no swap	(LIBOR + 0.12%)
Saving	2 basis points

Test your understanding 9 (Objective test question)

The answer is (B).

Solution:

Actual borrowing	(4.40%)
Payment to bank	(LIBOR)
Receipt from bank	4.10%
Net interest rate after swap	**(LIBOR + 0.30%)**

The interest fixing date is the start date of the year, so this overall net rate of LIBOR + 0.30% can be calculated as 4.25% (LIBOR on the year 2 start date) + 0.30% = 4.55%.

Hence, Spray Co pays 4.55% interest on its $10 million borrowing ($455,000 in the year) rather than the 4.40% fixed rate it would have paid without the swap ($440,000 in the year).

This is an extra cost of $15,000.

Test your understanding 10 (Objective test question)

The answer is (B).

Solution:

Actual borrowing	(LIBOR + 0.50%)
Payment to bank (higher rate)	(4.00%)
Receipt from bank	LIBOR
Net interest rate after swap	**(4.50%)**

The interest fixing date is the start date of the year (1 January 20X1), so the relevant LIBOR rate is 4.10%.

Hence, Ocean Co paid 4.50% overall net interest on its $5 million borrowing ($225,000 in the year) rather than the (4.10% + 0.50% =) 4.60% rate it would have paid without the swap ($230,000 in the year).

This is a saving of $5,000.

Test your understanding 11 (Integration question)

Timing	Explanation	Cash flows
Now	Exchange principals (at swap rate of CHF1 = USD 1.10)	Pay CHF 100m to the bank and receive USD 110m
6 mths' time	Pay swap interest to bank (5.5% × USD110m × 6/12)	Pay USD 3.025m
	Receive swap interest from bank (6% × CHF100m × 6/12)	Receive CHF 3m
	Pay Eurobond interest	Pay CHF 3m
End of year	Pay swap interest to bank (5.5% × USD110m × 6/12)	Pay USD 3.025m
	Receive swap interest from bank (6% × CHF100m × 6/12)	Receive CHF 3m
	Pay Eurobond interest (6% × CHF100m × 6/12)	Pay CHF 3m
	Swap back principals (at swap rate of CHF1 = USD 1.10)	Pay USD 110m to the bank and receive CHF 100m

The net result is that ABC Co has the use of the USD 110 million for the year, and effectively pays interest on this amount (in USD) at 5.5%.

Test your understanding 12 (Integration question)

Timing	Explanation	Cash flows
Now	Exchange principals (at swap rate of GBP1 = EUR 1.30)	Pay GBP 10m to the bank and receive EUR 13m
End of year	Pay swap interest to bank ((LIBOR + 0.50%) × EUR 13m)	Pay EUR 0.715m (on the assumption that the start date of the swap is the interest rate fixing date and hence LIBOR is 5%)
	Receive swap interest from bank (5.25% × GBP 10m)	Receive GBP 0.525m
	Pay interest on original borrowing (5.25% × GBP 10m)	Pay GBP 0.525m
	Swap back principals (at swap rate of GBP1 = EUR 1.30)	Pay EUR 13m to the bank and receive GBP 10m

The net result is that Smiths Co has the use of the EUR 13 million for the year, and effectively pays floating rate interest on this amount (in EUR) at LIBOR + 0.50%.

Test your understanding 13 (Objective test question)

The answer is (B).

The interest rate risk arises between the present day and when the loan is taken out – the rate may rise and cost the borrower more. A borrower should sell an interest rate future now at a low interest rate (100 – r where r is, say, 5% = 95) and buy it later at the higher rate (100 – r where r is say 10% = 90). Buying at 90 and selling at 95 creates the profit you will need to offset the increased borrowing cost.

Test your understanding 14 (Objective test question)

The answer is (B) and (E).

STIRS are standardised for 3 month notional deposits or loans, so the number of contracts = (20 million/500,000) × (9 months/3 months) = **120**

The company wishes to borrow funds so would set up a hedge on the futures market by **selling** futures.

Statement F is incorrect – given the loan is needed to be taken out on the 1 December, the company would still be exposed to **basis risk**.

Test your understanding 15 (Objective test question)

The answer is (C).

A cap sets an interest rate ceiling.

A floor sets an interest rate lower limit.

A collar sets a maximum and a minimum interest rate.

An interest rate guarantee is an alternative name for an interest rate option.

Test your understanding 16 (Objective test question)

The answer is (D).

A will effectively pay LIBOR + 0.2% − 0.15% (spread differential) = LIBOR + 0.05%

Test your understanding 17 (Objective test question)

The answer is (B), (C) and (D).

Forward contracts require the use of a third party such as a bank.

Test your understanding 18 (Objective test question)

The answer is (B).

By definition the answer is an FRA. Futures are for specific amounts and dates. Options require a premium to be paid up front and not upon settlement. Swaps do not require payment on settlement

Test your understanding 19 (Objective test question)

The answer is (C).

Note:

- A is false because interest rate futures have standardized sizes, which may not match the actual exposure
- B is false as options give the right but not the obligation
- D – in terms of interest rates matching involves ensuring assets and liabilities have a common type of interest rate (e.g. loan and investment both have floating rates)

Test your understanding 20 (Objective test question)

The answer is (D).

Brasil Co is currently paying LIBOR + 0.55%.

A swap rate of 2.86% for LIBOR means that Brasil Co will pay the bank 2.86% in the swap in exchange for LIBOR.

Therefore, Brasil Co's net payment is (LIBOR + 0.55%) + 2.86% − LIBOR = 3.41%.

Test your understanding 21 (Objective test question)

The answer is (D).

Actual borrowing	(4.35%)
Payment to bank	(LIBOR)
Receipt from bank (lower rate)	4.19%
Net interest rate after swap	**(LIBOR + 0.16%)**

The interest rate fixing date is normally the start date of the swap agreement, so LIBOR of 4.04% is the relevant value here.

Hence, interest payable at LIBOR + 0.16% amounts to (4.04% + 0.16% =) 4.20%.

Overall net interest is therefore 4.20% × $10 million = $420,000.

Test your understanding 22 – IR hedging (Case style question)

Briefing note

To: The finance director

From: The treasurer

Date: Today

Subject: Interest rate risk hedging

Dear finance director,

With all three methods of hedging interest rate risk, a time limit has to be decided for the period of the hedge. With a Forward Rate Agreement (FRA) or an interest rate guarantee (option/cap), the time limit must be specific, with an agreed settlement date or expiry date, say six months exactly from the contract/transaction date. With futures, the hedge would be for six months from any date up to the settlement date for the futures, which in this question would probably be September.

It is assumed here that the required hedge is for exactly six months in all three cases.

FRA

An FRA is an over-the-counter instrument that can be arranged with a bank, fixing the interest rate on a notional principal amount for a given period of time, in this case six months. The notional six-month interest period would start from an agreed date in September, in four months' time, so the FRA would be a 4v10 FRA. FRAs are only available for quite large principal amounts (at least USD 1 million) and can be arranged up to about two years into the future.

A company wishing to fix an interest rate for borrowing should buy an FRA. Here, AB should buy a 4v10 FRA on a notional principal amount of GBP 2 million. The bank would specify an interest rate for the FRA, which might be about 7.5% in this case.

The FRA is not an agreement to borrow the funds required. AB must arrange to borrow the GBP 2 million separately. AB will borrow GBP 2 million at the current market rate of interest in September, whatever this happens to be. The FRA would be settled by:

- a payment from the bank to AB if the benchmark interest rate (here probably the six-month LIBOR rate) is higher than the FRA rate; or

- a payment from AB to the bank if the benchmark rate is lower than the FRA rate.

The hedge works because the interest payment on the actual borrowing plus or minus the settlement amount for the FRA should fix the overall effective borrowing cost for AB. For example, if the interest rate does rise by 1.5 percentage points to 9% and AB borrows at this higher rate, it would receive a payment under the FRA agreement worth the equivalent of about 1.5%, thereby reducing the net borrowing cost to about 7.5% (depending on the actual rates that apply).

Interest rate futures

Short-term interest rate futures are exchange-traded instruments. A short sterling future is a notional three-month deposit of GBP 500,000, traded on LIFFE.

A company wishing to fix a rate for borrowing should sell interest rate futures. Since AB wants to hedge the borrowing cost for GBP 2 million for six months, it should sell 8 futures [(GBP 2 million/GBP 500,000) × (6 months/3 months)] and set up a 'short hedge'. It could sell either September or December futures, depending on when the interest period will begin, and when the September futures contract expires during the month.

The interest rate is in the price of the future. Prices are quoted at 100 minus the interest rate, so if AB were to sell September futures, say, at 92.50, this would 'fix' its borrowing rate at 7.5%. As the future approaches settlement date, if the interest rate has risen to 9%, the market price of September futures should have moved to about 91.00. AB could then close its position by buying 8 September futures, and making a profit of 1.50 (150 points) on each contract of its futures dealing. A profit of 150 points on 8 futures would be worth GBP 15,000 (150 points × 8 contracts × GBP 12.50 per point). This is equivalent to interest at 1.5% on GBP 2 million for six months.

AB would borrow GBP 2 million at the market rate. If this is 9%, the net borrowing cost would be 9% less the value of the profit on futures trading (1.5%) giving a net effective interest cost of 7.5%.

Since interest rate futures are only available in standardised amounts and dates, they are less flexible than FRAs, and so possibly less attractive to AB.

Interest rate guarantee

This is a type of borrower's option but with characteristics of an interest rate collar. Unlike an FRA or futures which are binding contracts on both parties, it is not a binding commitment on the option holder. If AB buys this instrument at a cap strike price of 7% (and a notional principal amount of GBP 2 million for six months), for expiry in September, it will exercise its option if the interest rate at expiry is higher than 7%. It will then receive the interest value of the difference (on GBP 2 million for six months) between the actual interest rate (six-month LIBOR) and the cap rate of 7%.

However, in this case, if the interest rate falls below 6%, the option counterparty (a bank) will exercise a floor option, and require AB to pay the difference between the actual interest rate and 6%.

As a result, AB is able to fix the benchmark interest rate between 6% and 7%. So if AB can borrow at, say, LIBOR + 0.50%, the interest rate guarantee would fix its actual borrowing cost between 6.5% and 7.5%, plus the cost of the guarantee.

Arranging this guarantee would cost GBP 2,000 (0.1% of GBP 2 million), which is equivalent to interest of 0.2% on GBP 2 million for six months. The premiums payable on interest rate guarantees can be expensive and must be paid up-front, which can be compared to an FRA on which no premium is payable.

Usefulness of the instruments to AB

All three instruments can help AB to hedge against the risk of a rise in interest rates.

FRAs and futures are binding contracts, so that the hedge effectively fixes the borrowing cost. The interest rate guarantee is a form of option, so that AB can benefit from lower interest rates if they are between 6% and 7%. However, the guarantee has to be paid for.

All three instruments are arranged for a fixed amount and a fixed borrowing period, which means that a hedge might not be perfect. For example, if it turns out that AB needs to borrow GBP 2.5 million for seven months starting in five months' time, none of the hedges would be perfect.

Test your understanding 23 – Gymbob (Case style question)

Email

To: Finance director

From: A.N. Accountant

Date: Today

Subject: Interest rate risk management

Dear finance director,

Forward rate agreements offer Gymbob the facility to fix the future interest rate on borrowings for a specified period. For example, if Gymbob entered into an FRA with a bank in 3 months' time one year at a guaranteed 7%, then if the interest rate rose the bank would have to pay Gymbob the difference. On the other hand, if the interest rate fell, Gymbob would still have to pay the bank the difference. No matter which way the interest rate moved, Gymbob would pay 7%.

FRAs do not involve any actual lending of the principal sum of GBP 5 million. This can be done with the same or a different bank, or other lender.

FRAs are usually for at least GBP 1 million, and can be arranged for up to 2 or 3 years in the future, so FRAs appear to be a suitable way for Gymbob to manage interest rate exposure.

Interest rate futures are binding contracts between seller and buyer to take delivery of a specified interest rate commitment on an agreed date at an agreed price. They can be used to protect against interest rate rises and are available for a maximum of 1 – 2 years.

Futures contracts are sold now in the expectation that, as interest rates rise the contract value will fall, and they can then be purchased at a lower price, generating a profit on the futures deal. The profit compensates for the actual rises in interest rates experienced by companies that have borrowed funds from banks and elsewhere. If the interest rate moves in the opposite direction to that expected, a futures loss will occur, but this will be offset by cheaper interest costs in the market.

All contracts require a small initial deposit or margin.

Futures should allow Gymbob to hedge successfully against increases in the interest rate, although a perfect hedge is rare.

Interest rate options such as caps, floors and collars guarantee that the interest rate will not rise above, or fall below, an agreed fixed level during a specified time period commencing sometime in the future. The interest rate protection for Gymbob is similar to that given by an FRA.

However, options involve the payment of a premium to the seller of the option, whether or not the option is exercised. No premium is payable with an FRA.

Also, whilst protecting downside risk (an interest rate rise), Gymbob can take full advantage of favourable interest rate movements.

For example, if interest rates fall, the option is left to lapse and Gymbob will borrow the GBP 5 million from the market at the lower rate. However, if rates rose, then Gymbob would exercise the option to guarantee a maximum cost of 7%.

However, the premium involved with an option can be prohibitively expensive. A way to lower this would be to take out a collar (a cap and a floor).

If you have any queries, please do not hesitate to ask.

Best wishes

A.N. Accountant

Test your understanding 24 – Swaps (Case style question)

Briefing note

To: The finance director

From: A.N. Accountant

Date: Today

Subject: Interest rate swaps

(a)   Interest rate swaps can have several uses.

–   They can be used by companies to arrange fixed rate borrowing, when direct access to fixed rate funding (the bond markets) is not possible, for example, if the company is too small or would not have a sufficiently good credit rating.

–   Occasionally, they can be used to obtain lower cost borrowing, through interest rate arbitrage. This opportunity exists in the case of RO and AB.

–   They can be used to alter the proportions of fixed and variable rate funding in a company's debt mix without the expense of redeeming existing debt and issuing new debt in its place, and so can be used to manage exposure to risk from possible future interest rate movements.

(b) AB is a larger company than RO, so we see that AB has cheaper borrowing rates in both the floating rate as well as the fixed rate market. However, while RO only has to pay 0.2% more in the floating rate market, it has to pay a full 1.0% more for fixed rate debt. This creates an opportunity to reduce their combined borrowing costs by 0.8% (1% − 0.2%).

AB has a comparative advantage in the fixed rate market, since it is cheaper by 1% than RO, compared to just 0.2% in the floating rate market. So, the companies could co-operate to their mutual benefit if:

– AB borrows at a fixed rate and swaps into floating rate; and

– RO borrows at a floating rate, where it can borrow comparatively more favourably than at a fixed rate (only 0.2% more), and swap into a fixed rate.

The opportunity for arbitrage is 0.8%, which means that if they share this equally, both will borrow 0.4% more cheaply than if they borrowed directly at a floating rate in the case of AB or at a fixed rate in the case of RO.

A swap could be arranged as follows:

– AB borrows in the fixed rate market at 7.5% and pays LIBOR to RO.

– RO borrows in the floating rate market at LIBOR + 0.5% and pays a fixed rate of 7.6% to AB.

The net effect is as follows:

AB pays 7.5% to the bank, receives 7.6% from RO and pays LIBOR to RO which equates to LIBOR − 0.1%.

RO pays LIBOR + 0.5% to the bank, receives LIBOR from AB, and pays 7.6% to AB which equates to a payment of 8.1%.

These net borrowing rates are each 0.4% less than AB could borrow at a floating rate or RO could borrow at a fixed rate

(c) In practice, most swaps are arranged through banks that run a 'swaps book'. There are several advantages in dealing with a bank rather than directly with another company.

– In dealing with a bank, there is no problem about finding a swaps counterparty with an equal and opposite swapping requirement. The bank will arrange a swap to meet the specific requirements of each individual customer, as to amount and duration of the swap.

– In dealing with a bank, the credit risk is that the bank might default, whereas in dealing directly with another company, the credit risk is that the other company might default. Banks are usually a much lower credit risk than corporations.

— Banks are specialists in swaps, and are able to provide standard legal swaps agreements. The operation of the swap is likely to be administratively more straightforward.

The significant drawback to using a bank is that the bank will want to make a profit from its operations. In practice, it will generally do this by charging different swap rates for fixed rate payments and fixed rate receipts on different swaps. In terms of the RO and AB situation, where there is a credit arbitrage opportunity of 0.8%, if a swaps bank were to be used to arrange a separate swap with each company, it might take a profit of, say, 0.2%, leaving just 0.6% of benefit to be shared between RO and AB.

Test your understanding 25 – QW (Case style question)

REPORT

To: The Board of QW plc

From: The Treasurer

Date: XX-XX-XX

Subject: Interest rate swaps

(i) A swap is an agreement between two parties to exchange the cash flows related to specific underlying obligations. In an interest rate swap, the cash flows are the interest payments arising on principal amounts. For example, company A might have outstanding borrowings of GBP 1m with annual interest fixed at 10%, whilst company B has borrowings of GBP 1m with annual interest paid at a floating rate of LIBOR + 1%.

If company A and company B agree on an interest rate swap, they agree to take on the other's interest obligations, so that company B will pay fixed annual interest of GBP 100,000 pa, while company A will now pay floating interest of LIBOR + 1% on GBP 1m. Such a swap might be entered into if company A thought that interest rates were going to fall, while company B thought they would rise.

A forward rate agreement (FRA) is a contract in which two parties agree on the interest rate to be paid for a period of time starting in the future, for example for a three-month period starting in six months' time. The contract is settled in cash; exposure is limited to the difference in interest rates between the FRA agreed rate and the actual rate, based on the notional agreed principal.

An interest rate futures contract is a standardised form of FRA traded on an investment exchange. Each contract is for a specified nominal amount of a specified financial instrument on a specified date.

The advantages of swaps compared to other forms of interest rate risk management are as follows:

- Swaps allow a company to restructure its capital profile without the expense of actually redeeming existing borrowings. Fixed borrowings can be changed to floating rate, or floating to fixed, without incurring the transaction costs and possible redemption penalties associated with actual redemption.

- Using the principle of comparative advantage, companies with different credit ratings can reduce their cost of borrowing, by borrowing at different costs in different markets.

- Swaps can offer access to capital markets for companies which would not normally be allowed to participate due to their low credit rating, by swapping borrowings with a company with a higher credit rating.

(ii) We (QW plc) could borrow at a fixed 8%, while ER plc borrows at a floating LIBOR + 0.5%, and then swap the interest obligations. Total interest paid by both parties is LIBOR + 8.5%.

The alternative is for us to borrow at a floating LIBOR + 0.2%, while ER plc borrows at a fixed 9.5%. Total interest then paid by both parties is LIBOR + 9.7%.

Clearly the swap is advantageous, since total interest is 1.2% less than the alternative. The bank's commission is 0.2%, leaving 1% (or GBP 100,000) as the net benefit to be shared between the two companies. ER plc has opportunistically proposed that the net benefit should be shared equally between the two companies. Since our credit rating is better than ER's, it would be fairer for us to receive more than 50%, though this is a matter for negotiation.

As a final point, it should be noted that, if we are confident that interest rates are going to fall over the next three years, it will probably be better to take out floating rate borrowings from the start, rather than take out fixed rate borrowings and swap these for floating rate. We would not have to share the benefits of falling interest rates with any third party or pay the swap's commission payment to the bank. The decision therefore depends on how confident we are that interest rates will fall as expected. Please contact me again if I can be of any further help to you in this or any other matter.

Financial and strategic implications of mergers and acquisitions

Chapter learning objectives

Lead outcome	Component outcome
D1: Discuss the context of valuation	Discuss: (a) Listing of firms (b) Mergers and acquisitions (M&A) (c) Demergers and divestment

Topics to be covered

- Reasons for M&A and divestments
- Taxation implications
- Process and implications of management buy-outs
- Acquisition by private equity and venture capitalist

1   Overview of chapter

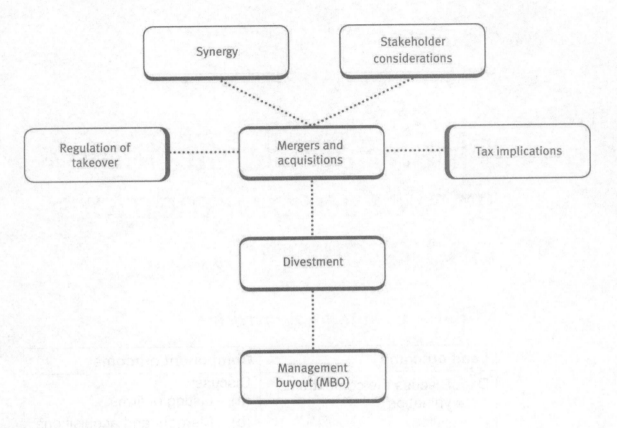

Terminology

The term 'merger' is usually used to describe the joining together of two or more entities.

Strictly, if one entity acquires a majority shareholding in another, the second is said to have been acquired (or 'taken over') by the first. If the two entities join together to submerge their separate identities into a new entity, the process is described as a merger.

In fact, the term 'merger' is often used even when an acquisition/takeover has actually occurred, because of the cultural impact on the acquired entity – the word merger makes the arrangement sound like a partnership between equals.

Types of merger/acquisition

Mergers and acquisitions can be classified to reflect the nature of the enlarged group:

- **Horizontal integration** results when two entities in the same line of business combine. For example, recent bank and building society mergers are a good example of this type of integration.

- **Vertical integration** results from the acquisition of one entity by another which is at a different level in the 'chain of supply' – as an example, UK breweries have moved heavily into the distribution of their product via public houses.

- **A conglomerate** results when two entities in unrelated businesses combine.

2 The reasons for growth by acquisition or merger

Specific reasons for merger/acquisition

The following reasons have been suggested as to why entities merge or acquire.

- **Increased market share/power.** In a market with limited product differentiation, price may be the main competitive weapon. In such a case, large market share may enable an entity to drive prices – for example reducing prices in the short term to eliminate competition before increasing prices later.

- **Economies of scale.** These result when expansion of the scale of productive capacity of an entity (or industry) causes total production costs to increase less than proportionately with output. It is clear that a merger which resulted in horizontal or vertical integration could give such economies since, at the very least, duplication would be avoided. But how could a conglomerate merger give economies? Possibly through central facilities such as offices, accounting departments and computer departments being rationalised. (Indeed, both sets of management are unlikely to be needed in their entirety.)

- **Combining complementary needs.** Many small entities have a unique product but lack the engineering and sales organisations necessary to produce and market it on a large scale. A natural course of action would be to merge with a larger entity. Both entities gain something – the small entity gets 'instant' engineering and marketing departments, and the large entity gains the revenue and other benefits which a unique product can bring. Also if, as is likely, the resources which each entity requires are complementary, the merger may well produce further opportunities that neither would see in isolation.

- **Improving efficiency.** A classic takeover target would be an entity operating in a potentially lucrative market but which, owing to poor management or inefficient operations, does not fully exploit its opportunities. Of course, being taken over would not be the only way of improving such a poor performer, but such an entity's managers may be unwilling to give themselves the sack.

- **A lack of profitable investment opportunities – surplus cash.** An entity may be generating a substantial volume of cash, but sees few profitable investment opportunities. If it does not wish to simply pay out the surplus cash as dividends (because of its long-term dividend policy, perhaps), it could use it to acquire other entities. A reason for doing so is that entities with excess cash are usually regarded as ideal targets for acquisition – a case of buy or be bought.

- **Tax relief.** An entity may be unable to claim tax relief because it does not generate sufficient profits. It may therefore wish to merge with another entity which does generate such profits.

- **Reduced competition.** It is often one benefit of merger activity – provided that it does not fall foul of the competition authorities.

- **Asset-stripping.** A predator acquires a target and sells the easily separable assets, perhaps closing down or disposing of some of its operations.

- **Big data opportunities.** When one entity takes over another, the knowledge and expertise of the target entity can increase the amount of big data available to the predator, to enable the combined firm to develop better competitive advantage.

 More on big data opportunities

What is Big Data?

There are several definitions of Big Data, the most commonly used referring to large volumes of data beyond the normal processing, storage and analysis capacity of typical database application tools.

Big Data will often include much more than simply financial information and can involve other organisational data which is operational in nature along with other internal and external data which is often unstructured in form.

One of the key challenges of dealing with Big Data is to identify repeatable business patterns in this unstructured data. Managing such data can lead to significant business benefits such as greater competitive advantage, improved productivity and increasing levels of innovation.

Why is Big Data so important?

Several major business benefits arise from the ability to manage Big Data successfully:

- Driving innovation by reducing time taken to answer key business questions and therefore make decisions

- Gaining competitive advantage

- Improving productivity

The relevance of Big Data in mergers / acquisitions

These points link directly into the reasons for merger / acquisition presented above.

For example even before considering Big Data specifically we stated that combining complementary needs is a key reason for merger / acquisition.

The acquisition of a company with a large database of customers (and potential customers) would be an example of this that also incorporates Big Data. The acquiring company would get access to this database, and also to the skills of the target company staff who have collected and analysed the Big Data.

Test your understanding 1 (Integration question)

MONEY is a company operating in the financial services industry offering high net worth client's private banking facilities and investment advice. It has recently been approached by the Board of CASH, a company providing business loans and other forms of borrowing to small businesses and start-up companies. The directors of CASH are looking to sell the company to raise the capital to start a new venture and believe the company would be a good strategic fit with MONEY.

Required:

Advise MONEY how the acquisition of CASH will give rise to Big Data opportunities.

The following reasons why entities merge are of questionable validity:

- Diversification, to reduce risk. While acquiring an entity in a different line of activity may diversify away risk for the entities involved, this is surely irrelevant to the shareholders. They could have performed exactly the same diversification simply by holding shares in both entities. The only real diversification produced is in the risk attaching to the managers' and employees' jobs, and this is likely to make them more complacent than before – to the detriment of shareholders' future returns.

- Shares of the target entity are undervalued. This may well be the case, although it would conflict with the efficient markets theory. However, the shareholders of the entity planning the takeover would derive as much benefit (at a lower administrative cost) from buying such undervalued shares themselves. This also assumes that the acquirer entity's management are better at valuing shares than professional investors in the market place.

Synergy

 Definition

Synergy may be defined as two or more entities coming together to produce a result not independently obtainable.

For example, a merged entity will only need one marketing department, so there may be savings generated compared to two separate entities.

Importance of synergy in mergers and acquisitions

For a successful business combination we should be looking for a situation where:

MV of combined company (AB) > MV of A + MV of B

Note: MV means Market Value here.

If this situation occurs we have experienced synergy, where the whole is worth more than the sum of the parts. This is often expressed as 2 + 2 = 5.

It is important to note that synergy is not automatic. In an efficient stock market A and B will be correctly valued before the combination, and we need to ask how synergy will be achieved, i.e. why any increase in value should occur.

Sources of synergy

There are several reasons why synergistic gains arise. These break down into the following:

- **operating economies**, such as economies of scale and elimination of inefficiency,

- **financial synergy**, such as the reduced risk caused by diversification,

- **other synergistic effects**, such as market power.

Detailed examples of synergy

Synergy from operating economies

Economies of scale – Horizontal combinations (acquisitions of a company in a similar line of business) are often claimed to reduce costs and therefore increase profits due to economies of scale. These can occur in the production, marketing or finance areas. Note that these gains are not automatic and diseconomies of scale may also be experienced. These benefits are sometimes also claimed for conglomerate combinations (acquisition of companies in unrelated areas of business) in financial and marketing costs.

Economies of vertical integration – Some acquisitions involve buying out other companies in the same production chain, e.g. a manufacturer buying out a raw material supplier or a retailer. This can increase profits by 'cutting out the middle man'.

Complementary resources – It is sometimes argued that by combining the strengths of two companies a synergistic result can be obtained. For example, combining a company specialising in research and development with a company strong in the marketing area could lead to gains.

Elimination of inefficiency – If the victim company is badly managed, its performance and hence its value can be improved by the elimination of inefficiencies. Improvements could be obtained particularly in the areas of production, marketing and finance.

Financial synergy

Several financial arguments are proposed in this area.

Diversification – The argument goes that diversification normally reduces risk. If the earnings of the merged companies simply stay the same (i.e. no operating economies are obtained), there could still be an increase in value of the company due to the lower risk.

Diversification and financing – If the future cash flow streams of the two companies are not perfectly positively correlated (i.e. if they are forecast to fluctuate in different ways) then, by combining the two companies, the variability of their operating cash flow may be reduced. A more stable cash flow is more attractive to creditors and this could lead to cheaper financing.

The 'boot strap' or P/E game – It is sometimes argued that companies with high P/E ratios are in a good position to acquire other companies as they can impose their high P/E ratio on the victim firm and increase its value.

Other synergistic effects

Surplus managerial talent – Companies with highly skilled managers can make use of this resource only if they have problems to solve. The acquisition of inefficient companies is sometimes the only way of fully utilising skilled managers.

Surplus cash – Companies with large amounts of surplus cash may see the acquisition of other companies as the only possible application for these funds. Of course, increased dividends could cure the problem of surplus cash, but this may be rejected for reasons of tax or dividend stability.

Market power – Horizontal combinations may enable the firm to obtain a degree of monopoly power that could increase its profitability. Removing competition from a market in this way could attract the attentions of the competition authorities, e.g. the Competition and Markets Authority in the UK, who could rule the acquisition unlawful.

Speed – Acquisition may be far faster than organic growth in obtaining a presence in a new and growing market.

By considering all the above sources of synergy, a company can work towards increasing the post-merger value of the newly formed joint company.

Test your understanding 2 (Case style question)

Williams Inc is the manufacturer of cosmetics, soaps and shower gels. It also markets its products using its own highly successful sales and marketing department. It is seen as an employer of choice and as such has a talented and loyal workforce with a history of developing new and exciting products which have sold well. It is now considering extending its range, however it has currently a build-up of unfulfilled orders due to a lack of capacity.

GSL is a well-known herbal remedy for skin problems. GSL Co was founded by three brothers in the 1950s and until the death of the remaining brother in 2007 has performed well – however the new Chairman has limited experience and the company has not performed well over recent years. GSL has a dedicated team of herbalists who have developed products, which would find a ready market – however, there is insufficient funds and expertise to correctly market these products and market share is low.

Williams' products and GSL's products are made using similar production technologies and their financial and administrative systems are similar and it is hoped savings can be made here.

Required:

Identify any potential synergy gains that would emerge from a merger of Williams and GSL.

(15 minutes)

The impact of mergers and acquisitions on stakeholders

Impact on acquiring company's shareholders

The existence of synergy has been discussed above as a key benefit to shareholders of an acquisition. All companies have a primary objective to maximise shareholder wealth, so it is clear that if synergy can be achieved, an acquisition should benefit the acquiring company's shareholders.

Impact on the target company's shareholders

The acquiring company will often pay a premium to the shareholders of the target company, to encourage them to sell their shares. Therefore there is also a financial benefit to them when a takeover happens.

Impact on lenders/debt holders

Debt will often be repayable in the event of a change in control. It all depends on whether the bank borrowings and bonds contain a change in control clause. With bank borrowings they almost certainly will. The risk profile of the acquirer may be quite different from that of the original borrower and the bank will not wish to become exposed to a higher credit risk. Bonds may be the same.

The acquirer is therefore likely to need to arrange new financing, debt and/or equity financing as appropriate in advance of the takeover.

Impact on managers and staff

In many acquisitions, an easy way to generate synergy is to make some staff redundant to avoid there being duplication of roles. Therefore, the managers and employees, particularly of the target company, often view a takeover with dread. However, the managers of the acquiring company often see takeovers as an opportunity, to demand higher salaries and bonuses now that they manage a larger company.

The acquirer may wish to retain many managers whose knowledge and skills may be essential to the successful continuation of the business, at least in the short term. In such a case, the acquirer may seek assurance and contractual tie-ins to ensure that such people remain with the business for a certain period of time.

Impact on society as a whole

Governments monitor takeovers carefully, and if they feel that a takeover will not be in the best interests of society as a whole, the takeover can be investigated and sometimes stopped. Competition law in most countries prevents monopolies being created which might be able to exploit their power to take advantage of customers.

Problems with acquisitions

If an acquisition generates the expected synergy, shareholders in both the acquiring company and the target should see an increase in wealth.

However, not all mergers and acquisitions are successful.

Synergy will not automatically arise. Unless the management of the two entities can work together effectively, there is a chance that any forecast benefits of the new arrangement might not be realised.

In many cases, the forecast synergy is not achieved, or is not as large as expected. It may be that the premium paid on acquisition by the acquirer was too high, so the shareholder value of the acquirer actually reduced as a result of the acquisition.

Also, cultural clashes between the two companies can make the integration of the two businesses very difficult.

Another reason for failure is that the opportunity cost of the investment could be too high. This means that the acquirer realises that the funds tied up in the acquisition could have been better used, to generate higher returns elsewhere.

Detailed reasons why mergers/acquisitions fail

The fit/lack of fit syndrome

There may be a good fit of products or services, but a serious lack of fit in terms of management styles or corporate structure.

Lack of industrial or commercial fit

Failure can result from a horizontal or vertical takeover where the acquired entity turns out not to have the product range or industrial position that the acquirer anticipated. Usually in the case where a customer or supplier is acquired, the acquirer knows a lot about the acquired entity; even so, there may be aspects of the acquired entity's operations which may cause unexpected problems for the acquirer, such that, even in these cases, a prospective acquisition should be planned very carefully and not be based solely on experience gained from a direct relationship with the acquired entity.

Lack of goal congruence

This may apply not only to the acquired entity but, more dangerously, to the acquirer, whereby disputes over the treatment of the acquired entity might well take away the benefits of an otherwise excellent acquisition.

'Cheap' purchases

The 'turn around' costs of an acquisition purchased at what seems to be a bargain price may well turn out to be a high multiple of that price. In these situations, the amount of resources in terms of cash and management time could well also damage the acquirer's core business. In preparing a bid, a would-be acquirer should always take into account the likely total cost of an acquisition, including the input of its own resources, before deciding on making an offer or setting an offer price.

Paying too much

The fact that a high premium is paid for an acquisition does not necessarily mean that it will fail. Failure would result only if the price paid is beyond that which the acquirer considers acceptable to increase satisfactorily the long-term wealth of its shareholders.

Failure to integrate effectively

An acquirer needs to have a workable and clear plan of the extent to which the acquired company is to be integrated, and the amount of autonomy to be granted. At best, the plan should be negotiated with the acquired entity's management and staff, but its essential requirements should be fairly but firmly carried out. The plan must address such problems as differences in management styles, incompatibilities in data information systems, and continued opposition to the acquisition by some of the acquired entity's staff. Failure to plan can – and often does – lead to failure of an acquisition, as it leads to drift and demotivation, not only within the acquired entity but also within the acquirer itself.

Every aspect of a prospective acquisition, as it will affect the would-be acquirer, should be weighed up before embarking on a bid. Problems of integration have a much better chance of being resolved before bidding action is taken than they do after the event, when many more complications can ensue.

Even if a product fit is satisfactory, the would-be acquirer should be satisfied that the aspects of its own operation affected by the bid will be properly adaptable to the new activities. Running the rule carefully over one's own operations may yield vital information as to areas which may need adaptation before a bid can be contemplated, and provide vital clues to appropriate areas for search when a bid has actually been launched. One factor of special importance is a clear assessment of the flexibility of one's own information systems.

> ### Inability to manage change
>
> Several of the above points stress the need for an acquirer to plan effectively before and after an acquisition if failure is to be avoided. But this in itself calls for the ability to accept change – perhaps even radical change – from established routines and practices. Indeed, many acquisitions fail mainly because the acquirer is unable – or unwilling – reasonably to adjust its own activities to help ensure a smooth takeover. One such situation is where the acquired company has a demonstrably better data information system than the acquirer, which it might be greatly in the acquirer's interest to adopt.

3 Tax implications of mergers and acquisitions

Introduction

There are several tax implications of mergers and acquisitions:

- differences in tax rates and double tax treaties

- group loss relief

- withholding tax.

Differences in tax rates and double tax treaties

Different countries around the world have different tax rates. Therefore, if one company acquires another company based in a different country, there are likely to be different tax rates for the two companies in the group.

The OECD (Organisation for Economic Cooperation and Development) is an organisation of developed countries whose main purpose is to maintain financial stability and the expansion of world trade.

In order to help avoid double taxation between countries, the OECD has published a model Double Taxation Convention with an accompanying commentary.

Significance of the OECD model double tax treaty

Whenever a double tax treaty is drawn up between two countries (or an old treaty is renegotiated) the OECD model is used as a guide.

Detailed knowledge of specific treaties is not required in your examination. The main function of any treaty is to avoid double taxation and to decide which country shall have the right to tax income.

Group loss relief

Members of a group of companies may surrender losses to other profitable group members for corresponding accounting periods.

Losses surrendered must be set against the claimant company's taxable total profits of a 'corresponding' accounting period.

(Note that in this context, a corresponding accounting period = any accounting period falling wholly or partly within the surrendering company's accounting period.)

Key considerations for group loss relief

Tax planning primarily seeks to ensure losses are used within the group to save the most tax. Accordingly, losses are first set against profits taxed at the highest rate.

Group relief is only available for losses and profits generated after a company joins a group. It is not possible to have group relief for preacquisition losses or to relieve preacquisition profits.

Group relief ceases to be available once arrangements are in place to sell the shares of a company. This will usually occur sometime before the actual legal sale of the shares.

Withholding tax

A withholding tax, also called a retention tax, is a government requirement for the payer of an item of income to withhold or deduct tax from the payment, and pay that tax to the government.

In the context of groups of companies, withholding taxes need to be considered when one company makes payments to another within the group (for example as dividends, or interest on loans).

Typically the withholding tax is treated as a payment on account of the recipient's final tax liability.

It may be refunded if it is determined, when a tax return is filed, that the recipient's tax liability to the government which received the withholding tax is less than the tax withheld, or additional tax may be due if it is determined that the recipient's tax liability is more than the withholding tax.

 ## 4   The role and scope of competition authorities

Introduction to competition authorities

During a takeover, it is important that the companies comply with relevant legislation and regulations.

Competition authorities monitor takeovers and mergers on behalf of national governments.

General principles

The role of the competition authorities varies from country to country but as a general rule their aims are:

- to strengthen competition
- to prevent or reduce anti-competitive activities
- to consider the public interest.

If the competition authorities find that a proposed merger or takeover is ant-competitive, they have the power to block the takeover completely, or to allow it to proceed subject to certain conditions being met (for example the combined entity might be required to sell off some of its retail outlets after the acquisition).

More detail on competition authorities

Many bids, because of their size, will require review by the competition authorities, and a limited number will subsequently be investigated if the authorities think that a merger might be anti-competitive or against the public interest.

Anti-competitive

An anti-competitive merger or acquisition can be defined as one that leads to a substantial lessening of competition or one that would significantly impede effective competition.

In many countries, 'anti-competitive' is deemed to be the creation of a new entity that will have 25% or more of the share of a market.

Public interest

To assess whether a merger or acquisition is in the 'public interest', the competition authorities will consider factors such as:

- National security (including security of energy and food supplies)
- Media quality
- Financial stability (e.g. protecting the stability of banks and financial services)

Investigations

Investigations may take several months to complete during which time the merger is put on hold, thus giving the target company valuable time to organise its defence. The acquirer may abandon its bid as it may not wish to become involved in a time consuming investigation.

The authorities may simply accept or reject the proposals or accept them subject to certain conditions.

Examples

In recent years, the competition authorities in the UK have investigated several UK energy company mergers and also mergers in the UK supermarket industry.

In 2018 they are investigating a potential merger between ASDA and Sainsbury's to decide whether the merger will be allowed to go ahead.

They also have put forward proposals to reduce the dominance of the 'Big Four' accountancy firms (KPMG, Deloitte, Ernst & Young and Pricewaterhouse Coopers) within the UK audit sector.

In addition, if the offer gives rises to a concentration (i.e. a potential monopoly) within the EU, the European Commission may initiate proceedings. This can result in considerable delay, and constitutes grounds for abandoning a bid.

In March 2017 the European Commission blocked a proposed merger of the London Stock Exchange and Deutsche Borse (who operate the Frankfurt stock exchange) due to this reason.

5   Divestment

 Definition

Divestment: Disposal of part of its activities by an entity. (CIMA Official Terminology, 2005).

Reasons for divestment

The reasons for divestment include:

The sum of the parts of the entity may be worth more than the whole

As identified earlier in this chapter, businesses which combine will attempt to find areas where resources can be combined to generate synergy. However, it may be that a business with many disparate parts actually ends up suffering from the opposite effect. For example, the company could be spending a lot of money trying to integrate business units together where there are no apparent benefits.

In such situations, the divestment of part of the business should be considered.

Divesting unwanted or less profitable parts

If there is an underperforming business unit which fails to meet general company performance targets, divestment should be considered. The opportunity cost of holding onto the underperforming business unit could be very high.

However, management should always consider the effect of the divestment on the other parts of the company. For example, if a division is sold off which previously performed some work for other business units within the company, disposing of that business unit will lead to the other parts of the business having to buy in goods and services from third parties.

Strategic change (e.g. to shift the strategic focus onto the core activities)

A part of the business which operates in a different market sector from the rest of the group may be considered for divestment. Increased focus on the company's core activities should help to develop the expertise of management and staff, and the strength of the company's brand.

A response to crisis

In a crisis, when cash is needed quickly, a part of the business might be divested if an attractive offer is received.

The most common examples of divestments are sell offs (trade sales), spin offs and management buyouts.

 More on divestment: Sell-offs and spin-offs

Sell-off (or trade sale)

A sell-off is the sale of part of an entity to a third party, usually in return for cash.

The most common reasons for a sell-off are:

- to divest of a less profitable business unit if an acceptable offer is received – this could be through a management buyout – see below;

- to protect the rest of the business from takeover – a part of the business which is attractive to a purchaser may be sold off to avoid the whole company being taken over;

- to generate cash in a time of crisis.

A sell-off may disrupt the rest of the organisation if key staff or products from within the organisation are part of the business unit sold off.

Spin-off (or demerger)

In a spin-off (or demerger) a new entity is created, where the shares of that new entity are owned by the shareholders of the entity that made the transfer of assets into the new entity. There are now two entities, each owning some of the assets of the original single entity. The ownership has not changed, and in theory the value of the two individual entities should be the same as the value of the original single entity.

Reasons for spin-offs

Spin-offs may be justified as follows

- they allow investors to identify the true value of a business that was hidden within a large conglomerate;
- they should lead to a clearer management structure;
- they reduce the risk of a takeover bid for the core entity.

6 Management buyouts

Definition

Definition of a management buyout (MBO): Purchase of a business from its existing owners by members of the management team, generally in association with a financing institution. (CIMA Official Terminology, 2005)

Overview of an MBO

In an MBO, the purchaser of the business is not another company (like in a sell-off/trade sale), but the existing management.

Usually the management provide some of the capital for the buyout, but the majority is provided by other financiers such as venture capitalists and financial institutions.

MBOs: Considerations for the divesting company

Members of the buyout team may possess detailed and confidential knowledge of other parts of the vendor's business and the vendor will therefore require satisfactory warranties over such aspects which it will not be able to control.

More seriously, key members of the MBO team may have skills vital to the vendor's operation, especially in regard to information services and networking.

A vendor may be reluctant to allow key players to end their contracts of service to take part in an MBO, because losing vital operational skills can hardly be compensated by forms of warranty.

MBOs: Considerations for the management team

Considerations before an MBO

MBOs are not dissimilar to other acquisitions and many of the factors to be considered will be the same.

- **Do the current owners wish to sell?** – The whole process will be much easier (and cheaper) if the current owners wish to sell. However, some MBOs have been concluded despite initial resistance from the current owners.

- **Potential of the business** – The management team engaged in the buyout will be making the switch from a relatively safe salaried position to a risky ownership position. They must, therefore, ensure that the victim business will be a long-run profit generator. This will involve analysing the performance of the business and drawing up a business plan (products, markets, required new investment, sources of finance, etc.) for future operations. Research shows that MBOs are less likely to fail than other types of new ventures, but several have collapsed, and managers must appreciate the risks they are taking and attempt to reduce them as far as possible.

- **Loss of head office support** – On becoming an independent firm many of the services that are taken for granted in a large organisation may be lost. The importance of these services varies from one industry to another but provision will have to be made for support in the areas of finance, computing, research and development, etc. Although head office fees might be saved, after the buyout these support services can involve considerable expense when purchased in the outside market.

- **Quality of the management team** – The success of any MBO will be greatly influenced by the quality of the management team. It is important to ensure that all functional areas (marketing, sales, production, finance) are represented and that all managers are prepared to take the required risks. A united approach is important in all negotiations and a clear responsibility structure should be established within the team.

- **The price** – As in any takeover situation the price paid will be crucial in determining the long-term success of the acquisition. The usual valuation techniques may be employed, often with more confidence as managers are likely to have a clearer idea of the future prospects of the firm. Care must be taken to ensure that all relevant aspects of the business are included in the package. For example, trademarks and patents may be as important as the physical assets of the firm. In a similar way, responsibilities for redundancy costs, etc. must be clearly defined.

Financing the MBO

In an MBO, unlike a corporate-backed takeover, the acquiring group usually lacks the financial resources to fund the acquisition.

For small buyouts the price may be within the capabilities of the management team, but it is unlikely that many managers could raise the large amounts involved in some buyouts.

Several institutions specialise in providing funds for MBOs. These include the following:

- venture capitalists;
- banks;
- private equity firms;
- other financial institutions.

Terminology: Leveraged buyout

A leveraged buyout occurs when an investor, typically a private equity firm, acquires a controlling interest in a company's equity and where a significant percentage of the purchase price is financed through leverage (borrowing).

Leveraged buyouts involve institutional investors and financial sponsors (like private equity firms) making large acquisitions without committing all the capital required for the acquisition.

The role of venture capitalists

Venture capitalists

Typically venture capitalists will be prepared to advance funds for five to ten years, and will expect annual returns on their funds of 25% or more (compounded and received at exit, rather than annually). They normally expect to take one or more seats on the board of directors (but not a majority).

The specific types of finance and conditions attached vary from one investment to another, but key points to be considered include the following.

The form of finance – The management team may need the venture capitalists to contribute more than 50% of the total funding, but will always want to keep at least 50% of the equity for themselves (a controlling stake). Therefore, this limits the amount of equity finance that can be raised from the venture capitalist.

However, raising too much from the venture capitalist as debt finance can lead to an unacceptable rise in the level of gearing in the business (perhaps for example if the company has debt covenants which limit the gearing level).

Therefore, venture capitalists often provide their funds as a mix of equity and debt, in order to give themselves security (the debt) while allowing them to participate if things go well (the equity).

As a compromise, convertible preference shares are often used. This ensures that the venture capitalist can benefit in the longer term if the company is successful (by converting to equity) but in the short term the control stays with the management team.

The preference shares usually carry covenants to protect the venture capitalist's position. These limit the actions that can be taken without the venture capitalist's approval. Examples might include paying dividends on ordinary shares, amending the Articles of Association or selling assets.

Exit strategy – The most important fact that any investing institution will want to know is how and when they will get their money back. The exit strategy is an important part of the agreement to advance money in the first place. Exit strategies are explained more fully later in this chapter.

Ongoing support – The management team should also consider the venture capitalist's willingness to provide funds for later expansion plans. Some venture capitalists also offer other services such as management consultancy to their clients.

The role of private equity firms

Private equity is sometimes confused with venture capital because both terms refer to firms that invest in companies and exit through selling their investments (often using methods such as initial public offerings (IPOs)).

However, there are major differences between private equity and venture capital firms.

Private equity firms mostly buy mature companies that are already established. The companies may be deteriorating or not making the profits they should be due to inefficiency. Private equity firms buy these companies and streamline operations to increase revenues. Venture capital firms, on the other hand, mostly invest in start-ups with high growth potential.

Private equity firms often buy 100% ownership of the companies in which they invest. As a result, the private equity firms are in total control of the company after the buyout. Venture capital firms invest in 50% or less of the equity of the companies.

Most venture capital firms prefer to spread out their risk and invest in many different companies. If one start-up fails, the entire fund in the venture capital firm is not affected substantially. By contrast, private equity firms prefer to concentrate all their efforts in a single company. Since they invest in already established and mature companies, the chances of absolute losses from such investments are minimal.

Details on financing MBOs

Financiers tend to favour established businesses with reliable cash flows (to pay down the debt) and a clear exit route.

They like definitive plans, but say they prefer them brief and to the point.

The emphasis should be on the competences of the team, and the market opportunity to be exploited, with detailed financial numbers (focussing on cash flow) put into an appendix. How services previously supplied by group departments, or fellow subsidiaries, will be replaced is likely to be a key item.

Managers will be required to invest some of their own money and this will take the form of shares with special features, for example a high proportion of any disposal value.

Suggested financial structure

Capital structures are inevitably complex, with several levels of risk/reward:

- **Secured borrowings** are usually obtained from a bank, with a first charge on the assets taken over by the venture.

- The provider of **senior debt** will require a first-ranking security over all the assets involved in the MBO venture and, usually, over the capital of the MBO as evidenced by shares in the new entity. Security will also involve undertakings from the MBO team regarding the provision of financial information and the setting of restrictions on the MBO's capacity to raise other debt finance and to dispose of assets.

- **Junior debt** is usually called mezzanine finance, which is an intermediate stage between senior debt and equity finance in relation to both risk and return. The return on mezzanine finance can comprise a mixture of debt interest and the ability to convert part of the debt into equity, perhaps by the conversion of warrants. By this means the lender can in time have a share in the premium resulting from eventual exit from the venture. The debt interest will carry a risk premium, as it is subordinate to the senior debt and with less security: it may even be unsecured.

- **Venture capital** is a form of equity provided mainly by institutional investors, whose reward will usually be in some form of dividends, probably preferential, combined with appreciation of their MBO equity holding which will build up a capital gain for when the investment is realised.

- The last link in the structural chain is the **equity holding granted to the MBO team** itself which, if their activities are successful, will provide a substantial capital gain when the venture is exited, either through flotation or by other means. Meanwhile, the MBO management will draw salaries or fees for their services.

MBOs: Considerations for the financiers

Key points for investors – usually banks or other institutions – in deciding whether to support an MBO are as follows:

- What is actually for sale, and why? It may be a division or subsidiary of an entity which no longer fits that entity's strategy, or it may be separable assets such as a factory or group of retail outlets.

- Whether the activities are profitable and enjoy a satisfactory cash flow. The prospective returns must justify the operational and financial risks involved. Profits must be sustainable and cash flow adequate to sustain the level of activities proposed.

- Whether the management is sufficiently strong. This point is particularly significant if the MBO relates to loss-making activities, although sufficient allowance must be made for the possibility that its existing owners may be burdening it with excessive overheads. Financial competence and marketing skills in the MBO's sector are especially important.

- Whether the price is reasonable and a sufficient contribution is being made by the managers. The managers should have some financial involvement and the future prospects for the new entity should be demonstrable, especially in a 'turn-around' situation.

These points are important as the main risks associated with MBOs, and hence the reasons why they may fail are:

- the bid price offered by the MBO team might be too high;

- a lack of experience in key areas such as financial management;

- a loss of key staff who either perceive the buyout as too risky, or do not have capital to invest;

- a lack of finance;

- problems in convincing employees and fellow colleagues of the need to change working practices or to accept redundancy.

Investors, probably institutions, backing the MBO will initially hold a majority of the equity, with a relatively small minority of shares held by the managers.

Although the backers must be prepared to hold their investment for the long term, they and the managers will be looking to the entity growing successfully to the point where it can be launched on the stock exchange. At this stage, a market value can be obtained for the equity and, if desired, some portion of the investment can be realised.

Where the backers desire a lower-risk element in their investment, they can require that some part of it will be in the form of redeemable convertible preference shares. This can give them priority in obtaining income through a preference dividend and preferential rights of repayment if the entity should fail. There is also the prospect of redemption if the entity does not develop satisfactorily, or conversely, the convertible aspect will allow backers eventually to increase their equity holding if the entity should prove successful.

7 Exit strategies

Overview of exit strategies

The investors and financiers in an MBO will want to realise a profit from their investment in the medium term.

Debt finance will normally have a specified repayment date, so the debt providers will have a clear exit route (assuming the borrowing company has performed in line with expectations and can afford to repay the debt as planned).

Exit strategies for equity holders

For the providers of equity, the exit route is not as easy to identify.

The most common exit route for an equity investor is the sale of the shares to another investor. This could be through one of the following methods:

Trade sale

If the MBO company receives an offer for all its shares from another company, the financiers will be able to realise their investment. However, in a trade sale, all the shares are normally acquired by the bidding company, so the management would have to sell their shares in their own company too. They may not be happy to do this, because the appeal of an MBO to managers is that they will own their own company rather than have to report to other shareholders.

IPO (Initial Public Offering)

An IPO or flotation on the stock market was introduced in the earlier chapter on 'Financing – Equity finance'.

An IPO gives the financiers who want to sell their shares the chance to do so on the stock market. If the managers want to keep hold of their shares, they will be able to do so.

The problem with an IPO is that the company will have to satisfy certain stringent criteria in order to join the stock exchange, and there will be significant costs associated with the listing.

After an IPO, the shares will be freely traded, which should increase their marketability and hence their value. On the other hand, the company becomes much more susceptible to takeover when its shares are listed.

Independent sale to another shareholder

The managers could try to increase their shareholdings in the company by 'buying out' the other financiers.

This would be expensive, but if the managers could afford it, it would prevent other external shareholders buying the shares and having a say in the running of the business.

8 End of chapter objective test questions

> ### Test your understanding 3 (Objective test question)
>
> BB is a listed company located in Country B. It is a retail clothing business which operates a large number of branded retail stores throughout Country B. Its functional currency is the B$. BB currently has five distinct brands, each owned and managed by a separate business unit. Each business unit runs its own chain of retail stores. BB is seeking to sell QQ, one of these business units, in a management buyout.
>
> A selling price of B$ 450 million has been agreed. It is anticipated that the effective date of the disposal will be 1 July 20X4.
>
> The managers of QQ have been in discussions with a bank and a venture capitalist regarding the financing for the MBO. The proposal is that the managers will put in B$45 million of equity, and the venture capitalist B$180 million (for class B equity shares with limited voting rights). Then the venture capitalist and the bank will each invest B$112.5 million as debt finance.
>
> The venture capitalist expects a return on the equity portion of its investment of at least 25% a year on a compound basis over the first 4 years of the MBO. No dividends are to be paid during this period.

What is the minimum total equity value of QQ on 30 June 20X8 required in order to satisfy the venture capitalist's expected return?

A   B$225.0 million

B   B$360.0 million

C   B$439.5 million

D   B$549.3 million

Test your understanding 4 (Objective test question)

The directors of a company are considering whether to dispose of one of its subsidiaries.

The directors of the subsidiary are interested in a management buy-out.

There is a potential conflict of interest if, during the negotiation phase of the management buy-out, the directors of the subsidiary company were to:

A   Lease some new vehicles to update the company's distribution facilities

B   Accept projects with high net present values

C   Perform a revaluation of assets

D   Employ more staff in the subsidiary's administration office

Test your understanding 5 (Objective test question)

Stan Co is a large multinational company. It has operations in several markets (including clothing, food and furniture) and geographical locations. Although Stan Co was originally a manufacturing company, it has expanded its operations into distribution and retailing in recent years.

The directors of Stan Co have decided to acquire the entire share capital of Ball Co, a small company that brews beer and sells it through its own network of bars.

What sort of business combination is this?

A   Vertical integration

B   Horizontal integration

C   A conglomerate

D   A management buyout

Test your understanding 6 (Objective test question)

NN sells electrical goods and operates a number of retail outlets in a particular region of the country. NN is in the process of acquiring the share capital of QQ, a company that sells the same type of products in the same region of the country through its own retail stores. Post-acquisition NN would be the largest retailer of electrical goods in that region. NN and QQ have perfectly positively correlated cash flow streams because they operate in the same market sector and location.

Which THREE of the following would be most likely to be synergistic benefits to NN of purchasing QQ?

A   Cash benefit by sale and leaseback of retail store property acquired

B   Increased sales due to owning a larger portfolio of retail outlets

C   Increased profit due to reduced competition in the region

D   Reduction in staff costs due to elimination of duplicated administrative roles

E   Cost savings due to economies of scale in purchasing activities

Test your understanding 7 (Objective test question)

The directors of GG Co have decided to sell off one of the company's subsidiaries, HH Co, for $100 million.

The managers of HH Co are keen to set up a management buyout in order to take control of their company.

They have proposed the following financing package, after lengthy discussions with bankers and venture capitalists:

	$ million
Equity invested by managers ($1 'A' shares carrying 1 vote each)	10
Equity invested by venture capitalist ($1 'B' shares carrying 1 vote for every 10 shares)	30
Borrowing from venture capitalist – unsecured, 10% interest rate, redeemable in five years	30
Borrowing from bank – secured, 6% interest rate, redeemable in five years	30
TOTAL	**100**

Which THREE of the following statements about the financing package are false?

A   The managers own enough of the equity to enable them to vote and carry decisions in a general meeting.

B   The venture capitalists own enough of the equity to prevent the managers from voting and carrying decisions in a general meeting.

C   If HH Co were to go into liquidation, the bank borrowing would take priority over all the other sources of finance.

D   The bank borrowing interest rate is lower than that on the borrowing from the venture capitalists because the bank borrowing is a mezzanine loan.

E   If HH Co were to go into liquidation, the borrowing from the venture capitalists would take priority over all the other sources of finance.

Test your understanding 8 (Objective test question)

Which THREE of the following reasons are often stated as valid justification for an acquisition, in that they help to increase shareholder wealth?

A   Diversification of risk

B   Reduction of competition

C   Big data opportunities

D   Better career prospects for directors

E   Asset stripping

Test your understanding 9 (Objective test question)

The directors of Hood Group have decided to sell off a loss-making subsidiary, Tucker Co. A management team from Tucker Co has expressed an interest in buying the company.

For which one of the following reasons would the parent company be likely to agree to sell Tucker Co to the management team rather than an external buyer, if the MBO team and the external buyer have both offered the same price?

A   To avoid redundancy costs

B   To avoid non-cooperation from management and employees hostile to the divestment

C   Because the MBO team knows more about the company than the external buyer

D   To raise the cash more quickly

9 End of chapter case style questions

Test your understanding 10 (Case style question)

Country T and Country V are separated by sea but linked by a rail tunnel. They have different currencies (T$ and V$ respectively) but are part of the same Trade Group which promotes free trade between its members and has authority over membership countries in matters relating to competition.

TNL is a public listed company, based in Country T, which owns and operates the rail link between Country T and Country V. Trains that travel through the tunnel carry passengers, cars and other vehicles such as trucks.

TNL was first listed on 1 June 20X4 by offer for sale of 100 million ordinary shares to the public at a price of T$ 3.70. Today, 21 November 20Y3, the share price is just T$ 2.95. The fall in the share price since 20X4 is largely the result of disappointing growth and market concerns about TNL's ability to renegotiate bank borrowings that are shortly due for repayment. The ordinary shares are held by a large number of individual shareholders as well as by large institutions and pension funds. The number of shares in issue remains unchanged since 20X4.

Debt funding is in the form of bank borrowings from a consortium of 10 banks to a total principal value of T$ 190 million. The borrowings were taken out on 1 June 20X4 and have a 10 year term. New borrowings are currently being negotiated to finance the repayment of the original borrowings on 1 June 20Y4.

There is strong price competition between TNL and two independent ferry companies, TT and VV which are based in Countries T and V respectively. Prices are generally low for travel by ferry since ferries are less convenient as they operate less frequently and have longer journey times than the rail tunnel link. TT has incurred losses in the past two years.

The board of TNL has approached ferry company TT with a view to acquiring it. The directors of TT are opposed to the bid and have referred the bid to the regional competition authorities of both Country T and the Trade Group.

Required:

Discuss the possible reasons why TNL may wish to acquire TT, and explain:

- Why the competition authorities in Country T and in the Trade Group might be concerned about the proposed acquisition.

- The possible actions that the competition authorities could take and the implications of these for TNL.

(30 minutes)

Advise TNL on:

- The factors that the banks are likely to consider when deciding whether or not to renew the loans made to TNL.

- Other appropriate sources of finance that should be considered.

(30 minutes)

 Test your understanding 11 (Case style question)

Country Y

Country Y is a large industrialised country with strong motor vehicle and construction industries. The glass industry supplies glass to these industries as well as to specialist users of glass such as contact lens manufacturers. There are five major glass manufacturing entities, each with market coverage in Country Y of between 5% and 40%.

Entity Q

Entity Q is a quoted entity and a major player in the glass industry. It has a market share in Country Y of approximately 35%. It is an old, well-established entity with a number of factories used to manufacture glass both locally and abroad. It has a stable, but unexciting, growth rate of 3% per annum and is facing increasing competition from new glass manufacturing entities setting up in its key markets. However, Q's high earnings levels of earlier years have resulted in relatively low levels of debt.

The head office building of Q is in the far north of Country Y in a remote geographical area. It is a considerable distance from the capital city and major centres of population in the south of the country. The building is much larger than the entity requires and several floors are unoccupied.

The management team of Q is highly experienced; the majority of the senior managers have worked for Q for the whole of their working lives.

The computer systems of Q were written especially for the entity, but are in need of replacement in favour of something more flexible and adaptable to changing circumstances.

Entity Z

Entity Z, with a market share in Country Y of 10%, is a comparatively new and small, but fast growing unquoted family-owned entity. It specialises in certain niche markets for high security and extra heat-resistant glass. The patents for this specialist glass were developed by the founder owner who now acts as Managing Director. The development of the business has largely been funded by high levels of borrowings at rates of interest well above standard market rates. In addition, the directors have often been required to provide personal guarantees against personal assets.

The management team of Z works in the capital city of Country Y, which is in the more prosperous southern part of the country. Z has a manufacturing base on the outskirts of the capital city.

The management team of Z is enthusiastic to grow the business, but is continually frustrated by a lack of financial and human resources and marketing network that would enable Z to expand into international markets. Also, on a personal level, many of the senior managers own a substantial number of shares in Z and are keen to realise some of their capital gains and become financially more secure.

The computer systems of Z consist of a basic accounting package and an internal network of PCs. Spreadsheet packages are widely used for budgeting and other financial reporting.

Takeover bid

The directors of Q have approached the directors of Z with a view to making a takeover bid for Z. A condition of the bid would be the retention of the current management team of Z, who have vital knowledge of the specialist manufacturing techniques required to manufacture the product range of Z. The directors of Z have been initially quite positive about the bid.

Both parties are concerned that the deal may be referred to Country Y's Competition Directorate, which regulates the country's competition policy, for approval and that conditions may be imposed that could make the takeover less attractive.

Required:

(a) Explain the role of competition authorities such as Country Y's Competition Directorate.

(15 minutes)

(b) Advise the directors of Q and Z on the potential problems of merging the management structure and systems of the two entities and how these could be minimised.

(15 minutes)

(c) Discuss whether the choice of capital structure for the new combined entity is likely to affect the overall value of the entity. Include references to Modigliani and Miller's (M & M's) theory of capital structure in your answer.

(30 minutes)

Test your understanding answers

Test your understanding 1 (Integration question)

Big Data management involves using sophisticated systems to gather, store and analyse large volumes of data in a variety of structured and unstructured formats. Companies are collecting increasing volumes of data through everyday transactions and marketing activity. If managed effectively this can lead to many business benefits although there are risks involved.

If MONEY acquires CASH it will get access to a significant amount of new data regarding a potentially brand new customer base. MONEY needs to consider whether this new data is going to be manageable and whether it will provide useful information.

If, following the acquisition, the two companies are going to continue to be managed as completely separate entities then it may be complicated to integrate the systems to be able to perform sophisticated analysis across the two sets of data. MONEY therefore need to be clear what the objective of such analysis may be and whether the business benefits make it worthwhile.

MONEY would need more information on the current customer base of CASH to identify if there are any likely cross-selling opportunities. Although CASH provides loans to small businesses and start-ups, it is quite possible that some of these companies will have entrepreneurs in control who will be high net worth individuals, if not now then at some point in the future. Having access to information about such individuals can allow MONEY to produce more targeted marketing activity and increase its client base relatively easily. This can work both ways as CASH can identify from MONEY's clients possible lending opportunities as some of these clients are likely to be business owners.

If the two companies are concerned that their individual clients may not like being targeted by other companies, another option is to use the data available to expand the product range for each entity. So MONEY could offer its clients an increased range of borrowing options and CASH could offer its clients investment advice.

Test your understanding 2 (Case style question)

- Operating efficiencies – the unused capacity at GSL can be used to produce Williams' products without adding to costs and capacity.

- Marketing synergies.

- If the cash flow streams of Williams and GSL are not perfectly positively correlated then by acquiring GSL – Williams may reduce the variability of their operating cash flow. This being more attractive to investors may lead to cheaper financing.

- The 'dedicated' herbalists of GSL and the R+D staff of Williams may be a complementary resource.

- Fixed operating and administrative costs savings.

- Consolidation of manufacturing capacity on fewer and larger sites.

- There may be bulk buying discounts.

- Possibility of joint advertising and distribution.

- GSL is badly managed – thus the elimination of inefficiency could allow for financial synergy.

Test your understanding 3 (Objective test question)

The answer is (D).

The VC is making a B$ 180 million equity investment. To generate a return of 25% a year on a compound basis this investment will need to grow to B$ 439.5 million (= B$ 180 million × (1.25)4) at the end of 4 years.

The VC investment represents 80% (= 180/(180 + 45) × 100%) of the equity, therefore the total equity value will need to be B$ 549.3 million (= B$ 439.5 million/0.80).

Test your understanding 4 (Objective test question)

The answer is (C).

All the other decisions are ones that would be perfectly acceptable in the normal course of business.

The value of the subsidiary's assets is likely to be a key issue when determining the consideration to be paid in the MBO, so revaluing assets could be contentious.

Test your understanding 5 (Objective test question)

The answer is (C).

The two businesses seem to have very little in common, so the combination would be referred to as a conglomerate.

Test your understanding 6 (Objective test question)

The answer is (C), (D) and (E).

The two businesses operate in the same region so combining them should lead to an opportunity to combine administrative roles (D), make more profit due to less competition (C) and wield greater purchasing power over suppliers (E).

Test your understanding 7 (Objective test question)

The answer is (B), (D) and (E).

The managers do own enough of the equity to enable them to vote and carry decisions in a general meeting; they have 10 million votes and the venture capitalists have 3 million votes (A).

If HH Co were to go into liquidation, the **secured** bank borrowing would take priority (C).

Test your understanding 8 (Objective test question)

The answer is (B), (C) and (E).

Diversification of risk (A) can be done more effectively by investors rather than companies.

Directors should only undertake acquisitions if there are benefits to shareholders, rather than considering their own career prospects (D).

Test your understanding 9 (Objective test question)

The answer is (B).

When an MBO team wants to buy a company, they will almost certainly be reluctant to co-operate with the sale to an outside buyer.

Although the MBO team will know more about the company than an outside buyer (C) this is not a matter of direct concern to the selling company.

Since the parent company has two potential buyers, avoiding redundancy costs (A) is not an issue either. Either purchaser would have to consider the need for redundancies after the takeover. There would be no cost to the parent.

There is no particular reason why a sale to an MBO team would be quicker than a sale to an external purchaser (D).

Test your understanding 10 (Case style question)

Answer to the first task

TNL may wish to acquire TT in order to:

- Gain economies of scale/synergistic benefits. For example, TNL and TT could share the same booking internet site.

- Increase market power. By offering ferry services as well as rail services, TNL will have increased influence over ferry prices in addition to rail prices. This increase in power could be used to its advantage.

- Increase customer loyalty. Marketing promotions (e.g. frequent traveller schemes) could be shared across TNL and TT, reducing marketing costs and increasing customer loyalty and convenience by offering a 'one-stop' shop for both rail and ferry tickets.

- Increase market share through cross subsidies or a price war. TNL could offer rail link passenger reduced cost ferry tickets or cross subsidise the ferry business by reducing fares for the ferries (financed by higher priced rail link tickets) in order to build its market share of the ferry business. TNL could use a price war in the ferry business to build market share and destroy competition, funding by profits from the rail link business.

- Obtain tax relief. TNL may be able to make use of tax losses incurred by TT by offsetting losses against any profits in TNL.

Competition authorities intervene where it is considered that the bid would have a serious effect on competition in the market by giving significant market power to a particular market participant or where the bid is contrary to public interest.

The competition authorities of the Trade Grouping would be particularly interested due to the reduction in competition that would arise in a key communication link between two countries in the Union. Country T's competition authorities may be less concerned as the move would give Country T a competitive advantage over Country V.

In this case, there is a high risk to TNL that the competition authorities find grounds to investigate the proposed acquisition further. If TNL were to own all ferry and rail links from Country T, it could be in a position to control prices and affect competition It already has a monopoly position in respect of the rail link and it may not be considered in the public interest to also allow TNL to acquire significant control over the ferry operation. For example, it could raise prices for rail link passengers and cross-subsidise the ferry business in an attempt to put VV out of business.

Whatever the final result, referring the bid to the regulatory authorities can be expected to significantly delay the bid and create uncertainty and costs for TNL at this key time when it needs to renegotiate bank borrowings. If they decide to intervene, the regulatory authorities would have the power to either prevent the acquisition going ahead or impose certain conditions on TNL. Such conditions might include, for example, price constraints or a requirement to operate the ferries from a port that is not so close to the rail link tunnel.

Answer to the second task

Issues that the banks are likely to consider:

- How will TNL pay back the original borrowings if the banks do not agree to renew the loans? Would the banks be likely to get any money back anyway?

- To what extent would the referral to the competition authorities affect TNL – for example, what price controls might be imposed and how would that affect TNL's profitability?

- What is the likely impact on TNL's future results of acquiring TT? Would it be likely, in practice, to realise synergistic benefits from the acquisition?

- Can TNL afford to buy TT; how would it be financed? Given that it is likely to be a hostile bid then TNL will need to pay a significant premium for TT.

- TNL's latest long term cash forecast and the sensitivity of cash flow to other possible government intervention (e.g. green taxes) or market prices (e.g. fuel and exchange rates, especially regarding V\$ costs and V\$ selling prices (regarding sales within Country V)).

- How do the credit ratings agencies view TNL? Have they put TNL on 'Negative outlook' to indicate the possibility of a downgrade in the next few months. How should this impact on the banks' willingness to lend and on the interest rate offered?

- Deterioration in gearing levels – and hence risk.

    - Gearing on 1 June 20X4: 34% (= 190/(190 + 370))

    - Current gearing: 39% (= 190/(295 + 190))

- Management reputation – has the original team left? What is the background and reputation of the current team?

- Impact of government assistance. If the tunnel is seen as strategically important for the Country might the Government step in and provide support to TNL. This would reduce the banks' risk.

Other sources of finance:

Rights issue

TNL may have to ask shareholders for cash by means of a rights issue if banks are unwilling to renew borrowings. However, investors may not be willing to invest additional sums of money in a company that has seen such a decline in the value of its shares in the last 10 years.

If the banks are unwilling or unable to rollover the borrowings, it is likely to be very difficult for TNL to be able to obtain finance from other sources such as, for example, bonds, because of its poor credit worthiness. Indeed, TNL may have no choice but to ask shareholders for cash by means of a rights issue if banks are unwilling to renew the bank borrowings.

Under a rights issue:

- Shareholders would be given the right to buy additional shares in proportion to their existing shareholding at a discount to the current share price.

- The share price is likely to fall, largely as a result of the discount.

However, a rights issue is a risky option in this case since the cash would be used to repay debt. Shareholders prefer to subscribe new capital to finance new projects and hence promote future growth and returns. Shareholders may not be willing to help finance the repayment of debt, especially since they have already seen their previous investment in TNL lose value.

The size of the rights issue could also be a problem – at a 20% discount shares would be issued at T$ 2.36 per share before taking issue costs into account. This equates to 80.5 million shares which is an 80.5% increase in the number of shares currently in issue. At this scale it is unlikely that any rights issue would be wholly successful. Even if the company were highly successful, shareholders may not have the funds or may be unwilling to make the additional investment.

Equity is more costly to service than debt and could lead to a reduction in the value of the company due to the loss of the tax benefit on debt interest.

Government funding

If the business is seen as key to Country T's trade position, then the government may be prepared to step in and offer funding as a last resort rather than see the company fail and the rail link cease to operate. This would result in conditions being imposed on TNL which might restrict its operations and future development.

Test your understanding 11 (Case style question)

(a) The Competition Directorate is a government-run or funded body which aims to protect competition within the local marketplace. Its brief will vary from country to country, but a Competition Directorate should consider the following issues:

– Whether a merger or acquisition is in the public interest. For example, there may be a policy to prevent all reservoirs being under one body for security reasons;

– Whether there would be substantial lessening of competition, leading to the risk of price setting and less competitive pricing so that the consumer is forced to pay an inflated price for goods or services;

– The ability to measure whether competition is still operating and prices set fairly after the merger has taken place. For example, for public utilities, there needs to be a sufficiently large number of utility entities to enable the regulator to compare prices with other entities in the same market.

(b) **Potential problems in merging the management structures and how to minimise them**

Potential problems that could be raised include the following:

– The importance of retaining the current management team. This is key to the success of the merger and plans to develop the business of Z;

– Different locations (opposing ends of the country);

– Spare capacity in the office building in the north of the country, but the management team of Z may well not be willing to move out of the capital. On the other hand, moving the management of Q down to the capital would result in an expensive empty office block in the north that may stand empty and, cost aside, there may not be a suitable office building to house the combined entity in or near to the capital city.

Possible solutions:

–   Offer the current management team an attractive salary package;

–   Obtain guarantees backed by financial incentives for management to stay with the business;

–   Determine which key employees and managers are willing to relocate and which operations need to be centralised and then identifies the lowest cost solution.

Potential problems in merging the systems and how to minimise them

Potential problems include:

–   Completely different type of systems at present: PC network for Z and bespoke system for Q. It is unlikely that Q could operate on a network of PCs and the transition would, in any case, be very problematic. On the other hand, it is unlikely that the different nature of the business of Z would fit well into the bespoke system that Q operates.

Possible solution:

–   The management may need to agree to run the systems independently and build an effective interface.

(c)   Under M & M, capital structure is irrelevant if you ignore taxes. However, if tax is included, debt becomes cheaper because of the tax shield and the value of the entity therefore increases as the proportion of debt increases. After a certain point, the entity reaches its debt capacity. That is, the level of debt at which there is a high risk of financial distress and both lenders and shareholders demand increased returns to compensate for the higher levels of risk.

From the information provided in the question, it would appear that Q is currently borrowing at levels well below its debt capacity and would therefore increase the value of the entity by taking on a higher proportion of debt.

Similarly, Z could well be borrowing in excess of its debt capacity and so its value would be enhanced by reducing the proportion of debt on its statement of financial position.

It is therefore highly likely that both entities would benefit from the improved capital structure that would result from a merger or takeover if Q were to fund the takeover of Z using debt or were to acquire Z together with its high levels of debt.

12

Business valuation

Chapter learning objectives

Lead outcome	Component outcome
D2: Evaluate the various valuation methods	(a) Evaluate different valuation methods
	(b) Discuss the strengths and weaknesses of each valuation method

Topics to be covered

- Asset valuation
- Valuation of intangibles
- Different methods of equity valuation (share prices, earnings valuation, dividend valuation, discounted cash flow valuation)
- Capital Asset Pricing Model (CAPM)
- Efficient market hypothesis

1 Overview of chapter

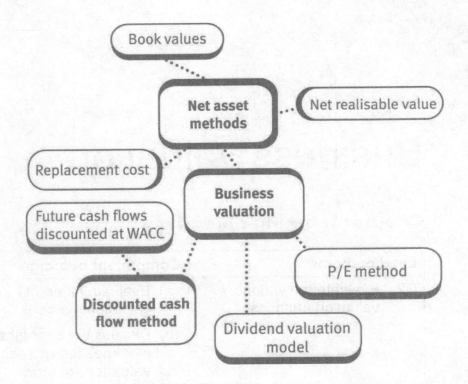

2 Introduction to business valuation

Business valuation is not a precise, scientific process. The value of a business is affected by:

- reported sales, profits and asset values

- forecast sales, profits and asset values

- type of industry

- level of competition

- range of products sold

- breadth of customer base

- perspective – the buyer and the seller will often have different expectations and hence may value the business differently.

The valuation methods covered in this chapter give suggested values of a business.

The final value is then agreed between buyer and seller after a process of negotiation.

Valuation of quoted and unquoted companies

Quoted (listed) companies

A quoted (or listed) company will have a stock market value (or market capitalisation).

If small numbers of shares are being traded on the stock market, this share price will be used by traders.

However, if one company is attempting to take over another by acquiring the majority of the shares, the market capitalisation value will not necessarily give a suitable value for the transaction, since the shareholders will not have any incentive to sell their shares at the current market price.

In order to encourage the shareholders in the target company to sell their shares, a premium is normally offered on top of the current stock market share price.

In conclusion, when valuing a listed company, the current stock market share price should be used as a starting point for the calculations rather than as a definitive final figure.

Unquoted (unlisted) companies

An unquoted (or unlisted) company has no stock market value. Also, there is likely to be less published information available which might help a purchaser to assess the value of an unlisted company. Unless there has been a recent private sale of the company's shares for a known value, the valuation process for an unlisted company is usually quite complex.

When valuing an unlisted company, estimates often have to be made, based on available information taken from similar listed companies ('proxy' companies).

The valuation methods shown below often value unlisted companies using data derived from proxy listed companies e.g. cost of equity, beta, dividend yield, P/E ratio.

In practice, it can be difficult to find a similar listed company.

The final answer may have to be discounted by 25% to 35% to account for:

- relative lack of marketability of unquoted shares – it is more difficult for investors to sell their shares if the company is not listed

- lower levels of scrutiny, therefore greater risk of poor quality financial information.

- higher risk of being a smaller, less well-regarded company with, possibly, a more volatile earnings record.

3 The different valuation methods

There are three basic ways of valuing a business:

Asset based valuation method

The business's assets form the basis for the valuation. Asset based valuation methods are difficult to apply to businesses with high levels of intangible assets, but this chapter covers methods of valuing intangible as well as tangible assets.

Earnings based valuation method

The projected earnings for a business will give an indication of the value of that business. For example, a business with high forecasted earnings will be attractive to a potential purchaser, and hence will be valued highly. In this chapter, we shall see how earnings can be used in business valuation.

Cash flow based methods

In theory, a business's value should be equal to the present value of its future cash flows, discounted at an appropriate cost of capital. This chapter explains how to identify and forecast future cash flows, and how to choose an appropriate discount rate.

Specifically, we shall see how the dividend valuation model can be used to value the business based on its expected dividend payments, and a discounted cash flow approach can be used to value the overall cash flows of the business.

 When should each method be used?

Although the most important thing is to know how to use the various methods to calculate values, it is also necessary to understand the circumstances in which each is most appropriate.

For example asset-based valuations have very limited relevance for entities which are going concerns especially if they have substantial intangible assets.

In each of the following sections, the various valuation methods are explained together with the circumstances in which they might be most appropriate.

 ## 4 Asset based valuation

In this method the company is viewed as being worth the sum of the value of its assets.

Remember to deduct borrowings when arriving at an asset value if just the equity is being acquired, but not if only the physical assets and related liabilities are being purchased without acquiring any liability for the borrowings.

An asset based valuation is most useful when a company is being broken up, rather than purchased as a going concern. Since the method does not incorporate the valuation of intangible assets, it usually gives a low valuation figure, which helps the parties to set a minimum price in a takeover situation.

Asset valuations are therefore likely to be more useful for capital-intensive businesses, than for service businesses, where many of the assets are intangible.

Alternative asset valuation bases

The asset valuation can be calculated in various ways:

Book value

This method suffers from being largely a function of depreciation policy, for example, some assets may be written down prematurely and others carried at values well above their real worth. Original costs may be of little use if assets are very old, or if asset replacement has been irregular over time.

Thus, this method is of little use in practice.

Replacement value

This method calculates the cost of replacing the business's assets, which may be relevant if the assets are going to be used on an on-going basis, or if the bidder wants to estimate the minimum price that would have to be paid to buy the assets and set up a similar business from scratch (especially if an estimate of intangible value can be added on).

Break-up value/Net realisable value

Individual assets are valued at the best price obtainable, which will depend partly on the second-hand market and partly on the urgency of realising the asset.

This method can be used to set a minimum selling price for the vendors, as they could liquidate the business as an alternative to selling the shares.

If a company has any tradable investments, including shares or digital assets such as cryptocurrency (e.g. Bitcoin, Litecoin), these should be valued at their current market price.

The strengths and weaknesses of asset based valuations

The main strengths of asset-based valuations are:

*   the valuations are fairly readily available;
*   they provide a minimum value of the entity.

The main weaknesses of asset-based valuations are:

*   future profitability expectations are ignored;

- statement of financial position valuations depend on accounting conventions, which may lead to valuations that are very different from market valuations;

- it is difficult to allow for the value of intangible assets. The valuation of intangibles is covered in detail below.

More detail on asset based valuation

An asset based valuation method for a listed company will usually give a value considerably lower than the market value of all the company's shares (the market capitalisation value).

So it should be obvious that shareholders/the market does not value the company on the basis of the statement of financial position's assets.

Shareholders are not buying the company for its assets but for the income those assets can produce.

This future income is generated from the use of the statement of financial position assets together with the intangible assets like highly skilled workforce, strong management team and competitive positioning of the company's products.

Thus assets in the crude sense of statement of financial position values are only one dimension of a company's overall value (in a normal going concern situation).

Test your understanding 1 (Integration question)

The summarised balance sheet (statement of financial position) of Owen at 31 December 20X7 is as follows:

Assets	$000
Non-current assets	23,600
Current assets	8,400
	32,000

Equity and liabilities	
Capital and reserves	
$1 Ordinary shares	8,000
Retained earnings	11,200
	19,200
Non-current liabilities	
6% Unsecured bond	8,000
Current liabilities	4,800
	32,000

Required:

Calculate the value of one ordinary share in Owen, using an asset based valuation method.

Fowler is wanting to make a bid for Owen.

It has estimated that the replacement cost of Owen's non-current assets is $40 million.

Required:

Calculate the value of a share in Owen from Fowler's perspective.

Test your understanding 2 (Integration question)

Ray plc, a UK listed manufacturing company, is considering a takeover bid for Ribbon Ltd, a smaller, unlisted company in the same industry.

Ribbon Ltd has been making losses in the last 2 years, so it is considered that an asset based method should be used to value the business.

Extracts from Ribbon Ltd's Statement of Financial Position

Assets	GBP000
Non-current assets (Note 1)	1,207
Current assets (Note 2)	564
	1,771

Equity and liabilities	
Capital and reserves	
GBP1 Ordinary shares	100
Retained earnings	553
	653
Non-current liabilities	
5% bonds	600
Current liabilities	518
	1,771

Note 1: The non-current assets comprise of specialised equipment. To replace the equipment would cost GBP1.5m, but if Ribbon Ltd were to be closed down, the assets would sell for no more than GBP1m.

Note 2: Receivables contain an amount of GBP120,000 from a large customer which has just gone into liquidation. A contract for the same customer, included in work in progress (inventory) at a value of GBP30,000 will now have to be scrapped.

Required:

Calculate the expected valuation of Ribbon Ltd, from the perspective of Ray plc. Explain and justify your figures.

5   Valuation of intangible assets

Definition of intangible assets

Intangible assets (intangibles) lack physical properties and represent legal rights or competitive advantages developed or acquired by an owner.

In order to have value, intangible assets should generate some measurable amount of economic benefit to the owner, such as incremental turnover or earnings (pricing, volume and better delivery, amongst others), cost savings (process economies and marketing cost savings) and increased market share or visibility.

Owners can exploit intangibles either in their own business (direct use) or through a licence fee or royalty (indirect use).

Characteristics of intangible assets

Intangible assets show the following four characteristics:

Identifiability

Intangible assets can be identified specifically with reasonably descriptive names and should see some evidence or manifestation of existence such as a written contract, licence, diskette, procedural documentation or customer list, amongst others. The intangible assets should have been created at an identifiable time (or event) and be subject to termination at an identified time (or event).

Manner of acquisition

Intangible assets can be purchased or developed internally.

Determinate or indeterminate life

A determinate life will usually be established by law or contract or by economic behaviour and should have come into existence at an identifiable time as the result of an identifiable event.

Transferability

Intangible assets may be bought, sold, licensed or rented and are subject to the rights of private ownership, ensuring a legal basis for transfer.

Specific examples of intangible assets

The "International Glossary of Business Valuation Terms" is a glossary of business valuation terms that defines intangible assets as "non-physical assets such as franchises, trademarks, patents, copyrights, goodwill, equities, mineral rights, securities and contracts (as distinguished from physical assets) that grant rights and privileges, and have value for the owner."

Many of these intangible assets are also referred to as intellectual capital, which can be defined as the value of an organisation's employee knowledge, skills, business training or any proprietary information that may provide the company with a competitive advantage.

More on intellectual capital

The term 'intellectual capital' has many complex connotations and is often used synonymously with intellectual property, intellectual assets and knowledge assets. Intellectual capital owned by a business is an important intangible asset.

Intellectual capital can be thought of as the total stock of capital or knowledge-based equity that the entity possesses. As such, intellectual capital can be both the end result of a knowledge transformation process or the knowledge itself that is transformed into intellectual property or intellectual assets of the firm. This can include information gathered through 'Big Data' analysis.

Intellectual capital includes:

- Human resources – The collective skills, experience and knowledge of employees. For a lot of service based businesses, this is likely to make up the bulk of the company's value

- Intellectual assets – Knowledge which is defined and codified such as drawing, computer program or collection of data

- Intellectual property – Intellectual assets which can be legally protected such as patents and copyrights.

Brands

Intellectual property is legally defined and assigns property rights to such things as patents, trademarks and copyrights.

These assets are the only form of intellectual capital that is regularly recognised for accounting purposes.

However, accounting conventions based upon historical costs often understate their value.

Companies can't recognise internally generated goodwill in their accounts, but on acquisition the value of any brand should be estimated and recognised.

Digital assets

Increasingly, digital assets are becoming a major part of many business's intangibles.

Digital assets include:

- Websites and apps
- Branding
- Cryptocurrency
- Domain Names
- And many more other forms of digital data

Valuation of intangibles (including digital assets) is covered in detail below, but there are additional considerations that make the valuation of digital assets even more complex than the valuation of other intangibles.

Changing regulations

Digital assets are a relatively new phenomenon and therefore as new assets and technologies develop, regulations surrounding the assets develop too.

When acquiring a business with lots of digital assets, the acquiring company needs to consider emerging regulations that could threaten future revenue streams

For example, governments and other regulatory authorities are currently consulting on potential regulatory models to shape the development of artificial intelligence, and are paying much closer attention to how an organisation's use of data affects both consumers and markets.

Usage rights

Digital assets are often created in partnership with third party consultants, so it is vital to consider usage rights when acquiring a company with digital assets.

Due diligence procedures should be designed to identify which party or parties have usage rights over the digital assets before the acquisition takes place. For example, uncertainty over the ownership of code created by contract consultants could cause the acquirer to pull out of the deal.

Valuation of intangible assets

It is recognised that intangible assets often have a significant value. Indeed many entities have intangible assets that are far more valuable than their tangible assets.

Intangibles may also be of significant importance to shareholders and other stakeholders, and are often a key part of integrated reporting.

The basic asset based methods covered earlier do not incorporate this value.

There are three basic ways of valuing the intangible assets of an entity:

1   **Market approach:**

Here the intangible asset is valued by comparing the asset to an identical (or very similar) one that has recently been traded in an arm's length transaction.

Unfortunately, for many intangible assets, such information is difficult if not impossible to obtain. Publicly available information usually reflects the market capitalisation of an entire business, not individual intangible assets.

However, it might be possible to find direct market evidence for intangibles such as carbon emission rights, internet domain names and licences (for radio stations, for example).

2   **Cost approach:**

For some intangibles like internally developed software (e.g. websites or apps) a cost approach to valuation can be used. Historic cost could be easy to identify, but in most cases, replacement cost new (the cost of a similar new asset) is the most direct and meaningful cost approach to estimating the value of an asset.

The problem with all cost approaches is that they ignore the amount, timing and duration of future economic benefits, as well as the risk of performance within a competitive environment.

3   **Income approach:**

Income based models are best used when the intangible asset is income producing or when it allows an asset to generate cash flow.

Just as in other valuation assignments (see later notes in this chapter), an income approach technique converts future benefits (such as cash flows or earnings) to a single, discounted amount, usually as a result of increased turnover or cost savings.

One of the main difficulties with an income approach method is distinguishing the cash flows uniquely related to the intangible asset from the cash flows related to the whole company.

Among the most common income based methods is the "Relief from royalty method", where the cost savings (or income enhancement) from using an intangible such as a trademark or patent are directly estimated. Under this "Relief from royalty method", value is based on the payment that would have been made had a third party licence been used (for the right to employ the asset to earn benefits).

Another common income based approach is a multi-period excess earnings model, such as the Calculated Intangible Value (CIV) method.

Calculated Intangible Value (CIV) method

The CIV method has been developed to estimate the value of a company's intangible assets that do not appear in its statement of financial position. It is used alongside the basic asset valuation to give a more accurate valuation of all the company's assets (both tangible and intangible).

The CIV method is based on a comparison of the total return that the company is producing against the return that would be expected based on industry average returns on tangible assets.

Any additional return is assumed to be the return on intangible assets.

This additional return is assumed to continue in perpetuity and can be converted into a present day value for intangibles (the Calculated Intangible Value, or CIV) by discounting at the company's cost of capital.

The value of intangible assets thus calculated is then added to the value of the tangible assets of the business to generate a total value.

i.e. Total value of the entity = Value of tangible assets + CIV

CIV is an adaption of the asset valuation method and suffers from the same drawback as the basic asset valuation method, in that it is based on historical figures. Unlike DCF valuations (covered later in this chapter) which look forward into the future and are based on forecast future outcomes when valuing a going concern.

Other drawbacks of CIV include:

– CIV assumes future growth in income from intangibles will be constant at the cost of capital.

– CIV is based on profit rather than cash flow.

– CIV is based on an industry average return which might not be representative of the company being valued.

Illustration of the CIV calculation (Objective test question)

UUU Co is a financial services company based in the USA.

It reported a profit before tax in the most recent financial year of USD 28.5 million, and the value of its tangible assets is USD 210 million.

The average return on tangible assets for firms in the financial services industry is 9%. The tax rate is 25% and UUU Co's cost of capital is 14%.

What is the value of UUU Co using the CIV approach?

A   USD 51.4 million

B   USD 217.2 million

C   USD 238.5 million

D   USD 261.4 million

Solution:

The answer is (D).

Workings:

		USDm
Current pre-tax profit		28.5
Less: Industry ROA × Tangible assets	9% × 210m	(18.9)
Excess annual return (pre-tax)		9.6
Post-tax excess annual return	9.6m × (1–0.25)	7.2
CIV (assuming constant perpetuity)	7.2m × 1/0.14	51.4

Therefore, the total value of UUU Co is estimated to be

$$210m + 51.4m = USD\ 261.4m$$

Test your understanding 3 (Objective test question)

Chapman Co has just reported a pre-tax profit of $24.29m, and the value of its tangible assets in its statement of financial position is $128.66m.

The average return on assets for companies in the same industry is 10%. The tax rate is 30% and Chapman Co's cost of capital is 16%.

What is the value of Chapman Co using the CIV approach?

A $179m

B $153m

C $137m

D $50m

6   Earnings based valuations

Introduction

In an earnings based valuation, the earnings of the business are forecasted and then an 'earnings multiple' is applied.

This earnings multiple could simply be a number negotiated between buyer and seller (e.g. a business could be valued at 3 times earnings), or it could be a perpetuity factor based on a suitable cost of capital. In this latter case, the earnings forecast is being taken as an approximation of cash flow and effectively a discounted cash flow approach is being used (see more details later in the chapter).

The most commonly used approach is to take a suitable P/E ratio as the earnings multiple.

P/E valuation method

The P/E valuation method is a very simple method which values the equity of a business by applying a suitable P/E ratio to the business's earnings (profit after tax).

Value of company's equity = Total post-tax earnings × P/E ratio

Value per share = EPS × P/E ratio

 Using the P/E valuation formula

The P/E ratio method is the simplest valuation method. It relies on just two figures (the post-tax earnings and the P/E ratio).

Post-tax earnings

The current post-tax earnings, or EPS, for a company can easily be found by looking at the most recent published accounts. However, these published figures will be historic, whereas the earnings figure needed for valuation purposes should be an expected, future earnings figure.

It is perfectly acceptable to use the published earnings figure as a starting point, but before performing the valuation, the historic earnings figure should be adjusted for factors such as:

- one-off items which will not recur in the coming year (e.g. debt write offs in the previous year);

- directors' salaries which might be adjusted after a takeover has been completed;

- any savings ('synergies') which might be made as part of a takeover.

P/E ratio

The P/E ratio for a listed company is a simple measure of the company's share price divided by its earnings per share.

The P/E indicates the market's perception of the company's current position and its future prospects. For example, if the P/E ratio is high, this indicates that the company has a relatively high share price compared to its current level of earnings, suggesting that the share price reflects good growth prospects of the company.

An unlisted company has no market share price, so has no readily available P/E ratio. Therefore, when valuing an unlisted company, a proxy P/E ratio from a similar listed company is often used.

Proxy P/E ratios

As explained above, an unlisted company will not have a market-driven P/E ratio, so an industry average P/E, or one for a similar company, will be used as a proxy.

However, proxy P/E ratios are also sometimes used when valuing a listed company – of course if a listed entity's own P/E ratio is applied to its own earnings figure, the calculation will just give the existing share price.

In particular, proxy P/E ratios are used in the context of bootstrapping, which is covered in the next chapter.

Test your understanding 4 (Objective test question)

Molier is an unquoted entity with a recently reported after-tax earnings of $3,840,000. It has issued 1 million ordinary shares with nominal value of $0.50 each. A similar listed entity has a P/E ratio of 9.

What is the current value of one ordinary share in Molier using the P/E basis of valuation?

A $34.56 million

B $69.12 million

C $34.56

D $69.12

The strengths and weaknesses of P/E method valuations

The main strengths of P/E method valuations are:

- they are commonly used and are well understood;
- they are relevant for valuing a controlling interest in an entity.

The main weaknesses of P/E method valuations are:

- they are based on accounting profits rather than cash flows;
- it is difficult to identify a suitable P/E ratio, particularly when valuing the shares of an unlisted entity;
- it is difficult to establish the relevant level of sustainable earnings.

Test your understanding 5 (Integration question)

Company X is considering a bid for Company Y.

X has earnings of $3m per annum, and Y has earnings of $1.5m per annum. The P/E ratio of X is 12 and that of Y is 8.

If the takeover proceeds, it is expected that synergies of $0.5m per annum will be generated, and that the combined company will have a P/E ratio of 11.

Required:

Calculate the maximum price that X should pay for Y, and the minimum price that Y should accept.

Earnings yield method

In some questions, you may not be given the P/E ratio, but you may be given the Earnings Yield instead.

The earnings yield is the reciprocal of the P/E ratio i.e. Earnings Yield = 1/ (P/E ratio).

Hence,

Value of company = Total earnings/Earnings Yield

Value per share = EPS/Earnings Yield

Understanding and interpretation of Earnings Yield

Some deeper analysis is desirable, for example examining the trend of share price over a number of quarters in the light of any events such as profits warnings and acquisitions (or rumours thereof), and the likely effect that they have had on earnings.

The stability of Earnings Yield is often as important as its growth, bearing in mind that in a general way the market is absorbing new information to try to assess a sustainable level of EPS on which to base growth for the future. Clearly, effective growth is dependent on a stable base, and the trend of Earnings Yield over time is to an extent a reflection of this factor.

A prospective acquirer would, of course, be concerned to assess the worth of a prospective target on the basis of its becoming part of the acquiring entity, and the valuation will especially need to take into account the expectations of the target's shareholders.

A further point relates to the acquirer's intentions regarding the target. If, for example the latter entity is to be partially demerged, that is certain parts disposed of other entities in which they would provide a better fit, then the share price valuation may well be greater than if the whole target entity was to be retained. Nevertheless, any such break-up considerations will need to take into account all the stakeholders, including employees, suppliers and customers of the target, as any serious demotivation will take away from the goodwill value of the acquisition and quite possibly damage that of the acquiring entity itself.

 ## 7 Cash flow valuation: The dividend valuation model

Dividend Valuation Model (DVM) Theory

The theory states that the value of the company/share is the present value of the expected future dividends, discounted at the shareholders' required rate of return.

This links to the NPV method covered earlier in your studies, where the discounted cash flows from a project represented the gain in wealth to shareholders if the project were undertaken – wealth (share value) is linked to discounted future cash flows.

If we assume that all cash flows to equity are paid out as dividends, the DVM would therefore give the same result as valuing a company by discounting cash flows to equity at the cost of equity.

DVM formula

Either $$P_0 = \frac{do}{k_e}$$ $$P_0 = \frac{do(1+g)}{k_e - g}$$

Assuming: a constant dividend **or** constant growth

Note that:

g = forecast future growth rate in dividends, and:

P_0 = Value of company, when do = Total dividends

P_0 = Value per share, when do = Dividends per share

Also, note that the simple formula (when assuming a constant dividend) is just a rearrangement of the standard dividend yield formula:

Dividend yield = (Dividend/Share price) × 100%

In fact, the formulae presented here are just short-cuts which can be applied if there is no growth, or if there is constant growth in dividends into perpetuity.

The dividend valuation model in its most basic form is just a cash flow discounting model, which can be used for any set of discrete future dividend cash flows even if they don't grow at a constant rate in perpetuity.

i.e. Value = (Dividend in 1 year × 1 year discount factor) + (Dividend in 2 years × 2 year discount factor) +....etc.

Test your understanding 6 (Integration question)

Target has just paid a dividend of EUR250,000. It has 2 million shares in issue.

The current return to shareholders in the same industry as Target is 12%, although it is expected that an additional risk premium of 2% will be applicable to Target, being a smaller and unlisted company.

Required:

Calculate the expected valuation of Target, if

(a)   dividends are expected to be constant

(b)   dividends are expected to grow at 4% per annum.

Forecasting growth – Gordon's growth model

Background

Gordon's growth model was developed by the economist Myron Gordon. It attempts to derive a future growth rate, rather than simply extrapolating the historical growth rate.

Gordon argued that an increase in the level of investment by a company will give rise to an increase in future dividends. Therefore, the two key elements in determining future dividend growth will be the rate of reinvestment by the company and the return generated by the investments.

Formula

Gordon's growth model formula is:

$g = r \times b$

where r = return on reinvested funds and b = proportion of funds retained.

Example

Bennett Co generates an average return on its investments of 10% per year. In recent years the company has paid out 40% of its earnings as a dividend.

Using Gordon's growth model, the expected future growth rate is:

$g = r \times b = 0.10 \times (1 - 0.40) = 0.06$ (6% per year)

Assumptions

There are a number of assumptions that underpin this model:

- the entity must be all equity financed;
- retained profits are the only source of additional investment;
- a constant proportion of each year's earnings is retained for reinvestment;
- projects financed from retained earnings earn a constant rate of return.

The strengths and weaknesses of dividend-based valuations

The strengths of dividend-based valuations are:

- value is based on the present value of the future dividend income stream (cash flow to an investor), so the method has a sound theoretical basis;
- they are useful for valuing minority shareholdings where the shareholder only receives dividends from the entity, over which he has no control.

The main weaknesses of using the dividend valuation model are:

- it is very difficult to forecast dividends and dividend growth, especially in perpetuity. For example, how can we predict whether there will be sufficient worthwhile projects to invest in over such a long term period? And what about the normal life cycle of a business – this could be the initial growth part of the cycle and not sustainable in the long term. Also, what about a new company that has yet to pay a dividend, that would be given a zero value under DVM but could actually be worth a considerable sum of money;

- particularly for unlisted companies, it can be difficult to estimate the cost of equity (note that in the exam, if you are not given the cost of equity, you should use CAPM to derive it, or use proxy company information). Also, for unlisted companies, a consistent dividend policy with constant growth rate is unlikely.

Uneven growth rates

The dividend valuation model formula cannot be used directly when the annual growth rate is expected to change.

In such cases, the entity's lifespan should be segmented into the periods for which the varying growth rates apply, and value each separately.

Illustration 1 (Integration question)

Target has just paid a dividend of EUR250,000. It has 2 million shares in issue.

The current return to shareholders in the same industry as Target is 12%, although it is expected that an additional risk premium of 2% will be applicable to Target, being a smaller and unquoted company.

Required:

Calculate the expected valuation of Target, if dividends are expected to stay constant for 3 years, then grow at 4% per annum thereafter.

Solution:

Separate the future dividend stream into two parts: first, the constant dividends for 3 years, then the growing perpetuity thereafter.

First 3 years

Present value of expected dividends = 250,000 × AF1–3 (14%) = EUR0.580m

Perpetuity from year 4:

Use the given DVM formula, then adjust for the fact that the dividend stream starts in year 4, not year 1 as normal:

[(250,000 × 1.04)/0.14–0.04)] × DF3 (14%) = EUR 1.755m

Total value = 0.580m + 1.755m = EUR 2.335m

or 2.335/2 = EUR1.17 per share.

Test your understanding 7 (Integration question)

Western Co has paid out a steadily growing dividend over the last few years, where dividends have grown at 2% per year. The company's cost of equity is 10% and the dividend just paid (at the most recent year end) was $1.5 million in total.

Western Co has 10 million shares in issue and its shares are valued at $1.91.

Change of future plans

A new chief executive has just been appointed. He has expressed his intention to change the dividend policy of Western Co, as follows:

> The next dividend (in 1 year's time) will be half of what it would have been under the previous dividend policy. Then, the chief executive hopes to be able to increase the dividend by 10% per year for the next three years, before increasing the dividend at 5% per year in perpetuity.

Required:

Calculate the likely change in share value if the new policy is introduced, on the assumption that the dividend valuation model is used to value the shares and that the proposed changes have been publicly announced to the market.

Concluding thoughts on the dividend valuation model (DVM)

The DVM demonstrates the underlying principle that a company is worth the sum of its discounted future cash flows.

However, DVM is based on very simplistic model, but does provide a useful analytical tool for investors to use to evaluate different assumptions about growth and future prospects.

The challenge is to make the model as applicable to reality as possible, which means using the most reliable assumptions available.

 ## 8 Cash flow valuation: Discounted cash flow method

Overview of the method

Under the discounted cash flow (DCF) method, a value for the equity of the entity is derived by estimating the future annual after-tax cash flows of the entity, and discounting these cash flows at an appropriate cost of capital. This is theoretically the best way of valuing a business, since the discounted value of future cash flows represents the wealth of the shareholders.

The cost of capital used to discount the cash flows should reflect the systematic risk of the cash flows.

Test your understanding 8 (Objective test question)

The expected after-tax cash flows of Thomas, an all equity financed company with 2 million shares in issue , will be as follows:

Year	GBP
1	120,000
2	100,000
3	140,000
4	50,000
5 onwards	130,000

A suitable cost of capital for evaluating Thomas is 12%.

What is the value of Thomas's equity (in total) using the DCF basis of valuation?

A   GBP 392,050

B   GBP 1,006,300

C   GBP 1,083,333

D   GBP 1,475,383

More details on cash flows and cost of capital

Cash flows to equity

Ideally, cash flows to equity should be used in DCF valuations rather than post-tax post-financing cash flows.

Cash flows to equity are similar to post-tax post-financing cash flows, except that they include average sustainable levels of capital and working capital net cash flow investments over the longer term rather than this year's figures.

Post-tax cash flows (after financing charges) are often used as an approximation for cash flows to equity.

However, where sufficient information is provided in a question to enable cash flows to equity to be calculated, cash flows to equity should be used in the DCF valuation instead of post-tax post-financing cash flows.

Free cash flow

The concept of 'free cash flow'

Free cash flow is the cash generated by the business that is 'freely' available for distribution to investors after having met all the immediate obligations of the business and investment in working capital and in non-current assets that is necessary to sustain on-going operations.

There are many different ways of defining free cash flow.

In CIMA materials and F3 OTQs you will find the following terms being used:

Cash flow to equity refers to cash flow generated by the company after tax, reinvestment needs and debt-related cash flows. That is, cash flow attributable to equity investors.

Cash flow to all investors refers to cash flow generated by the company after tax and reinvestment needs but before debt-related cash flows. That is, cash flow attributable to all investors, both debt and equity investors.

Free cash flow to equity is sustainable cash flow to equity, and free cash flow to all investors is sustainable cash flow to all investors.

Use of cash flows to equity

The value of the shareholders' stake (equity) in an entity is the sum of the future cash flows to equity discounted at the cost of equity.

Note that if we assume that a company pays out all of its cash flow to equity as a dividend, the DCF company valuation method (where cash flows to equity are discounted at cost of equity) will give exactly the same result as the DVM valuation method introduced earlier in the chapter, where the cash flows to equity used in the DCF calculation are assumed to grow at a constant rate and the same growth rate is used in the DVM valuation.

The problem of lack of information

In a project appraisal, the cash flows generated from the project are easily identifiable, but in a business valuation they can be harder to identify and quantify.

This is because there are so many of them, and because the necessary information does not usually exist in the public domain.

Therefore, for business valuation, we often have to estimate cash flows using readily-available accounting information.

How to calculate cash flow data from profit data

Cash flow to equity

1   Start with profit before interest and tax (PBIT).

2   Deduct tax for the year (see note, below) and interest to give profit for the year.

3   Adjust for non-cash items (e.g. add back depreciation).

4   Adjust for cash items such as capex/disposal of non-current assets; changes in working capital; new debt raised/debt repaid.

Note: Tax can be calculated as (PBIT – interest) × tax rate. Or, if tax depreciation allowances differ from depreciation, tax is: (PBIT + depreciation – tax depreciation allowances – interest) × tax rate.

Cash flow to all investors

1   Start with PBIT.

2   Deduct tax for the year, excluding tax relief on interest (see note, below).

3   Adjust for non-cash items (e.g. add back depreciation).

5   Adjust for cash items such as capex/disposal of non-current assets; changes in working capital.

Note: Tax can be calculated as PBIT × tax rate. Or, if tax depreciation allowances differ from depreciation, tax is: (PBIT + depreciation – tax depreciation allowances) × tax rate

Example of free cash flow to all investors

The recently published accounts of Matty show the following figures:

	$ million
Profit before interest and tax	220
Interest	40
Profit after interest but before tax	180
Tax expense (tax rate 20%)	36
Depreciation	8
Capital expenditure	70
Increase in working capital	10
Debt repayment	15

Required:

Calculate the free cash flow to all investors in the year.

Solution:

	$ million
Profit before interest and tax	220
Less tax expense based on PBIT: 20% × $220m	(44)
Plus depreciation	8
Less capital expenditure	(70)
Less increase in working capital	(10)
Free cash flow to all investors	104

Example of free cash flow to equity

The recently published accounts of Matty show the following figures:

	$ million
Profit before interest and tax	220
Interest	40
Profit after interest but before tax	180
Tax expense (tax rate 20%)	36
Depreciation	8
Capital expenditure	70
Increase in working capital	10
Debt repayment	15

Required:

Calculate the free cash flow to equity in the year.

Solution:

	$ million
Profit for the year (220 – 40 – 36)	144
Plus depreciation	8
Less capital expenditure	(70)
Less increase in working capital	(10)
Less debt repayment	(15)
Free cash flow to equity	57

Another example of free cash flow to equity

The recently published accounts of Carey show the following figures:

Operating profit (after deducting depreciation of USD 3m) = USD 32m

Interest paid = USD 2m

Taxation = USD 9m

Capital expenditure = USD 4m, which is assumed to represent a sustainable level of investment in non-current assets.

Required:

Calculate the free cash flow to equity in the year.

Solution:

Free cash flow to equity = 32m + 3m – 2m – 9m – 4m = USD 20m

An appropriate cost of capital

The introductory paragraph above explained that 'an appropriate cost of capital' should be used for discounting. In some exam questions, you will be told directly which cost of capital to use. However, in other cases you will be expected to either calculate or select an appropriate cost of capital. It is then important to understand the following relationships:

Use of cost of equity as a discount rate

The cost of equity can be used to discount the cash flows TO EQUITY (i.e. post-tax cash flows AFTER financing charges) in order to value the equity in a company directly.

Use of WACC as a discount rate

WACC can be used to discount the cash flows TO ALL INVESTORS (i.e. post-tax cash flows BEFORE financing charges) when valuing a project or an entity (debt + equity value). To find the company's equity value, the value of debt would need to be deducted.

In summary:

ENTITY VALUE	EQUITY VALUE / SHAREHOLDER VALUE
= equity value plus debt value	= entity value minus debt value
Discount cash flows attributable to all investors (i.e. after tax but before interest) at WACC	Discount cash flows attributable to equity investors (i.e. cash flows after tax and interest) at the cost of equity
	DEBT VALUE

Note that the equity valuation method is likely to more appropriate for divisions since they commonly report on a pre-financing basis. They do not have their own capital structure and therefore the cost of financing that is required to calculate entity value.

Use of proxy company information

The cost of capital used must reflect the risk of the entity's cash flows.

For listed companies, it is normally quite easy to identify the cost of capital, using the huge amount of information which is publicly known about the listed company. However, for an unlisted company, or perhaps a division of a company, it is much more difficult (due to lack of available information) to identify an appropriate cost of capital.

If a cost of capital is not given, or if is difficult to derive one, a proxy cost of capital from a similar listed company could be used instead. Much more detail on deriving a suitable cost of capital is presented in the next section below.

Test your understanding 9 (Integration question)

Chassagne Co is considering making a bid for Butler Co, a rival company.

The following information should be used to value Butler Co.

Statement of profit or loss for the most recent accounting period

	GBP m
Revenue	285.1
Cost of sales	(120.9)
Gross profit	164.2
Operating expenses (inc depreciation GBP 12.3m)	(66.9)
Profit from operations	97.3
Finance costs	(10.0)
Profit before tax	87.3
Taxation	(21.6)
Profit after tax	65.7

Other information

- selling prices are expected to rise at 3% per year for the next 3 years and then stay constant thereafter.

- sales volumes are expected to rise at 5% per year for the next 3 years and then stay constant thereafter.

- assume that cost of sales is a completely variable cost, and that other operating expenses (including depreciation) are expected to stay constant.

- Butler Co invested GBP 15m in non-current assets and GBP 2m in working capital last year. These annual amounts are expected to stay constant in future.

- Butler Co's financing costs are expected to stay constant each year in the future.

- the marginal rate of tax is 28%, payable in the year in which the liability arises.

- assume that book depreciation equals tax depreciation.

- Butler Co has 500 million shares in issue.

- the WACC of Butler Co is 9% and its cost of equity is 12%.

Required:

Calculate the value of the equity in Butler Co (in total and per share) by forecasting future cash flows to equity and discounting them to present value using cost of equity.

The strengths and weaknesses of cash-based valuations

The strengths of this method of valuation are:

- theoretically this is the best method of valuation;

- it can be used to place a maximum value on the entity;

- it considers the time value of money.

The weaknesses of this method are:

- it is difficult to forecast cash flows accurately;

- it is difficult to determine an appropriate discount rate;

- what time period should we evaluate in detail and then how do you value the company's worth beyond this period? i.e. the realisable value at the end of the planning period;

- the basic NPV method does not evaluate further options that may exist. However, the approach can be modified, by adding decision trees and probabilities to the analysis, to enable us to assess the sensitivity of the results to potential variations in cash flows;

- the basic model assumes that the discount rate and tax rates are constant through the period, although again this problem can be overcome by using sensitivity analysis and other methods of analysing risk such as probabilities and decision trees.

9 Deriving a suitable cost of capital for discounting

Introduction

In some questions, you will be told what the cost of capital of the entity is, so it will be clear what cost of capital to use for discounting the forecast cash flows.

However, in some questions you may only be given information for a proxy entity (if information for your chosen entity is not available).

When using a proxy cost of capital, care must be taken to ensure that it reflects the business risk and the capital structure of the entity being valued.

If necessary, a risk adjusted cost of capital could be used.

Risk adjusted cost of capital

In the earlier chapter on 'Financing – Capital structure' we saw how to use Modigliani and Miller's (M & M's) equations to adjust an entity's cost of equity or cost of capital to reflect a different capital structure.

In this chapter we shall revisit the M & M equations and also cover the Capital Asset Pricing Model (CAPM), which can also be used to derive a risk adjusted cost of capital for discounting.

Modigliani and Miller's (M & M's) equations

M & M's equations relating to cost of equity and cost of capital were introduced in the earlier chapter on 'Financing – Capital structure'. They are shown again below:

Cost of equity $\quad k_{eg} = k_{eu} + (k_{eu} - k_d) V_D(1 - t) / V_E$

WACC $\quad\quad\quad k_{adj} = k_{eu} [1 - (V_D t / (V_E + V_D)]$

where $\quad V_E$ = value of equity, V_D = value of debt

k_e = Cost of equity (k_{eg} = cost of equity in geared co, k_{eu} = cost of equity in ungeared co)

k_d = Cost of debt (must be gross of tax)

k_{adj} = the weighted average cost of capital in a geared company t = Corporation tax rate

WACC = weighted average cost of capital

Illustration 2 (Integration question)

Eamon Co is forecast to generate a constant stream of post-tax cash flows (after interest charges) of $10m per year.

The company is not listed, and no cost of equity has been calculated. However, a similar listed entity, Frank Co, which operates in the same business sector has a cost of equity of 10%.

Frank Co is all equity financed whereas Eamon Co has 20% debt and 80% equity by market values. The tax rate is 30%, and the yield on Eamon's debt is 4%.

Required:

Calculate the value of Eamon Co, using the discounted cash flow method.

Solution:

The given post-tax and post-interest cash flows need to be discounted using an appropriate cost of equity.

Although Frank Co operates in the same business sector, its gearing is different. Hence, a risk adjusted cost of equity (suitable to Eamon Co's circumstances) would be (using M & M's formula):

$$k_{eg} = k_{eu} + (k_{eu} - k_d)\,(1 - t)\,V_D / V_E$$

$$= 10\% + (10\% - 4\%)\,(1 - 0.30)\,20/80$$

$$= 11.05\%$$

Therefore, the value of Eamon Co's equity is $10m/0.1105 = $90.5m

The Capital Asset Pricing Model (CAPM)

The CAPM enables us to calculate the required return from an investment given the level of risk associated with the investment (measured by its beta factor).

Before showing how the CAPM formula can be used to derive a suitable risk-adjusted cost of capital for discounting, we first need to introduce the model and explain the terminology surrounding it.

In order to explain how the CAPM works, it is first necessary to introduce the concepts of systematic and unsystematic risk.

Systematic and unsystematic risk

There are two elements that make up the risk associated with a company:

- Unsystematic (or specific) risk is the risk of the company's cash flows being affected by specific factors like strikes, R&D successes, systems failures, etc.

- Systematic (or market) risk is the risk of the company's cash flows being affected to some extent by general macro-economic factors such as tax rates, unemployment or interest rates.

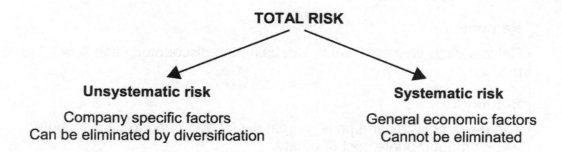

The impact of diversification

By holding a portfolio of investments, the unsystematic risk is diversified away but the systematic risk is not, so will be present in all portfolios.

For example, the return from a single investment in an ice-cream entity will be subject to changes in the weather – sunny weather producing good returns, cold weather poor returns. By itself the investment could be considered a high risk. If a second investment were made in an umbrella entity, which is also subject to weather changes, but in the opposite way, then the return from the portfolio of the two investments will have a much- reduced risk level. This process is known as diversification, and when continued can reduce portfolio risk to a minimum.

If an investor enlarges his portfolio to include approximately 25 shares the unsystematic risk is reduced to close to zero, the implication being that we may eliminate the unsystematic portion of overall risk by spreading investment over a sufficiently diversified portfolio.

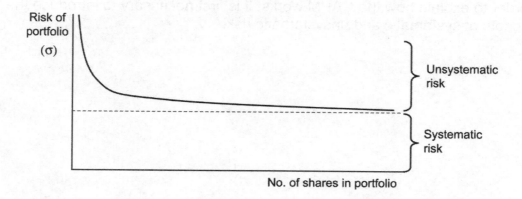

The capital asset pricing model (CAPM) enables us to calculate the required return for a well-diversified investor who is not subject to unsystematic risk.

If we can measure the systematic risk of a company or investment, the CAPM will enable us to calculate the level of required return.

β (beta) factor

The method adopted by CAPM to measure systematic risk is an index, β (beta). The β factor is the measure of a share's volatility in terms of market risk.

The β factor of the market as a whole is 1. Market risk makes market returns volatile and the ß factor is simply a yardstick against which the risk of other investments can be measured.

The β factor is critical to applying the CAPM; it illustrates the relationship of an individual security to the market as a whole, or conversely the market return given the return on an individual security.

Beta values fall into four categories, with the following meanings:

(i)   β > 1   The shares have **more** systematic risk than the stock market average.

(ii) β = 1   The shares have the **same** systematic risk as the stock market average.

(iii) β < 1   The shares have **less** systematic risk than the stock market average.

(iv) β = 0   The shares have no risk at all (if part of a well-diversified portfolio).

A share's beta value can be interpreted quite precisely:

β = 1.25   :   The shares have 25% **more** systematic risk than the average level on the stock market.

β = 0.80   :   The shares have 20% **less** systematic risks than the average. (i.e. they only have 80% of the average level).

The security market line (SML)

The security market line (SML) gives the relationship between systematic risk and return. We know two relationships:

1   **The risk-free security**

This carries no risk and therefore no systematic risk and therefore has a **beta** of zero.

2   **The market portfolio**

This represents the ultimate in diversification and therefore contains only systematic risk. It has a **beta** of 1.

The results may be plotted:

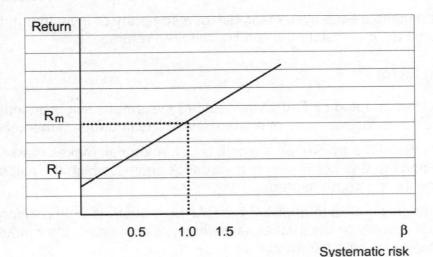

R_f is the point on the graph where the line intersects the axis, and then the higher the systematic risk, the higher the required rate of return.

The SML and the relationship between required return and risk can be shown using the formula shown below.

Formula – given in the exam

$$k_e = R_f + [R_m - R_f]\,\beta$$

where

k_e = required return from individual security

β = beta factor of individual security

R_f = risk-free rate of interest

R_m = return on market portfolio

Note: In exams, the question will sometimes refer to the market premium – this is the difference between Rm and Rf. It is the long term market premium that should be used in CAPM if this is different from current market rates.

 Calculating beta factors

Beta factors for a company are calculated statistically from past observed returns; for example the London Business School 'Risk Measurement Service' is published quarterly, using monthly returns from the previous five years to calculate each quoted share's beta.

Such an analysis begs two questions:

* Is it reasonable to use a beta factor, calculated from the past, as the basis of decision-making about the future?

* Are beta values observed to be stable over time?

Beta values tend to be more stable for highly diversified shares such as investment trusts than for more focused companies. Naturally beta will only be stable if the company's systematic risk remains the same, i.e. the company carries on the same areas of business in the long term.

Since betas are calculated statistically, the calculated beta value will be more reliable the more separate data went into its calculation. Therefore the longer the period underlying the calculations the better.

However if the beta will be used to estimate a required rate of return for a future project, it is important that the company's risk class in future will be more or less unchanged by accepting the project. Many businesses deal with this apparent paradox by using a sector average beta rather than using their own calculated beta.

The CAPM gives a required return for a given level of risk (measured by the beta factor).

Therefore, if we can estimate the level of risk associated with an entity (the beta of the entity), we can use CAPM to give a required return to shareholders.

This required return to shareholders is essentially the cost of equity which can then be used to derive an appropriate WACC for the entity.

Alpha values

If the CAPM stated that we should expect, on average, an annual return of 16.5%, this does not mean that the shares will produce a return (dividend yield plus capital gain) of 16.5% each year. Remember, shares are a risky investment which produces an uncertain annual return.

Suppose in one particular year, Company A shares produce an actual return of 18%. The shares are said to have produced a positive 'abnormal' return of 1.5% – that is, 1.5% higher than the expected return.

The alpha value of a share is simply its average abnormal return. Suppose Company A shares have an alpha value of +2%, this implies that in the recent past the shares have, on average, produced a return of 16.5% + 2% = 18.5%.

Alpha values can be either positive or negative, and in a perfect world they should be zero. In other words the average return that the shares actually do produce should be the same as the return indicated by CAPM. However, the world isn't perfect and so that will not always happen. Hence we get positive and negative alpha values.

Criticisms of the CAPM

1   CAPM is a single period model. This means that the values calculated are only valid for a finite period of time and will need to be recalculated or updated at regular intervals.

2   CAPM assumes no transaction costs associated with trading securities.

3   Any beta value calculated will be based on historic data which may not be appropriate currently. This is particularly so if the company has changed the capital structure of the business or the type of business it is trading in.

4   The risk free rate may change considerably over short periods of time. (5) CAPM assumes an efficient investment market where it is possible to diversify away risk. This is not necessarily the case, meaning that some unsystematic risk may remain.

6   Additionally, the idea that all unsystematic risk is diversified away will not hold true if stocks change in terms of volatility. As stocks change over time it is very likely that the portfolio becomes less than optimal.

7   CAPM assumes all stocks relate to going concerns, this may not be the case.

Asset betas, equity betas and debt betas

In order to calculate cost of equity and / or WACC for use in business valuation, we first need to expand our understanding of beta factors.

- The beta factor is a measure of the systematic risk of an entity relative to the market.

- This risk will be dependent on the level of business risk and the level of financial risk (gearing) associated with an entity.

- Hence, the beta factor for a geared company will be greater than the beta factor for an equivalent ungeared company.

The relationship between the beta factors for ungeared and geared companies is given by the following formula (given in the exam):

$$\beta_u = \beta_g \left[\frac{V_E}{V_E + V_D[1-t]} \right] + \beta_d \left[\frac{V_D[1-t]}{V_E + V_D[1-t]} \right]$$

where

β_g = the equity (geared) beta measures the systematic business risk and the systematic financial risk of a company's shares

β_u = the asset (ungeared) beta measures the systematic business risk only

β_d = the debt beta measures the risk associated with the debt finance. Usually we assume that debt is risk free and hence the debt beta is zero. If this is the case, the second term in the given formula disappears and the formula becomes:

$$\beta_u = \beta_g \left[\frac{V_E}{V_E + V_D[1-t]} \right]$$

More on systematic risk

The entity's systematic risk is important in the CAPM formula.

Remember:

- Shareholders are only interested in systematic risk because they hold well-diversified portfolios. Systematic risk of an entity is measured by its beta.

- Shareholders in a geared company suffer two types of systematic risk i.e. business and financial risk.

- The business risk of a company refers to the risk of the operating cash flows.

- Financial risk is the increased volatility of dividend payments to shareholders as gearing increases.

From the M & M analysis, we know that a share's systematic risk can be split up between the systematic **business** risk and the systematic **financial** risk.

Systematic business risk arises out of the risky nature of the company's business caused by:

- revenue sensitivity;

- proportion of fixed to variable production costs.

Systematic financial risk arises out of how the company has financed itself – its gearing or capital structure.

 Use of the formula: Degearing and regearing beta factors

For example, suppose a question tells you that the ABC company has a gearing ratio (D : E) of 1 : 2; the shares have a beta value of 1.45 (the equity beta); and the corporation tax rate is 30%. Then:

$$\beta_u = 1.45 \times \frac{2}{2 + 1 \times (1 - 0.30)} = 1.074$$

Note: If a question only states the beta, assume it is an equity beta. Also, if there is no mention of a debt beta, assume it is zero.

This indicates that shareholders in ABC have a beta value/systematic risk exposure of 1.45. Of this value, 1.074 arises out of the risky nature of the company's business (its business risk) and the rest (i.e. 1.45 − 1.074 = 0.376) arises out of the financial risk caused by the company's capital structure.

Notice four very important implications of this analysis:

1   A company's equity beta will always be greater than its asset beta, except

2   if it is all equity financed (and so has no financial risk), when its equity beta and asset beta will be the same.

3   Companies in the same 'area of business' (i.e. same business risk) will have the same asset beta, but

4   companies in the same area of business will not have the same equity beta unless they also happen to have the same capital structure.

As we shall see, the third of these points is particularly important.

Application to business valuation

There are two ways in which the gearing/degearing formula above can be used in order to derive a cost of equity and/or a WACC that can be used in business valuation.

Both methods start from the assumption that you have been given an equity beta for a proxy company.

- **Method 1:** Use the formula to derive the proxy entity's ungeared beta factor. Assume that this beta factor also reflects the business risk of the entity being valued, so regear this ungeared beta to reflect the capital structure of the entity being valued. Then use CAPM to derive a cost of equity for the entity being valued and (if necessary) use this ke in the standard WACC formula to find the entity's WACC.

- **Method 2:** Use the formula to derive the proxy entity's ungeared beta factor, then use CAPM to find an 'ungeared cost of equity' (keu) for the proxy entity. On the assumption that this keu is also a measure of the ungeared cost of equity of the entity being valued (same business risk), use M & M's WACC formula to calculate the WACC of the entity being valued.

(**Note:** Method 2 can only be used to calculate WACC, whereas Method 1 derives both cost of equity and WACC.)

Both methods will now be illustrated, to show that they give the same answer for WACC.

Illustration 3 (Integration question)

We are trying to value the company Garvey Co, an unlisted company with an estimated debt:equity ratio of 1:2. Post-tax cash flows before financing charges have been forecasted, so a suitable WACC is now needed for discounting. Since Garvey Co is an unlisted company, it has been difficult to derive a WACC for Garvey Co directly, because the necessary information is not readily available. Therefore, it has been decided to use proxy information as a starting point.

Information for Rocket Co, a listed company in the same business sector as Garvey Co is as follows:

	Rocket Co
Current geared (equity) beta	1.86
Current capital structure ratio (D:E by market value)	1:1

The tax rate is 30% and the return on the stock market has been 12% per annum in recent years. Debt is assumed to be risk free and has a pre-tax cost of 5% per annum.

Required:

Calculate a suitable WACC for Garvey Co.

Solution:

Method 1

Step 1

Rocket Co's ungeared / asset beta is calculated and then used as an estimate of Garvey Co's asset beta (because Garvey Co and Rocket Co are in the same area of business and so will have the same asset beta). Since debt is risk free, use

$$\beta_u = \beta_g \times \left[\frac{V_E}{V_E + V_D[1-t]}\right]$$

$$\beta_u = 1.86 \times \left[\frac{1}{1 + 1(1 - 0.30)}\right] = 1.09$$

Step 2

A geared / equity beta for Garvey Co is calculated next. As we know, an equity beta reflects both systematic business risk and systematic financial risk. Garvey Co's equity beta will reflect the business risk of Garvey Co and Rocket Co, and the capital structure of Garvey Co (1:2 D:E).

Using: $\beta_g = \beta_u [1 + (V_D (1 - t)/V_E)$

So: $\beta_g = 1.09 [1 + (1 \times (1 - 0.30)/2)]$

So: $\beta_g = 1.47$

Step 3

This equity beta is then input into the CAPM to give a cost of equity capital for Garvey Co:

$k_e = R_F + [R_M - R_F] \beta_g$

$k_e = 5\% + [12\% - 5\%] \times 1.47 = 15.3\%$

Step 4

The WACC is now calculated using the standard WACC formula:

$$k_o = k_{eg}\left[\frac{V_E}{V_E + V_D}\right] + k_d(1-t)\left[\frac{V_D}{V_E + V_D}\right]$$

$= 15.3\% \times (2/3) + 5\% \times (1 - 0.30) \times (1/3) = 11.4\%$

Method 2

Step 1

As above, the existing geared/equity beta of Rocket Co is degeared, to give an ungeared/asset beta of 1.09.

Step 2

Input this ungeared beta into the CAPM formula to give an ungeared cost of equity (k_{eu})

k_{eu} = 5% + [12% – 5%] × 1.09 = 12.6%

Step 3

Use the M & M WACC formula:

k_{adj} = k_{eu} (1 – tL)

= 12.6% (1 – 30% × (1/3)) = 11.4% as before.

Test your understanding 10 (Objective test question)

QQQ is planning a takeover bid for ABC, a telecoms company with a D : E ratio of 1 : 3.

The cash flows (after tax but before interest) for ABC have been forecasted, and now the directors of QQQ are trying to estimate a suitable WACC to use for discounting.

XYZ is a 'typical' listed telecoms company. It has an equity beta of 1.25 and a D : E ratio of 1 : 2.

Assume that RF = 6%, RM = 14%, and the tax rate is 30%. It is assumed that corporate debt is risk-free (and so the debt beta is zero).

Which of the following is a WACC that could be used in the valuation of ABC?

A   12.4%

B   14.8%

C   15.1%

D   18.3%

The EMH and business valuation

Implications of the Efficient Market Hypothesis (EMH) in business valuation

The level of efficiency in the market is very important when considering the value of a business.

According to the Efficient Market Hypothesis (EMH) the share price is a sum of all the known information about a company. As such the share price is always a 'fair price' and a true valuation – a particular share is neither under or over valued at any point in time.

This means that without additional information, currently not taken into account by the share price, no investor will be able to 'beat the market'. The only way to get higher returns, would be to invest in higher risk (higher beta factor) investments.

Weak form of efficiency

In the weak form of market efficiency, the share price will reflect any and all information that can be discerned by past trends in share prices. The day traders and other investors who attempt to speculate by studying past trends and predicting future movements will be wasting their time (and money) if markets are weak form efficient.

If such speculators can foresee movements then their actions will have the effect of updating the share price. The very fact of them, say, buying shares that are going to increase in price will push up the price.

Semi-strong form of efficiency

In the semi-strong form of the EMH, the share price will reflect all information that is publicly available. Analysts who study press reports, financial statements and economic figures in order to identify mispriced shares are wasting their time if the semi-strong form of the EMH is true.

Again, though, it could be possible to benefit from the ability to follow news in real time and to respond to events before they become public knowledge. Investors generally subscribe to information sources that give immediate access to news as soon as it is released, and before it has been broadcast. Again, their response to such news will enable the market to update itself because a flurry of sales by major investors will signal that "bad" news has become available.

Strong form of efficiency

In the strong form of the EMH, the share price will reflect all information, even if it has not been made publicly available. That may not seem credible, but information could be leaked because of, say, insider trading. The markets may not know why blocks of shares are being purchased or sold, but the fact that someone is trading will suggest that unknown person is in possession of some facts and the price may respond accordingly. Insider trading is illegal, but that does not always deter perpetrators.

Impact on business valuation

The EMH does not necessarily mean that it is wrong to pay a premium over the market price in order to acquire control. The bidder is usually hoping to benefit from an exploitable synergy. Even so, the EMH suggests that the markets will take the possibility of a future bid into account in setting prices.

Weak form efficiency might suggest that patterns of past trades can be a sign of a future bid. Semi-strong efficiency might suggest that any information that suggests the possibility of a bid (perhaps a loss-making company that requires the support that could only be obtained from being incorporated into a larger group) will affect the price. Strong-form efficiency suggests that share prices could rise because a dishonest employee who knows about an impending bid could start to buy shares in the target company and so signal the possibility of positive news.

Summary of valuation methods: When should each be used?

This chapter has covered the different valuation methods in turn, and has separately identified the strengths and weaknesses of each of the methods.

To conclude, we should consider the circumstances in which each valuation method is most useful.

Asset based methods

The asset based valuation methods are most appropriate when valuing capital intensive businesses with plenty of tangible assets.

For a service business, the asset based approach is likely to significantly undervalue the business, unless some effort is also made to value the intangible assets of the business.

Note however that in times of uncertainty, the asset based approach avoids the need to forecast future earnings or cash flows, so it may be favoured in these circumstances.

Dividend valuation model (DVM)

The DVM is a suitable valuation method when valuing a minority shareholding in a company, because if an investor purchases a minority stake, the dividends represent the forecast income from the investment, which will impact his wealth.

If the investor were to purchase a majority stake, it would be more relevant to consider overall company cash flows or asset values as a basis for the valuation.

P/E method and discounted cash flow method

Both these methods are based on forecasts of the future, and often use proxy information from proxy companies. These factors may be difficult to identify in practice.

Providing that the forecasts are accurate, these methods value the business based on its future prospects, so automatically include a measure of the goodwill / intangible assets associated with a business.

For service businesses, these methods are generally preferred to the asset based methods.

10 End of chapter objective test questions

Test your understanding 11 (Objective test question)

A company is planning to sell a wholly owned subsidiary (B) on 1 January 20X1 and is preparing a valuation for B as at that date using a discounted cash flow approach.

Additional information:

- The net operating cash flows of B are forecast to be $250 million in the year to 31 December 20X1 and are expected to remain at this level every year thereafter.

- New equipment at a cost of $200 million will need to be paid for on 1 January 20X1. Tax depreciation allowances can be claimed over 4 years on a straight line basis on this equipment.

- The corporate income tax rate is 30%. Tax is paid a year in arrears.

- Assume all cash flows arise at the end of the year unless stated otherwise.

- B has a financial year ending 31 December each year.

The trainee accountant has begun to produce an analysis of net cash flow for the valuation which is shown below. All figures are in $ million.

Select the TWO grid squares that contain an error.

Time (years)	0	1	2	3–5	6+
Net operating cash flow (NOCF)	–	250	250	250	250
Tax on NOCF	–	–	(75)	(75)	(75)
New equipment	(200)	–	–	–	–
Tax relief on new equipment	–	15	15	30	–

Test your understanding 12 (Objective test question)

Company XX is using the Calculated Intangible Value (CIV) company valuation method to value its intangible assets.

Key data:

- XX has a WACC of 12%, cost of debt of 7% and cost of equity of 14%

- Net profit before tax for XX is $50 million

- XX's tangible assets are $67 million

- Average industry return on tangible assets is 16%

- Corporate income tax is 20%

Complete the following CIV calculation:

CIV = [$50 million – ([UNKNOWN FIGURE 1] × $67 million)] × [UNKNOWN FIGURE 2]/0.12

[UNKNOWN FIGURE 1] is

A   0.16

B   0.12

C   0.07

D   0.14

[UNKNOWN FIGURE 2] is

E   0.80

F   0.20

G   1.20

H   1.80

Test your understanding 13 (Objective test question)

You are a management accountant working for Mega Co.

The directors of Mega Co have asked you to prepare some business valuation calculations for a potential target company, Mini Co.

They are particularly keen for you to use an asset based valuation method.

Which THREE of the following are potential problems with valuing Mini Co using an asset based method?

A   The asset based method might under-value Mini Co if it has significant intangible assets

B   The asset based method might over-value Mini Co if it has recently revalued its non-current assets

C   The asset based method will not be useful if Mini Co has been making losses in recent years

D   The asset based method ignores the future prospects and earnings potential of Mini Co

E   Mega Co, as the acquiring company, will be interested in the replacement cost valuation of Mini Co's assets, but replacement costs might not be readily available.

Test your understanding 14 (Objective test question)

You have been asked to calculate the equity beta factor for VERA.

Introductory data:

- BLAIZE is a listed company in the same industry as VERA. It has an equity beta of 1.45.

- Gearing levels – (debt/equity) by market value:

   – VERA   45/55

   – BLAIZE   30/70

- Tax rate is 25%. The beta of debt is 0.10.

Which one of the following shows the correct formula for ungearing the proxy company's equity beta (which would be the first step in trying to calculate an equity beta for VERA):

A $\quad \beta_u = 1.45 \times \dfrac{70}{100} + 0.10 \times \dfrac{30}{100}$

B $\quad \beta_u = 1.45 \times \dfrac{55}{55 + 45\,(1 - 0.25)} + 0.10 \times \dfrac{45\,(1 - 0.25)}{55 + 45\,(1 - 0.25)}$

C $\quad \beta_u = 1.45 \times \dfrac{40}{40 + 30\,(1 - 0.25)} + 0.10 \times \dfrac{30\,(1 - 0.25)}{40 + 30\,(1 - 0.25)}$

D $\quad \beta_u = 1.45 \times \dfrac{70}{70 + 30\,(1 - 0.25)} + 0.10 \times \dfrac{30\,(1 - 0.25)}{70 + 30\,(1 - 0.25)}$

Test your understanding 15 (Objective test question)

The systematic risk of an project's return is the result of uncertainties in the return caused by

A   factors unique to the project

B   factors unique to the entity undertaking the project

C   factors unique to the industry to which the project belongs

D   nationwide economic factors

11   End of chapter case style questions

Test your understanding 16 (Case style question)

The board of directors of Predator plc, a UK company, is considering making an offer to purchase Target Ltd, a private limited company in the same industry. If Target Ltd is purchased it is proposed to continue operating the company as a going concern in the same line of business.

Summarised details from the most recent financial statements (statements of financial position and statements of profit or loss) of Predator and Target are shown below:

	Predator plc as at 31 March		Target Ltd as at 31 March	
	£m	£m	£000	£000
Freehold property		33		460
Plant and equipment		58		1,310
Inventory	29		330	
Receivables	24		290	
Cash	3		20	
less current liabilities	(31)	25	(518)	122
		116		1,892
Financed by: Ordinary shares		35		160
Reserves		43		964
Shareholders' funds		78		1,124
Medium term bank borrowings		38		768
		116		1,892

Predator plc, 50 pence ordinary shares, Target Ltd, 25 pence ordinary.

	Predator plc		Target Ltd	
Year	PAT	Dividend	PAT	Dividend
	£m	£m	£000	£000
T5	14.30	9.01	143	85.0
T4	15.56	9.80	162	93.5
T3	16.93	10.67	151	93.5
T2	18.42	11.60	175	102.8
T1	20.04	12.62	183	113.1

NB: T5 is five years ago and T1 is the most recent year.

Target's shares are owned by a small number of private individuals. Its managing director, who receives an annual salary of £120,000, dominates the company. This is £40,000 more than the average salary received by managing directors of similar companies. The managing director would be replaced if Predator purchases Target.

The freehold property has not been revalued for several years and is believed to have a market value of £800,000.

The value of plant and equipment in the statement of financial position is thought to reflect its replacement cost fairly, but its value if sold is not likely to exceed £800,000. Approximately £55,000 of inventory is obsolete and could only be sold as scrap for £5,000.

The ordinary shares of Predator are currently trading at 430 pence ex-div. A suitable cost of equity for Target has been estimated at 15%.

Both companies are subject to corporation tax at 33%.

Required:

Estimate the value of Target Ltd using the different methods of valuation and advise the board of Predator as to how much it should offer for Target's shares.

(30 minutes)

Test your understanding 17 (Case style question)

AB is a telecommunications consultancy based in Europe that trades globally. It was established 15 years ago. The four founding shareholders own 25% of the issued share capital each and are also executive directors of the entity.

The shareholders are considering a flotation of AB on a European stock exchange and have started discussing the process and a value for the entity with financial advisors. The four founding shareholders, and many of the entity's employees, are technical experts in their field, but have little idea how entities such as theirs are valued.

Assume you are one of AB's financial advisors. You have been asked to estimate a value for the entity and explain your calculations and approach to the directors. You have obtained the following information.

Summary financial data for the past three years and forecast revenue and costs for the next two years is as follows:

Statements of profit or loss for the years ended 31 March

	20X4 (actual) EURm	20X5 (actual) EURm	20X6 (actual) EURm	20X7 (actual) EURm	20X8 (actual) EURm
Revenue	125.0	137.5	149.9	172.0	198.0
Cash operating costs	37.5	41.3	45.0	52.0	59.0
Depreciation	20.0	22.0	48.0	48.0	48.0
Pre-tax earnings	67.5	74.2	56.9	72.0	91.0
Taxation	20.3	22.3	17.1	22.0	27.0

Statements of financial position at 31 March

	20X4 EURm	20X5 EURm	20X6 EURm
Assets			
Non-current assets			
Property, plant and equipment	150	175	201
Current assets	48	54	62
	198	229	263
Equity and liabilities			
Equity			
Share capital (EUR 1 shares)	30	30	30
Retained earnings	148	179	203
	178	209	233
Current liabilities	20	20	30
	198	229	263

Note: The book valuations of non-current assets are considered to reflect current realisable values.

Other information/assumptions

- Growth in after tax cash flows for 20X9 and beyond (assume indefinitely) is expected to be 3% per annum. Cash operating costs can be assumed to remain at the same percentage of revenue as in previous years. Depreciation will fluctuate but, for purposes of evaluation, assume the 20X8 charge will continue indefinitely. Tax has been payable at 30% per annum for the last three years. This rate is expected to continue for the foreseeable future and tax will be payable in the year in which the liability arises.

- The average P/E ratio for telecommunication entities' shares quoted on European stock exchanges has been 12.5 over the past 12 months. However, there is a wide variation around this average and AB might be able to command a rating up to 30% higher than this;

- An estimated cost of equity capital for the industry is 10%;

- The average pre-tax return on total assets for the industry over the past 3 years has been 15%.

Required:

(a) Calculate a range of values for AB, in total and per share, using methods of valuation that you consider appropriate. Where relevant, include an estimate of value for intellectual capital.

(30 minutes)

(b) Discuss the methods of valuation you have used, explaining the relevance of each method to an entity such as AB. Conclude with a recommendation of an approximate flotation value for AB, in total and per share.

(30 minutes)

Note: A report format is not required for this question.

Test your understanding answers

Test your understanding 1 (Integration question)

Assuming the statement of financial position values are realistic, the valuation is:

	$000
Non-current assets	23,600
Current assets	8,400
Less: 6% Unsecured bond	(8,000)
Less: Current liabilities	(4,800)
	19,200

So the value per share is $19,200,000/8,000,000 = $2.40

(Note that the asset value of $19,200,000 is equal to the value of the ordinary share capital plus reserves.)

Fowler's perspective

Value per share = ($19,200,000 + $40,000,000 − $23,600,000)/8,000,000

= $4.45

Test your understanding 2 (Integration question)

GBP000		Explanation/justification
Non-current assets	1,500	Ray plc is buying the business, so would have to buy the machinery from scratch if it decided on the alternative of organic growth. The realisable value will be a useful minimum value from Ribbon Ltd's perspective, but it is not relevant to Ray plc.
Current assets (564–120–30)	414	The inventory and receivables relating to the bankrupt customer will not be acquired by Ray plc. They are therefore excluded from the valuation.
Less: 5% bonds	(600)	
Less: Current liabilities	(518)	In order for Ray plc to takeover Ribbon Ltd, it needs to buy the equity of the business. After the takeover, Ray plc will be responsible for meeting these liabilities, so they should be included in the valuation of Ribbon Ltd.
	796	

Value per share = GBP 796,000/100,000 = GBP 7.96

Test your understanding 3 (Objective test question)

The answer is (A).

Workings:

		$m
Current pre-tax profit		24.29
Less: Industry ROA × Tangible assets	10% × 128.66m	(12.87)
Excess annual return		11.42
Post-tax excess annual return	11.42m × (1–0.30)	7.99
CIV (assuming constant perpetuity)	7.99m × 1/0.16	49.94

Therefore, the total value of Chapman Co is estimated to be

128.66m + 49.94m = $178.60m (approx $179m)

Test your understanding 4 (Objective test question)

The answer is (C).

Workings:

EPS = 3,840,000/1,000,000 shares = $3.84

Value per share = P/E × EPS = 9 × $3.84 = $34.56

Test your understanding 5 (Integration question)

The maximum that X should be prepared to pay for Y is the total increase in value generated by taking over Y, i.e.

Value of combined	= 11 × (3m + 1.5m + 0.5m)	= $55m
Less value of X	= 12 × 3m	= $36m
Max. price to pay	= $19m.	

However, the shareholders of Y will value their company at 8 × 1.5m = $12m since they will not have enough information to enable them to value the expected synergies.

The price paid by X to take over Y is then likely to fall somewhere between these two valuations, depending upon the negotiating skills of the buyer and seller.

Test your understanding 6 (Integration question)

(a) $Po = \dfrac{250{,}000}{0.14}$

= EUR 1.786 million, or 1.786/2 = EUR 0.893 per share.

(b) $Po = \dfrac{250{,}000 \times 1.04}{0.14 - 0.04}$

= EUR 2.6 million, or 2.6/2 = EUR 1.30 per share.

Test your understanding 7 (Integration question)

Dividend in 1 year would have been $1.5 million × 1.02 = $1.53 million.

Therefore under the new policy it will be half of this i.e. $0.765 million.

So the present value of dividends for the next four years, discounted at 10%, will be:

(0.765 × 0.909) + (0.765 × 1.10 × 0.826) + (0.765 × 1.10^2 × 0.751) + (0.765 × 1.10^3 × 0.683)

= $2.780 million

After the first four years, the dividends will settle into a growing perpetuity, whose present value is:

[(0.765 × 1.10^3 × 1.05)/0.10 – 0.05] × 0.683 = $14.604 million

Therefore, the total value is $2.780 million + $14.604 million = $17.384 million, or approximately $1.74 per share for each of the 10 million shares.

This is a fall of $0.17 per share.

Test your understanding 8 (Objective test question)

The answer is (B).

Workings:

Year	GBP	DF (12%)	PV
1	120,000	0.893	107,160
2	100,000	0.797	79,700
3	140,000	0.712	99,680
4	50,000	0.636	31,800
5	130,000	0.567	73,710
		NPV	392,050

However, this ignores cash flows after year 5. Assuming the year 5 cash flow continues to infinity, this has a present value of:

130,000/0.12 = GBP 1,083,333

This has a present value today of:

GBP 1,083,333 × 0.567 = GBP 614,250

This gives a total present value (value of equity) of:

614,250 + 392,050 = GBP 1,006,300

Test your understanding 9 (Integration question)

GBPm	Year 1	Year 2	Year 3 etc
Sales (×1.03 ×1.05)	308.3	333.5	360.6
Cost of sales (×1.05)	(126.9)	(133.3)	(140.0)
Gross profit	181.4	200.2	220.6
Operating expenses	(66.9)	(66.9)	(66.9)
Financing costs	(10.0)	(10.0)	(10.0)
Forecast profit before tax	104.5	123.3	143.7
Less Taxation (28%)	(29.3)	(34.5)	(40.2)
Add back depreciation	12.3	12.3	12.3
Less Capital expenditure	(15.0)	(15.0)	(15.0)
Less Working capital investment	(2.0)	(2.0)	(2.0)
Forecast cash flows to equity	70.5	84.1	98.8
DF 12%	0.893	0.797	0.797/0.12
Present value	63.0	67.0	656.2

So the net present value = GBP786.2m

This is the total value of the equity in Butler Co.

With 500 million shares in issue, this corresponds to a value of

786.2/500 = GBP 1.57 per share.

Test your understanding 10 (Objective test question)

The answer is (A).

Workings:

Method 1

Step 1

XYZ's asset beta is calculated and then used as an estimate of ABC's asset beta (because ABC and XYZ are in the same area of business and so will have the same asset beta).

Using: $\beta_u = \beta_g \times \left[\dfrac{E}{E + D\,[1-t]}\right]$

$\beta_u = 1.25 \times \left[\dfrac{2}{2 + 1\,[1 - 0.30]}\right] = 0.926$

Step 2

An equity beta for ABC is calculated next. As we know, an equity beta reflects both systematic business risk and systematic financial risk. ABC's equity beta will reflect ABC's business risk and ABC's gearing of 1:3.

Using: $\beta_u = \beta_g \times \left[\dfrac{E}{E + D\,[1-t]}\right]$

$0.926 = \beta_g \times \left[\dfrac{3}{3 + 1\,[1 - 0.30]}\right]$

$0.926 = \beta_g \times 0.811$

$\dfrac{0.926}{0.811} = \beta_g = 1.14$

Step 3

This equity beta is then input into CAPM to give a cost of equity capital for ABC:

$k_e = R_F + [R_M - R_F]\,\beta_g$

$K_e = 6\% + [14\% - 6\%] \times 1.14 = 15.12\%$

Step 4

ABC's WACC is now calculated.

However, before we can do this calculation, we need to identify ABC's after-tax cost of debt capital. In many questions this information is given, but here it is not.

If you need a cost of debt in order to answer a question, but are not given one, then you can make use of the fact that we are allowed to assume 'corporate debt is risk-free'. In these circumstances:

$$k_d = R_F$$

and $k_d(1-t) = R_F(1-T)$

Therefore: $k_d(1-t) = 6\% \ (1 - 0.3) = 4.2\%$

Hence the WACC can be calculated using:

$$WACC = k_e \times \frac{E}{V} + k_d(1-t) \times \frac{D}{V} = 15.12\% \times \frac{3}{4} + 4.2\% \times \frac{1}{4} = 12.4\%$$

Alternatively: Method 2

Step 1

As above, the existing geared/equity beta of XYZ is degeared, to give an ungeared/asset beta of 0.926.

Step 2

Input this ungeared beta into the CAPM formula to give an ungeared cost of equity (k_{eu})

$$k_{eu} = 6\% + [14\% - 6\%] \times 0.926 = 13.4\%$$

Step 3

Use the M & M WACC formula $k_{adj} = k_{eu} (1 - tL)$

$=13.4\% \ (1 - 30\% \times (1/4)) = 12.4\%$ as before.

Test your understanding 11 (Objective test question)

The two cells containing errors are highlighted in bold below:

Time (years)	0	1	2	3–5	6+
Net operating cash flow (NOCF)	–	250	250	250	250
Tax on NOCF	–	–	(75)	(75)	(75)
New equipment	(200)	–	–	–	–
Tax relief on new equipment	–	**15**	15	**30**	–

The new machine is bought on 1 January 20X1, so the first tax depreciation allowance will be claimed at the end of 20X1. However, because tax is paid a year in arrears in this scenario, the tax relief on this first allowance would only be received one year later, at the end of 20X2 (corresponding to year 2 in the table).

The 30 in the 'year 3-5' column implies that $30m of tax relief would be received each year in year 3, 4 and 5. This is not the case. The figures should be split into separate columns for years 3, 4 and 5.

The tax relief figures should appear as $15m each year in years 2, 3, 4 and 5.

Test your understanding 12 (Objective test question)

[UNKNOWN FIGURE 1] is (A) 0.16 and [UNKNOWN FIGURE 2] is (E) 0.80

The missing figures were industry return on assets as [UNKNOWN FIGURE 1] and (1-tax rate) as [UNKNOWN FIGURE 2].

Test your understanding 13 (Objective test question)

The answer is (A), (D) and (E).

If Mini Co has recently revalued its assets, arguably the asset based method will be more accurate (B).

If Mini Co has been making losses recently, asset based valuations are unaffected (C). Admittedly earnings based valuations might be more problematic.

Test your understanding 14 (Objective test question)

The answer is (D).

Use the given formula, and make sure that Ve and Vd are the equity and debt values for the proxy company (BLAIZE in this case).

Test your understanding 15 (Objective test question)

The answer is (D).

Systematic risk reflects variations in the return of a security due to general market factors.

Test your understanding 16 (Case style question)

The approaches to use for valuation are:

1   Asset valuation

2   Dividend valuation model

3   P/E ratio/Earnings valuation.

1   **Asset valuation**

Target is being purchased as a going concern, so realisable values are irrelevant.

	£000
Net assets per accounts (1,892 – 768)	1,124
Adjustments to freehold property (800 – 460)	340
Adjustment to inventory	(50)
Valuation	**1,414**

Say £1.4m

2   **Dividend valuation model**

The average rate of growth in Target's dividends over the last four years is 7.4% on a compound basis.

Growth working: $(113.1/85.0)^{(1/4)} - 1 = 0.074$

The estimated value of Target using the dividend valuation model is therefore:

Valuation $\dfrac{£113,100 \times 1.074}{0.15 - 0.074} = £1,598,281$ **Say £1.6m**

3   **P/E ratio/Earnings valuation**

A suitable P/E ratio for Target will be based on the P/E ratio of Predator as both companies are in the same industry.

P/E of Predator: $\dfrac{70m \times £4.30}{£20.04}$ or $\dfrac{430}{28.63} = 15$

Target's maintainable earnings are:

£183,000 + (£40,000 × 67%) = £209,800 after adjusting for the savings in the director's remuneration.

The estimated value is therefore £209,800 × 15 = £3,147,000, **say £3.1m.**

Advice to the board

On the basis of its tangible assets the value of Target is £1.4m, which excludes any value for intangibles.

The dividend valuation gives a value of around £1.6m.

The earnings based valuation indicates a value of around £3.1m, which is based on the assumption that not only will the current earnings be maintained, but that they will increase by the savings in the director's remuneration. It is also based on a proxy P/E ratio of 15 which was taken from a much larger listed company with a higher level of historic growth. Arguably this P/E ratio is too high for the circumstances of Target.

On the basis of these valuations an offer of around £2m would appear to be most suitable. The directors should, however, be prepared to increase the offer to:

Maximum price:

It is worth noting that the maximum price Predator should be prepared to offer is:

The NPV of the combined group after the acquisition	X
The NPV of the acquiring company before the acquisition	(X)
Maximum price	**X**

If synergy occurs this could justify a higher price than shown by the valuation methods illustrated.

The comment on the maximum price is particularly appropriate in this question as this an example of horizontal integration where considerable synergies normally exist.

Test your understanding 17 (Case style question)

(a)   **Calculations**

Methods that could be considered are:

– Asset value

– Market capitalisation

– Dividend/earnings valuation model

– NPV

Each method is calculated as follows:

Asset value

The statement of financial position for 20X6 shows net assets of EUR233m (€233m). However, this entity clearly has substantial intellectual capital, which the value of tangible assets in the statement of financial position does not reflect. An estimate of the value of an intangible asset can be attempted as follows.

This method involves taking the excess returns on tangible assets and uses this figure as a basis for determining the proportion of return attributable to intangible assets.

1   Calculation of average pre-tax earnings for three years:

(€67.5m + €74.2m + €56.9m)/3 = €66.2m

2   From the statement of financial position the average year end tangible assets over the last three years is calculated as:

(€198m + €229m + €263m)/3 = €230m

3   The return on assets is calculated by dividing earnings by average assets as follows:

(€66.2m/€230m) × 100 = 28.8%

4   The industry's return on assets for this same three years is 15% (as per the scenario).

5   Multiply the industry average pre-tax return on assets by the entity's average tangible assets to show what the average telecoms entity would earn from that amount of tangible assets:

€230m × 15% = €34.5m

Subtract this from the entity's pre-tax earnings:

€66.2m – €34.5m = €31.7m

This figure shows how much more AB earns from its assets than the average telecommunications company.

6   The after tax premium attributable to intangible assets is calculated as follows:

    (a)   Three-year average income tax rate = 30%

    (b)   Excess return = €31.7m

    (c)   Multiply (i) by (ii) = €9.5m

    (d)   (ii)–(iii) = €22.2m

7   The NPV of the premium is calculated by dividing the premium by the entity's cost of capital as follows:

€22.2m/0.08 = €277m

If the NPV of the estimated value of intellectual capital is added to the value of net tangible assets we get €263m + €277m = €540m, less current liabilities gives a net figure of €510m.

Tutorial Note: Candidates would have gained credit for any valid attempt to place a value on intellectual capital.

Market capitalisation/PE method

If we use the industry average P/E of 12.5 the potential value is €497.5m. If AB can command a rating up to 30% higher, this value rises to €646.7m.

Note: €497.5m is calculated as €56.9m (20X6 pre-tax earnings) less €17.1m (taxation) multiplied by 12.5 (industry average P/E)

Dividend/earnings model

There is insufficient information to use the DVM, although earnings could be used as a proxy. However, as the future growth rate is not constant the simplified model cannot be used. The NPV approach would give broadly similar results.

NPV

	20X7 EURm	20X8 EURm
After tax profit	50	64
Add: Depreciation	48	48
Cash flow	98	112
DF 10%	0.909	0.826
PV	89	93

DCF of cash flows for 20X9 and beyond are

€112m × 1.03 × 0.826/(0.10 − 0.03) = €1.361m

NPV = €89m + €93m + €1,361m = €1,543m

Tutorial Note: The calculations here use the industry average cost of capital. An acceptable alternative would use 8%, the earnings yield (reciprocal of P/E ratio of 12.5). In this case the NPV would be €2,164m.

Summary of valuations

	Total EURm	Per share EUR
Asset value	233	7.70
Asset value including intellectual capital	510	17.00
PE method	497–647	16.57–21.57
NPV	1,543	51.43

(b) **Discussion of methods and recommendation**

Asset value

Asset value has little relevance except in specific circumstances such as a liquidation or disposal of parts of a business. Asset value is of even more limited usefulness in an entity such as AB, which earns a substantial proportion of its income from intellectual capital that generally does not feature in the statement of financial position.

Market capitalisation / PE method

The P/E basis of valuation has the advantage that it bases value on the future earnings of the entity. In a listed entity, the P/E ratio is used to describe the relationship between the share price (or market capitalisation) and earnings per share (or total earnings). It is calculated by dividing the price per share by the earnings per share. Market capitalisation is the share price multiplied by the number of shares in issue. Market capitalisation is not necessarily the true value of an entity as it can be affected by a variety of extraneous factors but for a listed entity it provides a benchmark that cannot be ignored in, say, a take-over situation.

In the case of an unlisted entity, a P/E ratio that is representative of similar quoted entities might be used as a starting point for arriving at an estimated market value, based upon the present earnings of the unlisted entity. The potential market capitalisation would be the entity's latest earnings multiplied by the benchmark P/E ratio.

AB is an unlisted entity so it does not have a market capitalisation or a quoted P/E ratio. Applying the industry average P/E provides a benchmark but not a very good one. As noted in the scenario, there is a wide variation around this average. Also, although not stated, the definition of the industry is likely to be very broad. A better approach might be to find an entity similar to AB and apply its P/E. Again, this is very rough and ready. As AB is unlisted there are arguments for both lowering and raising the P/E as compared with either a proxy entity or the industry average. The Financial Advisor's estimate is that AB could command a rating 30% higher than the industry average. It is not clear how this estimate was made, as an argument could be made for lowering the P/E ratio to reflect the higher risk and lower liquidity of such entities. It would be more appropriate to use the NPV method and adjust the discount rate – as discussed below.

NPV/Earnings method

Forecasting cash flows and discounting at a specific risk adjusted discount rate is the theoretically correct valuation method. The valuation here uses the industry average cost of equity. Using an industry average suffers from the problems noted above. Also, the cost of equity will include an element of return for financial risk if entities have debt in their capital structure. Many entities included in the industry average will have substantial debt finance.

What is needed here is an exercise to calculate a more accurate cost of capital. As with using the P/E ratio approach, discussed above, finding a proxy entity may be more reliable than using an industry average.

Recommendation

As shown in the summary table in part (a), the likely market value ranges from €233m (net tangible assets) to €1,543m (NPV). The NPV valuation is substantially higher than any of the others. While this method is theoretically correct, the reliability of the results does of course depend on the accuracy of the forecast cash flows and the discount rate used. Using growth in perpetuity (although a sensible simplification for examination purposes) is unrealistic.

None of the figures produced by this exercise is wholly reliable, neither is it expected to be, as this is simply an estimate based on incomplete information. The main recommendation must be to conduct a more detailed evaluation involving other advisors such as the entity that will be responsible for the flotation. It needs also to be established what percentage of their shareholding each director wishes to sell on flotation and how many new shares will need to be reissued. The calculations have been made on the current number of shares in issue to the directors/founding shareholders.

However, if a recommendation has to be made, a flotation value in the region of €600m or €20 per share would be conservative.

(**Tutorial Note:** Any sensible recommendation, or argument for not making one on the evidence available, would gain credit.)

A secondary recommendation would be to split the shares in readiness for a flotation. The share prices produced by all valuation methods, except asset value, are 'heavy' – that is buyers would not get many shares for their money. More shares would need to be in issue to allow a reasonably liquid market in them.

Pricing issues and post-transaction issues

Chapter learning objectives

Lead outcome	Component outcome
D3: Analyse pricing and bid issues	Analyse: (a) Pricing issues (b) Bid issues
D4: Discuss post transaction issues	Discuss: (a) Post transaction value (b) Benefit realisation

Topics to be covered

- Forms of consideration and terms of acquisition
- Target entity debt
- Methods of financing a cash offer and refinancing target entity debt
- Bid negotiation
- Post-transaction value incorporating effect of intended synergies
- M&A integration and synergy benefit realisation
- Exit strategies

1 Overview of chapter

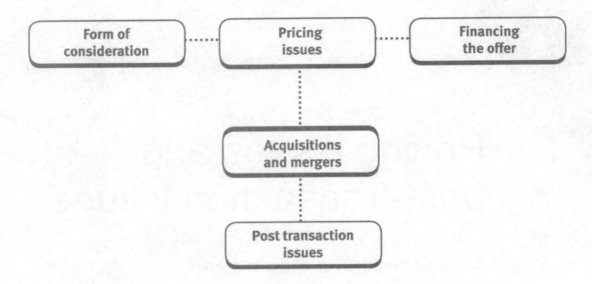

The last two chapters have covered business valuation and strategic issues associated with acquisitions and mergers, in particular the concept of synergy.

This chapter continues to look at acquisitions and mergers, but we now move on to look at practical matters such as what form of consideration should be used in an acquisition (for example cash or a share exchange) and the negotiation process that surrounds a bid.

2 Defences against hostile takeover bids

Any listed company needs to be aware that a bid might be received at any time.

The directors of a company subject to a hostile takeover bid should act in the best interests of their shareholders. However, in practice they will also consider the views of other stakeholders (such as employees, and themselves).

If the board of directors of a target company decides to fight a bid that appears to be financially attractive to their shareholders, then they should consider one of the following defences:

- Pre-bid defences
    - Communicate effectively with shareholders
    - Revalue non-current assets
    - Poison pill
    - Change the Articles of Association to require 'super majority' approval for a takeover

- Post-bid defences
  - Appeal to their own shareholders
  - Attack the bidder
  - White Knight
  - Counterbid – sometimes called a 'Pacman' defence
  - Refer the bid to the Competition authorities

 Details of takeover defences

Pre-bid defences

Communicate effectively with shareholders

This includes having a public relations officer specialising in financial matters liaising constantly with the entity's stockbrokers, keeping analysts fully informed, and speaking to journalists.

Revalue non-current assets

Non-current assets are revalued to current values to ensure that shareholders are aware of true asset value per share.

Poison pill strategy

Here a target company takes steps before a bid has been made to make itself less attractive to a potential bidder. The most common method is for existing shareholders to be given rights to buy future bonds or preference shares. If a bid is made before the date of exercise of the rights, then the rights will automatically be converted into full ordinary shares.

Super majority

The Articles of Association are altered to require that a higher percentage (say 80%) of shareholders have to vote for the takeover.

Post-bid defences

Appeal to their own shareholders

For example, by declaring that the value placed on the target company's shares is too low in relation to the real value and earning power of the company's assets, or alternatively that the market price of the bidder's shares is unjustifiably high and is not sustainable.

A well-managed defensive campaign would include:

(i) Aggressive publicity on behalf of the company preferably before a bid is received. Investors may be told of any good research ideas within the company and of the management potential or merely be made more aware of the company's achievements.

(ii) Direct communication with the shareholders in writing stressing the financial and strategic reasons for remaining independent.

Note: Under the City Code in the UK, any forecasts must be examined and reported on by the auditors or consultant accountants.

Attack the bidder

Typically concentrating on the bidder's management style, overall strategy, methods of increasing earnings per share, dubious accounting policies and lack of capital investment.

White Knight strategy

This is where the directors of the target company offer themselves to a more friendly outside interest. This tactic should only be adopted in the last resort as it means that the company will lose its independence. This tactic is acceptable provided that any information given to a preferred bidder is also given to a hostile bidder. The alternative company's management will be considered to be sympathetic to the target company's management.

Counterbid, or Pacman defence

Where the bidding company is itself the subject of a takeover bid by the target company.

Competition authorities

The target entity could seek government intervention by bringing in the Competition authorities. For this to be effective it would have to be proved that the takeover was against the public interest.

 ## 3 The form of consideration for a takeover

Introduction

When one firm acquires another, two questions must be addressed regarding the form of consideration for the takeover:

1 what form of consideration should be offered? Cash offer, or share exchange, or earn-out are the three main choices.

2 if a cash offer is to be made, how should the cash be raised? The choice is generally debt finance or a rights issue to generate the cash (if the entity does not have enough cash already).

The key considerations regarding these two questions are outlined below.

Form of consideration

Cash

In a cash offer, the target company shareholders are offered a fixed cash sum per share.

This method is likely to be suitable only for relatively small acquisitions, unless the bidding entity has an accumulation of cash.

Advantages:

- When the bidder has sufficient cash the takeover can be achieved quickly and at low cost.

- Target company shareholders have certainty about the bid's value i.e. there is less risk compared to accepting shares in the bidding company.

- There is increased liquidity to target company shareholders, i.e. accepting cash in a takeover, is a good way of realising an investment.

- The acceptable consideration is likely to be less than with a share exchange, as there is less risk to target company shareholders. This reduces the overall cost of the bid to the bidding company.

Disadvantages:

- With larger acquisitions the bidder must often borrow in the capital markets or issue new shares in order to raise the cash. This may have an adverse effect on gearing, and also cost of capital due to the increased financial risk.

- For target company shareholders, in some jurisdictions a taxable chargeable gain will arise if shares are sold for cash, but the gain may not be immediately chargeable to tax under a share exchange.

- Target company shareholders may be unhappy with a cash offer, since they are 'bought out' and do not participate in the new group. Of course, this could be seen as an advantage of a cash offer by the bidding company shareholders if they want to keep full control of the bidding company.

Share exchange

In a share exchange, the bidding company issues some new shares and then exchanges them with the target company shareholders. The target company shareholders therefore end up with shares in the bidding company, and the target company's shares all end up in the possession of the bidding company.

Large acquisitions almost always involve an exchange of shares, in whole or in part.

Advantages:

- The bidding company does not have to raise cash to make the payment.

- The bidding company can 'boot strap' earnings per share if it has a higher P/E ratio than the acquired entity (terminology explained later in this chapter).

- Shareholder capital is increased – and gearing similarly improved – as the shareholders of the acquired company become shareholders in the post-acquisition company.

- A share exchange can be used to finance very large acquisitions.

Disadvantages:

- The bidding company's shareholders have to share future gains with the acquired entity, and the current shareholders will have a lower proportionate control and share in profits of the combined entity than before.

- Price risk – there is a risk that the market price of the bidding company's shares will fall during the bidding process, which may result in the bid failing. For example, if a 1 for 2 share exchange is offered based on the fact that the bidding company's shares are worth approximately double the value of the target company's shares, the bid might fail if the value of the bidding company's shares falls before the acceptance date.

Earn-out

 Definition of an earn-out arrangement: A procedure whereby owners/managers selling an entity receive a portion of their consideration linked to the financial performance of the business during a specified period after the sale. The arrangement gives a measure of security to the new owners, who pass some of the financial risk associated with the purchase of a new entity to the sellers. *(CIMA Official Terminology, 2005)*

The purchase consideration is sometimes structured so that there is an initial amount paid at the time of acquisition, and the balance deferred.

Some of the deferred balance will usually only become payable if the target entity achieves specified performance targets.

More details on earn-out arrangements

Earn-out arrangements are often employed when the buyers and sellers disagree about the expected growth and future performance of the target company.

A typical earn-out takes place over a three to five year period after the acquisition and may involve 10% - 50% of the purchase price being deferred and paid across during that period.

Earn-outs are popular among private equity investors, who do not necessarily have the expertise to run a target business after acquiring it, as a way of keeping the previous owners involved following the acquisition.

Example:

An entrepreneur selling a business is asking $2 million based on projected earnings, but the buyer is willing to pay only $1 million based on historical performance.

An earn-out provision might structure the deal so that the entrepreneur receives more than the buyer's offer only if the business achieves certain targets. For example the earnout might set the purchase price at $1 million plus 10% of gross sales over the next three years.

Earn-out targets

The financial targets used in an earn-out calculation may include revenue, net income, EBITDA or EBIT targets.

Sellers tend to prefer revenue as the simplest measurement, but revenue can be boosted through business activities that hurt the bottom line of the company. On the other hand, buyers tend to prefer net income as the most accurate reflection of overall economic performance, but this number can be manipulated downward through extensive capital expenditures and other front-loaded business expenses.

Some earn-outs may be based on entirely non-financial targets such as the development of a product or the execution of a contract.

Limitations of earn-outs

Earn-outs have several fundamental limitations.

They generally work best when the business is operated as envisioned at the time of the transaction, rather than in circumstances where the business plan changes, often in response to a change in the business environment.

In some transactions, the buyer may have the ability to block the earn-out targets from being met. Outside factors may also impact the company's ability to achieve earn-out targets.

Sellers need to negotiate earn-out terms very carefully, taking into account all these issues.

Summary of the key issues relating to forms of consideration

Considerations of different stakeholders

In order to evaluate which form of consideration is appropriate in a particular case, it is important to assess the positions of both the target company's shareholders, and the bidding company and its shareholders.

Position of the target company's shareholders

The target company's shareholders may want to retain an interest in the business, in which case a cash offer would not be welcomed. However, there is a greater certainty of value with a cash offer (share prices fluctuate, so in a share exchange the target company's shareholders cannot be completely sure whether they are receiving an appropriate valuation for their shares).

Position of the bidding company and its shareholders

The bidding company will have to issue new shares if it is to undertake a share exchange. This may require the consent of shareholders in a general meeting. The shareholders may be concerned in a share exchange that their control of the bidding company will be diluted by the issue and exchange of shares.

Another key consideration is the impact of the takeover on the bidding company's financial statements. An issue of new shares could reduce the level of earnings per share (a measure which is often used as a key performance measure by market analysts). However, if a cash offer is made, the raising of the necessary cash could have a significant impact on the gearing of the bidding company.

Methods of financing a cash offer

If the bidding company has a large cash surplus, it might be able to make a cash offer without raising any new finance.

However, in most cases, this will not be the case, so various financing options will have to be considered by the bidding company. The main two options are debt or a rights issue.

Note that the amount of finance needed might be higher than expected if there is a plan to repay the target entity debt at the time of the takeover. This can sometimes be a requirement of the target entity's lenders, as stipulated in a debt covenant.

If target entity debt has to be repaid, the bidding company's total cash requirement will need to cover the cost of purchasing the equity shares and the value of the target entity debt.

Debt

The bidding company could borrow the required cash from the bank, or issue bonds in the market.

The advantage of using debt in this situation is the low cost of servicing the debt. However, raising new debt finance will increase the bidding company's gearing. This will increase the risk to the bidding company's shareholders, so might not be acceptable to the shareholders.

Rights issue

If the bidding company shareholders do not want to suffer the increased risk which debt finance would bring, the alternative would be for the bidding company to offer a rights issue to its existing shareholders. The funds raised can then be used to buy the shares in the company being acquired. Gearing levels are thereby protected.

From the shareholders' point of view, the problem with this financing option is that it is the shareholders themselves who have to find the money to invest.

 Evaluating a share for share exchange

One popular question is to comment on the likely acceptance of a share for share offer.

It is vitally important to be able to identify the likely synergy generated in the acquisition in order to assess the attractiveness of the offer accurately.

The procedure is as follows:

- Value the predator company as an independent entity and hence calculate the value of a share in that company.

- Repeat the procedure for the victim company.

- Calculate the value of the combined company post integration. This is calculated as:

Value of predator company as independent company	X
Value of victim company as independent company	X
Value of any synergy	X
Total value of combined company	X

- Calculate the number of shares post integration:

Number of shares originally in the predator company	X
Number of shares issued to victim company	X
Total shares post integration	X

- Calculate the value of a share in the combined company, and use this to assess the change in wealth of the shareholders after the takeover.

Company A has 200m shares with a current market value of GBP4 per share. Company B has 90m shares with a current market value of GBP2 per share.

A makes an offer of 3 new shares for every 5 currently held in B. A has worked out that the present value of synergies will be GBP40m.

Required:

Calculate the expected value of a share in the combined company (assuming that the given share prices have not yet moved to anticipate the takeover), and advise the shareholders in company B whether the offer should be accepted.

Solution:

MV of A = GBP800m

MV of B = GBP180m

PV of synergies = GBP40m

TOTAL = GBP1,020m

No. of new shares = 200m + (3/5) × 90m = 254m

New share price = 1,020m/254m = GBP4.02

	Shares	MV	Old wealth	Change
A	200m	GBP804m	GBP800m	GBP4m
B	(3/5) × 90m = 54m	GBP216m	GBP180m	GBP36m

The wealth of the shareholders in company B will increase by GBP36m as a consequence of the takeover. This is a (36/180) 20% increase in wealth.

Company B's shareholders should be advised to accept the 3 for 5 share for share offer.

Further numerical illustration (Integration question)

Initial example – cash offer

Summary of information regarding Entity A and Entity B, two UK companies (currency GBP, or £):

	Entity A	Entity B
Market price per share (£)	75	15
Number of shares	100,000	60,000
Market value (£)	7,500,000	900,000

Required:

If A intends to pay £1.2m cash for B, what is the cost premium if:

(a) the share price does not anticipate the takeover;

(b) the share price of Entity B includes a 'speculation' element of £2 per share?

Solution:

(a) The share price accurately reflects the true value of the entity (in theory).

Therefore, the cost to the bidder is simply £1,200,000 – £900,000, that is, £300,000.

Entity A is paying £300,000 for the identified benefits of the takeover.

(b) The cost is £300,000 + (60,000 × £2), or £420,000.

Follow up example – share exchange

Suppose A offers 16,000 shares (£1.2m/£75) instead of £1.2m cash. The cost appears to be £300,000 as before, but because B's shareholders will own part of A, they will benefit from any future gains of the combined entity. Their share will be (16,000/(16,000 + 100,000)), or 13.8%.

Further, suppose that the benefits of the combination have been identified by A to have a present value of £400,000 (i.e. A thinks that B is really worth £900,000 + £400,000, or £1.3m). Therefore, the combined entity of A and B is worth £7.5m + £1.3m, or £8.8m.

Required:

Calculate the true cost of the takeover to the acquirer's shareholders.

Solution:

	A	B
Market value: £8.8m × proportion	£7.586m	£1.214m
Number of shares currently in issue	100,000	60,000
Price per share (£)	100,000	20.23

What we are attempting to do here is to value the shares in the entity before the takeover is completed, based on estimates of what the entity will be worth after the merger. The valuation of each entity also recognises the split of the expected benefits which will accrue to the combined form once the merger has taken place.

The true cost to A can now be calculated as follows:

	£
60,000 B shares at £20.23	1,213,800
Less: Current market value	(900,000)
Benefits being paid to B's shareholders	313,800

Test your understanding 1 (Case style question)

Mavers Co and Power Co are listed on the Stock Exchange.

Relevant information is as follows:

	Mavers Co	Power Co
Share price today	$3.05	$6.80
Shares in issue	48 million	13 million

Mavers Co wants to acquire 100% of the shares of Power Co.

The directors are considering offering 2 new Mavers Co shares for every 1 Power Co share.

Required:

Evaluate whether the 2 for 1 share for share exchange will be likely to succeed.

If necessary, recommend revised terms for the offer which would be likely to succeed.

(30 minutes)

Bootstrapping and post-acquisition values

In the previous examples, we were told specifically what the values of the separate companies were before the takeover, and the synergy generated by the takeover was also given.

Sometimes we might have to derive these figures, using the bootstrapping method as in the following illustration.

 Illustration 2 (Case style question)

	Post-tax profit	P/E ratio	Pre-acquisition value
Company C	$10m	16	$160m
Company D	$1m	8	$8m

If Company C takes over Company D, the post-acquisition value of the combined company can be estimated by applying Company C's P/E ratio to the combined post-tax profit.

This is known as **bootstrapping**, and it is based on the assumption that the market will assume that the management of the larger company will be able to apply common approach to both companies after the takeover, thus improving the performance of the acquired company by using the methods that they have been using on their own company before the takeover.

Value of (C+D) post-acquisition = 16 × ($10m + $1m) = $176m

Thus, the value of the synergy is this combined value, less the values of the individual companies pre-acquisition, i.e.

$176m – $160m – $8m = $8m

4 Treatment of target entity debt

Introduction

In looking at forms of consideration above, we have assumed that the takeover bid will need to be sufficient to attract the target entity shareholders to want to sell their shares.

However, in many takeovers, the consideration needs to be greater than this, to deal with any 'material adverse change clauses' attached to the target entity's borrowings.

Treatment of debt in the target entity

A material adverse change clause is often used to make the target entity's borrowings repayable if the company is sold.

Therefore, when considering how to fund a takeover, the bidding company will have to ensure that sufficient funds are available to purchase the shares from the target entity's shareholders, and to repay the debt in the target entity.

Illustration 3

Example:

Company P is considering a takeover bid for Company H.

The $2.2 million borrowings in Company H are repayable if Company H is acquired.

Therefore, Company P is considering one of the following offers:

- P to pay $ 4.9 million in cash ($ 2.7 million cash to H's shareholders PLUS $ 2.2 million to finance the repayment of H's borrowings).

- Exchange two P $ 0.50 ordinary shares for each H ordinary share held PLUS P to pay H $ 2.2 million in cash to finance the repayment of H's borrowings.

Comments:

- Note that the bids look very similar to the ones seen earlier in the chapter, but they now contain a reference to the extra payment required to repay the debt

- We need to be careful with business valuation here. For example, in the previous chapter: 'Business valuation' we saw that:

  - applying an appropriate P/E ratio to the company's earnings, or discounting forecast cash flows to equity using cost of equity gives the value of the EQUITY, whereas:

  - discounting forecast cash flows to all investors using WACC gives the value of the WHOLE ENTITY (equity plus debt), and:

  - an asset valuation could be either an EQUITY valuation or an ENTITY valuation, depending what is included in the valuation calculation.

- Therefore, when deciding what size of offer should be made, it is critical to assess whether the valuation figure already includes the value of both debt and equity or whether it is just an equity valuation.

- Note that in the circumstances described in the offer above, P would need to consider how to finance the cash offer of $4.9 million (e.g. by borrowing), but it would also have to consider the possibility of borrowing under the share for share exchange offer.

Test your understanding 2 (Objective test question)

BB is considering a takeover bid for QQ.

BB has prepared a valuation of QQ based on a forecast of cash flows before financing charges, discounted at an appropriate weighted average cost of capital. The valuation is $130 million.

If BB does acquire QQ, QQ's debt of $20 million will become repayable.

If BB wants to make a cash offer, what should the value of the cash offer be in total?

A $20 million

B $110 million

C $130 million

D $150 million

5   The post-merger or post-acquisition integration process

Introduction to the post-merger or post-acquisition process

Mergers and acquisitions often fail to deliver the anticipated synergies as a result of failing to effectively integrate the newly acquired entity into the parent.

Poor planning and a lack of information to guide the integration plans ahead of the acquisition will lead to post-acquisition integration problems.

Druker's Golden Rules

P. F. Druker (1981) identified five Golden Rules to apply to post-acquisition integration.

1   Ensure a 'common core of unity' is shared by the acquired entity and acquirer. Shared technologies or markets are an essential element.

2   The acquirer should not just think 'What is in it for us?', but also 'What can we offer them?'.

3   The acquirer must treat the products, markets and customers of the acquired entity with respect.

4   Within 1 year, the acquirer should provide appropriately skilled top management for the acquired company.

5   Within 1 year, the acquirer should make several cross-entity promotions of staff.

Post-acquisition value enhancing strategies

The following are key points to consider when determining strategy for the combined entity:

- The integration strategy must be in place before the acquisition is finalised.

- Review each of the business units for potential cost cuttings/ synergies or potential asset disposals. It is possible there are outlets more valuable to another entity, but it is important they are in good shape before they are sold. However, more than this is needed for a full effective enhancement programme and a position audit could be carried out.

- Consider the effect on the workforce and determine how many, if any redundancies are likely and what the cost will be.

- Risk diversification may well lower the cost of capital and therefore increase the value of the entity.

- The entity's cost of capital should be re-evaluated.

- Make a positive effort to communicate the post-acquisition intentions within the entity to prevent de-motivation and avoid adverse post-acquisition effects on staff morale.

- There may be economies of scale to identify and evaluate.

- Undertake a review of assets, or resource audit, and consider selling non-core elements or redundant assets.

- There may well be a need to pursue a more aggressive marketing strategy.

- The risks of the acquisition need to be evaluated.

- There needs to be harmonisation of corporate objectives.

Impact on ratios or performance measures

Following the completion of an acquisition the purchaser will need to examine thoroughly the financial and management accounting records of each business unit of the acquired entity.

Thus, the directors of the acquirer will be particularly interested in the financial condition of those units which they might plan to dispose of.

From a strategic point of view these are likely to be of more use to another entity with whom they would form a better fit. However, it is still essential that financially and operationally they should be in as good shape as possible to ensure that a good price can be obtained for them.

Illustration 4

Hall Co has just acquired a subsidiary called Wodgits as part of a larger acquisition. Hall Co has no other subsidiaries in the same business sector as Wodgits, so management are considering disposing of Wodgits.

A small listed company called Bigwodge, whose core business is similar to Wodgits, has been identified, and by using all published and any other information reasonably available, the following analysis has been prepared:

	Wodgits	Bigwodge
Return on Capital Employed (ROCE)	14.9%	25.0%
Asset turnover	1.3 times	1.8 times
Net profit margin	11.5%	13.9%
Current ratio	1.5 times	2.2 times
Inventory holding period	68 days	57 days
Receivables collection period	54 days	43 days
Payables payment period	49 days	37 days

Other key information:

- Bigwodge has a P/E ratio of 18.

- Wodgits made an operating profit of $860,000 last year.

- Wodgits has total non-current assets of $4.87m, out of which land and buildings comprise $2.5m. Its net assets at book value are $5.77m.

- The tax rate is 33%.

Required:

As the management accountant of Hall Co, prepare a report to the directors in which you analyse the performance of Wodgits compared with Bigwodge, and recommend a price which Hall Co ought to seek for the disposal of Wodgits.

Solution:

Report to the directors of Hall Co

Return on capital employed (ROCE)

Wodgits' inadequate ROCE seems to be mainly due to a low rate of asset turnover, which we must carefully investigate.

We know that land and buildings account for $2.5m of Wodgits' fixed asset total of $4.87m and it is important to establish how much of this property value represents redundant assets. As to plant and machinery, it may be that this is substantially new or revalued, in which case the assets may be of good value and the faults may lie mainly in under-capacity working or production inefficiencies.

Much more serious, however, would be a situation where the plant is old and requiring heavy maintenance, and would be hard put to cope with increased volume of throughput.

If the first of these plant scenarios is correct, then Wodgits may well fetch a reasonable price, as a bidder, possibly Bigwodge themselves, would be obtaining good assets to add to their own evidently successful performance in their sector. If the second scenario applies, then we might find it difficult to obtain net asset value for the assets remaining after sale of the redundant properties.

Current ratio

Wodgits' current ratio and inventory holding period are fairly good, but before we put the unit up for sale, we would improve our prospects for a reasonable price by taking early action in regard to both receivables and payables. Both are too high and we should aim to tighten up credit control and also bring payables down to the more acceptable level which Bigwodge's payables payment period indicates is appropriate for the industry sector.

Conclusions

Assuming that we can find that, say, $1.5m of land and buildings are redundant and can be separately sold, and that the plant scenario is favourable or can be made so, then it would not seem to be too difficult to make the remainder of Wodgits a saleable proposition.

Thus if we can assume no debt interest, and taxation of 33%, then after-tax profits could be $576,000 ($860,000 × 0.67), and as Bigwodge's current P/E is 18, we might achieve for Wodgits a P/E of 9 or 10 which suggests a price of between $5.2 and $5.8m, which is comfortably above an asset value of $4.3m ($5.8m – $1.5m assets sold).

 The impact of an acquisition on the acquirer's post-acquisition share price

A very important aspect for an acquirer is the post-acquisition effect on its earnings per share (EPS), and the impact on the share price and P/E ratio arising from the market's perceived views on the acquisition.

Once again, detailed analysis of the accounts, and comparison to other companies in similar business sectors can help to assess whether the likely impact will be favourable.

Simple example of the impact on EPS

Assume that the new entity starts with a prospective EPS of 13.1 cents based on combined profits of acquirer and acquired of $8.4m, and 64m shares in issue, and if these earnings could be maintained in year 1 (post-acquisition) they would appear not to be diluted.

However, if the acquirer is expected from its previous performances to attain 10% per annum growth in normal (money) terms, then for year 1 EPS of 13.1 cents × 1.10 would be 14.4 cents, and arguably if this is not attained then dilution will seem to have taken place.

A serious threat to an acquirer's EPS is the 'getting to know you' costs and also the 'reverse synergy' effects of 2 + 2 = 3, which sadly seems to be the fate of numerous acquisitions.

A major question is whether the present value of the combined earnings, including assumed longer-term profit improvements, really takes into account all the downside costs of putting two different entities together, each with its own management style.

Illustration of strategic issues

You are acting as financial adviser to a public entity, H plc, in the hotel business. H plc is considering a takeover bid for the shares of G Limited. Information relating to G Ltd is given in the table below.

G Limited operates in the gaming and betting industry.

The company was established 7 years ago, and the two founder directors still provide the necessary technical and marketing skills. They own 60% of the issued share capital, the balance plus the long-term loan capital having been subscribed by a firm of venture capitalists.

Extracts from the annual reports of G Limited are given below.

Required:

Discuss the extent to which each of the following six reasons might apply to the proposed acquisition of G Limited by H plc. Support your answers with appropriate analysis of the data provided.

(i)   Access to innovation

(ii)   Growth in earnings per share

(iii)   Achievement of operating economies

(iv)   Reduction of risk through diversification

(v)   Access to liquid funds

(vi)   Improved asset backing for borrowing.

Data relating to G Ltd – extracts from annual reports

Year to 30 June	20X8	20X7	20X6
	£000	£000	£000
	860	684	547
Operating profit	55	68	16
Loan interest	(20)	(14)	(12)
Taxation	(9)	(6)	–
Net profit	26	48	4
Tangible non-current assets:			
Cost	224	174	133
Less depreciation	54	34	23
	170	140	110
Development costs			
Cost	254	189	129
Less written off	176	109	53
	78	80	76
Current assets			
Inventory	30	40	31
Receivables	109	72	57
Cash	1	14	5
	140	126	93
TOTAL ASSETS	388	346	279
Equity			
Share capital (25p shares)	100	100	100
Retained profit reserve	61	35	(13)
	161	135	87
Long-term liabilities	160	160	160
Current liabilities	67	51	32
TOTAL EQUITY AND LIABILITIES	388	346	279

Solution:

(i) Access to innovation

To comment upon this fully would require detailed statement of profit or loss information. However, the development costs capitalised on the statement of financial position give an indication of considerable increase in development as opposed to research expenditure which has been undertaken, assuming that this does not reflect changes in accounting policy.

Against this, the high rate of write-off suggests that the life of developed products may well be short.

As innovation depends on people, H plc should identify and take steps to retain key staff in the event of a takeover.

(ii) Growth in earnings per share

The impact of the acquisition on the earnings per share of H plc will depend upon the price paid and whether the price included shares of H plc.

The past profit performance of G Limited and forecast earnings are certainly erratic and lower in relation to revenue. This may be due to poor management, in which case the firm could be turned around and earnings improved or it could be uncontrollable factors in which case earnings might be low and volatile in the future.

The counter-view would be to suggest that if the rapid growth of the past 3 years can be maintained, then there must be opportunities for boosting earnings even if the profit forecasts do not reflect this.

(iii) Achievement of operating economies

The achievement of such economies depends upon integration of similar businesses. Given that hotels and gaming and betting are closely linked there may be scope for such economies if gambling operations already occur or are planned at the hotels of H plc.

(iv) Reduction of risk through diversification

G Limited has volatile earnings and is more likely to increase the risk profile of H plc than reduce it.

(v) Access to liquid funds

Although there is no ready cash in G Limited, the entity has had a satisfactory liquidity position for several years with current ratios of between 2.9 (20X6) and 2.1 (20X8).

However, it should be noted that the position has worsened slightly over recent years. It is probable that since the hotel industry typically has fairly low liquidity, acquiring G Limited will improve the liquidity position of the combined entity as compared with H plc.

(vi) **Improved asset backing for borrowings**

Tangible non-current assets at cost less depreciation have increased dramatically during the period 20X6–20X8.

Obviously comments which can be made are limited due to a lack of categorisation of assets and detail of movements. However, the low depreciation charge suggests that there is land and buildings or long leasehold property among the assets.

Such assets provide good security for borrowing, and as assets are at cost the borrowing capacity may well be higher as it will reflect market values.

6 End of chapter objective test questions

Test your understanding 3 (Objective test question)

Mr A and Mr B incorporated a new company five years ago.

The company has grown extremely quickly and Mr A and Mr B still own 100% of the share capital in the company.

They now feel that the company needs an injection of funds to enable it to grow further. Mr A and Mr B want to keep a controlling interest in their company, and they feel that the company's growth prospects would be damaged by disposing of any part of it.

Which TWO of the following strategies could Mr A and Mr B consider?

A   Spin off

B   Initial public offering (IPO)

C   Private equity buy-in

D   Management buy-out

E   Trade sale of the whole company to a competitor

Test your understanding 4 (Objective test question)

Ravenglass Co is the subject of a takeover bid from Irton Co. An offer of $5 per share has been made to the Ravenglass Co shareholders.

Irton Co has recently taken over several other companies and has gained a reputation as an asset stripper. The directors of Ravenglass Co don't feel that the takeover would be in the best interests of the shareholders and other stakeholders of Ravenglass Co, so they are keen to prevent the takeover from going ahead.

Which THREE of the following strategic defence methods could be used by the directors of Ravenglass Co in this situation?

A   Poison pill

B   Super majority

C   White knight

D   Pacman

E   Appeal to the shareholders

Test your understanding 5 (Objective test question)

Paolo Co acquires another company and pays a price that represents a higher P/E valuation than the current P/E of Paolo Co.

The purchase consideration is paid by issuing new Paolo Co shares. There is no synergy arising from the takeover. Paolo Co has some debt in its capital structure.

Which of the following would be the LEAST likely consequence of this takeover?

A   A reduction in gearing for Paolo Co

B   A dilution of earnings of Paolo Co

C   An increase in the share price after the takeover

D   A reduction in the proportionate stake in the company of existing Paolo Co shareholders

Test your understanding 6 (Objective test question)

ASH Co has made a bid for GIANT Co, in an attempt to take it over.

The bid is a 1 for 2 share for share exchange.

Currently, ASH Co has 1 million shares in issue, trading at $6.33. GIANT Co has 200,000 shares in issue trading at $2.96.

It is expected that $100,000 of synergy will be generated by the takeover.

What is the expected share price in the combined company after the takeover?

A $5.92

B $6.33

C $6.38

D $7.02

Test your understanding 7 (Objective test question)

In Co is hoping to make a successful takeover offer for Out Co.

In Co is a successful company but it has relatively low cash reserves. Its gearing ratio has stayed fairly constant at around 15% in recent years (measured as debt/(debt + equity) by market values) and its interest cover is 5.50. 55% of the equity in In Co is still owned by the founding family. This holding has reduced from 75% in the last three years, as the family has sold off shares to generate much-needed income.

Which of the following is likely to be the best way of structuring an offer for Out Co?

A   Cash offer, funded from existing cash resources

B   Cash offer, funded by a rights issue

C   Cash offer, funded by borrowings

D   Share for share exchange

Test your understanding 8 (Objective test question)

Alpha Co has a P/E ratio of 16 and post-tax earnings of $200,000.

Beta Co has a P/E ratio of 21 and post-tax earnings of $800,000.

Beta's directors estimate that if they were to acquire Alpha they could save $100,000 (after tax) annually on administrative costs in running the new combined company. Additionally they estimate that the P/E ratio of the new company would be 20.

On the basis of these estimates, what is the maximum that Beta should pay for the entire share capital of Alpha?

A $6.3 million

B $5.2 million

C $4.2 million

D $2.0 million

Test your understanding 9 (Objective test question)

Two all-equity financed companies, R and S, have identical business risks.

Company R is valued at $40 million and Company S at $8 million. The two companies merge via a share exchange which results in R shareholders holding 80% of the shares of the new merged company.

As a result of synergy, surplus assets of $5 million are sold immediately without affecting the future profitability of the merged company. Half of the proceeds of the disposal are invested in a project with a net present value of $1 million.

What will be the gains to the shareholders of Company R?

A $4.8 million

B $3.2 million

C $1.2 million

D $0.8 million

7   End of chapter case style questions

Test your understanding 10 (Case style question)

(a)   One theoretical method of valuing a company's shares is to calculate the present value of future dividends using a discount rate that reflects the risk of the business. In respect of large, listed companies, current evidence suggests that this is far too simplistic a view of how company values and share prices are determined.

Required:

Comment on the reasons why share prices may be substantially different from the level suggested by theory. Include brief comments on the relevance of P/E ratios and asset values in share price determination.

(15 minutes)

(b)   ML Co is an expanding clothes retailing company. It is all equity financed by ordinary share capital of $10 million in shares of 50 cents nominal. The company's results to the end of March 20X9 have just been announced. Pre-tax profits were $4.6 million. The chair's statement included a forecast that earnings might be expected to rise by 5% per annum in the coming year and for the foreseeable future.

CO, a children's clothes group, has an issued ordinary share capital of $33 million in $1 shares. Pre-tax profits for the year to 31 March 20X9 were $5.2 million. Because of a recent programme of reorganisation and rationalisation, no growth is forecast for the current year but subsequently constant growth in earnings of approximately 6% per annum is predicted. CO has had an erratic growth and earnings record in the past and has not always achieved it's often ambitious forecasts.

ML Co has approached the shareholders of CO with a bid of two new shares in ML Co for every three CO shares. There is a cash alternative of 135 cents per share.

Following the announcement of the bid, the market price of ML Co shares fell while the price of shares in CO rose. Statistics for ML Co, CO and two other listed companies in the same industry immediately prior to the bid announcement are shown below. All share prices are in cents.

20X8		Company	Dividend yield %	P/E
High	Low			
225	185	ML Co	3.4	15
145	115	CO	3.6	13
187	122	HR	6	12
230	159	SZ	2.4	17

Both ML Co and CO pay tax at 33%. ML Co's cost of capital is 12% per annum and CO's is 11% per annum.

Required:

Assume you are a financial analyst with a major fund manager. You have funds invested in both ML Co and CO.

– Assess whether the proposed share for share offer is likely to be beneficial to the shareholders in ML Co and CO, and recommend an investment strategy based on your calculations.

– Comment on other information that would be useful in your assessment of the bid. Assume that the estimates of growth given above are achieved and that the new company plans no further issues of equity.

State any assumptions that you make.

(30 minutes)

Test your understanding 11 (Case style question)

Oscar Wills is the chief executive of OW plc, a UK listed company. The entity has been trading for 5 years. Oscar is ambitious and aims to make his entity market leader within 5 years.

He makes an offer to acquire Wilde plc, an older quoted entity of similar size to OW but with a profit record that has been erratic in recent years. Wills is of the opinion that Wilde lacks marketing strength and feels that he could make the entity much more profitable.

A summary of the financial data before the bid is as follows:

	OW	Wilde
Number of shares in issue	40m	44m
Earnings available to ordinary shareholders	£4m	£4.4m
P/E ratio	20	10

OW – estimated financial data post-acquisition

Estimated market capitalisation	£167.7m
Estimated share price	262 p
Estimated EPS	13.1 p
Estimated equivalent value of one old Wilde share	143 p

- The offer is six OW shares for eleven Wilde shares.

- The offer is not expected to result in any immediate savings or increases in operational cash flows, but in future, Oscar Wills expects the EPS to grow by 10% per annum.

Required:

(a) Show how Oscar Wills calculated his estimate of post-acquisition values. Discuss the assumptions made by Oscar Wills, and calculate an alternative post-acquisition value for the company. State any assumptions that you make.

(15 minutes)

(b) If Wilde's shareholders rejected the bid, calculate the maximum price OW could afford pay without reducing its shareholders' wealth (assuming Oscar Wills' estimate of post-bid market value is correct).

(15 minutes)

(c) Explain why OW would wish to make the acquisition and comment on likely post-acquisition effects on the P/E ratio.

(15 minutes)

(d) Discuss other post-acquisition impacts that the directors of OW plc should consider.

(15 minutes)

Test your understanding answers

Test your understanding 1 (Case style question)

Calculations

Value of Mavers Co = $3.05 × 48m shares = $146.4m

Value of Power Co = $6.80 × 13m shares = $88.4m

Total value (assuming no synergistic gains) = 146.4 + 88.4 = $234.8m

Number of shares post-integration = 48 million + (2 × 13 million) = 74 million

So the post-integration share price will be:

$234.8m/74 million = $3.173

	Shares	MV	Old wealth	Change
Mavers	48m	$152.3m	$146.4m	+$5.9m
Power	2 × 13m = 26m	$82.5m	$88.4m	−$5.9m

Advice

The Power Co shareholders will not accept a 2 for 1 share for share exchange since it causes their wealth to reduce.

Recommendation

In order for the Power Co shareholders to be encouraged to accept the offer, it must offer them a gain in wealth.

To make sure that Mavers Co is valuing Power Co at its current market value, the value of the offer needs to be ($6.80 × 13m shares) $88.4m in total.

Given the current Mavers Co share price of $3.05, this amounts to $88.4m/$3.05 = 28.98m shares in Mavers Co.

An exchange of 28.98m Mavers Co shares for the 13m Power Co shares represents a ratio of 28.98m to 13m or 2.23 to 1.

However, if the terms of the offer were to be exactly 2.23 Mavers Co shares for every 1 share in Power Co, there would be no incentive for the Power Co shareholders to sell (financially, they'd be indifferent between keeping their existing shares and exchanging them for Mavers Co shares).

In order to encourage Power Co's shareholders to sell, a premium would have to be offered.

Hence, an offer of (say) 2.5 Mavers Co shares for every 1 share in Power Co would probably be needed to encourage the Power Co shareholders to sell.

Position of Mavers Co shareholders

In this situation, where no synergistic gains are included in the calculations, a gain to Power Co's shareholders will result in a corresponding loss to the Mavers Co shareholders. Clearly Mavers Co would not want to proceed with the takeover in these circumstances.

Unless some synergies can be generated, to improve the wealth of the overall company after the acquisition, there is no way of structuring the deal so that both sets of shareholders will be satisfied.

Test your understanding 2 (Objective test question)

The answer is (C).

A forecast of cash flows before financing charges, discounted at an appropriate weighted average cost of capital, gives a valuation for the whole entity, both debt and equity.

Therefore, to acquire the shares and pay off the debt, this value ($130 million) should be paid.

Test your understanding 3 (Objective test question)

The answer is (B) and (C).

A spin-off would not actually generate any cash and a management buyout would split the business up or (if it was to be for the whole company) take a controlling interest away from Mr A and Mr B. A trade sale of the whole company would not leave Mr A and Mr B with a controlling interest.

Test your understanding 4 (Objective test question)

The answer is (C), (D) and (E).

(A) and (B) are defences that would have to be set up **before** a bid was made.

Chapter 13

Test your understanding 5 (Objective test question)

The answer is (C).

If Paolo Co buys another company and values the target company on a higher P/E ratio, and if there is no synergy, there will be a reduction in the earnings per share of Paolo Co (B). Since the acquisition is paid for by using new shares, the gearing ratio of Paolo Co will fall (A), and existing shareholders will own a smaller proportionate stake in the company (D). It is unlikely that the share price will increase; in view of the reduction in earnings per share, it is more likely that the share price will fall after the takeover.

Test your understanding 6 (Objective test question)

The answer is (C).

Total value of the combined company will be:

$(1m \times \$6.33) + (200,000 \times \$2.96) + 100,000 = \$7,022,000$

The number of shares in the combined company will be:

$1 \text{ million} + [(1/2) \times 200,000] = 1,100,000$

Therefore the share price will be $\$7,022,000/1,100,000 = \$6.38$

Test your understanding 7 (Objective test question)

The answer is (C).

In Co's gearing appears to be quite low and interest cover is quite high, so it shouldn't cause any problems to increase borrowings (C).

Low cash reserves would rule out a straight cash offer (A), and the fact that the family owners have been selling off shares would seem to rule out a rights issue (B).

A share for share exchange (D) would change the control of In Co, and would probably reduce the family's holding to lower than 50%, so should not be undertaken unless the family owners accept that they will lose their control of the company.

567

Test your understanding 8 (Objective test question)

The answer is (B).

Expected value of Alpha and Beta combined is:

20 × (200,000 + 800,000 + 100,000) = $22 million

Beta's current value is

21 × 800,000 = $16.8 million.

Therefore the value of Alpha to Beta is the difference between these two figures, i.e. $5.2 million.

Test your understanding 9 (Objective test question)

The answer is (B).

Value of merged company ($ million) = 40 + 8 + 5 + 1 = $54 million

R's shareholders have 80% (i.e. $43.2 million)

This is a gain of $3.2 million.

Test your understanding 10 (Case style question)

(a) Given the wording, you really need to explain why the dividend valuation model may break down, as it is the 'theory' specifically mentioned in the question. You probably have time only to mention a couple of drawbacks with each approach.

A common way of valuing the ordinary shares in a company is discounting all future dividends anticipated from holding the shares. Although having a ring of truth, it often fails to give a price which corresponds to the current market price, due to its inherent flaws:

– It requires constant dividend growth, which in turn implies a constant retention ratio and return on re-invested funds. It is possible to cope with varying growth rates but the calculation is awkward.

– It requires a continuous supply of investment opportunities through time to justify retention.

– It can give nonsensical results e.g. zero current dividend generates zero value, thus ignoring the value of the firm's assets and/or its earnings stream.

– It is only suitable for valuing minority stakes in a firm because it ignores the opportunities for managers to restructure firms to improve earnings and cash flow. The key to value is not the portion of profit paid out to shareholders but the earning power of the business.

Price earnings (P/E) ratios

This is not a method of valuing shares of quoted firms – P/E ratios are the product of valuation. When the market sets a value, the resulting share price divided by the last reported earnings gives the P/E ratio. Generally, a high P/E ratio indicates that a company is expected to grow its earnings rapidly in the future.

The P/E ratio can be used to cross-check against the value of other companies – if their relative P/E ratios look out of line, it may suggest under- or overvaluation somewhere. P/E ratios can also be used when valuing the shares of unquoted companies, taking due care when interpreting the accounting data used.

Asset Value (AV)

The AV is the value per share of the firm's assets net of all liabilities i.e. the owners' stake in the firm. It has some merit for unlisted companies whose shares are not traded, but it is highly unreliable for many reasons:

– Based on IFRS, asset values in the Statement of Financial Position are primarily designed to satisfy the directors' duty to account for past performance.

– It can be distorted by accounting practices e.g. different depreciation policies.

– Revaluation of assets is not mandatory (except in the property sector) so asset values could seriously understate market values.

– It is only valid at one point in time, the statement of financial position date.

– It (usually) ignores intangibles such as brands and market standing.

– It may exclude some liabilities – 'off-balance sheet' debts like operating lease obligations and warranty commitments.

– Inventory values quickly outdate in some industries, and some receivables / debtors may be doubtful.

The AV provides merely a floor to equity value – usually, the market value is many times the AV because the market is valuing future earnings capacity. A discounted cash flow approach is the most appropriate method of valuation.

(b) The length of answer that you can offer will be limited. The bulk of your time will be spent on computation. The solution presented here gives a step-by-step guide that you would need to follow, rather than just a summary of the results.

Basic information

	ML	CO	Combined
Profit after tax (PAT) for each firm is			
ML: (0.67 × $4.6m)	$3.082m	$3.484m	$6.566m
CO: (0.67 × $5.2m)			
Given respective P/E ratios, market values are:			
ML: (15 × $3.082)	$46.23m	$45.29m	$91.52m
CO: (13 × $3.484)			
Given the number of shares, share price is:			
ML: ($46.23m/20,000)	$2.31	$1.37	
CO: ($45.29m/33,000)			
EPS:			
ML: ($3.082/20,000)	15.41c	10.56c	
CO: ($3.484/33,000)			

Analysis

No. of shares post-bid: 20,000 + (2/3 × 33,000)	= 42,000
Expected market prices post-bid	= Total market value/no of shares
	= (91,520/42,000) = $2.18
Value of bid at post-issue price = (2 shares × $2.18)	= $4.36
Cash value of bid per 3 shares offered: ($1.35 × 3)	= $4.05

Assessment

Assuming no changes in the level of market prices, and no re-rating of the sector, ML share price would fall post-acquisition to $2.18. At this price, the value of the 2-for-3 share offer should attract CO shareholders. They would be getting shares worth (2 × 2.18) = $4.36 in exchange for shares currently worth (3 × 1.37) = $4.11.

The share-for-share offer is also worth more than the cash alternative: $4.36 vs $4.05.

This is a 'reverse takeover', where the shareholders of the target end up holding a majority stake in the expanded company – but who gains from this?

Former CO shareholders would hold (22,000/42,000) × 91.52m = $47.939m of the value of the expanded firm, a gain of (47.939m – 45.290m pre-bid value of CO) = $2.649m.

ML shareholders would lose $2.649m, making the share-financed deal distinctly unattractive to them.

Conversely, the cash offer would create wealth for ML shareholders i.e. they give $4.05 for something worth $4.11 pre-bid.

The advice to the fund manager is: 'accept the bid in respect of CO shares and sell ML shares in the market if you can achieve a price above $2.18'.

Other information required

The advice given hinges on the behaviour of ML's share price – it has already fallen on the announcement, but by how much? It may already be too late if the market is efficient, as it would already have digested the information contained in the announcement.

Also:

–   What benefits are expected from the merger i.e. cost savings and synergies? To make sense of the bid, ML must be setting the PV of these benefits above $2.649m to yield a positive NPV for the acquisition.

–   How quickly are these benefits likely to show through? Any delay in exploiting these lowers the NPV.

–   It is feasible that the market might apply a higher P/E ratio to the expanded company – maybe not as high as ML's but possibly at the market average, currently 14.25, compared to the weighted average P/E ratio for ML/CO of 14.

–   Is ML likely to sell part of CO's operations? And to whom? If ML has already lined up a buyer, it must expect to turn a profit on the deal.

> – Is the bid likely to be defended by the target's managers, fearful for their jobs? If so, a higher bid might be expected.
>
> – Is a White Knight likely to appear with a higher bid on more favourable terms?
>
> – Are there competition implications likely to attract the interest of the authorities?

Test your understanding 11 (Case style question)

(a)

	OW	Wilde	OW + Wilde
Earnings (£m)	4	4.4	8.4
Number of shares (m)	40	44	64
EPS (p)	10	10	13.1
P/E ratio	20	10	20
Share price (p)	200	100	262
MV (£m)	80	44	167.7 (estimate)

Post-acquisition:

% of entity owned by OW (40/64)	62.5%	
% of entity owned by Wilde (24/64)		37.5%
Market value (% × £167.7m)	104.8	62.9
No. of shares pre-acquisition (m)	40	44
Post-acquisition price per existing share (p)	262	143

Oscar Wills has applied his own pre-acquisition P/E ratio to the combined earnings of the new entity.

The difference between the combined market values pre-acquisition (£124m) and the estimated market value post-acquisition (£167.7m) is £43.7m.

This is Wilde's pre-acquisition earnings multiplied by the difference between the entity's pre-acquisition P/E and the combined post-acquisition P/E (20 – 10 = 10). EPS for Oscar Wills appears to have increased from 10 p to 13.1p because of this 'bootstrapping' effect.

In the absence of any immediate commercial benefits, or the disclosure of new information during the bid, there is no reason why the market value of the combined entity should be any different from the total of the two individual entities' market values – that is, £124m. This would suggest the following post-acquisition prices per existing share:

Wills: £124m × 62.5% = £77.5m or 194p per existing share compared with 200p per share now.

Wilde: £124m × 37.5% = £46.5m or 106p per existing share compared with 100p per share now.

There is a transfer of wealth from Wills' shareholders to Wilde's, because the terms of the offer are slightly more generous than the ratio of the old share prices.

The pre-acquisition prices suggest 1-for-2, not 6-for-11.

(b)   –   Estimated value of combined firm (per OW) £168m

     –   Value of OW before merger £80m

     –   Maximum price £88m

This is £44m over the existing value of Wilde's shares. It can be reconciled by multiplying the historic earnings by the difference between Wilde's P/E and OW's P/E – that is £4.4m × (20 – 10).

(c)   OW plc may have had the following among their reasons for making a bid for Wilde plc:

     –   **Expectation of growth.** OW is an ambitious entity and it sees in Wilde a means of growing faster and more cheaply than by internal expansion, especially as Wilde seems to be a 'slumbering heavyweight' relative to OW.

     –   **Management and technical staff.** Wilde's results may be erratic, but OW is aware that in terms of size and quality of main products Wilde is a significant player in its market sector. It is reasonable to assume therefore that Wilde may be suffering from poor administrative as well as marketing management, which could considerably undervalue the earning potential of its products. By means of more aggressive marketing and improved administration, OW believes that dramatic profit improvements are possible. Also Wilde may possess strong technical expertise which OW might find difficult and expensive to obtain by internal development.

     –   **Market share.** If Wilde is in the same industry sector as OW, this could well be a main reason for the bid, in which case OW's shareholders might have less reason to be concerned over the price. Thus if the acquisition led to OW's market share rising fairly quickly to make the new entity second or third in its sector, and not excessively far below the leader, it could begin to wield significantly greater influence in that sector.

     –   **Synergy savings.** Wilde may have a number of 'dogs' (Boston Consulting Group term for bad failure) among its business units, which OW may be much less prepared to pour resources into, even though some may be the Wilde chairman's 'pets'. However, if this aspect is known to the market, then the synergy savings may well attract a higher bidder.

– **Risk reduction.** From the comparative P/E ratios it seems evident that Wilde is regarded by the market as being much riskier than OW, and this could well be due to Wilde being an acquirer of struggling entities, bought at cheap prices, possibly even in sectors only remotely related to Wilde's core business. Such entities often turn out to be disasters, taking up disproportionate amounts of the acquirer's valuable management time. At OW, Mr Wills does not believe in keeping a 'kennelful of dogs'! and the profit improvement suggested is likely to come not only from more aggressive marketing but from a concentration of resources on key products, thereby reducing risk in the new entity.

Next, the acquirer needs to be concerned at the post-acquisition effects on its P/E ratio.

On the basis of the pre-acquisition estimates, Mr Wills looked to maintain OW's own P/E ratio of 20 (262p/13.1p), but on the more realistic basis of assuming a value of 194 p per share – which assumes that OW inherits the greater risks of Wilde's current operations – then, as shown above, for the new entity the market capitalisations should be simply added together, making £124m and the P/E ratio becomes 194p/13.1p = 14.8.

However, we must now consider the possibility of downside costs in year 1; thus even assuming that OW has taken several steps to improve Wilde's operations and perhaps made some significant asset sales, an upset to earnings caused by 'teething troubles' could do more than offset the effect of the improvements. Thus, EPS of, say, 13.5p for year 1 (instead of 14.4p, showing 10% expected growth), which one would expect to yield a P/E ratio of approximately 15.2 (13.5p/13.1p × 14.8), might well fall back to about 13, or even 12. Downside factors often seem to the market to be more significant than improvements.

Clearly then, at the time of making its bid, it would have been most unwise for OW to pay excessively for 'synergy savings' and not to give due regard to possible adverse post-acquisition impacts.

(d) **Further post-acquisition aspects**

Position audit

As an initial move, OW will need to do much more than analyse key financial factors of each of Wilde's units. OW's management will need to get a proper understanding of the main 'stakeholders' of each Wilde unit, for example, staff, customers and suppliers, and an appreciation of the products or services provided. In company planning, this wide-ranging survey is of the nature of a 'position audit', which should help considerably in speeding up the 'getting to know you' aspect which is so important if the full benefits of the acquisition are to be obtained.

Improving efficiency

It is better for OW to approach Wilde more as a management consultant rather than to demand immediate changes without adequate explanation. Administrative savings mainly involve people, and OW must try to ensure that the logic of its proposals is clearly explained to Wilde's management and staff, and as far as possible their cooperation gained.

Redundancies need to be worked out fairly but firmly with an emphasis on voluntary redundancy as far as possible; the main purpose must be to reduce the resentment of those who are losing their jobs and to provide as much help as possible by way of counselling or assistance in job seeking. In these situations uncertainty should be avoided, as it tends to demotivate the entire workforce, and rumour is liable to feed greedily on rumour.

Even if Mr Wills is convinced that Wilde's marketing needs to be more aggressive, he should first of all make himself fully aware of the nature of Wilde's marketing policies and of their customers and competitors. If Wilde is substantially in the same market sector as OW, there may be certain valuable niches occupied by Wilde which OW would do well to retain.

Profit improvement

The financial analysis of Wilde's units suggested above will help to pinpoint the areas where profit improvements can be obtained, but it is essential that a comprehensive action plan is then prepared, as far as possible in co-operation with Wilde's management, and reasonable time allowed for the phasing-in of significant changes.

It is not helpful to go 'stomping around' offices and factories, thereby emphasising the perceived incompetencies of Wilde personnel. It may be that many faults, especially of inadequate systems, may already be recognised by Wilde staff and, faced with the necessity of correcting them, they may be quite willing to join in making appropriate changes. Sadly, it is often the case that obstinate managers may be standing in the way of improvement, and in this situation OW is in a good position to take quick but fair and firm action, possibly by grasping the nettle of making major changes in Wilde's organisation structure if this is seen to be necessary for a more profitable operation.

Asset sales

Here it is often the reluctance of top management to dispose of redundant assets and 'dog' units, even though it is recognised that keeping them represents a serious waste of management time and scarce resources. OW will need to make it quite clear as to which activities are to be retained, which merged with OW units and which disposed of, but in all cases the logic of each move should be clearly explained to the Wilde management and staff affected. This assumes, of course, that OW has thought through what it intends to do, which again is a good reason for first carrying out a position audit before taking action on Wilde's operations.

Effective communication

Finally, a qualitative factor of the utmost importance, as by effective communication we mean that OW must do all possible to ensure that Wilde is on the same 'wavelength' as itself. New reporting systems and procedures should only be introduced after proper consultation, in which OW will need to make clear their purposes and ensure that changes will not cause serious disruption to Wilde's operations. This is especially true in seeking computer system compatibility, which will call not only for careful planning but an acceptance by OW that in this, as with other system changes, a sufficient period of parallel running may be an essential procedure.

There should be reasonable opportunities for Wilde staff to have contact with those of OW and vice versa, especially through participation in training procedures and conferences; also Wilde staff should be encouraged to feel that promotional prospects throughout the new entity will be open to them.

All the points made in this section concerning redundancies, changes and reorganisation created by the acquisition of Wilde apply equally to the need for OW to keep its own staff properly informed, otherwise demotivation may also affect OW with consequent damage to its own profitability whatever happens with Wilde.

Perhaps, in the end, the most effective post-acquisition strategy that OW can apply to Wilde and itself is to provide an atmosphere in which both sides are able to talk freely with each other, seeking co-operation wherever possible, and even though some of OW's actions – improving profitability and making asset sales – may be very hurtful to Wilde, at least things can probably be made somewhat more acceptable if the justification for them is properly explained to all concerned, and that includes any of OW's own staff who may also be affected.

Index

Index